Graham

with best wishes

Richard

18 April 2009

EVANGELICALS
in the
ROYAL NAVY
1775–1815

Blue Lights & Psalm-Singers

EVANGELICALS
in the
ROYAL NAVY
1775–1815

Blue Lights & Psalm-Singers

Richard Blake

Richard Blake

THE BOYDELL PRESS

© Richard Blake 2008

All rights reserved. Except as permitted under current legislation
no part of this work may be photocopied, stored in a retrieval system,
published, performed in public, adapted, broadcast,
transmitted, recorded or reproduced in any form or by any means,
without the prior permission of the copyright owner

The right of Richard Blake to be identified as
the author of this work has been asserted in accordance with
sections 77 and 78 of the Copyright, Designs and Patents act 1988

First published 2008
The Boydell Press, Woodbridge

ISBN 978-1-84383-359-8

The Boydell Press is an imprint of Boydell & Brewer Ltd
PO Box 9, Woodbridge, Suffolk IP12 3DF, UK
and of Boydell & Brewer Inc.
668 Mt Hope Avenue, Rochester, NY 14620, USA
website: www.boydellandbrewer.com

A CIP record for this book is available
from the British Library

This publication is printed on acid-free paper

Designed and typeset
in Adobe Caslon Pro and Academy Engraved by
David Roberts, Pershore, Worcestershire

Printed in Great Britain by
Antony Rowe Ltd, Chippenham, Wiltshire

Contents

List of illustrations vi

Preface vii

Abbreviations viii

Introduction 1

I A Century of Neglect and a Call to Revival 5

II The Genesis of a Movement: Middleton, Kempenfelt and Ramsay 35

III Gathering Momentum: Divine Service at Sea in the Later Eighteenth Century 69

IV The Blue Lights during the French Revolutionary War, 1793–1802: A Change of Emphasis 105

V Developing the Ethos of the Officer Corps 140

VI The Impact of Evangelical Enthusiasm on Fighting Determination: Quarter-Deck or Organ Loft 174

VII Evangelical Activity on the Lower Deck: The Psalm-Singers 225

VIII Evangelicalism at the End of the Napoleonic War: A Flare in the Darkness? 268

Bibliography 294

Index 309

Illustrations

1. Admiral Charles Middleton. Oil painting, British School, 19th century (detail)   37
2. Rear-Admiral Richard Kempenfelt. Oil painting by Tilly Kettle   51
3. The Reverend James Ramsay. Oil painting by Carl Frederik von Breda   59
4. Lord George Graham in his cabin celebrating the capture of privateers, *c.* 1745. Oil painting by William Hogarth   78
5. Title-page of *The Seaman's Monitor* by Josiah Woodward, 1705 edition   97
6. HMS *Defence* at the Battle of the Glorious First of June, 1794. Oil painting by Nicholas Pocock   121
7. Admiral Adam Duncan, 1st Viscount Duncan. Oil painting by Henry Pierre Danloux   135
8. 'Britons! Your Nelson is dead!' Poster of 1806   152
9. Vice-Admiral Sir Charles Vinicombe Penrose. Oil painting by W. Sharp   164
10. Vice-Admiral Sir James Saumarez. Oil painting by Edwin Williams   176
11. 'Sternhold and Hopkins at Sea or a Stave out of Tune', 1809. Satirical etching by C. Williams   191
12. James, Lord Gambier. Oil painting by Sir William Beechey   197
13. Sketch map of the Aix Roads action 1809   216
14. Bible-reading on board a British frigate, *c.* 1830. Oil painting by Augustus Earle   270–1

Preface

This work has been a long time on the slipway. In some ways the keel was laid unwittingly in my childhood by a Guernsey sea captain who gave my father a fine engraving of Admiral Lord de Saumarez and a copy of Ross's two-volume biography. I passed that portrait every time I went up or down stairs. In time I turned to the books and noticed that the admiral had professed just the same kind of evangelical faith that my parents held. My father was a master mariner who had served with the navy in both world wars. Amongst his close Christian friends were the Guernseyman – former Commodore of the British India Steam Navigation Company – and a senior master in the Union Castle line. The connection between faith and seafaring seemed something to explore, and accordingly I undertook part-time research into aspects of this at Southampton University under the skilled and generous supervision of the late Professor John Bromley. When at last I retired from a career in teaching I found time to develop my earlier work and to prepare it for publication.

Over forty years I have valued the help and encouragement of many people. I am grateful to the governors of Monkton Combe School for allowing me a term's leave of absence to start my research, and of Luckley Oakfield School for granting me a sabbatical term in 1999 to begin more focused writing. The staff of the National Maritime Museum, the National Archive at Kew, the British Library, the Naval Historical Library, Southampton University Library, the SPCK and the Scripture Gift Mission made my researches a pleasure. Professor N. A. M. Rodger, who knows so much about every aspect of naval history, and Surgeon Vice-Admiral Sir James Watt who understands the correlation between Christian faith, medicine and the navy better than any living authority, have both encouraged this study and helped with their advice and expertise. Dr Roald Kverndal with his unrivalled knowledge of seafarers' missions both British and global has been a particular inspiration.

The present Lord de Saumarez has kindly given permission to publish extracts from the private papers of Admiral Sir James Saumarez. I am grateful to Peter Sowden for all the encouragement, advice and practical help he has given me in preparing the book for publication.

Without the understanding and support of my wife Margaret and our family the work could never have been finished. On and off this study has accompanied all the years of our marriage, and throughout she has given a warm welcome to the seafarers of ages past who have intruded into our home and absorbed great tracts of my time. I gladly pay her this affectionate tribute of thanks.

Abbreviations

Adm.	Admiral
BDEB	*Blackwell Dictionary of Evangelical Biography*
BL	British Library
BP	*The Barham Papers, edited for the Navy Records Society*
Capt.	Captain
CB	Companion of the Order of the Bath
Cdr.	Commander
Cdre	Commodore
C-in-C	Commander-in-Chief
CMS	Church Missionary Society
DNB	*Dictionary of National Biography*
GCB	Knight Grand Cross of the Order of the Bath
KB	Knight of the Order of the Bath
KCB	Knight Commander of the Order of the Bath
Lieut.	Lieutenant
MM	*The Mariner's Mirror*
MS	The Marine Society
NC	*The Naval Chronicle*
NHL	Naval Historical Library
NMBS	Naval and Military Bible Society
NMBS	*Anniversary Report of the Naval and Military Bible Society*
NMM	National Maritime Museum
NRS	Navy Records Society
NSM	*The New Sailor's Magazine*
ODNB	*Oxford Dictionary of National Biography*
PRO	Public Record Office
RAI	*Regulations and Instructions Relating to His Majesty's Service at Sea*
RN	Royal Navy
RM	Royal Marines
RTS	Religious Tract Society
RUSI	Royal United Services Institute
SPCK	Society for Promoting Christian Knowledge
SPG	Society for Propagating the Gospel
USJ	*The United Service Journal*

Introduction

HISTORIANS have always known that Evangelicalism got into the navy because it is linked with one of the most dramatic – and notorious – episodes of the Napoleonic Wars. In 1809 a British fleet had the French at their mercy in Aix Roads and might have destroyed the entire battle squadron as it lay stranded and keeling over in shoal water – had the Evangelical commander-in-chief, Lord Gambier, shown as much concern for winning the war as for spreading his religion. That was the opinion expressed fiercely and publicly by Lord Cochrane, the young captain of genius who had personally created the opportunity for victory. The echoes of that argument have reverberated to the present, with Gambier invariably seen as an eccentric who might have made a bishop but was incompetent as a fighting admiral.

The navy never seemed the right place for evangelical fervour – religion maybe, but not zealotry – and during the Revolutionary and Napoleonic Wars officers with these opinions were commonly seen as misfits, with enough collective identity to earn the pejorative 'Blue Lights'. Gambier, the best known of them, by missing his call to greatness at Aix Roads showed that he was unsuited for command, while his family link with the able but unpopular Sir Charles Middleton (later Lord Barham, First Lord in 1805–6) invites the conclusion that eminence came through nepotism not ability. Religion of this kind – so the line runs – should have stayed in pulpits ashore: afloat it was risibly irrelevant and damaging.

And yet there is something astray with this evaluation. For a start, it underestimates the strength of religious practice in the navy. While Jervis was more of a martinet than a pastor he was scarcely less zealous than Gambier in holding church services at sea even in the presence of the enemy. Nelson's Christianity was not Gambier's, but it fed an essential part of his persona. Neither Jervis nor Nelson were Blue Lights, but Nelson was just as ready as they to invoke the aid of the Almighty and to attribute victory to his intervention. All three of the British flag officers at Trafalgar were supporters of the Bible societies and distributed religious literature to their crews – just as Gambier is so slated for doing.

Then again, the movement cannot be understood by referring only to Middleton and Gambier, for there was a strong supporting cast. Their contribution to the navy was a great deal wider and more subtle than the moralising proselytism for which they are known. A reappraisal is needed. For one thing, some were outstanding combat commanders – Duncan, Saumarez, Pellew – and for another, taken as a group they generated humane reforms and far-sighted analyses of what the navy needed, as seen in Kempenfelt's letters, Penrose's ideas in *The Naval Chronicle*, Pellew's prototype punishment returns, and Barham's *Regulations*. Their thinking on social issues proved seminal.

Most of the material used here is familiar enough. Other historians have noticed – for example – that the SPCK was supplying ships with Bibles and prayer books, that Duncan was a profoundly God-fearing man, and that Bo'sun Smith became the most conspicuous agitator for sailors' moral reformation in the post-war period. Where this study breaks new ground is by relating disparate elements to one another and to the familiar evangelical revival, so that its coherence as well as its development can be seen. The starting date is 1775 when the War of American Independence broke out, and it ends when the wartime fleets were paid off in 1815. My basic argument is that the Blue Lights initially tried to restore religion to its traditional prominence, and then came to recognise that the navy was a huge unevangelised mission field. Responding to this challenge during the Napoleonic War, they worked to spread the Christian message through voluntary prayer groups in scores of ships. The Blue Light programme aimed for more than individual salvation: it nurtured a compassionate awareness of lower deck needs which in turn developed into workable schemes of humanitarian reform.

Fortunately for the Blue Lights, some of their concerns were shared by admirals and captains who made no claim to piety. For reasons more to do with discipline than the Kingdom of God, Sir John Jervis insisted on regular religious observance. The expanded demand for manpower had brought into the navy elements which could not readily be tamed by well-proven methods, and commanders were willing to try what religion could do. Naval Regulations specified copious applications of compulsory worship but the prescription had been neglected for decades. While the Evangelicals were recalling the officer corps to its religious and pastoral obligations, the outbreak of the 1797 mutinies underlined the wisdom of trying gentler forms of social control. Blue Lights steadily gained attention, not for their eccentricity, but for the compelling evidence of their success in running ships' companies under captains such as Brenton, Penrose or Hillyar.

Independently of this process, wartime lower-deck seamen with Methodist-type convictions were forming their own gatherings, derisively termed 'psalm-singers'. The two movements became aware of each other during the Napoleonic Wars – officers and men sharing a common faith, and meeting for prayer and Bible study in voluntary off-duty gatherings. In ships without Blue Lights they appear to have struggled, but where officers (and especially captains) encouraged piety, they had significant influence. Eventually no less than eighty ships of the fleet supported praying groups of this kind. In parallel to what was happening afloat, a striking work developed amongst prisoners in France.

At each stage evangelicals came up with the tools needed. For church services afloat, there were prayer books and Bibles; when the focus moved to evangelism, they gave tracts and New Testaments for personal use. The cell groups were a revolutionary device working voluntarily in off-duty hours, often bringing together officers and men. And once peace came – beyond the scope of this book – they devised the recognised apparatus of missions to seamen, with floating chapels, mariners' churches, sailors' hostels, leisure facilities, and welfare measures for dependants.

The focus of this book is evangelicalism. It is a not a comprehensive study of religion in the navy. There were many Scots whose Presbyterianism was given no special treatment, and there was a strong body of Catholics, principally from Ireland, whose religious needs were callously disregarded. My neglect of other creeds and traditions results from constraints of space and perspective, and does not imply that they were too few or unimportant to deserve notice. This study might also have been enriched by exploring more thoroughly the religious climate of the eighteenth century, but again I must plead the limits of space. Furthermore, as shall become apparent, the quality of naval religion depended relatively little on the vigour of the Hanoverian clergy ashore. The recruitment of chaplains and their freedom to exercise any kind of ministry aboard ship were in the hands of ships' captains: until commanding officers saw much point in religion there was little that a clergyman could do. A major part of this book concerns the process whereby senior officers began to see value in religious observance.

To go beyond 1815 in a single volume would have resulted in an unwieldy study, and yet it cannot really be left there. How did the movement continue in its mission to sailors, and how durable was its influence in the navy? After the war the Blue Lights and their allies turned to social and evangelistic action to reform maritime society. Since the lower deck was manned from the national pool of seamen, this programme did not leave the navy unaffected. Furthermore, evangelicalism had not yet done with the navy. While it lacked the prominence it had enjoyed under Barham, its influence was still felt through *Regulations,* through agitation over particular questions (notably punishment and prostitution), and through the quiet example of a new generation of young officers.

From 1775 to 1815 the Blue Lights consistently promoted religion and morality, so that the navy would be strengthened. In the process they found ways to elevate the self-respect of the lower deck. As the next half-century would show, they imparted an ethical tone to the officer corps, and they managed to give to the whole service something of their own moral purpose. From a high Victorian vantage point, those early Blue Lights begin to look remarkably far-sighted.

This treatment complements Gordon Taylor, *The Sea Chaplains* (Oxford, 1978), and Roald Kverndal, *Seamen's Missions: Their Origin and Early Growth* (Pasadena, 1986). While Taylor gave a valuable study of the chaplains, he made no detailed assessment of the spiritual value of sea-going clergy, and left out much concerning lay religion As my study seeks to show, the clergy could not be the sole or even the principal force for evangelism, if only because of their shortage of numbers. Kverndal's monumental work takes note of wartime naval developments but is properly focused on maritime mission, largely amongst merchant seamen and principally after the Napoleonic War. I believe we need a study of evangelical mission in the Royal Navy – and here it is.

A note on three stylistic conventions

1. Evangelical and evangelical. Spelt with a capital it denotes the Church of England party that emphasised Bible preaching and conversion – associated with Whitefield, Wilberforce, Newton, and Simeon. When it appears lower case, 'evangelical' refers to the same doctrines in a non-denominational or a free church sense. Followers of the new piety were all *evangelical* but only Anglicans were *Evangelical*.

2. The Reverend George Charles Smith (1786–1863), a Baptist minister, once served in the navy as a boatswain's mate. He became famous under the incorrect title of Bo'sun Smith. It is how contemporaries knew him, and I often refer to him thus.

3. Where warships are given a figure in parentheses after the name it is an indication of the armament and size. For example, the *Defence* (74) carried 74 guns and was a third rate line of battle ship.

I

A Century of Neglect and a Call to Revival

Prelude

THE American War was not going well in late 1779. The quarrel with the Colonies had brought both France and Spain into hostilities with Britain, and there was danger of invasion as well as a threat to her worldwide possessions. The Channel Fleet's chief of staff in the *Victory* had pressing concerns over the conduct of the war, which he often expressed in private letters to his friend the Comptroller of the Navy, Sir Charles Middleton, who carried heavy burdens of his own for the proper equipping of Britain's fleets. In December, taking advantage of the winter period when a first-rate flagship would not be at sea, Richard Kempenfelt wrote again, and this time he included some remarks about collective worship.

> Divine service should ... be performed every Sunday; and I think a short form of prayer for mornings and evenings, to be used every day, would be proper ... The French and Spaniards, in their ships, have their matins and vespers every day. Our seamen people are more licentious than those of other nations. The reason is, they have less religion. Don't let anyone imagine that this discipline will disgust the men, and give them a dislike to the service, for the very reverse will be the consequence.[1]

This may be seen as the foundation document of a reform movement aiming to bring Christianity into mainstream naval life in the late eighteenth century. In time Kempenfelt, Middleton and officers who thought as they did would be called Blue Lights or 'Methodists' and psalm-singers.

Amidst their wartime responsibilities these two senior officers were prepared to give mental space to something so apparently marginal as sailors' morals and religion, but to Kempenfelt and Middleton these were far from being secondary matters; they were at the heart of their personal values, and in their judgement ought to be at the core of naval life. Although staunch in their Protestantism they found inspiration from contemporary Catholic practice, where religious observance at sea remained strong. The French and Spanish ships of the 1770s were following the common practice of all European mariners in the early sixteenth

---

[1] J. K. Laughton (ed.), *The Letters and Papers of Charles, Lord Barham, 1758–1813* [hereafter *BP*], 3 vols., NRS (1907–11), I, p. 308.

century, but why had such observances died out in British ships? Where Catholic practice had withered away in a Protestant climate, what spirituality had taken its place? Was Kempenfelt justified in his assumptions that orthodox practice was essential not just for morality but for discipline as well, and would British sailors really welcome more religion?

This chapter will give context for Kempenfelt's remarks by exploring links between seafaring and religion, and then more specifically considering how Protestant England lost the hold that the Pre-Reformation Church had exercised over maritime culture.

The Sea-Going Environment

IN every age the sea has been cruel and unforgiving. It has not lost its force today, even when technology has taken much of the unpredictability out of storm and current, and when position-fixing by satellite signal has become an exact science. For the centuries when wind and muscle were the only source of power at sea the dangers were immeasurably multiplied. Pilotage required close observation of tide and shore, while oceanic navigation depended on sightings of sun and stars, together with the technical knowledge to turn sightings into measurement and measurement into position lines on a chart. Seafaring was notoriously perilous and mariners of all kinds, whether coastal or deep-sea, faced dangers that emptied voyaging of romanticism. People who earned their living this way became hardy and self-reliant, inured both to hardship and shoreward refinements.

Ocean-going sailors seemed to others like a race apart, a breed of men whose habits, dress, appearance and language were distinctive. Seafaring left a man on the outskirts of the community ashore, ill at ease amongst land folks. It was a way of life that took him to the far reaches of the globe but kept him isolated from most of his fellow countrymen. To work aloft amongst a world of rope and canvas in constant movement demanded confident agility which came more naturally to youngsters. Most sailors went to sea when quite young – eleven years old was not uncommon – and their education suffered. They learned their skills at an age when other children were in school, but then few seamen valued book learning as highly as practical competence. They acquired the arcane vocabulary of the sea in a community of men, with little feminine influence. Sea-going broke the ties of upbringing, along with habits of church going. Family life had little opportunity to flourish during intervals ashore, and sailors were notorious for their casual sexual liaisons. It could hardly be otherwise amongst hardy young men with strong instincts which had to be restrained for months at sea. Once ashore, their taste for liquor and women maintained a dark trade in all the world's ports – ancient and modern – condoned or even encouraged as palliatives for the rigours of life at sea.

To natural dangers were added the risks of disease. Fresh produce would last for brief voyages only, and deep water seafarers had to get used to a diet of salt meat and ship's biscuit, inevitably lacking in vitamin C. In the eighteenth century a better understanding of how to combat scurvy began to save lives, but not before huge numbers had fallen victim. Foreign voyages brought close encounters with malaria, or fevers and fluxes inadequately understood, and venereal diseases whose origins were no mystery at all.

Life already at risk was constrained further by the customs of shipboard routine. Stern discipline was recognised as essential for the preservation of ship and cargo. Sailors must work aloft in all weathers whatever the risk to individual safety. When candles were the only form of artificial light the danger of fire was ever-present, and strict guard against carelessness was essential. With numbers of men cooped up in crowded proximity, rules had to be enforced about cleanliness of person and deck area. Quarrels could easily arise, and regulations against fighting, gambling and abusive language were common. Disorder might jeopardise the ship and her company. Strong discipline was in fact perceived as essential, and generally was not resented by seamen so long as it conformed to the accepted customs of the sea.

Sanctions there had to be, and in every sailing fleet they included corporal punishment, a common means of enforcing laws ashore. There is no need to suppose that sea-going bred a peculiar type of cruelty. Flogging was widely used, but what after all were the alternatives? To put a man in confinement meant his duties had to be done by his shipmates. To deprive a sailor of food or leisure would hardly distinguish the guilty from the innocent, and to fine him when pay was a distant prospect and there was nothing to spend his money on at sea would have seemed no punishment at all. Baffling and deplorable as it may be to modern taste, sailors commonly accepted beating as a necessary evil, but they were perfectly capable of seeing the difference between reasonable force and tyranny.

In their harsh life, sailors commonly made space for a rudimentary kind of spirituality. They might know little of orthodox piety but they commonly retained some sense of religion. How could it be otherwise? In ways more dramatically dangerous than landsmen, they felt themselves at the mercy of the elements and instinctively grasped at anything offering hope of security. Evidence for this kind of natural religion is not hard to find from ancient times to the present. It may not be profound or theological, and often it is scarcely distinguishable from superstition.

Marcus Rediker and Peter Earle have researched the life and beliefs of seamen generally in the eighteenth century, focusing primarily on merchant sailors. Rediker found 'an amalgam of religion and irreligion, magic and materialism, superstition and self-help' overlaying a substratum of scepticism and anti-clericalism that was not uncommon amongst the uneducated. He attributes their well-founded reputation for irreligion to their isolation from family life and shore-based religious observance; work at sea obliterated the rhythms of the church calendar, both Sundays and religious festivals. Sailors belonged to the enclosed world of a ship at the mercy of the elements: they were, he says, 'always perched on the curling lip of disaster'. The only way to combat danger was through exertion and co-operation. 'Self-help and solidarity, so utterly essential to survival, eclipsed religion in cultural importance and value. Irreligion became a basis for community.'[2]

It is a compelling view, substantiated by contemporary opinion that seafarers were amongst the most abandoned and profane of men. But it must not pass without qualification. Many sailors were troubled by defiance of God, by blasphemers who invoked divine judgement upon ship and crew, and they retained a moral code, rudimentary and easy-going perhaps, but essential to preserve the harmony of a close-packed community. Earle came across plenty of evidence that sailors possessed Bibles and devotional books, that masters recognised Sunday with lighter duties if not with devotions, and that prayers were occasionally held in a good many ships. 'Scattered evidence suggests that religious observance was not unusual on merchant ships, though regular prayers may well have been commoner in the seventeenth than in the eighteenth century. Much no doubt rested on the piety or otherwise of the captain' – assisted perhaps by a clergyman passenger or ship's officer.[3]

Even where sailors lacked religious knowledge or awareness of God, they still quite often showed respect for the supernatural. They looked out for omens, premonitions or signs of disturbance in nature – birds, fish, astronomical phenomena – that might give warning of storm or danger. They clutched at ways of protecting themselves against their harsh environment, by prizing an infant's caul as a guard against drowning, for instance, or by avoiding inauspicious days for setting sail. They found nature awe-inspiring but that might lead as readily to superstition as to worship.

At the risk of imposing overmuch coherence on a complex picture of subtle developments and local exceptions, a provisional chronology is offered. The Catholic Church had devised tangible means of reminding sailors of their religious duties, with shrines and images aboard ship; a liturgy of prayer marked

---

[2] Marcus Rediker, *Between the Devil and the Deep Blue Sea: Merchant Seamen, Pirates and the Anglo-American Maritime World, 1700–1750* (Cambridge, 1987), pp. 169–85.

[3] Peter Earle, *Sailors: English Merchant Seamen, 1650–1775* (1998), p. 105.

the passing hours at sea, while church-based fraternities cared for sailors ashore. The Reformation changed all this, and left the care of souls in the hands of ship masters. Through most of the seventeenth century prayers were commonly said at sea, sometimes daily or twice daily, and often on Sundays: afloat as ashore, it was still an age that treated religion with respect. The eighteenth-century mindset was more wary of religious controversy, and the reasonably educated classes from which ship's officers were drawn, increasingly sceptical themselves, attached less importance to maintaining a pattern of prayers for ships' crews. As long-distance voyaging became more usual, absence from home and family influence became increasingly protracted, and links with shore-based religious observance more tenuous. In consequence sailors tended to develop their own medley of syncretistic elements, blended according to taste from piety and paganism. Half-forgotten childhood Christianity might surface at times of danger, but deism, superstition and unbelief had plenty of adherents. It was not a world without religion, but it was a long way from the orthodoxy of Anglican parish life.

There were no port chaplains, no visiting ship evangelists, no clergy embarked specifically to minister to merchant crews. The largest East Indiamen were supposed to carry a chaplain but the company rated all its mid-eighteenth-century trading ships at 499 tons, just too small to require a clergyman. The quality of naval chaplains will be considered in more detail in due course, but the general picture will not greatly change. The eighteenth-century seafarer had little enough religion, and even when he called himself Christian he had scant knowledge of what that implied, and allowed it to impose few demands upon time or conduct.

Constantly aware of dangers at sea, sailors ashore were renowned for their reckless pursuit of transient pleasures such as drink, sex, conviviality, brawling or gambling, with scant regard for moral convention. One eighteenth-century sailor described his colleagues' shallow fickleness and abandoned conduct: 'no trouble softens their obdurate hearts, but as soon as the danger is past they return in the greatest avidity to practise wickedness and blaspheme their Maker and preserver.' [4] Undoubtedly there were many men like that. Sailors' idiosyncratic spirituality sustained a pliant moral code, but that is not the whole story. They prized the values that made for community. Loyalty to messmates was the cardinal virtue, carrying with it a set of social obligations such as basic honesty with colleagues, and an overriding duty to give every support when lives were at risk. Those who knew them well were deeply impressed with crewmen's faithfulness to fellow seamen

---

[4] Samuel Kelly, quoted in W. R. Hunt, 'Nautical Autobiography in the Age of Sail', *The Mariner's Mirror* [hereafter *MM*], LVII (1971), p. 142. Caul: skin membrane protecting a baby's head in the womb, discarded at birth. Alternative beliefs in Angelo S. Rappoport, *Superstitions of Sailors* (1928).

and their officers, their generosity and warmth of affection. Sea-going demanded hardihood and courage. Both qualities were characteristic of sailors, especially in defence of their colleagues or in pursuit of money. Often they dispensed with ordered family life, and settled instead for undemanding sexual liaisons in ports ashore, slipping into and out of such relationships like a vessel picking up or dropping moorings. A lack of formal education placed them at a disadvantage when faced with Government officials, lawyers, swindlers and crimps. They were bad at saving money, easily conned by rogue salesmen, and notoriously in thrall to publicans. They had a moral code of a kind, but it did not cover women or drink. Sailors became ready stereotypes, the courageous, resourceful man of the sea, who became a pathetic spendthrift ashore, unable to make a responsible life for himself in that unfamiliar environment.[5]

No simple character summary will suffice. There was a spectrum of beliefs and conduct, ranging from the irreligion that Rediker has identified as typical, to the latent Christian orthodoxy that the Blue Lights hoped for. Middleton and Kempenfelt were obviously right to recognise that sailors lacked pastors, teaching and opportunity for worship, and they began to address the problem. But if Rediker is right, if the predominant mindset of seafarers was unbelief, a different strategy of evangelism and persuasion would eventually be required. Did the secularised maritime culture of the eighteenth century represent the choice of sailors for a life without religious constraint, or was it a by-product of neglect by the Christian community ashore? A brief survey will show how closely related seafaring and religion had once been, and will explore how those links had been loosened if not wholly discarded, creating a massive challenge for naval evangelicalism.

Reformation England and its Navy

The medieval Church evolved a complex apparatus of pastoral and moral care for the sailor which largely perished in post-Reformation England and was not adequately replaced by anything equivalent – until the time of the Blue

---

[5] Vice-Admiral Sir Jahleel Brenton gives an example of this view: 'The sufferings of seamen have but too generally been … viewed as the inevitable consequences of intemperance and profligacy. … The sailor is thoughtless, reckless and improvident to a degree which will scarcely be credited by those who are unacquainted with his character. … From early youth the water becomes his element. … From this circumstance he is necessarily unsettled in his views, has no conception of a permanent home. … Dangers and hardships … he meets and suffers … with a steadfastness and endurance of which so tender an age would scarcely be thought capable. … All who are familiar with the habits of the seaman will readily give him credit for a large portion of kindness and generosity.' *An Appeal to the British Nation on Behalf of Her Sailors* (1838), pp. 7, 15, 35.

Lights. Claiming supreme spiritual authority over the lands and seas of Western Europe, the Church necessarily concerned itself with sailors who might be outside normal episcopal oversight but who were not outside the Christian polity. Sea-going ships were perceived as a part of Christendom where the Church had a major role in shaping offences and their punishment, morals, contracts and immunities. With its supra-national authority it gave a measure of protection to women, pilgrims and non-combatants; most ships carried a shrine at which some right of sanctuary was probably recognised. With its interest in pilgrim ships, crusading fleets and international trade in ecclesiastical goods the Church had a practical investment in seafaring, and addressed issues of safety and welfare as well as law.[6]

Monasteries and hermitages accepted an obligation to provide navigation beacons on dangerous stretches of coast. Early English lights, such as those on Bardsey or the Farnes, were hermit cells where monks maintained a prayer vigil as well as a night-time beacon. The Benedictines of Tynemouth Priory rang the church bell in time of fog as a warning to mariners. Sailors' gilds were often partially religious in character, and the Church provided much of the charitable support for their widows and orphans, and care for sick mariners. When a society of Bristol sailors set up St Bartholomew's hospital in 1445, for example, they provided beds for the medical care of twelve seamen, and money for a priest to minister to them. Coastal churches displayed *ex-voto* ship models as thanksgiving for deliverance from shipwreck, and memorial walls commemorated lives lost at sea. Each port held its patronal feast day with rituals, processions and celebrations. Ships were often given the names of saints to invoke heavenly protection, and services of blessing were held before crews left for distant voyages – and for fisheries, as still today in Brittany.[7]

Religion, then, gave structure to maritime law, customs and charities, but it faced a harder task in pastoring sailors once they had put to sea. Crews of pilgrim vessels or in a war squadron might have the benefit of a priest aboard to hear

---

[6] R. F. Wright, 'The High Seas and the Church in the Middle Ages', *MM*, LIII (1967), pp. 3–31, 115–35.

[7] Peter F. Anson, *The Church and the Sailor* (1948), pp. 31–7; Robert Miller, *From Shore to Shore: A History of the Church and the Merchant Seafarer* (privately printed, 1989), pp. 7–24; J. J. Keevil, *Medicine and the Navy, 1200–1900*, I: *1200–1649* (1957), p. 11 (and *passim*, pp. 1–54). French Catholic practices are well treated in Alain Cabantous and Françoise Hildersheimer (eds.), *Foi chretienne et milieux maritimes (XVe–XXe siècles), Actes du colloque, Paris, College de France, Sept. 1987* (Paris, 1989), and Alain Cabantous, *Le Ciel dans la mer, christianisme et civilisation maritime XVIe–XIXe siècle* (Paris, 1990).

confession and celebrate the Mass (normally the 'dry Mass' without the sacred elements – for fear of spillage), but trading ships rarely embarked one. Nevertheless religion had an honoured place in daily routine. The crucifix or a religious image was placed conspicuously on the upper deck where all were expected to show reverence. Prayers were to be recited when the watch was changed and all hands were summoned for matins and vespers. In the England of Henry VIII, before the break with Rome, it was customary for an evening hymn to be sung before the image of Our Lady, and Queen Mary required that prayers should be said twice a day at sea, as had long been traditional practice. Two and a half centuries later these customs were still being faithfully observed aboard the ships of France and Spain (as Kempenfelt observed), where the ancient Catholic traditions had not been severed.[8]

In England the Reformation profoundly altered the religion of seafarers. The old rituals fell into disuse ashore, and the shrines and crucifixes lost their place aboard ship: with them went the most obvious focus for religious practice. With the disbanding of religious orders there no longer existed any organised fraternity to care for spiritual life afloat. And yet the break with Rome made religion more significant then ever in the culture of the sea. It became the test of loyalty and heresy – potentially matters of life and death. English merchants in contempt of papal decrees who forced their way into Spanish trading preserves were risking a heretic's death. Across Christendom and beyond, religion embodied corporate loyalties, and in England it pre-eminently defined nationhood. Since the fleet was the principal safeguard against any continental Catholic attempt to reverse the English Reformation, the navy's religious leaning determined whether or not Henry's measures would survive. If sailors forsook the new beliefs in favour of the old Catholic creed, the Tudor state would perish, along with the Church of England, the new land settlement and the Protestant succession.

The ancient custom of the sea punctuated the day with prayers, and might therefore leave a place for the old liturgy and beliefs. It was an important area to claim for Protestantism. Political prudence as much as piety led the Crown to demand definite religious observance – not just prayers, but the new Anglican liturgy, preferably conducted by a clergyman of the established church. In his orders of 1578 Frobisher directed that prayers must be said 'with the services usual in the Churches of England'. On his voyage of circumnavigation Drake took a chaplain to lead prayers for the crew and to celebrate Holy Communion

---

[8] Gordon Taylor, *The Sea Chaplains: A History of the Chaplains in the Royal Navy* (Oxford, 1978), p. 12; Wright, 'The High Seas', p. 29; J. S. Corbett (ed.), *Signals and Instructions, 1776–1794*, NRS (1908), p. 366.

in accordance with the Elizabethan Book of Common Prayer; even after the two men had clashed and the chaplain had been publicly disgraced, the twice-daily ceremony of prayer continued, with Drake reading the service with the officers and Fletcher taking the service for the crew. To possess the Scriptures and to join in devotions from the English Book of Common Prayer were badges of the new Protestantism: when Lord Sheffield's surgeon was suspected of Catholic sympathies in 1588 he was able to clear himself by showing his New Testament and Anglican prayer book, together with a psalter 'which he daily sang with the company'. Where no clergy were carried, the master was expected to read psalms and intercessions, using, of course, the Anglican liturgy. The traditional custom of the sea survived, but in a manner that reinforced each day the new religion of the Tudors.[9]

N. A. M. Rodger has identified Protestantism as a key element in the emergence of British sea-power; the creation of a formidable fleet in the sixteenth and seventeenth centuries grew out of Protestant England's isolation from mainland Europe and the danger that came of it. 'The governing classes were obsessed with the Popish menace ... It is impossible to imagine that a Catholic England would have been, or felt, so isolated and imperilled. It was because she became Protestant that she had so many reasons to build up a fleet.'[10] If the Enterprise of England in 1588 was perceived by the Spanish as a holy war, the English were equally convinced that it was a struggle for the true faith. 'Their fleet consisteth of mighty ships and great strength', wrote Howard to Walsingham, 'yet we doubt not, by God's good assistance, to oppress them.' 'We shall be able, with God's favour, to weary them out of the sea and confound them', wrote Hawkins, and Drake too saw the campaign in similar terms: 'God give us grace to depend upon him; so shall we not doubt victory, for our cause is good.'[11] The political elite willingly accepted the tax burden of a huge maritime establishment because it perceived continental Catholic Europe as a threat to its survival. Ideology fuelled the rise of sea-power and, as Peter Padfield has intriguingly shown, fed upon it. The ocean was not a neutral milieu but an arena of conceptual conflict as well as national

[9] Miller, p. 18: note Frobisher's emphasis on moral conduct 'to banish swearing, dice and card playing, and filthy communication'; Anon., 'Drake's Voyage Round the World', pp. 143–67, in J. Hampden (ed.), *The Tudor Venturers* (1970), p. 164 (Folio Society edn of Richard Hakluyt, *Principal Navigations, Voyages, Traffics and Discoveries of the English Nation*, 1589); Taylor, pp. 33f.; Keevil, I, p. 68.

[10] N. A. M. Rodger, *A Naval History of Britain*, II: *The Command of the Ocean, 1649–1815* (2004), p. 577.

[11] J. K. Laughton (ed.), *State Papers Relating to the Defeat of the Spanish Armada, 1588*, 2 vols., NRS (1895–1900, reissued 1981), I, pp. 241, 360, 365.

rivalry. New ideas travelled with river-borne and sea-going traders, exposing sailors to radical thinking.[12] No Government – particularly a Protestant English one – could willingly abandon the moral and religious guardianship of its navy.

Daily prayer continued to be routine well into the seventeenth century. Privy Council instructions to the Earl of Rutland in 1623 referred to 'common prayer and the singing of psalms' as 'the ancient custom of relieving and setting of watches', and this applied in every ship whether a clergyman was embarked or not. There is no reason to suppose that such prayers were unwelcome to crews. After all, the prevailing culture believed in a God who answered prayer, the Creator who controlled wind strength and sea state. When the *Golden Hind* was stranded on a Pacific reef in 1580 Drake called the chaplain to celebrate Communion for the crew before a last desperate effort to free her; when the ship was saved he led them in thanksgiving. It was usual for fleets going on war service to be accompanied by chaplains – Cadiz 1596, Algiers 1620, Buckingham's expeditions to the Île de Rhé and La Rochelle 1627 and 1628 – and for prayers to be offered before battle. Who would wish to die without the comfort of religion? As the *Constant Reformation* began to founder in heavy seas in 1651, those who could not escape in the boats joined her chaplain to partake of Holy Communion before they perished.[13]

Religion reinforced morale; it also carried a powerful political message. The unsettling ambiguities of Charles I's policies towards Catholicism were partially resolved by his recruiting Anglican clergy as 'preachers' for every ship. When liturgy and ministers changed after the first civil war, a new order of worship was provided: *A Supply of Prayer for the Ships of this Kingdom that want* [i.e. lack] *Ministers to pray with them* (1646) took the place of the now discredited Book of Common Prayer. It remained important that the navy's religious stance should be uncompromisingly Protestant and yet as devout as it had been in Catholic times. As Lord High Admiral the Earl of Warwick, in his fleet orders, called for daily prayer, Sunday services and respect for religion, regulations which were superseded by Parliament's Articles of War in 1652; with similar wording they demanded that 'preaching and praying and other religious duties be exercised … and the Lord's Day religiously observed.' Cromwell's navy saw itself as the sword of the Lord against Catholic Spain, Islamic Algerines and even those errant Protestants the Dutch. Before the action off Dungeness in 1652 prayers were said in every ship; a

---

[12] Peter Padfield, *Maritime Supremacy and the Opening of the Western Mind* (1999), pp. 1–6.

[13] Taylor, p. 64; John Cummins, *Francis Drake* (1995; pbk edn 1997), pp. 121f.; Waldo E. L. Smith, *The Navy and its Chaplains in the Days of Sail* (Toronto, 1961), p. 18; W. Laird Clowes, *The Royal Navy, a History from the Earliest Times to the Present*, 7 vols. (1897–1903), I, pp. 429f.; Taylor, pp. 62, 66f.

day of humiliation before God was observed before the fleet sailed to the attack on Porto Farina in 1655. In anticipation of battle at Santa Cruz in 1657 there was 'earnest seeking to the Lord for His presence', and after his victory Blake wrote in his official despatch, 'we desire the Lord may have the praise and glory, to whom alone it is due.' Those Puritan sailors had come to identify their naval operations as the service of God, in terms that might have been echoed by their Victorian successors, but perhaps by few individuals before the mid-nineteenth century.[14]

Soon after his return to the throne Charles II defined the religious stance of the new Royal Navy in the 1661 Articles of War. It was to be as Protestant and Anglican as the king himself at that time. The first regulation required commanding officers to cause the public worship of Almighty God to be 'solemnly, orderly and reverently' conducted according to the liturgy of the Church of England. 'Prayers and preachings' were to be diligently performed by chaplains in holy orders, and the Lord's Day was to be observed. These measures replaced Parliament's Articles from 1652 but kept the fervour of its wording. The navy's Protestantism was an amalgam of conviction, prejudice, xenophobia and tradition. After James II's conversion he advanced a few Catholic officers but made little headway in altering the culture afloat. In 1688 the navy's essential Protestantism was personified by Admiral Herbert – devoid of both charm and piety – who was crucial in switching the fleet's loyalty from James II to William of Orange. In his Anglican days as Lord High Admiral James had been a brave and successful commander, but reputation could not help him once he embarked on his Catholic policies. By choosing to avoid battle with the Dutch in 1688, the predominantly Protestant fleet became England's king-maker, and its support for the Protestant Succession thereafter was key to the survival of William III and Anne, and the transfer of the Crown to the Hanoverian dynasty.[15]

Religion, then, which had been so important in the creation of a powerful fleet, was a prominent component of the naval profession. It flaunted its Protestantism and Anglican liturgy. Nonetheless there are reasons to doubt whether there was much depth of piety in this religion. How far was anything being done for

14 Taylor, pp. 66, 72; Michael Oppenheim, *A History of the Administration of the Royal Navy from 1509 to 1660* (1896), pp. 311f.; A. G. Kealy, *Chaplains of the Royal Navy, 1626–1903* (Portsmouth, 1905), p. 13; J. R. Powell, *Robert Blake, General-at-Sea* (1972), pp. 187, 261; J. R. Powell (ed.), *The Letters of Robert Blake*, NRS (1937), pp. 368f. – his will, p. 342.

15 An Act for the Establishing Articles and Orders for the regulating and better Government of His Majesties Navies Ships of Warr and Forces by Sea: 13 Car. II, c.9, *Statutes of the Realm* (1819), v, pp. 311–14.

the souls of sailors? Examination of this question must begin once more with the Reformation, and the changed relationship between the Church and seafarers.

The Pastoral Care of Sailors

THE Reformation dismantled the sophisticated apparatus for the care of sailors which the Catholic Church had developed over centuries. Removing images from ships was the most obvious but not the most significant of the changes. With the disbandment of religious fraternities much was lost in the way of practical care for sick and destitute seafarers and of support for their dependants. There were no friars to go to sea, no corps of priests to minister afloat, no religious order to look out for sailors, no voice to speak consistently for their spiritual needs. When captains or fleet commanders recruited clergy to serve afloat, it was for a specific expedition or an individual ship, never for general naval service. The Bishop of London licensed clergy to serve afloat, but that was as far as organisation went. The Church of England was slow to recognise any general responsibility for the care of maritime souls.

This was partly a result of reformed theology. In Catholic thinking, the sacraments were needful for salvation, and only priests could administer them: unless the Church were to regard all sailors as lost souls it had to find ways of keeping them in touch with a sacramental ministry, with opportunity for confession and the Mass. Protestant teaching stressed the need for personal faith rather than reception of the sacraments as the way of salvation: there was therefore less urgency about appointing clergy to sea service. Let prayers be said at sea, of course, but look to the parish church for teaching, baptism and communion. This strategy was flawed for two main reasons. First, the scrapping of so many rituals and festivals connected with the sea had left the sailor with fewer links to parish life, and secondly the character of seafaring was changing, as the range of maritime trade increased, making regular worship ashore more difficult for the sailor.

Coastal fishermen and short-haul seamen would return to their home ports at frequent intervals, and might reasonably keep in touch with local life including church. As lengthy deep-water voyaging became more typical of English merchant shipping in the seventeenth and eighteenth centuries, seafarers could expect longer absence from home, and attenuated contact with worship ashore. Normal parish life did not fit with the rhythms of seafaring which reflected wind and tide, the fishing season or availability of cargo in preference to the church calendar. Clergy ashore had relatively little influence over men whose adolescence (and perhaps even childhood) was spent on the high seas, who were inevitably away from home for most of their working lives, and who did not readily settle to family life. French coastal fishermen returning to port after relatively brief intervals preserved their church-going, and priests working with mothers and families ashore had some success in keeping up religious observance amongst their menfolk as well. Reformation England risked secularising the seafaring community by dismantling the shrines and images, and by scrapping so many of the earlier rituals of blessings, fasts and festivals that used to punctuate the life of the seafaring community.[16]

The Reformers were clear in their own minds that religious ceremonies were harmful unless accompanied by faith: they led a man to trust in the efficacy of what he was doing rather than what Christ had done. There was therefore no loss in the removal of pictures and carvings which could lead the ignorant into virtual idolatry or superstition. But what would take their place? The answer of the Reformed theologians was clear: it must be the Scriptures, the Word of God made accessible to all in language they could understand. It is significant that chaplains in Howard's fleet were described as 'preachers', but sailors needed more than sermons.[17] At sea they endured risk as a daily reality; in port they faced the lure of taverns and brothels away from the steadying influence of family or parish. Their hard drinking, loose living, gambling and recklessness with money created self-inflicted hardships, but these vices owed much to a lack of moral nurturing in youth. They needed all the help that religion and charity could bring. Protestant sailors had the same material needs as before, but the ancient structures of social security had gone when the spiritual orders had been dissolved. There is room for some detailed comparison of welfare arrangements for destitute and sick sailors and for their dependants before and after the break with Rome. Did private charity and the Chatham Chest adequately compensate for the old gilds and fraternities, the *maisons dieu* and hospitals? Perhaps they did, but the lingering suspicion remains that the new focus on preaching and faith was not accompanied by so much social activity as before. When the Blue Lights took up what was known as the Sailor's Cause more than two centuries later, they found plenty of human suffering in the maritime community, and little being done by church or state to alleviate it. Greenwich Hospital served a fortunate few, but there were plenty of destitute sailors and impoverished families in every port.

Even the directly religious ministry was patchy. In time of war clergy could be found to accompany the fleet, but once the fighting was over, ships' companies were left too often to the religion of established routine – Sunday service, daily prayers and psalms as long as they were in vogue, but rarely a sermon, a tract, or a

---

[16] For French customs, see Cabantous, *Le Ciel dans la mer*.

[17] At least six 'preachers' were embarked for operations against the Armada, and were awarded a pay rise: Laughton, *Spanish Armada*, II, p. 231.

service of Holy Communion. In Commonwealth times, when the Puritan experiment relied on the loyalty of its navy, Parliament sent ministers to preach and new services of prayer to be used in ships without chaplains, giving the most sustained attention yet to the spiritual needs of the whole fleet. The central Government had seen how important it was to send good pastors afloat and to maintain the old routines of sea-going religion, for one of their ships had been lost to the cause in 1648 because of the random whims and inconsistencies of well-intentioned ministers who did not understand sailors: 'we had no settled form of Divine Worship', protested a group who went off to join the Royalists, 'no Communions, little or no Preaching on board but by illiterate and mechanical persons.' The terms of the protest demonstrate how mid-century sailors acknowledged spiritual needs that went deeper than liturgical repetition.[18]

However widespread such fervour may have been in the 1650s, it was checked by the Restoration. In the King's ships a few chaplains were found, but according to Pepys their numbers were small and quality poor. In default of ministers to do the work, the pastoral care of sailors would fall upon their officers, and particularly the captain. As we have seen, there was a long tradition of religious observance at sea, and codes of conduct approved by the Church: in any ship the master was expected to uphold both. When Charles II promulgated the Articles of War in 1661, it seemed entirely appropriate for commanding officers to be made responsible for the moral and religious welfare of crews, but what in practice would it mean? There were fine words about the public worship of Almighty God, with 'prayers and preachings' from the chaplains, and general observance of the Lord's Day; profanity and 'scandalous actions in derogation of God's honour and corruption of good manners' were subject to punishment. Although these measures gave authority to chaplains and insisted on Sunday prayers, they did not go far to ensure depth of pastoral care. In a ship without a chaplain, would there be any religious instruction for the boys in her crew? Daily prayers were not mentioned: had they begun to disappear already, together with the Puritan fervour that had probably kept the practice alive for the last decade? Since, in Pepys's judgement, far too few captains troubled to find a chaplain, how would religion fare at sea when left in the hands of laymen? Any ship master might enforce acceptable conduct but only a handful would ever have made spiritual guides. There was every danger that sailors who went to sea ignorant of religion would stay that way.[19]

[18] Taylor, p. 74.

[19] J. R. Tanner (ed.), *A Descriptive Catalogue of the Naval Manuscripts in the Pepysian Library at Magdalene College, Cambridge*, NRS, 4 vols. (1903–23), I, p. 219; see n. 15 above.

Scattered evidence suggests that in places religious practice was faithfully observed. The Quaker seaman Edward Coxere describes evening prayers being led by the master in a merchantman well after the Restoration, and the chaplain Henry Teonge managed to hold divine service most Sundays in a warship during Charles II's reign. Taking a view of the service as a whole, however, Pepys the Secretary of the Navy believed that morality and religion were both in decline: in the 1670s he noted the 'debauchery and impiety ... too generally found in the navy', and he attributed this to a lack of chaplains. He deplored how few captains troubled to take a clergyman to sea, and 'the ill choice generally made of those that are entertained, both for ignorance and debauches, to the great dishonour of God and the Government, and the encouragement of profaneness and dissolutions [dissoluteness] in the fleet.' Keen to ensure that every ship of fifth rate and larger should have its own chaplain, Pepys recommended better screening by the church authorities and better payment from the Admiralty. Helpful as these reforms were, they failed to bring sufficient clergy aboard. Frustrating as it seemed to Pepys, the appointing of chaplains depended on ships' captains, and if lay interest in religion was flagging there was little that the Secretary of the Admiralty could do. Teonge's diary tells of Sunday services usually with a sermon, but there is no reference to daily prayer. Occasional pamphlet writers such as Robert Crosfield in 1693 and a former Commonwealth sea-captain in 1707 deplored the decline of religion, fearing the divine judgement which might be incurred and calling for a mending of morals 'lest otherwise Heaven as well as the Common Enemy be engag'd against you.' While Pepys and pamphleteers may have exaggerated, their picture of neglect was not fanciful.[20]

During the wars that closed the seventeenth and opened the eighteenth centuries naval religion underwent something of a revival. Perhaps to reaffirm

[20] E. H. W. Meyerstein (ed.), *Adventures by Sea of Edward Coxere* [written between 1685 and 1694] (Oxford, 1945), p. 88; G. E. Manwaring (ed.), *The Diary of Henry Teonge, Chaplain on board HM Ships Assistance, Bristol and Royal Oak, 1675–79* (1927), *passim*; Tanner, IV, pp. 383, 400ff.; R. Crosfield, 'England's Glory Revived' (1693), in J. S. Bromley (ed.), *The Manning of the Royal Navy, Selected Public Pamphlets, 1693–1873* (1976), p. 3; Anon., *An Inquiry into the Causes of our Naval Miscarriages* (2nd edn, London, 1710), p. 27 [originally *The Old and True Way of Manning the Fleet*, 1707]. Compare Rodger, *Command of the Ocean*, p. 215: there is some evidence that religious observance in the fighting fleet declined after the Restoration but it should be used with caution. One ex-Commonwealth sea captain noticed the difference when religion was neglected and speech corrupted – 'nothing but damning and sinking and coarse obscene conversation to be heard aboard our men-o'-war': there was, he felt, no need to search further for causes of England's eclipse at sea: *Naval Miscarriages*, p. 12. Rodger explains that some

England's Protestantism and to shore up the loyalty of the fleet, the Church ashore thought kindly of its sailors and provided them with clergy. It may have owed something to William III's Proclamation against Vice in 1692, and the renewed religious spirit which created both the Society for Promoting Christian Knowledge in 1698 and the Society for the Propagation of the Gospel in Foreign Parts in 1701. A fresh concern for religious observance is found in the Mediterranean fleet when the Rev. John Hext became chaplain to Sir George Rooke; with the admiral's encouragement he held prayers twice a day in the flagship, and hoped the practice would spread to other ships. All chaplains in the squadron in priests' orders were expected to celebrate Communion, once again at Rooke's behest. At last an admiral was accepting a responsibility for spiritual welfare that went beyond routine prayers, and now that the SPCK was beginning its activities, there was an agency to give help. In 1700 the Rev. Patrick Gordon, chaplain of the *Salisbury*, became SPCK Correspondent for the Navy, and it appears to have been his idea to have a tract commissioned especially for issue to seamen. As a result Dr Josiah Woodward wrote *The Seaman's Monitor*, destined to be the longest lived of all sailors' tracts, and a powerful call to Christian faith and commitment. The SPCK supplied the fleets of Rooke and Shovell with 14,000 copies in 1701, aiming to provide one for every pair of sailors. Where chaplains were reluctant to distribute them, Rooke ordered it done. Bearing in mind the overt evangelistic purpose of *The Seaman's Monitor*, this surely means that Rooke had some notion, however vague, that sailors needed the Gospel. Where admirals led captains followed, and in this new climate 350 chaplains were appointed to warships during the War of Spanish Succession. Recruitment was helped no doubt by a measure of 1697, allowing a naval chaplaincy to be held without abandoning a living ashore: it was a concession which helped with a temporary shortage, but it further emphasised the navy's lack of a dedicated profession of sea-going clergy who would identify with sailors and be truly accepted by them.[21]

criticisms of naval administration were couched in religious terms as an acceptable code understood by contemporaries; even so, the force of the argument would disappear if there were no basis in fact.

[21] David Ogg, *England in the Reigns of James II and William III* (Oxford, 1955; pbk edn 1969), pp. 530ff.; Taylor, p. 123; A. E. Barker, *The SPCK and the Armed Forces*, SPCK leaflet (n.d.); Josiah Woodward, *The Seaman's Monitor, or Advice to Sea-faring Men, with Reference to their Behaviour before, in and after their Voyage* (1700); Mark Harris, 'Naval Chaplains in the late Seventeenth and early Eighteenth Century', *MM*, LXXXI (1995), p. 208. The official seal of the SPG showed a clergyman arriving by sea in response to the prayers of the people of North America: the first

A Century of Neglect and a Call to Revival

How much of this revival was due to a genuine care for souls, motivated by spiritual zeal, and how far was it aimed at ensuring the Protestant Succession in England? With the state and religion so intertwined it becomes impossible to distinguish clearly between piety and politics. On a private level religion could help with personal moral issues and a sense of well-being. In a letter to the SPCK Gordon explained that he was concerned for 'the reformation of the seamen', meaning their moral improvement, and to make righteousness more appealing he proposed to distribute tobacco along with his tracts. Was all this to promote high morale, or good discipline, or to win converts? Perhaps all three, for religion could serve more than one purpose.[22]

Whatever the driving force behind this new burst of piety, its energies were soon spent. After 1714 there were few approaches to the SPCK for its literature. The request of the captain of the *Princess Amelia* for 'some Books of Divinity' in 1739 broke a lengthy silence. Clergy largely avoided going to sea: barely ten chaplains a year entered the navy between the Treaty of Utrecht and the start of the American War, and few stayed beyond a single commission. As a type they lacked commitment to the navy, but the problem ran much deeper than that, as quite a proportion showed little sense of vocation. Sea-going religion – as will be demonstrated – slid further into an obsolescence which its paid representatives failed to halt. The Church of England whether at sea or on land largely neglected seafarers and did little either for their practical needs or for the good of their souls. The Admiralty left their spiritual health in the hands of captains who might or might not choose to ship a clergyman, and responsibility for general welfare – health, accommodation, pay, family – pretty well ended when they were discharged ashore at the end of a commission.[23]

Who might befriend him, educate and better him? The answer is compellingly obvious. Jack's officers – not Admiralty officials but his own ship's captain and lieutenants, perhaps the master and warrant officers, the people he learned to trust through shared danger, the people who knew and liked him in return – these were almost the only ones who consistently looked after sailors and protected their interests. Blue Lights came from this sector of the profession, but their interest in sailors' welfare was by no means unusual. Nelson as a young captain was prepared

---

Anglican missionary to America was given passage in the fourth rate *Centurion*. William's Proclamation was renewed by Queen Anne, and by George III. The text of the 1760 Proclamation is given in *The Bye-Laws and Regulations of the Marine Society* (1772; 4th edn 1792), pp. xi–xiv.

[22] Barker, p. 1.

[23] SPCK Minutes Books, 1739; General Meeting of 25 September.

to stretch legality to breaking point on behalf of his boatswain in trouble, and Collingwood was once found in tears after paying off a ship's company whom he regarded as family. Compared with such personal interest from those who knew him best, the sailor had poor support from the organised Church ashore and its ordained representatives afloat. A vigorous movement of lay piety in the fleet might yet reach seamen with the Gospel, and bring this unevangelised class into the Christian orbit.[24]

Eighteenth-Century Naval Regulations

IN view of declining interest in the SPCK and the slump in both numbers and quality of chaplains, it is surprising to find religion given prominence once more when *Regulations and Instructions Relating to His Majesty's Service at Sea* were first issued by the Admiralty in 1731, to define obligations for its commanding officers. This document was reissued with some emendations until the thirteenth edition of 1790; it was not superseded until 1806. Unaltered throughout this period were requirements for divine service to be held twice a day according to the Anglican liturgy, with a sermon on Sunday. Swearing and cursing, frequently directed against authority, could be understood as offences against discipline, but blasphemy – contempt for God – was also to be punished, by fines and the wearing of a 'wooden collar or some other shameful badge of distinction'. Later Blue Lights saw an opportunity for spiritual renewal in these measures, but it must be highly doubtful that they were framed with such deliberate purpose.[25]

Did they reflect the customs of the time, when church going was normal and daily prayers were routine in many households ashore? Perhaps they were the product of administrative inertia, if the Secretary who framed them, Thomas Corbett, merely transcribed the provisions of Charles II's day when religion had been more of an issue. We cannot be sure of the motive but religious revival is unlikely since chaplains were almost totally ignored. No instructions were included for them, and they gained only a brief reference to their pay (19 shillings a [lunar] month) and entitlement to a servant. Nor would crusading zeal fit Lord Torrington, First Lord from 1727 to 1733: he had hitched his wagon to the Protestant cause, but he is not usually regarded as strongly driven by religion. Yet while creed was still an issue in the nation at large it made sense to reaffirm the navy's Protestantism, as a bulwark against Jacobite claimants and their Catholic allies.

---

[24] John Sugden, *Nelson: A Dream of Glory* (2004), pp. 320–9; Rodger, *Command of the Ocean*, p. 491.

[25] Rules of Discipline and Good Government, article 4, *Regulations and Instructions Relating to His Majesty's Service at Sea* (1731) [hereafter *RAI* 1731], p. 44.

Whatever the intention behind the *Regulations*, they did not usher in a period of religious zeal in the navy's public life.[26]

In the succeeding three decades it became a matter of note when an admiral insisted on regular public worship or took measures to curb profanity – as Norris in 1735 and later both Anson and Hawke. Samples of ships' logs tell the same story of infrequent Sunday services. If the Lord's Day was neglected despite official direction, it is surely safe to infer that daily prayer had disappeared. Scattered references in ships' records, published reminiscences and private correspondence give a coherent story of religion retreating into personal conviction, still guiding morality and giving inner strength perhaps, but no longer the focus for collective shipboard life. Had it been otherwise, the Blue Lights would have lacked a cause to promote.[27]

By 1742, when Charles Middleton went to sea, the religious part of *Regulations* had become a dead letter, with daily prayer unknown and Sunday services a rarity. As he recalled:

> I was sixteen years in the sea service before I was made a captain, and never, during that time, heard prayers or divine service performed a-board of ship, nor any pains taken to check vice or immorality further than they interfered with the common duty of the ship. As soon as I became a captain I began reading prayers myself to the ship's company of a Sunday and also a sermon. I continued this practice as long as I was in commission and without a chaplain, and it never was omitted when I had one. I did not indeed venture to carry it further than Sundays, because the practice was confined to those days by the very few ships who had chaplains, when followed at all; and I should only have acquired the name of methodist or enthusiast if I attempted it.[28]

How is this disregard for *Regulations* to be explained? Captains still took seriously their responsibility for the conduct of crews, as their instructions required, but they had come to see this as a disciplinary rather than moral charge. Samples of ships' logs from the 1760s contain only occasional references to Sunday worship – although duties were habitually lightened for one day in seven. In unconscious

---

[26] As Sir George Byng, Torrington had been a wartime flag officer under Rooke, and the *Regulations* reflect the good practice in his fleet.

[27] G. Hinchliffe, 'Some Letters of Sir John Norris', *MM*, LVI (1970), pp. 77–84; also S. W. C. Pack, *Admiral Lord Anson* (1960), p. 12; and Ruddock F. Mackay, *Admiral Hawke* (Oxford, 1965), p. 2.

[28] *BP*, II, p. 163.

parody of a solemn assembly for the Lord's Day, hands were regularly mustered for a reading of the Articles of War, which spelt out the awesome authority of commanding officers, reminded officers and men of their duty to obey and rehearsed the penalty for non-compliance. A stern litany it was, with death the normal punishment for mutiny, desertion or wilful defiance, while the captain was to punish lesser offences according to the custom of the sea. There was nothing here to lift the spirits, not even a rudimentary effort to acknowledge the Creator. Religion as a definition of loyalty had been displaced by secular controls. After 1745, when the chance of a Catholic restoration had dwindled to vanishing, the new Hanoverian security could safely neglect religion.

The intellectual climate of the age suited these rearranged priorities. Enlightened thought made scepticism congenial: educated minds were turning to rational enquiry and empirical science instead of revealed religion. Doubt was becoming fashionable, not just doubt as to which religion might be true, but doubt concerning all religions. The officer corps prided itself on technical expertise, scientific outlook, mathematical skill and modern thinking as parts of its professionalism. The navy used the most advanced technology to keep its fleets at sea; its explorers were using cutting-edge navigational and cartographic skills; its physicians were increasingly mastering age-old problems of medicine and diet, and sea-going surgeons were often outstanding practitioners. In such a world of new doubts and fresh discoveries, thoughtful officers were becoming more interested in deism than old beliefs. John Newton and Andrew Burn felt its allure, and Richard Marks found it still active in the early 1800s. Deism was a popular form of agnostic religion: it accepted the existence of God as an explanation of origins and guarantor of ethics, but doubted any divine intervention in the affairs of mankind. While it could coexist quite happily with Enlightened thinking, it saw little point in intercessory prayer and was embarrassed by fervent piety. With doubt and deism gaining ground amongst the educated classes, the navy's growing secularism probably owed as much to Enlightenment values as to negligence or overriding duties.[29]

If captains were unwilling to fulfil their pastoral and religious tasks, the chaplains, lacking both in numbers and authority, were unable to fill the breach. In the first place there were not enough to staff the ships entitled to one, and in the second they were entirely dependent upon their captains for the right to carry out their ministry. Even if we allow that the few chaplains who served many years and several commissions in the navy were men of spiritual effectiveness – and that

---

[29] The Rev. John Newton (1725–1807); Major General Andrew Burn, Royal Marines (1742–1814); Lieutenant the Rev. Richard Marks (1778–1847); see p. 282 below for Newton, p. 109 for Burn, and p. 253 for Marks.

is not proven – their influence would have been confined to a small number of ships. There were no Admiralty Instructions to guide and empower the chaplain. He had no career structure and no archdeacon to care for his interests or to keep him up to the mark. Appointed by Admiralty warrant, he belonged not to the chaplains' branch or to the navy in general, but to one specific ship. Once that ship's commission ended, the chaplain, like all her foremast hands, was discharged ashore, unemployed until another captain might apply for him. Aboard ship he held an anomalous position. A gentleman by education, his social rank was equivalent to the commissioned officers of the wardroom, but he had no rights there: he must normally eat and live amongst his social inferiors, the warrant officers of the gunroom. The largest part of his floating parish was made up of lower-deck sailors, but the social hierarchy of the ship and the complexities of her layout made it hard for him to mingle with them, to create enough trust to bridge the social divide and enable him to counsel men's souls.[30]

According to Middleton, few chaplains were in priests' orders, and so had no authority to celebrate Holy Communion. No clergy were likely to be attracted to naval service because of the opportunities for ministry. All was so dependent upon the captain, who could readily find an excuse to forbid service in the state of the weather or the demands of naval necessity. Nor were the material compensations large enough. The chaplain was paid at the rate of an able seaman, supplemented by 'groats' of four pence per month deducted from the pay of each member of the crew, and enhanced perhaps by prize money. He had a cramped cabin to himself amongst the other warrant officers of the gunroom, with a swinging cot, small desk and a chair, set about with removable walls of canvas and light wood.[31]

None of this might have deterred a man with vocation, but the problems ran deeper still. He was essentially an interloper who did not truly belong. By background and training he was a landsman who had strayed aboard. One eighteenth-century chaplain who was refused protracted leave of absence wrote in astonishment that he had not expected to 'be obliged to be near the ship or on board'. The simple fact was that he had no permanent place in the navy, no career structure afloat, and, unless he was fortunate in his friends ashore, no ready way

[30] For chaplains, the standard work is by Taylor. See also the important study, N. A. M. Rodger, 'The Naval Chaplain in the Eighteenth Century', *British Journal for Eighteenth-Century Studies*, XVIII (1995), pp. 33–45, and Smith, *The Navy and its Chaplains*.

[31] Chaplain's cabin in HMS *Gloucester*, 1812, depicted in 'The Rev. Edward Mangin's Journal', in H. G. Thursfield (ed.), *Five Naval Journals, 1789–1817*, NRS (1951), facing p. 10.

of advancing his clerical career on land. Chaplains were all too often men who had failed in their vocation and had no other way of finding a living: seeking a short-term solution to problems ashore, they might well end up with a further one afloat. Unable to secure a parish ashore and deprived of a satisfying ministry at sea, some settled into the gregarious life of the gunroom, earning a reputation for conviviality rather than spirituality – if they were accorded even that degree of acceptance. Superstitious sailors regarded a clergyman as an unlucky shipmate, a Jonah whose presence would never be welcome.[32]

Only a determined pastor with a deep sense of vocation could surmount such discouragements. But what if chaplains themselves were unsure of their calling, or given to indolence, or troubled by doubt? We know that some went to sea for reasons that had nothing to do with the ministry – to experience for a time a life of action, to recover health, to escape gambling debts, or to travel (say) to the East Indies at state expense. Others had vocation but no living: being wanted for a ship gave sufficient title to be ordained a deacon. Some were undeniably lazy, and no doubt preferred an undemanding captain to a bishop's oversight. And how many had theological doubts of their own which might be left aside at sea when there was nothing more unsettling than a few prayers or a homily to be read from time to time? Later 'friends of religion' were generally contemptuous of naval clergy as a breed – often compromised by speech and character, pursuing philosophy in preference to biblical theology, and peddling beliefs that trailed off into deism or speculation. Contemporary memoirs do not cancel this impression. When chaplains appear – in the recollections of James Anthony Gardner, for instance – they may be congenial company but hardly men of God driven by a sense of mission. While prevailing culture was propelling the navy towards secularism, chaplains of this kind had no resistance to offer.[33]

But fervour was springing back to life. A new movement of piety began to revitalise parts of the Church of England and old Dissent in the eighteenth century – the Methodist awakening and the Evangelical revival – developments on shore which would impact on the navy, clergy and laity, officers and men. The primary impulse afloat came from laymen whose piety had been kindled by the Evangelical Awakening, and who became widely known as 'Blue Lights'.

---

[32] Rodger, 'The Naval Chaplain', p. 40, quoting Percival Stockdale in 1776.

[33] Rodger, 'The Naval Chaplain', pp. 35–8; Smith, *The Navy and its Chaplains*, pp. 67, 70; Harris, p. 209; James Anthony Gardner, *Above and Under Hatches*, ed. Christopher Lloyd (1955), pp. 84, 113; Harris, pp. 207–10.

The Evangelical Awakening

THE Great Awakening had its origins in New England under the preaching of Jonathan Edwards and others from 1734. George Whitefield's preaching extended it to England. When John and Charles Wesley caught the vision a spiritual revival resulted which through their itinerant ministry brought 'vital religion' to many thousands of the marginalised and unchurched, hitherto untouched or unimpressed by the parish life of the Church of England. New wineskins were needed for this new wine. Although Wesley never intended to break from the national Church, his Methodist movement was eventually obliged to find an ecclesiastical home of its own. The genius of John Wesley set up a self-propagating movement based on local cells with lay leadership, the class system loosely linked into a national organisation. Yet the Methodist leadership was not primarily interested in church organisation but in rediscovering and proclaiming the Christian message.[34]

Reinvigorated by the Methodist example, a section of the Church of England responded with the Evangelical Movement, Christian believers who held just as passionately as the Wesleys the Gospel of God's redeeming love in Christ but who had no wish to secede from the national Church. They wished instead to see the Church of England revived by ardent Gospel preaching in its parish churches. From the twin centres of Cambridge, where Charles Simeon ministered, and Clapham, where many of their most notable members lived, the Evangelical Movement spread its influence into pulpit and Parliament.

Like the Methodists they preached the need for conversion. Sin, they taught, was not just a matter of moral lapse, still less of abandoned wrong-doing, but a state of alienation from God to which all were subject. God had provided the remedy for this most universal of human needs through the incarnation of the Son of God as Jesus of Nazareth. His death had paid for the guilt of humanity, making possible a fellowship with God which would transcend death and bring the believer into Heaven's immortal glory. All this could be received by simple faith, by believing in Jesus Christ as Saviour and Lord. By faith alone,

---

[34] Studies of the Evangelical Movement abound. Mention might be made of Mark A. Noll, *The Rise of Evangelicalism* (Leicester, 2004), and A. Skevington Wood, *The Inextinguishable Blaze: Spiritual Renewal and Advance in the Eighteenth Century* (1960) – both favourable studies. Biographies of Wilberforce include Robin Furneaux, *William Wilberforce* (1974), and John Pollock, *Wilberforce* (1977). The Clapham Sect, parliamentary arm of the movement, is well covered by Ernest Marshall Howse, *Saints in Politics: The 'Clapham Sect' and the Growth of Freedom* (Toronto, 1952; reissued as Open University pbk 1971).

they stressed, following the Apostle Paul and the teachings of Luther and the English Reformers; but such a faith, to be accounted real, had to bring forth the fruits of repentance in a changed way of life, with honesty and uprightness the evidence that living faith existed. This change they called conversion, and their sermons were directed to the achievement of it. Such a task of evangelism was, they believed, fundamental to the calling of the Church, and every member ought to be active in witnessing to its truth.

One theological difference which distinguished Anglican Evangelicals from Wesleyan Methodists concerned free will and election. At some risk of oversimplification, it may be stated that Whitefield, Simeon and their colleagues in the Church of England believed that the human will unaided was too far disabled by sin to make a real choice for God and repentance; only the intervention of the Holy Spirit, calling and convicting, could overcome this natural repugnance towards the things of God and enable repentance to take place. Conversion must therefore be seen as God's work, choosing, empowering, granting the gift of saving faith. The same grace of God which saved the lost would keep the believer true to his faith and deliver him safe into his eternal home. Wesley and his followers dissented from this Calvinistic view of election. To them, the human mind enlightened by the Gospel had a choice: to choose faith and repentance would lead to salvation, while deliberate rejection of the message would lead to hell. Furthermore the believer must keep himself in his faith through the grace of God available to him, lest by wilful persistence in sin or by deliberate denial of faith he should forfeit his salvation. Such a position is sometimes described as Arminian. Occasionally in the heat of debate Wesleyans would denounce their opponents as Antinomian, a technical theological term from antiquity implying an easy view of morality; by this they meant that, by separating salvation from good works entirely, Calvinists might encourage loose living. Evangelicals did not intentionally condone wrongdoing, of course, but believed no one could lose salvation through misconduct any more than he could gain it by right behaviour. When compared with latitudinarian Anglicanism, with Deism or Unitarianism, with friends of formalism and opponents of 'enthusiasm', Wesleyans and Evangelicals had a vast amount in common. Indeed, some individuals like the Countess of Huntingdon or John Fletcher of Madeley for a time tried to hold a bridge between the two positions. In spite of such efforts and all that the leaders might do to promote harmony, the rift existed, and for years it soured relations between Whitefield and Wesley. Where less gracious and theologically subtle minds were involved, the differences could be sharp and the divisions bitter. Yet still the new piety spread.

Terms need to be defined. *Evangel*, the Greek word for Gospel, gives rise to *evangelism*, the proclamation of the message. Wesley and the Methodists, together with all who believed similarly in this *evangelical* faith, would engage in *evangelistic* activity. The *Evangelical* Movement is its Anglican wing, comprising believers within the Established Church. The Blue Lights were Evangelicals afloat.

At sea as on land, their preferred methods were the same. The message had to be circulated through the spread of the Scriptures, and applied by persuasive preaching and literature. The religious tract was a powerful instrument, and skilled writers like Hannah More achieved a huge circulation. Stories of everyday life could attract the reader, who was then led on to face the need for personal response, for the exercise of faith in Christ and conversion of life. Printed sermons were popular, either for use in the pulpit or more usually for private devotions in the household. They were strong supporters of preaching – of godly preaching, that is – scripturally based, Gospel-oriented, Christ-centred. Such preaching they looked for in the parish churches of the land, and to get it they were happy to use whatever patronage their more wealthy members might have.

A seeming contradiction lay at the heart of Evangelicalism ashore and afloat. On the one hand they distanced themselves from the formalism of much contemporary religion, effectively stressing the novelty and radicalism of the Awakening. On the other hand they were reassured to find that their beliefs had been the historic convictions of the English Reformers. They did not wish to undermine the national Church but to recall it to its ancient roots. Nor did they want to see the ordered society of Georgian Britain brought down by radical Jacobinism. By religious conviction and by social status they were conservative. Nevertheless they were certain that the *status quo* would not do, tainted as it was with religious lethargy and moral decline. They could never ally with the political Radicals, who also despised the *status quo*, because they did not share the same spiritual vision. Both wanted England changed but whereas the Radicals thought of the franchise, the press and the law, the Evangelicals concentrated on faith, morality and the Bible.

They were not social reformers by inclination, but they knew the Gospel command to love their neighbour obliged them to help those in need. To their credit they saw slavery as a monstrous wrong but were slower to perceive the injustices of a harsh penal code and a social structure that tolerated privilege and destitution. They preferred compassion and charity to political action. They were instinctively but not unthinkingly conservative: they knew they were under orders to put God's claims before Caesar's. It might not be apparent to everyone when this moment of supreme choice had been reached, and some felt they could go on supporting existing institutions such as slavery or impressment longer than others. Every Evangelical agreed, however, that the demands of the Kingdom of Heaven transcended those of earth. At the same time they rejoiced that Providence had placed them in a land of Protestant liberties where godliness could flourish, and King George had no more loyal subjects than they.

In its 'methodist' lower-deck form, the new movement had the potential of stirring up radical notions with echoes of Puritanism – spiritual egalitarianism, religious exclusivism, moral censoriousness – all guaranteed to end the messdeck truce over religion, and to alarm the authorities by threatening division in the closed society of a ship's company. It created plenty of local controversy but, like its counterpart in the commissioned ranks, it preferred piety to politics and worked for conversion rather than subversion. Had this movement of spiritual rejuvenation lacked officer leadership, would it have remained so docile? It simultaneously moderated lower-deck radicalism and stimulated reforming activity in commissioned ranks, until Blue Lights from the officer corps became proponents of structural change. Christian teachings promoted socially desirable characteristics such as sobriety, honesty, charity, reliability and mutual respect. Groups of officers and men discovered a religious unity that bridged social class. Whatever general truth there may be in Rediker's thesis, the new piety afloat became one workable basis for community.

The Blue Lights Appear

MEN of this kind attracted nicknames, the lower deck generally being labelled Methodists or psalm-singers, and the officers either Blue Lights or psalm-singers. It is not clear when the term 'Blue Light' was first applied. Admiral Wauchope used it after the Napoleonic War as an established description well understood in naval circles. When Whitefield visited Gibraltar in 1738 he found a group of Methodist soldiers who were called 'the New Lights' by their colleagues. One may speculate that their seafaring counterparts were given a nickname which neatly altered the religious term to a naval one. Blue lights were pyrotechnics used for ship-to-ship signals at night, drawing attention to danger, course alteration or some pre-arranged meaning. Rather less derisory than 'Psalm singer', it was probably used in a politely contemptuous way, as these night-time flares gave gloomy light and soon passed away. Supporters found the term serviceable, for a light shining in the darkness is a frequent Christian motif, all the more appropriate if they were marking out the route. But they do not appear to have selected the name for themselves. In a sense the Blue Lights were those who were so defined by others. They were officers, normally in positions of seniority, who used their influence to promote their own narrow view of religion. They were, of course, Protestants, since all commissioned officers were obliged to forswear Rome and the Pope before they could be appointed. Like most of the wardroom they came from the propertied classes. They supported the Crown and the Church of England, were suspicious of dissent and opposed to Radicalism, republicanism, atheism and anything else that bore the taint of the French Revolution, including the United Irish movement. In all this they were in no way different from their brother officers.[35]

What principally distinguished them was their proselytism. Not content with maintaining their private piety and morality, they hoped to make converts amongst both officers and men. They promoted religious practice but were never content with external observance. Ultimately their goal was nothing less than to introduce individuals to a personal knowledge of God. Faith of this kind if genuine would be life-transforming, and would need to express itself in conduct. But the evangelicals went further. Of course, they expected converts to live by an exalted moral code, but, in the belief that God had revealed standards for all humanity, they looked for ethical conduct in the whole community. They were driven by an inner compulsion, a missionary spirit. Their perceived obligation to remedy society's vices made them uncomfortable colleagues, apparently judging others inadequate in religion and morals. This went way beyond personal devotion. The particularity of evangelicalism was that it made demands in the public sphere. It was not content to be a private matter. Piety came out of the shadows, seeking converts and promoting – even demanding – changes in public conduct.

Its true temper can be seen in Wilberforce, the 'lay archbishop' of the movement. Once he had come to his own understanding of salvation, he dedicated his life to proclaiming the Christian message. Evangelicals acknowledged a responsibility to spread their faith. They were also deeply concerned for the honour owing to God. They sought godliness in their own lives and in society at large; they looked for righteousness in personal conduct and in the laws of the nation. It therefore became part of evangelical thought that private and public life should follow biblical standards, and that immorality should be checked. Royal proclamations against vice had been issued by successive sovereigns since William III as general statements of corporate national values: Wilberforce, through the Proclamation Society which originated with him, aimed to turn moral aspirations into rules for personal and national behaviour, by invoking legal process to enforce morality. Their creed did not stop at personal piety, but had an intrusive element that gained enemies as readily as friends.

---

35 Admiral Robert Wauchope, *A Short Narrative of God's Merciful Dealings* (printed for private circulation, 1862), p. 93; The Rev. George Whitefield, *Journals, 1738–1741* (1960), p. 131.

Fearing the results of religious conflict, eighteenth-century England had become profoundly wary of fervour, preferring detachment and even indifference to overheated conviction. The Church of England had developed a theory of Establishment which suited a mixed constitution of monarchy, aristocracy and landowning elite, along with their dependants. It offered them the comfort of a religious view of life, with the blessing of God on the social and political order. It made less appeal to those on the make, the upwardly mobile classes who were suspicious of the prevailing structure of society, those mercantile and manufacturing communities who found Nonconformist culture more congenial. The Church of England had learned to tolerate Dissent so long as it stayed on the periphery of power. Neither Anglicanism nor old Dissent had much to offer people on the margins of communal life – the miners and new urban migrants of industrial change, the dispossessed, the unchurched, the criminal – or the Catholics, especially the Irish. The Wesleyan and Evangelical Awakening would have something to say to the neglected classes, and this movement eventually impacted on the navy.

Michael Snape has shown that Methodism in the mid-eighteenth century made substantial inroads into the rank and file of the army, for reasons which only partially hold good for the lower deck. He points out the appeal that 'raw supernaturalism' made to the class from which private soldiers were drawn; men who lived with danger had reason to think about issues of life and death. Religious tracts circulated quite widely and aroused interest. Doddridge's biography of the life and heroic death of Colonel Gardiner was a popular book for soldiers and an inspiration to many redcoats who sought to combine their faith and their secular calling. Pious officers of whom there were a few had some effect on their units, while the dearth of Anglican chaplains left the field open to lay preachers inside the army or dissenting ministers near military encampments. Civilian influence which nurtured army Methodism had fewer points of contact with sailors, especially at times when shore leave was a rarity. The basic social unit afloat was the mess, and large gatherings were only possible when hands were mustered by order: in the constricted world of a man-of-war, Methodism would have been perceived as divisive, whereas gatherings of soldiers off duty for hymn-singing and testimony may have produced the reverse effect. Snape points to the sense of comradeship in these meetings, which reinforced the faith of members and attracted enquirers. There was a religious revival in Flanders in 1745, and significant conversions amongst officers during the Seven Years War. He argues that Methodism may have become the dominant form of piety amongst the rank and file. That could never have been said of the lower deck. Individual sailors were labelled Methodist; as we shall see, there were sometimes enough of them in a large ship to form their own mess, but there is little indication of widespread interest.[36]

From time to time we encounter officers and men of sincere Christian piety in the Georgian navy, natural allies of the Blue Lights, whose faith guided conduct in life and brought consolation in death, but whose convictions remained personal and private. The present study is not primarily concerned with them. Blue Lights had to be seen: their mission was to shine; their intention was to influence; their aim whether stated or implied was conversion. Others shared some of their concerns, and even looked uncommonly like them in important respects, but unless they were promoting the salvation of souls they cannot truly be regarded as Blue Lights. Thus St Vincent's determination to see regular worship enforced does not qualify him, nor Nelson's regular reliance on the SPCK for supplies of prayer books and Scriptures. Collingwood presents more of a problem: his personal piety was evident to his secretary and biographer who noted his attendance at public worship and his invariable habit of privately reading prayers, lessons and a devotional book if Sunday service could not be held. He may have distributed Bibles and New Testaments to his crews – a speaker at the NMBS anniversary meeting claimed to have seen an application from him; certainly his post-Trafalgar order for a thanksgiving service is particularly striking, with its reference to seeking God's mercy and forgiveness for sins – all thoroughly congenial to the Blue Lights – and yet it would be hard to number him amongst them unless there is further evidence that he was concerned for Gospel preaching and conversion. Sir William Hoste similarly was a God-fearing man of profound personal piety, but not (it seems) associated with evangelistic activity.[37]

Evangelicals in the navy were not an organised party, yet they were distinctive enough to be labelled 'enthusiasts' or 'methodists' in the early days, and eventually Blue Lights. They shared the values of a society of property and privilege. They belonged to a profession which prided itself on its progressive modernity, and had welcomed technological innovation, but where continuity was more obvious than change. Its officers were largely drawn from gentry families, socially conservative;

---

36 Michael Snape, *The Redcoat and Religion* (2005), pp. 34, 36, 41, 64, 67. James Gardiner (1688–1745) was a pious colonel in the light dragoons who died heroically in the battle of Prestonpans.

37 Newnham Collingwood, *Correspondence of Admiral Lord Collingwood* (1829; 4th edn 1829), pp. 567f.; Captain Francis Maude, as reported in *Anniversary Report of the Naval and Military Bible Society* [hereafter *NMBS*] (1839), p. 27; Trafalgar signal: PRO ADM 1/411, Part 5, fol. 568; Lady Hoste (ed.), *Memoirs and Letters of Captain Sir William Hoste, Bart., RN, KCB, KMT*, in 2 vols. (1833), I, pp. 206, 244, 311; II, pp. 89, 177, 290, 292.

its seamen and petty officers came from the seaports and coastal districts which traditionally provided men for the nation's shipping whether engaged in trade, fisheries or the fighting fleet. Improvements in diet, medicine and navigation offset similarity in so much else – provisioning, pilotage, armament, architecture, even pay for an ordinary seaman had altered little since Pepys. Like all naval officers the Blue Lights were aware of such continuity, and initially appeared more old-fashioned than progressive. When faced with the spiritual needs of the American War their first response was to invoke the traditional values of the 1731 orders. They called for chaplains and literature, Admiralty *Regulations* and Sunday observance; they looked to captains to fulfil a moral and spiritual role. Eventually they got their way, and in so doing became a force for change. This study will demonstrate how a socially conservative movement of piety developed such radical energies that it achieved lasting reform, and then in its turn became the new tradition of the Victorian navy.

II

The Genesis of a Movement: Middleton, Kempenfelt and Ramsay

Captain Charles Middleton: A 'Methodist' Afloat

ONCE the new evangelical piety spread on shore it was only a matter of time before it seeped into the navy through several entry points. Chaplains were one; commissioned sea officers were another, as quite a high proportion of entrants were sons of clergy, some of whom were touched by the religious revival. Lower-deck seamen were drawn in high numbers from the seaport areas where Wesley had preached – Plymouth, Portsmouth, Dover and Cornwall generally. The philanthropic Marine Society of Hanway and Fielding gave a steady stream of destitute youngsters the opportunity to sign on at sea, and they had been well drilled in their religious duties first. Since sailors were normally allowed to choose their own messmates, a group of like-minded believers could form a small community to sustain their own faith and perhaps have an improving effect upon the moral tone of the ship's company. In any of these ways some localised influence might have been anticipated from the evangelical awakening. As this study will show, its impact came to be felt on a much wider scale, not just in particular warships but throughout the ranks of the navy. How a minority creed of private faith acquired such leverage demands explanation.[1]

The whole movement began when an undistinguished commander who had embraced the new piety was appointed captain of a modest-sized warship on the West Indies station in 1757. From the start he began reading the service of Morning Prayer to his ship's company on Sundays at sea, with a sermon as well. In spite

---

[1] John Wesley, *The Journal of the Rev. John Wesley, 1735–1790* (Everyman edn, 4 vols., n.d.), II, p. 171; III, pp. 307, 425, etc.; 'What a desire to hear runs through all the seaport towns whenever we come! Surely God is besieging this nation and attacking it at all the entrances' – after preaching at Dover, 30 Nov 1768, ibid., III, p. 354. For Marine Society, see James Stephen Taylor, *Jonas Hanway: Founder of the Marine Society* (1985). *The Bye-Laws and Regulations of the Marine Society, incorporated in 1772* (4th edn 1792), includes tracts and religious books (amongst list of clothing), along with references to religious practices, including an injunction to say prayers twice a day with at least one other besides the Lord's Prayer – 'say them slowly and secretly in your hammock when you cannot kneel.' Although associated with the Evangelicals Hanway seems to have kept his distance from its more 'enthusiastic' elements and was therefore critical of Whitefield's preaching: Taylor, p. 139.

of what the Articles of War and the *Regulations* stated, it was unusual even for a chaplain to hold divine service regularly; sermons were rarer still, and for a layman to conduct worship in this way was entirely exceptional. But Charles Middleton, unremarkable in 1757, would become a figure of outstanding significance as naval administrator and reformer.[2]

The influence he exerted is the primary reason why the new piety became strong in the navy. By exploiting his position he ensured wide currency for his creed, but how far it was accepted by the naval profession is a question to be explored. We shall examine how he came to hold this faith, how it shaped his character, and how in turn his convictions helped form the evolving ethos of the officer corps. In time Middleton became the central figure amongst a group of captains and admirals who shared his beliefs and helped to spread them in the navy; they became known by the slightly pejorative term of the Blue Lights. He filed away amongst his papers a private memorandum on the duty of captains: it was in effect a programme for religious reform, little more than a distant aspiration when composed, but one that he brought to fulfilment before his long life of public service was over. He dreamt of a navy where church services were held each Sunday after the pattern of his first command, where chaplains preached sermons and Bibles were made available, where morality flourished and piety could thrive. It deserves to be regarded as the manifesto of the Blue Lights.

In later life Middleton claimed that he began taking Sunday service at sea as soon as he became a captain, sixteen years after joining the navy. Since he had entered as a captain's servant in 1741, this would mean that he instituted divine worship in February 1757 when made commander of the *Speaker*, a 12-gun brig, on the Leeward Islands station. The next year he shifted to another brig before taking over the *Arundel* (24) as post-captain in March 1759. All three ships were employed in commerce raiding and protection. He recalled having gone through the whole order of service with all who could be spared, while the watch on duty maintained pursuit of an enemy sail. He knew that religious activity of this kind

---

[2] *BP*, II, p. 163. Middleton's career is summarised in John Charnock, *Biographia Navalis*, 6 vols. (1794–8), VI, p. 330, and is surveyed in *BP*, I, pp. vii–xlvi; II, pp. vii–xx and III, pp. vii–xxxviii. The only full biography is John E. Talbott, *The Pen and Ink Sailor: Charles Middleton and the King's Navy, 1778–1813* (1998), but there is an extensive biographical appreciation by Roger Morriss, 'Charles Middleton, Lord Barham, 1726–1813', in Peter Le Fevre and Richard Harding (ed.), *Precursors of Nelson: British Admirals of the Eighteenth Century* (2000). His work at the Navy Board and the Admiralty flavours two works by N. A. M. Rodger, *The Insatiable Earl: A Life of John Montagu, Fourth Earl of Sandwich, 1718–1792* (1993), and *The Admiralty* (Lavenham, 1979).

1 Admiral Charles Middleton (1726–1813). An outstanding naval administrator and the most influential of the Blue Lights, he was created Lord Barham in 1805. (Oil painting (detail), British School, 19th century)   © National Maritime Museum, London BHC2529

would expose him to notice in the navy, and not wishing to be labelled a fanatic – 'Methodist or enthusiast' – he did not try to introduce the daily prayers specified by *Regulations*.[3]

Middleton had not grown up with piety like this, and his religion owed much to romance. Before he could afford to marry a girl with no dowry he needed an income, and active service against privateers provided opportunity for enrichment. As captain of the fast 28-gun frigate *Emerald* (July 1760 – October 1761) he was successful in several operations, taking eleven laden merchantmen and five

[3] *BP*, II, p. 163.

privateers as prizes, a haul that brought him a substantial sum in prize money, enough to set up his own establishment. Now a successful captain of thirty-six, he returned to his homeland and to the girl he had not seen for at least six years; after six more weeks they were married. This interval of shore leave was soon over, and they were parted by a further year of war service off the coast of Normandy. When at last he came home from the sea to married life and fatherhood, Middleton settled down as an innovative farmer. His profits from agriculture and prize money were invested in the East India Company to supplement his half-pay, but he had no direct links with the sea for the next twelve years.

Many found him difficult, a man of strong opinions, critical and irascible when stirred. He was not swayed by fashion or popularity, and he felt little need to cultivate personal charm. From his grandfather, the principal of King's College Aberdeen, came a keen intellect; to his father, collector of customs at Bo'ness, he owed a strong business sense and a commitment to public service. Yet the character which most truly defined him, his Christian piety, was not inherited from family but derived from Margaret Gambier, the young woman who became his wife in late 1761. Shortly after her death in 1792 Middleton wrote to a friend, 'it was to my dear wife's perseverance, as a means, that I owe all I possess of religion, and in that blessing she has left me more than herself.' Then he added a few poignant words that hinted at how much he depended on her and how faith sustained him in distress. 'It is to that source of every comfort that I owe the serenity which I now feel – and but for the great prospect which it holds out to poor believing sinners, I should this moment feel nothing but despondency and despair.'[4]

Margaret, daughter of the warden of the Fleet Prison and member of a substantial Huguenot family, was the niece of Middleton's first captain. Further information is provided by Sir John Deas Thomson, a civil servant and sometime secretary to Middleton, who assembled materials for a biography never completed. According to him, Middleton met Margaret when he was twenty-one (1747). The girl preferred him to someone else the family had in mind for her, and a ten-year dispute with her father followed, culminating in her leaving home disinherited and taking up residence with a friend, Elizabeth Bouverie, on her estate at Teston in Kent. Something more durable than pique or girlish romance must account for such a breach.

The two young women had been friends since schooldays and shared an interest in painting, but what really drew them together was their commitment to the new piety. The biographer John Pollock concluded that Margaret Gambier had come to evangelical faith under the influence of the great preacher George Whitefield.

---

4 NMM MID/2/28 (2) to Rev. C. I. Latrobe, 17 Dec 1792.

As an orator, he attracted huge crowds of working people in England, Scotland and North America, but was equally capable of holding high-society congregations spellbound. With fair plausibility Pollock suggests that Margaret took her naval lieutenant to hear Whitefield preach, and gave her heart to him once she was sure that his faith matched hers. We may surmise that Margaret resolved to marry no one who did not share her creed and that this caused the alienation from her own family. Middleton's reference to 'her perseverance' implies that he did not have an immediate conversion; nor did they have a whirlwind romance. Perhaps the sequence went something like this: an initial meeting when Charles was twenty-one led to three or four years of cautious courtship with his Christian understanding developing under Margaret's prompting. Any hopes they may have had of marriage at this stage were dashed when her father refused Middleton's suit and countered with an advantageous match of his own devising. Margaret was obdurate and her father unyielding. She had to leave the family home with no hope of a dowry, and Middleton was faced with nine years of saving his naval pay before he could afford to marry.[5]

If this reconstruction is correct, Middleton became committed to the new piety sometime between his first meeting with Margaret Gambier in 1747 and his return to sea, in the *Anson*, in 1753. Her first lieutenant was Richard Kempenfelt, another of the pioneer Blue Lights, who became a close friend and confidant in due course. There are grounds for thinking that Kempenfelt had not yet found his faith at this stage. It can scarcely be doubted that they talked about religion: did Middleton, emboldened by his new convictions and his slow-burning romance, share his beliefs with his friend and thus prepare him for his own conversion a few years later? Middleton first, Kempenfelt second: this order makes sense of what can be deduced about Kempenfelt's faith, and it does justice to Charles's testimony that he owed his conversion entirely to Margaret. If Charles and Margaret, already at one in their Christian conviction, had reached an understanding, an unofficial engagement to marry, before he embarked on his long period of sea service, it also makes the ten-year estrangement from her father more comprehensible. She must have been very sure of her man to reject one offer of marriage, break with her father and lose her inheritance for his sake. But if she had shared her beliefs with

---

5 Sir John Deas Thomson served as Middleton's secretary and planned a biography of him. He gathered materials but never achieved a finished work. The Rev. John Pollock has written biographies of leading Evangelicals, *Wilberforce* (1977), *George Whitefield and the Great Awakening* (1972), and *Amazing Grace: John Newton's Story* (1981). His speculation concerning Middleton's conversion appeared in a brief essay on Barham for the Officers' Christian Union, 'Trafalgar, Admiral Lord Barham', *Practical Christianity*, Nov–Dec 1955, pp. 1–5.

him, prayed for him, and introduced him to preaching that brought him to the same conviction, her constancy can be more readily understood. Once they were married she had the further task of introducing her husband to evangelical circles. Not much could be done during the three months they had together before the navy whisked him away for another year at sea, but the following twelve years on half-pay gave time for a whole new way of life to develop. They kept up their links with Mrs Bouverie at Barham Court and often stayed there; they found a London house in Mayfair, where Margaret became a noted hostess. In all this they were not unlike many a couple with money and social contacts, but with an unusual twist: they were adjusting to life in the evangelical subculture which came to define so much about them.

At first glance the landward side of Middleton's life might seem far removed from the navy: Sir John Laughton, who edited his papers, describes these twelve years as a blank involving nothing of general interest. In fact this was the time when his faith became so blended with his character that it is impossible to separate the man from his religion. In his secular life hereafter he would have a spiritual take on any issue – exasperating to those who suspected hypocrisy or a spurious claim to moral advantage. Without his religious views Middleton might still have been an efficient administrator, perhaps a reformer, but his evangelical piety gave him something else – a confident assurance that he was doing God's will. That conviction bestowed astonishing powers of perseverance in the face of difficulty; it gave him concentration of energy and intellect, for he believed that the work in hand was a God-given task. Nothing could be mundane, no detail insignificant, if it belonged in some fashion to the service of the Almighty. While aiming that truth and honesty should be present like a watermark in all his dealings, he seemed unwilling to admit that any public servant might be as principled as he was, and where he suspected unrighteousness in policy or conduct he exposed it. He could be harsh in his judgements and inflexible in opinion. Some of this was due to his personality, some derived from his background, but most of it came from his faith. This close integration of religion and character was noted by contemporaries and has been readily apparent to those who have studied his role in naval affairs: he has been justly described as 'the Evangelical Administrator'.[6]

In those twelve years on half-pay Middleton was inducted into evangelicalism, with its doctrines, personalities, attitudes to public life and principles of personal self-discipline. Neither of the Middletons had grown up in the evangelical world;

---

[6] Ian Lloyd Phillips, 'The Evangelical Administrator: Sir Charles Middleton at the Navy Board, 1778–1790' (DPhil thesis, Oxford University, 1978).

after entering it they had to construct a network of supportive relationships outside their families. Keenly conscious of the gap between their own values and those of the world, evangelicals were adept at creating communities of interest. Margaret's friendship with Elizabeth Bouverie was now widened to include Charles, and the couple were always welcome at Barham Court, her residence in Kent, which became a second home to them and was left to Middleton on her death in 1798 – by which time the inheritance had been greatly enriched by his business and farming skills on her behalf. As Margaret had talent for painting and literature, they entertained a cultured circle of visitors, including Johnson, Boswell, Garrick and Reynolds. At a greater level of intimacy they made close friends with like-minded believers, Kempenfelt (perhaps only by letter) and James Ramsay from naval days, Ambrose Serle and John Newton who had both been at sea, social reformers Jonas Hanway and John Howard, Bishop Porteus and the More sisters, the Moravian pastor Benjamin La Trobe and his son. This vigorous social life is not well represented in the Barham volumes, for Sir Charles had a habit of destroying purely personal papers, but the reminiscences of Wilberforce and Hannah More contain many references to dinners with the Middletons, often in company with evangelicals and a broader mix of opinion. Wilberforce became a close friend; Granville Sharp, Thomas Clarkson and the other leading Abolitionists often met at Barham Court to refine their strategy. As Middleton became more closely involved with politics, both through the Abolition movement and through the governance of the navy, another circle joined the list of visitors – his cousin Dundas, his wife's more distant relative Pitt, and Grenville, leading statesmen of the time. And Middleton became a welcome member of the so-called Clapham Sect, a group of wealthy, influential evangelicals who clustered around the Rev. John Venn and his parish church. They came to see their social rank as an opportunity to spread their faith and values more widely through political and philanthropic action. Like them, Charles and Margaret shared a world-view where Christianity was central and its implications clear – evangelism, abolition of slavery, and the moral reformation of society – and where high office gave singular opportunities for these goals to be attempted.[7]

---

7 For the Middletons' social circle, see R. I. and S. Wilberforce, *Life of William Wilberforce*, 5 vols. (1838), III, pp. 223, 370f., 460, and IV, p. 122, and William Roberts, *Memoirs of the Life and Correpsondence of Mrs Hannah More* (2nd edn, 4 vols., 1834), I, pp. 77, 93, 146 ('good Jonas Hanway of the party'), 185, 207, 238, 253 ('the captain of one of Commodore Johnson's Dutch prizes breakfasted at Sir Charles Middleton's' – 1782), 277, 317, 398; II, pp. 13, 24, 81('whole day at Middletons – entirely spent on negro business'), 106, 110 (More met Wilberforce at Middletons'), 156 ('Mr Wilberforce and his myrmidons are still shut up at Mrs Bouverie's, at Teston,

Sir Charles Middleton: The Evangelical Administrator

The American War of Independence ended Middleton's peaceful years of progressive farming and brought him back into the navy. Initially he held no post of great distinction – he became captain of the *Ardent*, the guard ship at the Nore in 1775 – but he immediately put the stamp of evangelicalism upon his command. His order book is proof that he had not lost his earlier concern for the moral and religious welfare of his ship's company. Laughton finds evidence here of 'an enlightened mind, singularly in advance of his day'.[8] The ship's company was organised into four divisions, each under a lieutenant; measures were put in place to combat vice and the perennial problems of drunkenness, swearing, fighting and leave-breaking. Officers were given delegated powers to punish minor offences, and thus avoid undue recourse to flogging. Only married women were allowed to stay on board, but shore leave was to be given to well-behaved men. The chaplain was to be treated with proper respect and given every support for his ministry. The complete set of regulations shows a captain determined to have a well-ordered company, efficient, healthy and clean living. They were just the kind of measures that Kempenfelt would wish to see extended throughout the navy a few years later. Upholding religion and curbing vice could both could be treated as elements of discipline, but how to persuade the unconverted and how to tackle unbelief were problems of a different order, still beyond the grasp of the Blue Lights.

A couple more home-based assignments were an undistinguished prelude to his true life's work in naval administration which began in 1778. On the death of Nelson's uncle Maurice Suckling, Sandwich the First Lord of the Admiralty had to find a new Comptroller for the navy – and surprisingly he invited Middleton to take the post. The two men had probably met from time to time at music concerts. The straight-laced Scotsman impressed Sandwich: he was clearly a master of business as his agriculture proved. He had excellent financial acumen and seemed incapable of dishonesty. He was immensely industrious, well connected amongst various useful people outside the Sandwich circle, and of course he had wartime experience at sea. He was acquainted with British interests in Asia through the East India Company, and he knew the West Indies from his own service there.

---

to write'), 226, 253 (Newton); III, pp. 9, 15, 53, 96 (Porteus) and 226. Also Pollock, *Wilberforce* (pbk edn 1978), pp. 50, 52, 56, and James Watt, 'James Ramsay, 1733–1789: Naval Surgeon, Naval Chaplain and Morning Star of the Anti-Slavery Movement', MM, LXXXI (1995), p. 163.

[8] *BP*, I, pp. 39–45 and xix.

The Genesis of a Movement

Sandwich found quite enough to persuade him that this man could do the job; he chose well.

As Comptroller of the Navy from 1778 to 1790, Middleton was head of the Navy Board with its wide-ranging responsibilities for stores and provisions and for the design, construction and refitting of warships. In this role he was answerable to the Admiralty and its head, the First Lord, but Middleton developed his own particular view of the relationship between them. The First Lord might be either an admiral like Anson, Howe or St. Vincent, or a politician such as Sandwich, Chatham or Melville; as a member of the Cabinet, he must expect to lose office whenever there was a change of administration. Three experienced sea officers assisted with specifically naval affairs, and the four men together comprised the Board of Admiralty, responsible for appointments and promotions, for policy and ship deployment, for discipline, tactical principles and war strategy. While successive administrations came and went, Middleton's long tenure of office gave him the sense of being a permanent servant of the state, above politics. Furthermore he recognised that the exercise of sea power rested on the possession of adequate material resources. The Navy Board was therefore essential to British national policy, and his own position at its head gave him peculiar responsibility; because his role was technically subordinate to the Admiralty and always subject to political control, he became extremely tenacious of his authority. His mastery of the intricacies of all the departments he controlled gave him a clear view of where reforms were needed; his own integrity and commitment gave him exacting standards by which to measure both his subordinates and his political masters, Sandwich included.

What effect did religion have upon his character? His faith may have had a slow and difficult birth, but once in place it became part of the essence of the man; without entirely altering his personality, it helped him to self-mastery, and particularly over his anger. Once as a lieutenant, when confronted by an insolent sailor with a group of supporters, he reached for a pike in a dangerously disproportionate reaction. Later, when a captain, he cuffed and kicked a defiant carpenter; again that fiery temper is evident – but less savage than some historians have supposed. Talbott alleges that Middleton kicked the carpenter 'in the crotch': instead, the mate gave evidence that he 'saw the Captain strike the carpenter with his open hand, and at the same time struck him with his foot on the britch' – no doubt an undignified and even improper application of a shoe to the seat of his trousers, but less than the assault alleged![9]

---

[9] PRO ADM 1/5299, fol. 32; cf. Talbott, p. 9, and Rodger, *The Wooden World, An Anatomy of the Georgian Navy* (1986), p. 212.

Dundas noted his irritability, and even Hannah More, a personal friend, recorded that 'Sir Charles … has the stern and simple virtues of the old school', suggesting an austere and distant man.[10] In 1805, when First Lord of the Admiralty and largely responsible for national defence, he still had a reputation for bad temper – the reason why his staff did not rouse him from sleep with crucial intelligence about the French fleet. He could be harshly critical, but he was essentially fair-minded too. He had sharp words for Sandwich over what he considered his dilatory hours, but he later wrote him warm words of appreciation. Although he was appointed to replace his cousin, the disgraced Lord Melville (the title taken by Dundas), as First Lord in 1805, Middleton remained on good personal terms with him: he congratulated him on being cleared by the Lords of fraud (Middleton could well distinguish between negligence and malversation) and hoped he would soon be back in public office, while a little later he offered him a 'quiet retreat after all the persecution and agitation of mind your lordship has gone through'.[11] This is the considerate, thoughtful man rarely glimpsed in his published papers and his public life, where the purpose-driven man predominates, an enemy to incompetence, indolence and iniquity; such attitudes made him censorious and perhaps self-righteous, but neither malicious nor vengeful. In his private dealings he retained lifelong friendships with a surprisingly wide circle of intimates, but much is still inaccessible – how he dealt with his tenants, for instance, or treated his staff. And yet there surely was a gentler, affectionate side to the man, revealed particularly in letters written just after Lady Middleton's death (but omitted from *The Barham Papers*).[12]

Margaret his wife was renowned for practical kindness towards the vulnerable and destitute, and her sympathy for Negro slaves. Under her influence he became more amiable. His fiery temper cooled into an irascibility that he never completely lost, but patience, self-mastery and concern for others seem to have developed through his nearness to her. While it is difficult to characterise a man who has left so little record of his inner thoughts, it appears that he was not a warm-hearted philanthropist by instinct but through persuasion. As we shall see, it was Margaret who prompted him to initiate the Abolition struggle in Parliament, and under her tutelage his humanitarian sense developed. No doubt parenthood helped the process. Their only child was a daughter, Diana, born in September 1762, ten months after their wedding – Middleton kept fond ties with her even when she was married – and they brought up their nephew James Gambier like

---

[10] Roberts, II, p. 24.

[11] BL Add MSS Melville Papers (Series II) I, fols. 133, 135.

[12] *BP*, II, pp. xix–xx.

an adopted son, a bond made even closer by his full acceptance of evangelical faith.[13]

This Middleton is less accessible than the formidable administrator. Historians since Deas Thomson who have studied his papers most closely have found a personality more powerful than appealing, confident, critical, outspoken (Laughton), priggish (Murray, Rodger), irritable, oppressive and at times cruelly judgemental (Morriss), self-righteous and unwilling to admit his own mistakes (Talbott). In his own day he was respected for his abilities but was not well liked. Howe clashed with him over his demand for promotion to flag rank; a later First Lord, Spencer, found him obdurate on a point of principle; St Vincent disliked the man and his methods – 'a compound of paper and pack-thread' – while the politician and diarist Creevey despised him as a 'superannuated Methodist'.[14] Dundas (then secretary at war) modified praise for his 'great official talents and merits' with the caveat that he was 'a little difficult to act with from an anxiety, I had almost said an irritability of temper, and he requires to have a great deal of his own way of doing business in order to do it well.'[15] Yet despite the drawbacks of such a personality, he stayed long as Comptroller because of his recognised ability. His capacity for sustained and highly focused work was outstanding, with energy maintained for years at a stretch. Capable of mastering vast quantities of detail, he could also take a long-term and widely ranging view of policy and strategy, making him, in Pitt's opinion, 'the best man of business' he knew.[16]

Middleton had a distant family link and, through his friendship with Wilberforce, a further informal route to the attentions of William Pitt the Younger, who came to trust his judgement on practically all naval matters whether within the competence of the Navy Board or beyond it: in fact, in or out of office Pitt would seek Middleton's opinions, and if he failed to ask for his views Sir Charles would provide them nonetheless. Any Government, and particularly Pitt's, was keen to see a better navy for less money, and Middleton used this concern to promote

---

[13] www.thepeerage.com/p.5349.

[14] J. K. Laughton's introduction to *BP* and in *DNB*; Oswyn A. R. Murray, 'The Admiralty' Part VI in *MM*, XXIV (1938), p. 335, quoted in Talbott, p. xv; Talbott, p. 107 (for example); Morriss in Le Fevre and Harding, *Precursors of Nelson*, p. 304; Rodger, *Command of the Ocean*, p. 373; St Vincent to Markham, 17 May 1806: 'the said admiral [Young] is, like Lord Barham and Admiral Gambier, a compound of paper and packthread': Sir Clements Markham (ed.), *Selections from the Correspondence of Admiral John Markham, 1801–04, 1806–07*, NRS (1904); Creevey quoted in Talbott, p. 14.

[15] Quoted in Morriss, p. 319.

[16] Wilberforce, II, p. 212.

his own view of necessary reforms. He wanted to see a more modern concept of salaries for public servants replacing the older customs, fees, exemptions and privileges, which were rather the style of the eighteenth century. He supported Pitt's Commission of Inquiry into Fees in Public Office (1785), gave evidence to another one on the Navy Board and Dockyards (1788), and at intervals directed the Commission for Revising the Civil Affairs of the Navy. At every stage he showed himself master of his brief, pressing for coherent structures and streamlined management. He came to regard himself as the lynch-pin of administrative reform, the irreplaceable official, incorruptible and conscientious. It became all too easy for him to see his critics as self-serving and perhaps dishonest, and so to move to the obvious remedy, his own over-arching control. He pressed for the authority of the Comptroller to be affirmed, for the Navy Board's indispensable role to be recognised by giving its head a seat at the Admiralty, and for his own personal position to be confirmed by promotion to flag rank while serving as Comptroller in Somerset House, and finally by elevation to the peerage when he became First Lord in 1805.

Morriss refers to his determination to advance himself, quoting the view of David Syrett: 'he was nakedly ambitious ... a bureaucratic imperialist.'[17] When placed in the context of what national security demanded, and his frustration at lacking the resources or authority to do what good sense required, his self-promotion can be better understood and more easily forgiven. It was not prompted by mere selfishness, a lust for power or money, but by his desire to advance a cause much greater than himself. He was impatient with administrative inertia and the system which protected it – the lack of a career structure to attract and reward ambitious and capable officials – and he was fearful of the consequences. Middleton never forgot the perils of 1779–82, and how close the country had come to a disaster even greater than the loss of the Thirteen Colonies: Canada, India, the West Indies, Gibraltar, all were at risk, together with the safety of Ireland and the British mainland. And politicians or even fighting admirals had a maddening tendency to forget that strategy is eventually shaped by inconvenient details so easily overlooked – the availability of stores or merchant shipping, the capacity of shipyards both royal and commercial, workers, nails, spars, rations, accurate charts. It is part of his greatness that he could sense how policies and war plans impacted upon individual ships at sea, and he could visualise the link between seemingly trivial detail and broader strategy.

In many ways he foreshadowed the Victorian concerns for public probity and administrative efficiency, for bureaucratic structure and accountability. In spite

---

[17] Morriss, p. 302.

of the ground-breaking role that Talbott gives to Middleton, he still locates him firmly in the eighteenth century: 'he is sometimes said to have been ahead of his day, to have prefigured the great Victorian reformers. I disagree. He was as much a figure of Georgian society and culture as Samuel Johnson.'[18] By contrast Morriss enlarges his significance by stretching the perspective into the next century: 'the administrative machine he worked to improve between 1778 and his death in 1813 was the basis for British naval power well into the nineteenth century ... his contribution to the organisational foundation of that ascendancy was greater than that of any other single man.'[19] When Talbott insists that he was 'a person of the second tier, a moderately influential man who had the ear of the most powerful men in the kingdom',[20] he overlooks his role in shaping the ethos of the naval profession where only Pepys and Anson compare with him. This study will demonstrate that his religious outlook spread far beyond the Navy Office and the Admiralty, and helped to shape the values of the officer corps. In this respect unquestionably Barham's touch reached well into the succeeding century. What he thought were important insights – the spiritual obligations of captains, the pastoral responsibilities of officers, the duties of chaplains, the concept of the navy itself as an instrument of high moral purpose – became in some measure hardwired into the naval profession, and in this regard he must be placed in the first echelon.

In all this public service Middleton had a sense of divine calling, giving him peace of mind and motivation. 'I have, however, I thank God, a peace within, which the world cannot give nor take away, and as long as my own conscience does not condemn me, I am indifferent about further fame.'[21] That is how it might have seemed to him, but his critics perceived a temperament less than serene and an ambition for rank and recognition. 'Without religion', he asserted, 'there can be no public principle' – an attitude bound to offend more secular minded servants of the state, who in their turn found reasons to be critical of him.[22]

Contemporaries and historians have suspected him of favouritism. Pitt once alleged that Middleton would do anything for a Methodist, but whom did he have in mind? A possible candidate is Ambrose Serle, who had proved himself in the transport service during the American War, and whom Middleton appointed to head the Sick and Hurt Board when that department was brought under the

[18] Talbott, p. xvi.
[19] Morriss, p. 323.
[20] Talbott, p. xvi.
[21] *BP*, III, p. 9.
[22] Middleton to Sandwich, *BP*, II, p. 10.

Navy Office – part of his 'bureaucratic imperialism'. With posts to fill, Middleton may well have turned to his co-religionists, the people he believed he could trust. This was how patronage worked before the civil service was opened to competitive examination; until then many posts were filled by personal recommendation from men of substance who could vouch for the character of their nominees. The process was not meant to be an easy route for incompetence, but in practice were there examples of inadequate or corrupt officials maintained in office by the Comptroller? Hardly – such folly on his part would have jeopardised his own position just as surely as it would have damaged the reputation of his religion. Talbott draws attention to his request to the First Lord for his unqualified brother to be appointed as purser; it was turned down, but it should not be seen as an improper application. Pursers did not have a regular professional training beyond fairly rudimentary book-keeping, and they were expected to learn on the job. It would be hard to think of a better training than to keep a purser's office under the hawk eye of Charles Middleton, who would be held responsible along with his brother for any irregularity.[23]

More seriously it is sometimes alleged that James Gambier was over-promoted at the insistence of his uncle, who acquired a compliant family member on the Board of Admiralty but a man not up to the job. In due course the question of Gambier's competence will be faced, but Middleton cannot be held responsible for his advancement. When Gambier first came to Whitehall it was at Howe's invitation; he was already well into a second term before his uncle took over the Admiralty, and the third came after Barham's retirement. If family interest promoted Gambier, it surely came from his links with Pitt and Melville rather than Middleton's interference.[24]

On two occasions Middleton resigned office on a point of principle, and in both instances he gave reasons that went far beyond the immediate disagreements. In 1790 he left the Navy Board, frustrated at the slow pace of change. The enquiries into fees for public office had closed with his two reports proposing an 'energetic and judicious system' for reform of the Navy Office and the dockyards, but after two years nothing had been done. Middleton cited dark forces at work

[23] Wilberforce, II, p. 212. Ambrose Serle (1742–1814) was a civil servant and theological writer, friend of noted Evangelicals William Romaine and John Newton; had been in the navy before becoming under-secretary to the Secretary of State for Colonies in 1772; served in America during War of Independence; clerk of reports 1776; commissioner of transport service with care of prisoners-of-war 1795. Talbott, pp. 23, 34.

[24] Brian Tunstall, *Naval Warfare in the Age of Sail: The Evolution of Fighting Tactics, 1650–1815*, ed. Nicholas Tracy (1990), p. 227.

frustrating the 'necessary reformation': he referred to 'the private ferment which had been raised against every kind of reform by those whose prejudice, whose ignorance, or whose particular interest it was to oppose it.'[25] The indignant Hannah More no doubt reflected the views of the Middleton household when she wrote that ministers 'would not consent to help and forward his excellent plans of reform in that important branch of the Government, and an honest man does not feel happy in a situation where he sees a great deal of good to be done, which he is not allowed to do.'[26]

A sense of moral outrage provoked his second resignation, this time from the Admiralty Board in 1795, when he refused to countenance the First Lord's order to recall a senior admiral from his command in the West Indies. In fact he came dangerously close to disputing the principle of political control over the military, and now Spencer, the new First Lord, had his own position to consider. If his principal service colleague on the Board were to take an independent line whenever he disagreed with the political head of the navy, where would the authority of the First Lord be, and how would the principles of political supremacy and collective responsibility survive? Spencer demanded that Middleton add his signature to the order of recall if he intended to remain on the Board. Middleton resigned, claiming that his seniority and experience should have exempted him from rubber-stamping ministerial decrees. 'I did not till then understand that I was to dwindle into the wretched insignificance of sitting as a numerical member of a naval board, to receive a salary for signing my name to whatever might be put before me; to concur in all measures without question or hesitation, whether dictated by ignorance or pride.'[27] Collegiality with such a man of inflexible opinion would have been impossible for the youthful Spencer – and Middleton had to go. It had become an issue of principle, a matter of conscience, and he did not shrink from putting it on the very highest level: 'no consideration on earth will induce me to concur in what I think is an unjust measure, because I know myself to be amenable to a much higher tribunal than any on earth.'[28]

Alongside his ostentatious willingness to invoke moral principle went a quiet inner piety. He was a man who valued prayer. After he became First Lord, Hannah More rejoiced that the country now had 'a cabinet minister who, we know, prays for the success of his measures.'[29] He was prepared to recognise his

[25] *BP*, II, p. 350; see pp. 347–50 for whole document.
[26] Roberts, II, p. 226.
[27] *BP*, II, p. 429. Dispute over Admiral Laforey's recall, pp. 414–30.
[28] *BP*, II, p. 422.
[29] Roberts, II, p. 226.

vulnerability as he sought the prayers of close friends on his behalf. To La Trobe he admitted feeling inadequate when appointed to the Navy Office: he gratefully acknowledged how God had strengthened his weakness and what he called his 'diffidence'.[30] Reeling under the shock of his wife's unexpected death, he asked that La Trobe and John Newton should pray for him. As First Lord he begged prayer support from Wilberforce to help in public duties which were both arduous and 'hazardous beyond conception' – and the very next day he received intelligence that the French fleet had passed through the Straits of Gibraltar into the Atlantic, the opening moves of the Trafalgar campaign.[31]

Over the years Middleton became increasingly involved with the proclamation of the Christian message to the unconverted. A lifelong membership of the SPCK began in 1775, the year of his return to active duty. He became deeply interested in the work of the Moravian Brethren who ran the only mission specifically for West Indian slaves. When the Church of England set up its own missionary society he became one of the earliest members, and at home he supported the More sisters' Mendip schools. Such concerns gradually grew, particularly under the influence of his wife, and it would be unrealistic to look for a narrowly dated dawning. Nonetheless a profound change in his thinking really did take place as the evangelistic impulse grew stronger. The junior captain of the Seven Years War, enforcing religious observance, matured into the elder statesman of the Blue Lights who saw more need for persuasion. He was making his own religious journey from enforcement to evangelism, as his later career will show.[32]

The Influence of Rear-Admiral Richard Kempenfelt

RICHARD Kempenfelt prompted Middleton at a key point in the evolution of his thinking about naval religion. While Middleton was at the Navy Office he preserved a number of confidential letters from his friend and former shipmate. One part of this wide-ranging correspondence resonated with the Comptroller's religious programme, but whereas Middleton had done no more than hold services aboard any ship he happened to command, Kempenfelt was advocating an extension of the principle to the entire fleet. Middleton had felt diffident over his first reading of prayers in the Seven Years War, but by the time he took over the *Ardent* in 1775 he was ready to formulate a moral and religious regimen in standing orders, but of course it had no currency in any ship but his

---

[30] Middleton to Latrobe, 11 Oct 1792. NMM MID/2/28/1.

[31] Pollock, 1978, p. 193.

[32] List of subscribers, *SPCK Report* 1811; Roberts, III, p. 397.

2 Rear-Admiral Richard Kempenfelt (1718–82). The unusual octagonal telescope hints at his fascination with new thinking. (Oil painting by Tilly Kettle, 1735–86)

© National Maritime Museum, London BHC2818

own. Now, four or five years on, Kempenfelt was proposing just such a scheme as a remedy for general indiscipline, with daily prayers and Sunday services throughout the navy. This was an astonishing proposal to come from such a progressive officer, at a time when religious observance was little countenanced afloat, but the writer had thought deeply about the management of men and fleets, and he was a man of profound if private piety.[33]

Before considering the correspondence we must examine Kempenfelt's credentials as a Blue Light. He was first lieutenant of the *Anson* (60) when Middleton joined her in January 1753, and a lasting friendship grew out of their experience of wardroom and watch-keeping over the next two years. We have seen that probably Middleton was already committed to the new piety, but such evidence as there is suggests that Kempenfelt was not yet convinced. The principal indication of his religious views comes from a slim volume of verse published in 1777 under the pseudonym 'Philotheorus', and dedicated to the Rev. John Fletcher, a Swiss-born theologian who became the Anglican vicar of Madeley in 1760.[34]

One poem is in the style of George Herbert, others reminiscent of Charles Wesley. There are verses describing a meeting at Gwenap, where Wesley preached to thousands, and there is a powerful piece about the Last Judgement. This book of verse furnishes the best clues we have regarding Kempenfelt's spiritual development. The fact that he addressed them to Fletcher suggests that he regarded him as his spiritual mentor, perhaps the instrument of his conversion. In 1771 Fletcher wrote a book in support of Wesley's teaching about sanctification, upholding the view that full holiness of life may be attained this side of heaven. Wesley's insistence on the possibility of perfection split him from Calvinistic Anglicans such as Whitefield and Newton, but Kempenfelt aligned himself with Wesley and Fletcher, as his poem 'The Soul Longing for Holiness' shows:

---

33 For Kempenfelt's service, see Charnock, VI, pp. 246–51; James Ralfe, *The Naval Biography of Great Britain*, 4 vols. (1828), I, p. 215. Laughton wrote the entry in *DNB*, and a brief introduction to the Kempenfelt letters in *BP*, I, pp. xxxiii–xxxvii. A more recent article is Ake Lindwall, 'The Kempenfelt Family', *MM*, LVII (1971), pp. 379–83. Gardner, *Above and Under Hatches*, ed. Lloyd, p. 15.

34 Richard Kempenfelt [under pseudonym 'Philotheorus'], *Original Hymns and Poems* (first published 1777; Exeter, 1861). For Fletcher: see entries in Timothy Larsen (ed.), *Biographical Dictionary of Evangelicals* (Leicester, 2003), pp. 228–30, and Donald M. Lewis, *Blackwell Dictionary of Evangelical Biography, 1730–1860*, [hereafter *BDEB*] 2 vols. (Oxford, 1993), I, pp. 393f. Middleton–Kempenfelt correspondence, *BP* I, pp. 288–365.

> Crown me with the true perfection,
> Previous to the stroke of death …
> O, my agonizing spirit!
> Thou shalt surely enter in,
> Pluck the fruit of Jesu's merit
> And expel the poison Sin.

Worn out by controversy Fletcher withdrew to Switzerland in 1777 to recover his health – the date when the verses were published. If Kempenfelt truly attributed to Fletcher his spiritual awakening we may tentatively sketch some further possibilities. It cannot have happened before 1754, the date of Fletcher's conversion, and probably not until he embarked on parish work. By then Kempenfelt was out east until 1764. Five years later, off Sicily, he was moved to write the only poem which carries a date:

> Sweet is the face of night, and scarce a breeze
> Disturbs the silent surface of the seas;
> Straight let my wandering soul with rapture gaze,
> And read thy works, O Nature! with amaze:
> Cast off awhile the load of earthly cares,
> And view the Eternal in yon round of stars …

Other compositions are more Christ-centred than this celebration of the God of nature, which may well be the earliest of what he calls 'juvenile attempts at sacred poesy'. Perhaps then we should place his conversion sometime between his return from the East Indies in 1764 and his dabbling in theological debate about sanctification around 1771. The fact that he preserves the date of his Sicilian poem may well be significant: perhaps 1769 was the decisive time.

As a staunch Anglican Middleton had little time for sinless perfection. When Kempenfelt wrote to him about naval religion in the American War he was conscious of standing on the other side of a theological divide. That would account for the cautious tone of his expression, so different from the warmth of his poetry. 'Religion is particularly necessary … to preserve morals', he wrote rather stiffly, and the remedy of regular prayers seems equally formal. Nevertheless they were thinking along congruent lines. Middleton's starting point had been his own faith and the spiritual needs of his ship's company, a localised answer to a particular situation. By contrast Kempenfelt had been assessing the manpower problems of the navy at large, and he specified religion as part of the cure. His ideas need to be placed in the context of his career and wider contribution to the sea service.

Although he made his way rather ponderously through the ranks of the navy and was sixty-two before he achieved flag rank, Kempenfelt was widely esteemed for his tactical theories and his work on signal codes. He was a keen student of French writers in both disciplines. As chief of staff to the commander of the Channel Fleet, he witnessed the fumbling efforts of first Admiral Hardy and then Admiral Geary in 1779–80, and he poured out his frustrations and fears in a series of confidential letters to his friend Middleton at the Navy Office. Far from underestimating the French, as his contemporaries were inclined to do, Kempenfelt allowed that they had brought their ship-handling and fleet-manœuvring skills to a high level of excellence. Granted also that the combined fleets of France and Spain outnumbered the British in the Channel, the international situation was grave indeed – the American colonies in full revolt, war in the West Indies, fighting off the East Indies, Gibraltar threatened, a hostile coalition of European powers forming, and England itself menaced with invasion. He had no illusions about the assumed superiority of British courage and the celebrated national ability to muddle through crises. 'There is also a vulgar notion that prevails amongst us, and that even with our gentry, that our seamen are braver than the French. Ridiculous to suppose courage dependent upon climate. The men who are best disciplined, of whatever country they be, will always fight the best.'[35]

Kempenfelt searched for ways to maximise the navy's force at this time of national peril. He noted down ideas about signalling, armament and ship-construction, but some of his most perceptive comments concerned the quality of the human resource brought into the fleet by the demands of war. Whereas 20,000 volunteers would suffice for peacetime manning, hostilities required many more ships at sea with five or six times the number of sailors. Such a figure could not be achieved by waiting for voluntary enlistment: there was neither the time for such a luxury nor any hope of finding so many willing hands. There was no practicable alternative to the compulsory enlistment known as impressment, with all the attendant problems which arose. Pressed seamen might be reluctant to serve and anxious to desert: the one problem could be checked by stern discipline and the other by withholding shore leave or pay. But such hard terms of service deterred further volunteering. Thus there was created a cycle of resentment and mistrust which was extremely difficult to break. Inspired leadership, success in battle, good fortune in capturing prizes – experience showed how these might forge a ship's company out of indifferent human material. But Kempenfelt

---

[35] *BP*, I, p. 311.

believed there were other measures which should be tried – one organisational and the other religious.

'If six, seven or eight hundred men are left in a mass together, without divisions, and the officers assigned no particular charge over any part of them ... such a crew must remain a disorderly mob ... and the people, thus left to themselves, become sottish, slovenly and lazy, form cabals, and spirit each other up to insolence and mutiny.'[36] The remedy was to divide the whole crew amongst the lieutenants, placing each group of men under the particular supervision of one officer. He knew that such a scheme had been tried already, but now the time had come for it to be implemented in every ship. Over the next decades the divisional system would become the basis for shipboard organisation, the prime collective unit of welfare and discipline.[37]

Still on the track of good order, Kempenfelt believed that religion should move out of the shadows and back into the routine of everyday naval life. 'Religion is particularly necessary in the common people to preserve morals. It should in a plan of discipline make a part.' He was actually calling for a return to the religious provisions of the 1731 *Regulations*, still current, but he did not base his reasoning on them. 'Divine service should therefore be performed every Sunday; and I think a short form of prayer for mornings and evenings, to be used every day, would be proper. It would take up but a short time.' Noting that French and Spanish ships observed twice daily prayers, Kempenfelt drew a critical comparison with the British: 'our seamen people are more licentious than those of other nations. The reason is, they have less religion.' He was sure that sailors would be quick to recognise the advantages from the 'sobriety, cleanliness, order and regularity' of a well-disciplined ship with a divisional system and regular worship. 'With order and discipline you would increase your force; cleanliness and sobriety would keep your men healthy; and punishments would be seldom, as crimes would be rare.'[38]

In due course the Blue Lights came to adopt such a programme, with its salient features of moral regulation, religious observance, concern for health and humane discipline, but they came to appreciate the need for a teaching ministry as well, to instruct the ignorant and to appeal for conversion. For this, good chaplains and Christian literature were at least as important as routine prayers. At this early

[36] *BP*, I, pp. 305f.

[37] The introduction of the divisional system is credited to Vice-Admiral Thomas Smith in 1755; Rodger, *Wooden World*, p. 216. Middleton had copied the idea for the *Ardent* in 1755: 'Captain's Order Book' in *BP* I, p. 39.

[38] *BP*, I, pp. 308f.

stage Kempenfelt was more concerned with discipline than persuasion, but it is possible that he eventually came to favour a more pastoral approach, as his flagship was the first warship to be supplied by the Naval and Military Bible Society with several hundred copies of the Scriptures, most probably at his request in 1782.[39]

The would-be reformer proved himself as a combat commander. In December 1781, when flying his flag in the *Victory* with eleven other sail of the line, he encountered the premier tactician of the French Navy, Admiral de Guichen, off Ushant. Since the French numbered nineteen to his twelve, Kempenfelt rightly concluded that attack would be folly. By a masterpiece of movement, however, he gained the weather gauge and slipped his own fleet between de Guichen and the convoy he was supposed to be guarding. Using part of his force to ward off the French fleet, Kempenfelt was able to capture fifteen of the laden cargo ships and to bring them safely into a British port as prizes without loss to himself. It was a feat which proved him to be much more than a theoretician and which fully endorsed the practical value of the new scheme of signals. Appointed second-in-command to Howe, he helped prepare for the expedition to relieve Gibraltar in 1782, but before it set sail he was drowned when his flagship, the *Royal George*, sank at Spithead with heavy loss of life.

Had he lived, perhaps he and Middleton would have collaborated in efforts to promote religion, but it is hard to see what they could have achieved at this stage. Middleton had shown to his own satisfaction that a ship could be run with strict regard for morality and collective worship, but he had no authority to spread the pattern more widely. Even an admiral with Kempenfelt's prestige could have insisted on religious observance only in ships under his command. Referring to his package of proposals, Kempenfelt wanted it 'commanded, enforced by authority, to be practised in every ship', but so long as a secular spirit prevailed at the Admiralty it was a vain hope.[40] Nonetheless Middleton cherished the idea and allowed it to surface again in his private papers during the 1780s. In an important memorandum on the duty of captains (to which we shall return) he took a fresh look at the link between discipline and religion. He claimed that his orders for the *Ardent* were fully practicable and might serve for other ships, and he wished that all captains might be instructed to take care of their men's spiritual and moral needs. He must have known, however, that only a widespread shift of opinion amongst the commanding ranks would have made his programme possible, and that seemed out of the question in the decade of peace between

---

[39] *NMBS* 1804, p. 12; 1847, p. 19.

[40] *BP*, I, p. 309.

the end of the American and the start of the French Revolutionary Wars. The whole Blue Light programme might have remained only pious aspiration if James Ramsay had not become his secretary. Ramsay dealt with words and arguments; in the 1780s he was attempting to change public perceptions of slavery, and with it the whole climate of British opinion. He was just the man to be at Middleton's right hand as they looked for ways to shift the secular mind-set of the naval profession.

The Reverend James Ramsay

AT the Navy Office Middleton had staff to attend to official business, but he did an immense amount of further, confidential work at Barham Court. A good deal of this concerned his inquiries into naval governance. By the time his series of reports on the civil administration were complete, he had proposed little less than the wholesale modernisation of its methods and ruling principles. His mind was also working on ways of improving the discipline of the fleet by updating its regulations. When engaged on this project he enjoyed the collaboration of Ramsay as his confidential secretary, the fellow Scot who had once served under his command in the West Indies and was now his neighbour and parish priest. He was a man of exceptional versatility and wide experience, by turns a ship's surgeon, Anglican clergyman, naval chaplain, author of books and pamphlets, and a pioneer of the movement to abolish slavery.

Born in Fraserburgh in 1733, Ramsay's hopes of training for the ministry of the church were frustrated by his family's scarce means, and he took up a medical apprenticeship instead. In the event his outstanding abilities earned him bursaries to pursue two courses of study more or less simultaneously, learning surgery and obstetrics from an eminent London doctor, and taking a degree in mathematics, science and literature at Aberdeen. In 1757 Ramsay passed the examination set by the Company of Surgeons and entered naval service. Appointed to the 24-gun *Arundel* on the sickly Leeward Islands station, he became responsible for the health of her 160 men. Over a three-year period she suffered thirty-two deaths, but only five of these were due to illness aboard ship; her daily sick list at sea was never more than nine, and frequently zero, a worthy record. In view of the attacks later made on his reputation, it is worth stressing that Ramsay was a highly proficient sea surgeon.

Two notable events in 1759 shaped his future career. In March Charles Middleton was appointed captain of the *Arundel*, the beginning of a thirty-year friendship, and in November Ramsay encountered for the first time the brutal reality of the Atlantic slave trade. This was the event (as we shall see) that turned him into an Abolitionist and indirectly recruited Middleton to the cause.[41]

When Ramsay left the sea for holy orders Middleton helped him to his first living in the West Indies. It may well have been the Comptroller's recommendation that secured for Ramsay a wartime appointment to Admiral Barrington's flagship as chaplain in 1778 and allowed him to forward secret intelligence about the loyalties of plantation owners. When Ramsay was forced to leave St Kitt's in 1781, Middleton found another living for him at Teston, where he had the right of appointment. Middleton invited his help with sensitive material related to reform of the Navy Office, a strange job to combine with parish responsibilities, but one approved by Government and rewarded with a salary. When Ramsay publicised the injustice and cruelty of plantation slavery, Middleton hosted meetings of the leading Abolitionists; he spoke up for him in the Commons, and offered his London home as a refuge. It was there that Ramsay died in 1789, exhausted by the struggle. At every stage Ramsay relied on Middleton's patronage and protection, but their relationship was much more interdependent than that implies.

While Middleton was preoccupied with reforming the Navy Office in the 1780s Ramsay worked alongside him, copying memoranda, editing documents, and occasionally initiating preliminary drafts. It is not possible to be sure which ideas originated with whom: some documents appear to be drafts prepared on Middleton's behalf; others are drawn up by Ramsay and endorsed by Middleton, sometimes with negligible alteration. Other memoranda carry comments and modifications in both sets of handwriting. Clearly the two men were working in partnership to hone each other's thinking. The fruit of their collaboration did not appear during Ramsay's lifetime, but when the revised *Regulations and Instructions* were published in 1806, they showed how Middleton's thinking had been shaped by the issues that mattered so much to Ramsay – the influence of ships' officers generally, and the role of chaplains and surgeons in particular.[42]

Back in 1765, when Middleton was a half-pay captain more obviously interested in agriculture than seafaring, Ramsay published a book for junior officers. Many years before Middleton wrote anything of consequence on the subject, his surgeon had become the noted author of *An Essay on the Duties and Qualifications*

[41] Folarin Shyllon, *James Ramsay: The Unknown Abolitionist* (Edinburgh 1977); Watt, (1995), pp. 156–70, and his contribution to *Oxford Dictionary of National Biography* (2004). See also: 'Statement of public services performed by the Reverend James Ramsay, vicar of Teston, in Kent', written by Major P. Mitchell and enclosed by Middleton to Pitt, 7 Aug 1787, *BP*, II, pp. 250–4.

[42] *Regulations and Instructions Relating to His Majesty's Service at Sea* (1806) [hereafter *RAI* 1806].

3 The Reverend James Ramsay (1733–89). Naval surgeon, chaplain, pioneer of the Abolition movement, and confidential secretary to Sir Charles Middleton. (Oil painting by Carl Frederik von Breda, 1759–1818) © National Portrait Gallery, London NPG 2559

of a Sea Officer. The book was well received and ran to three English editions as well as translations. There was an obvious need for something like this, as various admirals noted at the time. The navy was good at providing a rigorous practical training in seamanship for its midshipmen – at sea, on the job under the eye of a captain patron – but there was no staff college or forum for theoretical dissection of the principles of command. That too had to be learned by observation. The nearest the naval profession came to a handbook was the 1731 edition of *Regulations and Instructions*, but it was more of a reference manual than an inspirational text, with its Rules of Discipline and Government, pay scales and punishments. It gave no room to discourse about the management of men, or the principles of justice, or the rationale of shipboard routine. Ramsay's book fleshed out the bare text of *Regulations*, and it apparently became the kind of thing that senior officers gave their protégés to induct them into some higher thinking about their profession. One section dealt with flag signals and their importance, but since no copy has come to light the rest of the contents must be inferred from the title and the comments of others.[43]

It is significant that it was written by a surgeon, as the navy's medical officers were customarily respected as confidants and counsellors to the crew. In contrast, chaplains were few in number and seen as remote members of a learned profession. Even more significantly, chaplains were associated with righteousness, while the surgeons dealt with men in the raw and the dirt, quite often presenting the evidence of unrighteousness such as injuries from drink or fighting, venereal disease – or all too often the bloody backs of men punished at the gangway. Surgeons if any good were approachable and trusted members of a profession with standards of humanity and at least rudimentary ideas of confidentiality. Coming from this respected profession, Ramsay was well placed to influence the attitudes of young officers. His later volume of *Sea Sermons* added a pastor's insight to the problems of communal life, with advice relevant to all ranks. A contemporary military officer wrote of him, 'he has done everything in his power by his writings to suggest and introduce method, manners and religion into the royal navy.'[44]

Ramsay was constantly using words to shape opinion and change attitudes. As a preacher in St Kitts he tried to modify white attitudes towards the blacks. His pamphlets on economics and slavery deployed evidence and arguments to shift people's thinking from a held position to a more enlightened one. His sermons for seamen aimed to sweeten relationships aboard ship. Words well used could persuade and so change conduct. This was Ramsay's special skill, and it seems to have given Middleton the fresh thinking he needed in the 1780s when the two men were gathering material for the revision of outdated regulations. If the work were rightly done it could reshape attitudes throughout the navy. Instructions for

---

[43] No copy has been found in BL, NMM or Rhodes House.

[44] *BP*, II, p. 254. For comments on the role of surgeons I am indebted to Surgeon Vice-Admiral Sir James Watt.

captains, lieutenants, surgeons and chaplains formed a mechanism for change, to influence the commissioned ranks, and to set standards of conduct for everyone. Taken on their own, the printed rules would probably not do much for morality and would certainly not bring revival of religion, but they could provide opportunity for godly chaplains and officers to hold divine service and distribute Christian literature. Once sanctioned by the Admiralty Board and followed throughout the service, new regulations might then become the means of making the example of the *Ardent* and the aspirations of Kempenfelt normative for the fleet.

Evidence for Middleton's thinking comes from a document headed 'Memoranda – Duty of Captains in the Navy', undated but placed by Laughton between letters of December 1783 and July 1784. It shows that in searching for the best way to correct and establish the morals of seamen he recognised the captain as the essential figure. The existing regulations called upon him to uphold religion and good conduct, with prayers twice daily and a full service with sermon on Sundays whenever practicable. Middleton's conclusion was clear: 'the captain of a king's ship has full authority to govern those who are placed under him; and if the admiralty would furnish the means and the captain execute his instructions, no set of men in the community can be better placed for religious instruction than seamen.'[45] Evidently this paper was intended to find a place in a new issue of *Regulations and Instructions*. Middleton refers to this project a few years later, in a memorandum they prepared together, where he expresses impatience over delays: he had already done his part, of course – 'the navy board part of those instructions has been revised and sent to the admiralty upwards of two years' – but other parts remained obsolete, unchanged and confusing. 'No time ought to be lost in regulating the whole for the approval of the king in council.'[46] The administration then in power did not give it sufficient priority to bring to completion before Ramsay's death in 1789 and the Comptroller's resignation the year after. After Middleton became First Lord in 1805 he took the long-delayed opportunity to publish the revised edition. It will be necessary to consider its fuller significance in a later chapter, but here we are looking for indications of Ramsay's influence.

The great innovation was the inclusion of Instructions for the Chaplain which set the standard required for his ministry – his tone of conduct, his regular leading of prayers, the obligation to preach intelligible sermons, the duty of visiting the sick and supervising aspects of the ship's educational programme. Similarly the directions for the surgeon have something to say about the emotional aspects of patient care and their contribution to recovery. Both these sections deal with

[45] *BP*, II, p. 162.
[46] *BP*, II, pp. 298f.

departments familiar to Ramsay, and it seems likely that Middleton had absorbed his friend's thinking here. Even more remarkable was the moral climate of the new *Regulations*, for they insisted that it was part of an officer's duty and particularly the captain's to suppress profanity, to promote respect for religion and to curb immorality. These measures recalled the neglected principles of 1731, and the responsibilities in Ramsay's mind as he wrote his treatise for young officers in 1765. When the new edition of *Regulations and Instructions* appeared in 1806, it had a warmer feel to it than its predecessor, with compassionate elements embedded in rules about health, discipline and religion.

While there is no hard proof to credit Ramsay rather than Middleton with these humane touches, it is beyond doubt that Ramsay had written or contributed to literature on officer values, medical reform and sea chaplains years before Middleton, and it seems a fair inference that his thinking influenced Middleton's. There was often something visionary about Ramsay's ideas that complemented Middleton's pragmatism, and made their collaboration so effective. Ramsay led the way over opposition to slavery, and Middleton followed as a facilitator. They worked together over plans for the First Fleet to Botany Bay: while the Comptroller was responsible for finding the shipping, Ramsay selected a team of naval surgeons for the voyage and for establishing the medical facilities in the new settlement. Again Ramsay proposed that a free black community in West Africa should be made economically viable with British help and protection: the idea appealed to Pitt and eventually inspired the Sierra Leone project beloved of the Clapham philanthropists, who included Middleton. In material terms Ramsay depended on Middleton's patronage, but in the realm of ideas Ramsay showed the way.

The memorandum on the duty of captains neatly blends what we know about the approaches of the two men. There is the voice of Middleton, calling for commanding officers to set a high example, for the morals of sailors to be corrected by their captains, and for the suppression of 'all dissolute, immoral and disorderly practices'. His layman's approach to religion is complemented by Ramsay's confidence in the good that can be done by a clergyman and the power of literature to change lives. To attract men of the right calibre Middleton was keen to see them properly rewarded, and in a far-sighted proposal which did not take full effect until the 1840s, he wanted more chaplains in priests' orders so that Holy Communion might be more widely celebrated. The memorandum concludes in ringing hope:

> I am confident – if good chaplains were appointed to the king's ships, and the regulations I have pointed out enforced by the admiralty, and carried punctually into execution by the clergymen ...; if he had the power of

distributing bibles and other good books amongst the seamen as he saw occasion, to be paid for by themselves at pay day – I have little doubt but our seamen would be amongst the foremost of the lower classes of the people in examples of piety and good conduct. Much – very much will depend on the character of the captain.[47]

Here then is the manifesto of the Blue Lights. In a conservative way it was recalling the navy to its past observances, with captains fulfilling their pastoral duties. It aimed to reform sailors' conduct and present them with a proper Anglican ministry of daily prayer, Sunday services, Bibles and Christian literature. Blue Lights saw no impropriety in making such observance compulsory, and they felt no need to address the religious concerns of Dissenters or Catholics, let alone other faiths altogether. It was prescriptive religion well in line with the attitudes of the landed gentry and the underlying assumptions of Establishment.

If the admiralty would furnish the means, and the captain execute his instructions, no set of men in the community can be better placed for religious instruction than seamen.[48]

Middleton, didactic and authoritarian, was invoking Admiralty regulation and captains' powers to impart religion through instruction. But what if unbelief were a greater problem than ignorance? Time would show that explanation and pastoral application were necessary if souls were to be converted to God. Public worship was a good place to start, but the Blue Lights would have to go much further to christianise the navy.

The Origins of the Abolition Movement

No study of evangelicals in the navy can disregard their part in the abolition of slavery. In a sense this movement represents a digression from the Blue Light programme of bringing religion back into the fleet, but it cannot be omitted. For one thing, his support for this campaign became part of Middleton's persona, just as it furnished the dynamic for much of Ramsay's career. For another, it established the credentials of the Blue Lights as humanitarians. Above all, since sea power was the essential mechanism for suppressing the Atlantic slave trade, the attitude of naval officers who would be called upon to risk their lives would determine if it could be done.

While the parliamentary struggle for the abolition of the slave trade in 1807 and for emancipation of all slaves in the British Empire in 1833 is well known, the

---

[47] 'Memoranda – Duty of Captains in the Navy', *BP*, II, pp. 161–5.
[48] Ibid., pp. 164f.

pioneering role of the navy is frequently overlooked. English sailors played the largest part in launching this gruesome trade in the sixteenth century by purchasing men and women in West Africa, shipping them across the Atlantic to the West Indies and selling them to plantation owners to work on the cultivation of sugar. At first the planters were Spanish, but the struggle for imperial possession gradually excluded them in favour of the British and French. Bristol and Liverpool formed the apex of the triangular trade in which goods were shipped out from Britain, to be exchanged for human cargo in West Africa, and then in turn traded for sugar and rum in the West Indies for the return voyage to Europe. For the sailors it involved high risk of disease and mortality, but there were huge profits to be made by surviving slaving captains and successful sugar merchants. The human cost was appalling, and estimates of more than 3 million Africans unwillingly shipped into slavery by British vessels, and hundreds of thousands perishing on passage, hardly begin to convey the incalculable weight of misery and suffering.

It is particularly chilling to find enlightened European opinion in the seventeenth and eighteenth centuries deploying an array of arguments in its favour. History, philosophy, economics, natural science and religion were all quarried for proof of the legitimacy and inevitability of slavery. So long as Hume and Jefferson were questioning whether African slaves belonged to the human race, there could be little but scorn for the few idealists, Quakers and others, who questioned its morality. When English seafarers had done so much to establish and maintain the Atlantic trade, and when the naval interest was convinced that its sailors provided essential manpower for the fighting fleet, there is something ironic about the part the navy played in kindling the movement to abolish it. Again the chief advocates were Ramsay and Middleton.

On 21 November 1759, in the course of her commerce protection duties, the *Arundel* came up with the slaver *Swift* of Bristol, originally on passage from Guinea to Barbados, but plagued with dysentery and left adrift by a French privateer which had boarded her to remove her marketable slaves and healthy crew. It seems that none of the other British surgeons in the squadron was keen to risk infection by treating her sick, but Ramsay went aboard. He found men shackled on the slave deck in unimaginable conditions of squalor brought on by dysentery and vomiting, with several of them close to death. He gave what relief he could. He left behind instructions to help the sick, but he brought away with him a passionate hatred for the inhumanity of the slave trade. Back aboard his own ship – distracted, perhaps, by what he had witnessed – he lost his footing and fell heavily, fracturing his femur. To recover he needed time ashore in the naval hospital in Antigua followed by ten months confined to his cabin. From this point onwards a sea-going career became impracticable, for any protracted voyage on salt provisions might make him prone to scurvy, and dissolution of the mended bones would follow. Ramsay saw in this calamity an opportunity to pursue his original hope of becoming a clergyman – only now, with his eyes newly opened to the plight of slaves, he planned to take a living in the West Indies so that he might minister to them in particular.

Middleton helped launch his friend on his new career, by commending him to the Bishop of London, and by searching out a living that he might take up in the Leeward Islands. Ramsay returned to England in the *Ardent* in July 1761, left the navy in September and took Anglican orders in November. The next year he began a new life at Capisterre in St Christopher's, married a few months later the daughter of a planter, Rebecca Akers, and reared a family of a son and three girls. Yet from the start there was something unusual about his ministry, a restless energy and breadth of vision that could not be simply constrained by preaching and visiting parishioners. He used his medical skills first as a free service to the poor, and then in a proper practice which included midwifery and attending various plantations as visiting surgeon. Very soon he witnessed the brutalities of West Indian slavery to add to what he had already seen of the slave trade. Aware that he would need documented facts if he were to do anything to remedy abuses, he began to keep detailed accounts of what he saw. His Christian humanity was outraged by things he witnessed – savage punishments, callous overworking of undernourished blacks, lack of concern for pregnant and newly delivered mothers, inadequate rest and disregard for basic human rights – a system that at best was harsh and at its worst plumbed the depths of cruelty.

A fire was kindled in Ramsay's soul turning him into a fighter. First by example and specific teaching – he had his pulpit and a congregation of planters to hear him preach – he aimed to promote kindlier treatment for blacks; he urged the need for their conversion, for their legal rights to be respected, for amelioration of their working conditions. When he realised the stubbornness of the property owners and the futility of merely appealing to their better nature, he began to marshal arguments against the institution of slavery. He was quite prepared to concede that many owners of sugar estates treated their workforce considerately, but he knew of appalling excesses as well. He believed that eventually economic forces would bring about an end to slavery and its replacement by paid employment. In the meantime he urged that considerate treatment would be more profitable than harshness. He recognised that immediate emancipation of people uneducated and untrained to manage their own lives would not be wise, but in his burning desire to see slaves treated more humanely he urged progressive improvements in schooling and health care, combined with the protection of their human rights by law. Ramsay's call was ignored. He became convinced that plantation owners would never see the economic value of treating their human resource with consideration so long as fresh supplies of African labour could be imported to replace any wastage. He began to devise a strategy for throttling West Indian slavery by depriving it of its oxygen supply, the Atlantic slave trade. By nature gentle and humane, Ramsay was also shrewd and well informed, energetic, articulate and, above all, courageous. He came to see that no lasting good would come until the evils of cruelty and neglect were faced head on. By degrees he became a crusader for ending the whole vile system of imported kidnapped labour: the gradualist became an abolitionist.

His pamphlet of 1784, *An Essay on the Treatment and Conversion of African Slaves in the British Sugar Colonies*, opened a new era of debate, forcing the slavery issue out of polite philosophical discussion, readily ignored, into the public arena by one who knew what he was talking about, whether it was the theology, philosophy, economics or practical outworking of the system that was under scrutiny. The public was interested, politicians were stirred, the West India faction aroused. Slavery became a topic of coffee-house conversation: how had the sugar been produced? Uneasy consciences could no longer bypass the issue when it was presented by someone so well informed as Ramsay – son-in-law of a planter, surgeon to several plantations, physician and pastor to blacks as well as whites. Other voices had been raised against slavery from time to time – a sermon here, a tract there: Granville Sharp's pioneering protest in 1769, Wesley's *Thoughts upon Slavery* in 1774, protests from Quakers and Moravian missionaries – but no one else had been so fully committed to its eradication, so convinced of the practicality of ending it, so equipped with telling detail, and so exposed to the wrath of the West Indian vested interest. His lonely stand makes Ramsay the pioneer Abolitionist. His first battles were not comparatively civilised pamphlet exchanges but confrontations, eyeball to eyeball, with the planter aristocracy on their own ground, with press and magistracy on their side. His *Essay on Interest* showed up the unscrupulous efforts of the planters to lower the rate they paid for their loans, even though it would have ruined the many poor businesses to which they owed money. For this pamphlet, for his church services at which blacks were welcome, and for his sermons which called for justice and kind treatment for slaves, they loathed him with a passionate, visceral hatred that generated lies to besmirch his name, and pursued him to England with a torrent of denunciation that continued even after his death. But they never silenced his argument.[49]

[49] Ramsay's *Essay* is well summarised with comment in Shyllon, *James Ramsay*, pp. 20–37.

Although a major player in the Abolition movement, Middleton said and wrote little on the subject in public. In spite of his personal knowledge of the West Indies and the slave trade which underpinned their sugar economy, he wrote no pamphlets in condemnation, and made little impact in Parliament beyond a brief speech in the Commons. Nevertheless his central role is undeniable, from the time he got Mrs Bouverie to present Ramsay to the living at Teston in 1781, to the calling of meetings at Barham Court, where early strategies were devised. With encouragement from Sir Charles and more urgent prompting from Lady Middleton, Ramsay launched his 1784 pamphlet as first salvo in a ferocious literary war. In July 1786 the Middletons brought together four important allies for Ramsay, the Virginian-born Bishop Porteus of Chester, the Moravian minister Benjamin La Trobe, his son Ignatius, and Thomas Clarkson, author of a prize-winning Cambridge essay attacking slavery as 'commerce of the human species' (1786). After these Barham Court discussions Clarkson committed himself to full-time campaigning against slavery.[50]

Public opinion now roused by Ramsay and Clarkson would prove a mighty force, but at some point there would have to be legislation: Parliament must become involved. According to La Trobe's account, Margaret Middleton rather than her husband was the first to grasp what had to be done: she urged him to use his position as MP for Rochester to demand a parliamentary inquiry into the slave trade. He felt his ability in debate was too limited, but had hopes of the young Member from Yorkshire, William Wilberforce, an accomplished public speaker. Middleton wrote to him and received at first a tentative reply, but in due course there followed other meetings at Barham Court with the Middletons and Ramsay, until Wilberforce agreed to lead the parliamentary attack in the autumn of 1786. In later life he acknowledged their urging as one of the impulses – and perhaps the crucial one – in driving him to take up the Abolition cause at this stage. Without assuming any leadership role in the Abolition movement, Middleton supported it as a facilitator. He was present when Clarkson called a

---

50 Anon., *An Answer to the Rev. James Ramsay's Essay, by Some Gentlemen of St. Christopher* (Basseterre, 1784); J. P. Bateman, *Remarks on a Pamphlet written by J. Ramsay*, 1784; Rev. James Ramsay, *An Inquiry into the Effects of Putting a Stop to the African Slave Trade* (1784); James Tobin [under pseudonym 'A Friend to the West India Colonies'], *Cursory Remarks upon the Rev. Mr. Ramsay's Essay*, 1785; Anon. [probably James Tobin], *A Short Rejoinder to Mr. Ramsay's Reply*, 1787; Rev. James Ramsay, *An Address on the Proposed Bill for the Abolition of the Slave Trade* (1788); *An Examination of Mr. Harris's Scriptural Researches on the Licitness of the Slave Trade* (1788); *Objections to the Abolition of the Slave Trade, with Answers* (1788); J. Tobin, *A Farewell Address to the Rev. Mr. James Ramsay* (1788).

few people together with Ramsay, Sharp and Wilberforce to plan the next moves early in 1787. His home at Barham Court became the headquarters where the Abolitionists met to prepare their parliamentary strategy in 1789, leading Hannah More to hope that 'Teston will be the Runnymede of the negroes, and that the great charter of African liberties will be there completed.'[51]

In spite of such hopes, Emancipation for plantation slaves was only a distant prospect. Unfolding events in France were soon to trigger bloody risings in the French Caribbean, and raise fears that talk of freedom might stir up violence in the British West Indies. The planter interest allied to the sugar merchants of Liverpool and Bristol was too strong in Parliament, but the slave trade was more vulnerable to political assault, as the Abolitionists recognised. Their case was powerfully strengthened when they proved that, far from being a nursery of seamen as commonly claimed, the Atlantic slave trade was a graveyard of sailors as well as slaves in transit. English crews suffered severe rates of mortality through exposure to disease ashore in West Africa and on the Middle Passage from the Bight of Benin to the Caribbean. This discovery was made by Clarkson's brother John, a naval lieutenant, during his researches in Liverpool in 1787. The men who could confirm his findings and appreciate their significance were the Teston seafarers Middleton, Ramsay and Newton, who knew that any struggle against the Atlantic trade must necessarily be a naval enterprise.[52]

Olaudah Equiano, the former slave who met Ramsay in St Kitts and knew of his efforts to combat slavery, ranked him with Granville Sharp and Thomas Clarkson as 'our approved friends, men of virtue, ... and benefactors to mankind.'[53] With his further contribution to naval medicine, religion and officer values, this unassuming man must be accounted with Middleton one of the two originators of the Blue Light movement.

---

[51] Roberts, II, p. 156.

[52] Furneaux, p. 74; Simon Schama, *Rough Crossings: Britain, the Slaves and the American Revolution* (2005; New York edn 2006), p. 176.

[53] Olaudah Equiano, *The Interesting Narrative of the Life of Olaudah Equiano, or Gustavus Vassa, the African, Written by Himself* (1789; pbk edn 2001), p. 176n. Equiano was formerly a seafarer who had served in the navy, and had once been owned by a naval officer.

III

Gathering Momentum: Divine Service at Sea in the Later Eighteenth Century

The Testimony of Ships' Log Books

IF Kempenfelt and Middleton were correct in diagnosing religious neglect, this should become evident from a perusal of ships' log books. Similarly the same source should give some indication, however imprecise, of religious revival. Each ship was obliged to keep a record of navigational details and weather conditions, with further information about the employment of the crew, major punishments, deaths and burials at sea, and frequently a wealth of additional matter concerning ships in company, signals observed, stores embarked and of course any operations of war. Separate logs were written up each day by the captain and by the sailing master, where both officers were carried, while admirals kept their independent journals. At intervals these carefully maintained documents were forwarded to the Admiralty for official scrutiny and preservation in the archives. Although they were susceptible to a degree of editing, even of collusion by captain and master, they provide a wealth of objective, cryptic information about life in individual ships. It would have been proper for any general assembly of the hands to be recorded, whether to witness punishment, to muster at their quarters, to exercise gunnery skills, or to attend divine service.

How far was religion publicly observed in HM ships in the mid-eighteenth century and onwards? According to Middleton, Sunday services were sometimes held in ships with chaplains, but almost never in ships without. A dip into logs of the 1740s and the Seven Years War confirms the picture. In the *Arundel* under Captain Reynolds (1747–9), or under Captain Sankerson ten years later, there are occasional references to a muster of the ship's company for the reading of the Articles of War, but no specific mention of divine service. Sundays pass with the normal business of a man-of-war at sea or in harbour; it is a day to exercise the great guns, to survey boatswain's stores, to overhaul the rigging, to issue fishing lines, to fire a salute in honour of the king's accession – a day for general duties devoid of organised worship. Perhaps more might be expected from a ship commanded by an officer known for his piety, but neither the captain's nor the master's log for Captain Adam Duncan's *Valiant* shows any more taint of religion than Charles Colby's *Torbay*, even though Duncan had a chaplain aboard and signed a certificate for his pay. Middleton claimed that he began to read prayers with his men when he obtained his captaincy, but the *Arundel* log does not show it. Instead the silence concerning divine service continues as before, even when Middleton had taken command.[1]

How are we to understand this evidence? It is possible that Middleton wanted to exaggerate the contribution he personally had made to a revival of religion in the Seven Years War or that his memory had let him down. Maybe he did not log a muster for worship, either out of fear of Admiralty displeasure when the record was scrutinised or because it seemed inappropriate to record the event. After all, there were plenty of routine happenings at sea that never got into any logs, and some extraordinary ones such as punishments that should have been recorded but were not always. A more likely explanation is to be found in his recollection of holding prayers while the ship was in chase of an enemy: a sizeable proportion of both officers and men would have been involved in tending the sails, while the captain read prayers with the watch off duty. He may have felt that such an informal service did not warrant an entry in the log.[2]

It is, of course, quite possible that religious observance of this kind was going on in the navy, with prayers being offered by captain or chaplain in the presence of an off-duty group of officers and men. Later on, in the 1790s, we know that Captain Gambier held daily prayers with his midshipmen and with his officers before battle (on the testimony of one of them), and that Admiral Duncan held extempore prayer with his staff on the quarterdeck of his flagship before the Battle of Camperdown, but these occasions are not reflected in the official logs. Even in this earlier period groups of men may have shared from time to time in public prayers, especially in ships with a chaplain, but there is nothing to show it. And anyway, pious happenings on this scale fell far short of what divine service had meant in the Anglo-Dutch wars of the seventeenth century, with vessels hove to and ships' companies mustered for psalms, Bible reading, prayers and preaching, under the protection of the church pennant which combined the English and Dutch colours. It was this kind of gathering that Middleton and Kempenfelt wished to see reinstated to its place in naval routine.[3]

The widespread neglect continued into the American War as a further sample of logs demonstrates. Take the *Formidable*, Admiral Rodney's flagship at the Battle of the Saints: from mid-April 1782 to mid-March 1783 there is no reference

---

[1] PRO ADM 51/3770, 51/3771 *Arundel*; 51/3998, 52/1086 *Valiant*; 51/1001 *Torbay*.

[2] *BP*, II, p. 163.

[3] Michael A. Lewis (ed.), *A Narrative of my Professional Adventures, by Vice-Admiral Sir Willam Henry Dillon (1790–1839)* [hereafter *Dillon*], 2 vols. (1953–6), I, p. 128; Neil Duncan, *Duncan of Camperdown* (Diss, 1995), p. 105.

to divine service. The *Barfleur* was a second rate, sometimes used as a flagship: she was favoured with four services between March and July 1781, the only instances of public worship during three and a half years. The *Bedford* was a 74-gun third rate, with her logs recording the events of a commission of four years and two months on war service, but never a reference to public worship. The sloop *Fortune* was a much smaller vessel based at Gibraltar and involved in active operations against the Spanish from April to October 1782. In slightly over six months her crew listened to the Articles of War three times, had fourteen musters for a check of clothing and physical presence, and occasionally 'parades as required', but no evidence of divine service.[4]

In summary, a first-rate flagship, a second and a third rate, all ships of the line, and a sloop to represent smaller men-of-war, chronicle between them four instances of divine service across a cumulative period of eight years, ten months – four Sundays out of 450! Yet the same war gave the first Blue Lights their chance to shine. Middleton took command of the guardship *Ardent* in March 1775. The master's log shows that one Sunday in April part of the ship's company was sent 'to attend divine service on board the Church Ship' – presumably a commissioned warship with chaplain embarked. In May there were two services held in the *Ardent*, one led by her own chaplain, the next by a chaplain from Sheerness. Over a nineteen-month period the log records eighteen instances of public worship, most conducted by the ship's chaplain John Frew. In a stationary guardship it was perhaps not so difficult to hold to a routine of monthly services, but could the same thing happen at sea in the teeth of wind and weather on demanding war service? Kempenfelt was about to find out. His ship, the *Victory*, emerged from dockyard refit in March 1780 to become Admiral Geary's flagship at the end of May, with Kempenfelt captain of the fleet. During twelve weeks at sea there were four church services in this ship without a chaplain. Having recommended more religion for sailors to his friend Middleton, Kempenfelt was apparently putting theory into practice during a wartime cruise.[5]

As congregations were expected to share in the Anglican liturgy, prayer books and psalters were needed for public worship. The SPCK had a long tradition of supplying them for ships' companies when asked by captain or chaplain, but it seems to have been rarely approached during the American War. Alongside Middleton's testimony and Kempenfelt's corroboration, the record of ships' logs confirms the claim that public worship afloat had become a rarity. In March 1776

---

4 PRO ADM 51/4193 *Formidable*; 51/88 *Barfleur*; 51/94 *Bedford*; 51/4193 *Fortune*.

5 PRO ADM 51/56, 52/1568 *Ardent*; 51/1086 *Victory*.

Lieutenant Andrew Burn of the Marines attended a service for the ship's company held in the great cabin of the frigate *Milford* as she crossed the Atlantic: it was, he says, the first time divine worship had taken place since she had been commissioned several months before, and probably the first opportunity her crew had had to look at the prayer books supplied.[6]

From the start of the French Revolutionary War a better rate of religious observance may be seen, no doubt reflecting the ideological character of war against atheistic, republican France. James Saumarez, Guernseyman and notable frigate captain, held public worship in the *Crescent* once a month from June to December 1793. He was a Blue Light to whom these things mattered greatly; on the other hand Admiral Richard Howe, though decent and godfearing, was certainly not an Evangelical, yet his flagship the *Queen Charlotte* showed a comparable record – rather better if her winter spell in port is excluded. From April 1794 to May 1797 her captain's logs show the ship's company mustered for worship on thirty occasions, including the Sunday following the Battle of the Glorious First of June and a tense day during the Spithead Mutiny. The 74-gun *Bellerophon* had a chaplain, the loquacious John Fresselicque, who would surely not have missed an opportunity for a public platform; from January to November 1794 the captain's log shows twelve entries for divine service.[7]

Once a month is beginning to look like a reasonable average in ships which made some show of religion, either because they had a chaplain or a pious commander. Elsewhere there was often a religious desert. During much the same stage of the war the ship's company of the fifth rate *Adventure* was mustered at quarters on twenty-eight occasions, and once more to have the Articles of War read to them, but they apparently went nigh on two years with never a public prayer. Inspection of Captain Gambier's record in the *Defence* shows at once why he was regarded as eccentric and even excessive in his regard for religion, for in this ship on average only one Sunday a month was ever missed. On those occasions it seems fairly clear why church had not been rigged: fleet manoeuvres in squally weather, a ticklish passage in shoaling water, an alarm that an enemy force had put to sea, and fleet action on the Glorious First of June account for one-third of the gaps. On one particular Sunday it was recorded that the chaplain performed divine service both morning and evening. Surprisingly the log kept by her fifth lieutenant only notes two instances in a twelvemonth, a

---

[6] Andrew Burn, *Memoirs of the Life of the late Major General Andrew Burn of the Royal Marines, collected from his Journals, with copious Extracts from his Principal Works on Religious Subjects*, 2 vols. (1815), I, entry for 11 March 1776.

[7] PRO ADM 51/1159 *Crescent*; 51/1198, 51/4490 *Queen Charlotte*; 51/1162 *Bellerophon*.

further warning that more religion may have been happening than the records suggest.[8]

As hostilities wore on, there are signs of a quickened regard for religion, and not just when Earl St Vincent was around. In Admiral Duncan's flagship of the North Sea Fleet, often at sea, sometimes at anchor off the Texel, facing the possibility of mutiny, divine worship was regularly performed by the chaplain, thirty-one times in eighteen months. This is in sharp contrast to Duncan's record as a captain in the *Valiant* many years before, when he either did not hold prayers or did not record it if he did. Perhaps the man himself had changed from personal piety to proselytising Blue Light; or perhaps the changing temper of the times had made religion more acceptable.[9]

In 1801 the *Courageux* was a heavy frigate (technically a cut-down line of battle ship) operating in the Channel on attachment to Sir Edward Pellew's squadron. Her captain, Thomas Bowen, does not seem to have been an evangelical, but even in the arduous role these ships had, he managed to hold a service every fortnight or so. While Pellew was or became a supporter of the new piety, he cannot be held responsible for what was going on in a vessel on detached service. Although it may be right to see the distant influence of grim St Vincent, the probable explanation is that Bowen thought religion was good for his ship's company.[10]

To round off this sample of logs, two instances from the Napoleonic War offer another standard of comparison; the further issues they raise about the influence of the Blue Lights are for later discussion. The *Conqueror* had a sympathetic captain, Sir Israel Pellew, Edward's brother and a veteran of Trafalgar. He invited Richard Marks, one of his junior lieutenants, to read the Sunday service to the ship's company, and the practice soon became a standard part of routine. Divine service makes its appearance in the captain's log on Sunday 14 June 1807, a significant date in the history of the Blue Lights' movement, the day when Marks first led prayers at sea. Thereafter over almost one year the *Conqueror* had thirty more services, quite often at the rate of three a month (except during winter months). Sir Harry Neale was captain of the Channel Fleet in 1808–9 and Admiral Gambier's chief of staff. His log for the *Caledonia* records the church services for which Admiral Gambier was famous, and the dramatic action in Aix Roads for which he is infamous. There was a Sunday without service in December 1808, the only gap in twenty-three, but that was a day when storm staysails were set.[11]

---

[8] PRO ADM 51/1162 *Adventure*; 51/4435, 52/3505 *Defence*.

[9] PRO ADM 51/1214 *Venerable*.

[10] PRO ADM 51/1369 *Courageux*.

[11] PRO ADM 51/1734 *Conqueror*; 51/1908 *Caledonia*.

The evidence of the logs inspected bears out the testimony of memoirs and the records of the Bible Societies: religion became more prominent in the navy of the 1790s, until it established itself in the routine of a good many ships in the Napoleonic War. Until the records have been more thoroughly searched it is not possible to judge what proportion of captains were holding prayers and with what frequency, but it is clear the custom had ceased to be unusual. How and why did this revival of religion take place?

The Sea Chaplains in the Eighteenth Century

PARADOXICALLY this unfolding story of naval religion must focus on laymen not clergy. Naturally the chaplains have a part in it, but particularly in the earlier stages it was a subsidiary one. Lay control was so powerful afloat that it determined the pace of any revival of religion. If Admiralty and commanding officers decided to encourage religion, they had the power to implement change by appointing chaplains and allowing them to minister effectively. Then services would be held and literature distributed. If, on the other hand, they had no interest in religion, indifferent clergy would be appointed, or none at all, and public worship would have no place. A brief survey of the eighteenth-century chaplains will show how limited their authority was, and therefore how dependent naval religion was upon its lay friends. The Blue Lights were not painting on a blank canvas: their encouragement of religion had to take account of the existing chaplains. Bad clergy would discredit faith, but the right men, with a sense of vocation and gift of communication, if properly supported by commanding officers, could bring the aims of the Blue Lights to fulfilment.

Ever since 1677, when Pepys tried to ensure that every sea-going fifth rate and larger should have its own chaplain as part of the complement, the navy had never been able to find enough clergy. Candidates had first to be approved by the Bishop of London or the Archbishop of Canterbury, yet that did not prevent some dubiously qualified or motivated men getting themselves to sea. Quite simply the navy lacked the drawing power to attract men sufficient in quantity or quality. The reasons are not hard to find, and were neatly summarised for Pepys by a couple of chaplains in a memorandum of about 1685. They admit that motivation is a problem: 'few betake themselves to the sea out of choice but necessity. They want a comfortable subsistence by land and therefore seek their bread upon the waters.' They believed the Bishop of London had weeded out men of scandalous unsuitability, but nevertheless the chaplain still lacked respect. Since his pay was the same as an ordinary seaman's, the lower deck reckoned themselves his equal. With no executive authority, he could scarcely be reckoned an officer at all. No service could be held without the captain's agreement; times of service were not fixed and as a result might often be omitted from the ship's programme. Sailors had to contribute four pence a month out of their own scanty wages to supplement the chaplain's pay, and they were apt to tell the parson that he did nothing to earn their money.[12]

The four-penny payment of 'groats' was strongly disliked. Without it, the basic wage of 19 shillings a month would hardly have attracted even the most dedicated clergyman. It was a due payable from those who benefited from the chaplain's ministry, much like tithes in every parish ashore. It took account of the varying size of the flock, so that the chaplain of a first rate had a very respectable rate of remuneration. Groats emphasised the personal responsibility of minister to congregation. But if the chaplain could not afford to be without his groats, the sailor could scarcely afford to pay them, and resentment rather than respect was the obvious result. There was therefore an economic reason why sailors disliked having a parson aboard, but the objection was often expressed as a traditional superstition: clergymen wore black, the colour of mourning, and the presence of one aboard was an unlucky omen.

Parsons were hard to attract and to keep. Judging from the number who served for only one commission, it seems likely that many wanted an appointment to give them title to a curacy and had no real vocation for the sea. And of course it is quite possible that closer acquaintance with realities afloat deterred some from a second chaplaincy. Quite apart from the rigours of the life – sea-sickness, over-crowding, continual damp and cold – there were the problems of career. The navy did not attempt to offer one. A clergyman belonged to a ship for one commission, at the end of which he went back on the beach like every foremast hand. If he wished to serve again he must find a captain to apply for an Admiralty warrant. The few chaplains who served many years may have been fortunate in finding commanders or unfortunate in getting livings ashore. Since every chaplaincy was to some degree a private arrangement with a commanding officer, unofficial understandings were occasionally made, even to the extent of exempting the minister from living aboard. Some far-sighted clergy, having obtained a living ashore, were quite unwilling to give it up, even while holding a chaplaincy. Then it was anyone's guess as to which field of ministry would suffer, the parish afloat or the church at home. While the Rev. Alexander Scott was giving outstanding service to Hyde Parker and then to Nelson as confidential secretary and translator, at sea in the Atlantic, at Copenhagen and off Spain, he was technically vicar of St John's,

---

[12] Thos. Hughes and G. Dunlope to Pepys, 'The Causes of the General Disreputation and Disesteem that Chaplains of H.M. Ships lie under', undated; Bodleian Library, Oxford, Rawlinson A 171, fols. 2–3 [transcribed by J. S. Bromley].

Jamaica – and very put out to discover that the Governor had tried to give away his living to someone else during his protracted absence. In that case the navy won over the land.[13]

A sea chaplain was very much on his own professionally, hard to fit into a normal ecclesiastical career and equally hard to fit into a ministry afloat. What, after all, was he supposed to do? The 1731 *Regulations* that specified the duties of commissioned and warrant officers gave him no guidance at all. Customarily he was expected to take services when they were held and preach sermons. Most chaplains would visit the sick, and many assisted the surgeon with casualties in action. They would read the burial service, all too frequent a duty when disease was the prime killer at sea. They were expected to give spiritual support to anyone condemned to death. There was scarcely any opportunity to administer the sacraments: confirmation classes were unknown until the 1840s and Holy Communion was rarely held, perhaps (as Middleton believed) because so few chaplains were in priests' orders. In truth almost every task might have been performed by a layman.[14]

Many clergy felt themselves nothing but a spare hand at sea, or as one put it, 'somewhat like a pet bear on board. I was fed, coaxed and stared at – if in my den, forgotten; if at large in every body's way; of no manner of use – and at best, endured.'[15] Another chaplain, Joshua Larwood, writing to *The Naval Chronicle* in 1802, suggested that he and his kind would be more appreciated if they were not 'idlers' for six days a week, and that it would be much more satisfactory for everyone of the chaplain were also to be the ship's schoolmaster. ('Idlers' does not express contempt but describes men who did not have to turn out when the watch was called.) Larwood got his wish in 1812, when chaplains were given financial encouragement to combine the two posts.[16]

It is hardly surprising that sea parsons are sometimes found performing additional duties, as admirals' secretaries, or even judge advocates; both Ramsay and Scott were involved with intelligence work. In action they might well give assistance to the surgeon in his makeshift operating theatre in the cockpit, but not everyone could cope there; at the Battle of Quiberon Bay Hawke's chaplain was apparently on deck taking notes, and it was not totally unknown for a chaplain to stray onto the gundeck, like Samuel Cole who served a quarterdeck cannon at

[13] Rodger, 'The Naval Chaplain', p. 40; Taylor, pp. 200ff., 206.

[14] *RAI* 1731, pp. 145, 147.

[15] Thursfield, p. 22.

[16] Joshua Larwood, 'Navy Chaplain Schoolmasters', *The Naval Chronicle* [hereafter *NC*] VII (1802), pp. 372–87.

Camperdown or John Frowd at Algiers in 1816. An unusual service was performed by the *Britannia*'s chaplain at Trafalgar: he used his powerful voice and a speaking trumpet to relay the captain's orders above the din of battle. But then Laurence Halloran was an unusual kind of clergyman, a poet with a knack for getting the wrong side of people: he was later banished from South Africa and eventually transported to Australia for fraud.[17]

Custom and conscience had to be their guide for lack of any Admiralty direction. Even then, much depended on the captain. Hogarth painted a famous group portrait in about 1745 showing Lord George Graham celebrating in his cabin the capture of privateers (illus. 4): here the chaplain is seated at table with the captain, very obviously a privileged member of his entourage.[18] Nelson, a parson's son, tried to deter his brother from taking up what he called 'such a disagreeable station in life'; in 1781 he wrote, 'if you get with a good man and with gentlemen, it will be tolerable; if not you will soon detest it.'[19] Unless a commander deliberately made opportunity for ministry, it might easily be overlooked amidst the pressure of life's round at sea, with competition from weather conditions as well as duty. 'Divine Service', records one chaplain's log in 1782, 'which was grown quite a novelty in the *Superbe* from the continual hurry and bustle unavoidable in war.'[20]

The quality of the men who served was varied, some struggling to find scope for their ministry, others to find any useful purpose at all, and a few earning high credit. The Rev. Evan Halliday took up a self-appointed role as 'prisoner's friend', being always ready to speak in favour of men under discipline: he had found a most effective way of entering the world of the lower deck and winning their confidence, but sadly he was far from typical.[21] Most naval chaplains – to judge from contemporary accounts – were men of shallow spirituality whose ministry

---

[17] Cole served in the *Monarch* at Camperdown. His naval service began in 1790; he was pretty well continuously at sea until 1802. From 1813 he was chaplain first at Haslar and then Plymouth Hospital. In 1816 he became chaplain at Greenwich and exercised the powers of senior chaplain, to the disapproval of evangelicals. Frowd (1786–1865) was in the flagship *Queen Charlotte* at Algiers; he held six chaplaincies from 1811 to 1823 before becoming senior dean and librarian at Corpus Christi College, Oxford. Taylor, pp. 211–14.

[18] *Lord George Graham in his Cabin*; painting by William Hogarth, c. 1745; National Maritime Museum.

[19] Quoted in Oliver Warner, *A Portrait of Lord Nelson* (1958; Reprint Society edn 1959), p. 26.

[20] Benjamin Millingchamp in *Superbe*, 1782; Taylor, p. 183.

[21] Vice-Admiral Sir Jahleel Brenton, *The Hope of the Navy* (1839), pp. 274f.

4 Lord George Graham (1715–47) in his cabin celebrating the capture of privateers, c. 1745. The chaplain on the left of the picture is portrayed as part of the nobleman's retinue, a friend of the captain. (Oil painting by William Hogarth, 1697–1764) © National Maritime Museum, London BHC2720

achieved little. The picture is not greatly different if we take up the memoirs of an officer like Commander Gardner, or lower-deck reminiscences, or the dismissive statements of George Charles Smith, once a boatswain's mate, and Marks, a former lieutenant, men whose search for God received no help from sea-borne clergy. 'Few ships ever had a chaplain on board', wrote Marks, 'and several which had them would have been better off without them; with very few exceptions they were the butt of the officers' jokes, and furnished too many sad objects for their contempt and ridicule.'[22] From experience he expected such a man to 'discredit himself and his profession, and hurl contempt on every thing like real religion', and even when he found an agreeable and dignified man who obtained the respect of his colleagues, he was profoundly disappointed in his theology – speculative and unscriptural.[23] Smith was ruthlessly critical of the whole set. And churchmen in their turn could find plenty to complain about.

The disillusioned comments of a short-serving chaplain in 1812 may stand for many clergy who found their sea-going parishioners uncongenial and unresponsive. Years of genteel ministry in Bath had never prepared the Rev. Edward Mangin for what he found afloat, and in the end he could find neither enough sympathy nor regard for his shipmates to keep him in the navy:

> I did not see the smallest likelihood of effecting any material change in the morals of such an assemblage. To leave them unreproved and vicious was possible; and I dare say it was equally possible to have transformed them all into Methodists, or madmen and hypocrites of some other kind: but to convert a man-of-war's crew into Christians would be a task to which the courage of Loyola, the philanthropy of Howard, and the eloquence of St Paul united would prove inadequate.[24]

While, of course, there were plenty of officers who would have agreed with him that a warship was an inappropriate environment for religious ministry, an influential minority had begun to attempt the widespread evangelisation of the navy. Whatever the quality of clergy available, there would never have been enough of them for the task. Middleton's original vision always depended on laymen seeing what ought to be done: it was a remote hope in the American War, but that was before the evangelical influence was strongly felt.

---

[22] Roald Kverndal, *Seamen's Missions: Their Origin and Early Growth* (Pasadena, 1986), p. 664 n. 141.

[23] 'Aliquis' [The Rev. Richard Marks], *The Retrospect, or Review of Providential Mercies* (1816; 20th edn 1842) [hereafter *Retrospect*], p. 208.

[24] Thursfield, p. 14.

in 1793 they were ready to serve at sea again – and to bring with them the influence of the new piety. It was especially relevant to the new conflict.

The war that broke out in 1793 was profoundly different from the American revolution which had repudiated the crown in the name of republican liberty but had not set out to turn British society upside down. Jacobinism aimed to create a whole new order, an aggressive kind of liberty with no respect for frontiers or faith. However admirable the constitutional stage of the Revolution had been, it had become something very different in the hands of Robespierre the regicide. Freedom French-style looked bloody and anarchic to the British ruling class, and the Assembly's promise to topple tyranny seemed to threaten the liberty and prosperity which the English and Scots, but not perhaps the Irish, were convinced they enjoyed already. British society might have stomached the anti-clericalism of the Civil Constitution of the Clergy: it found some sympathy in England, where not everyone rejoiced to pay their tithe, but the militant atheism that butchered priests and desecrated churches was repellent to all, including the Irish. While earlier wars against the French had been about trade or possessions, the Revolutionary War seemed to be a struggle for the soul of Europe.

As John Sugden has shown, there was in Nelson's mind an easy merging of religion and patriotism into what he calls the 'sacrosanct trinity: God, king and country'.[27] Many minds less subtle than Nelson's saw monarchy and social rank as divinely given, and the laws invested with more than human authority. Loyalty to king and Church of England seemed to go together, while Dissent invited caution, and Romanism downright suspicion. With England's laws and liberties at risk from atheistic republicanism, it was natural for Church and Crown to draw even closer, and for popular loyalty to fasten itself to both. On this basis, of course, religion had more to do with the security of the state than the salvation of souls, but that does not mean it lacked sincerity. With the nation's survival at stake many heartfelt prayers were offered for deliverance.

To a degree unknown in the American War commanding officers began to take their religious duties seriously. As new ships were brought into commission in 1793, requests to the SPCK came from fourteen captains or chaplains in that year alone. The normal response was a large copy of Bible and Prayer Book for use in leading worship, together with a number of smaller New Testaments or Bibles and Prayer Books with separate copies of the Psalms, in sufficient quantity to allow each mess to be supplied. The books were a grant to the ship and were not for private possession. Quantities of *The Seaman's Monitor* were enclosed and sometimes other tracts or prayers on pasteboard were given for individual use. Although there was

---

[27] Sugden, p. 401.

some evangelistic potential behind these pieces of literature, the primary intention of the Society was the promotion of public worship. Presumably that is what most applicants intended, but there remains another possibility – that the books were seen as a possible resource for difficult days, when the burial service would be needed for battle casualties or a New Testament to administer an oath: on at least one occasion a court martial had to be postponed when no Bible could be found.[28] In the first four years of hostilities forty-nine ships received grants. The letters recorded in SPCK minutes show that the books were appreciated, though not always for evidently religious reasons: politics and shipboard discipline had a role as well. Captain John Duckworth of the *Orion* in 1794 believed there never had been such a time when 'the circulating of religion and morality appeared more evidently necessary, especially among the lower orders of people, than the present.'[29] He therefore sought a supply of prayer books and Bibles to facilitate public worship and – presumably – combat the radical philosophies that France had spawned. Captain William Bedford of the *Royal Sovereign* was sure that 'a packet of books ... received from the Society [had] caused a happy change on the mind and conduct' of his last ship's company, and the chaplain of the *Formidable* reported 'general satisfaction' with the donation received in 1798.[30] On several occasions Nelson was equally emphatic that the books had been well used and that regular worship made a measurable difference to conduct. His claim that men were invariably better behaved when Sunday prayers had been held echoes Kempenfelt's hope, that more religion would mean less punishment. There is room for a study of ships' logs to correlate frequency of prayers and incidence of punishment: did public worship act as a brake on disorderly conduct, or were captains inclined to write what they thought the Society would like to hear?[31]

---

[28] SPCK Minutes Book XXXI lists ships supplied in 1793: January: *Powerful* (Capt. Hicks); *Britannia* (Capt. Hallowell); February: *Queen* (Hutt); March: *Agamemnon* (Nelson); April: *Victory* (Capt. Knight), *Alcide* (Capt. Linzee); May: *Sceptre* (Dawe), *Colossus* (Pole), *Lord Mulgrave* (Maxwell) [prob. HEIC]; June: *Trimmer* (Craven), *Queen* sloop (Ramsey); October: *Sandwich* (Mosse); September: *La Nymphe* (Pellew), *Resolution* (Pinder) [listed but not found]; October: *Amphion* (Sawyer). Recollection of Captain R. J. Elliot at NMBS anniversary meeting, referring to incident in a frigate where he was serving thirty years before. The trial was delayed until a New Testament was procured from another ship. *NMBS* 1836, p. 26.

[29] SPCK Minutes, XXXI, p. 234 (Duckworth).

[30] SPCK Minutes, XXXII, pp. 238 (chaplain Ward), 253 (Bedford).

[31] SPCK Minutes, XXXIV, p. 22 (Nelson). See also XXXI, p. 128; XXXII, p. 260; XXXIII, pp. 93, 370 for further Nelson correspondence.

Public worship was a method of humane control appealing to some commanders who were looking for ways to knit together a ship's company of mixed ages, origins and race. Public worship did several things. It gathered the crew together for something less ominous than the reading of the Articles of War – although that useful bit of warning could well be included. Public worship implicitly recognised the common humanity of everyone involved: from captain to idler and swabber, all stood answerable to Almighty God and acknowledged the binding nature of a moral code. Each was called to listen to the voice of conscience and reason. For believers there was the additional psychological support of addressing fears and concerns with hope of divine help. There were good reasons why any captain might want to see what religion could do for his ship.

Public Worship in Wartime

ADMIRAL Sir John Jervis, ennobled as Earl St Vincent, while no friend to the Evangelicals, recognised the utility of religion, and demanded a regularity of worship that would have appealed even to their high standards. And yet there was a profound dissimilarity between his punctiliousness and their piety. To him religion was an aspect of discipline. Like Kempenfelt (and many others) he realised that ordered cohesion and obedience to a common purpose would turn a collection of fighting ships into a formidable engine of war, and his unflinching commitment to this goal helped to produce the finest navy of the sailing era. He knew how difficult it was to fashion such a fleet once impressment brought in men of mixed quality and motivation. The mutinies of 1797 drew out his unflinching courage and resolution, but emphasised less appealing traits as well. There was a quirky side to his character that suddenly softened into kindness and generosity – the source of several endearing anecdotes cherished by his biographers – but could equally turn to harshness. A shrewd judge of men, he recognised and brought forward some of the most illustrious officers of the time, such as Nelson, Troubridge, Pellew and Saumarez. He recognised that there were injustices about the way seamen were treated, and he saw the importance of health reforms, good rations and regular pay. On the other hand, he was merciless towards any mutinous airing of grievance, and his passion for discipline makes him appear unreasonably pitiless.

When he took command of the Mediterranean Fleet in 1795 and when he moved his flag to the Channel command four years later, Jervis made religious observance obligatory. His contempt for Middleton and Gambier precludes any thought that he was driven by their example. He could see advantage in using Anglican services to promote loyalty to the crown. As long as the standing instructions for the navy demanded Sunday worship he would insist on it as a point of compliance: although the expressed purpose of the clause was to reverence God, the way he set about it honoured discipline more. In an incident of July 1797, Jervis ordered that the sentence of death, passed on four men by court martial, should be carried out the next day, even though it was Sunday. In the case of two of them, facing charges of mutinous behaviour, some of the most incriminating evidence was obtained through confession to a chaplain, normally sacrosanct. Jervis was deaf to the plea that they should be given more time to make their peace with God; he dismissed Vice-Admiral Thompson's protest against profaning the Sabbath by sending him home, and in a heartless parody of the spirit of worship he had ships' companies at prayer with the corpses left swinging at the yardarm. Nelson approved, but he, like Jervis, was inclined to value public religion for its social utility rather than as food for the soul.[32]

St Vincent's true view is shown by what he directed his chaplain to preach on:

> The Morning Service – Prayer to defend us against our enemies. One Thanksgiving Prayer and the Ordinary Prayers used at Sea, with a Moral Discourse of between Ten and Fifteen minutes, viz. Either on Obedience to Superiors, On Temperance and Sobriety. Against Profane Swearing, Obscene and Vulgar conversation. On forgiveness of injuries. And on Benevolence to Shipmates. Against sudden and violent gusts of passion, revenge and becoming Judge and Executioner in one's own Cause and thereby becoming the offender instead of calmly remonstrating and persuading the person who first offered the injury to make reparation – Exhortation to Courage and Perseverance in the day of Battle the way to be rewarded by both God and Man – And alacrity or cheerfulness in carrying on the common duties of the ship the sure Road to Promotion.[33]

This schedule of sermons never considers whether seamen are sinners in need of salvation. Bounded by issues of conduct, with never a hint of eternity, it is pragmatism devoid of piety. Jervis saw that chaplains could do good as welfare officers and moral police, but there is little to suggest he respected them as men of God. Hence the tale, reliable or not, of his summoning fleet clergy in a lively sea, giving them a long wet row to the flagship in open boats – a piece of practical joking that verged on mockery. He found real abuses amongst the clergy, including one

---

[32] For Jervis see Admiral Sir William James, *Old Oak: The Life of John Jervis, Earl of St. Vincent* (1950); P. K. Crimmin, 'John Jervis, Earl of St Vincent' in Le Fevre and Harding, *Precursors of Nelson*, pp. 325–50, and Rodger, *Command of the Ocean*, pp. 476f., 479, 525f., etc. Roger Knight, *The Pursuit of Victory: The Life and Achievement of Horatio Nelson* (2005), pp. 239f.

[33] RUSI MSS A29B N.M. 35.

selling spirits to the lower deck, and imagined others. A few had their names entered in the Admiralty black book of officers not to be employed again: one long-serving chaplain had sought to be discharged from his ship when a request for leave was refused, and another stood condemned for 'shuffling behaviour'.[34] With more justice he described some others as a disgrace to their profession, for they lacked honesty, sobriety or commitment to the sea service, but he made no attempt to evaluate them as pastors and theologians.

All this fits well enough with St Vincent's religious orientation. While not given to church-going ashore, he could see merit in the Established Church when it gave support to the social order; in Ireland, where the same religious structure created antagonism and where toleration might secure loyalty to the Crown, he supported Catholic Emancipation. There was a force here to be harnessed. Religion as medicine for sick souls would have been incomprehensible to him, but as the cement of society it had obvious utilitarian value. At sea it might bind together a heterogeneous collection of ranks, trades, classes and even races in one community with a single acknowledged allegiance. Those regular prayers for 'our Sovereign Lord King George III and all who are set in authority under him' carried a definite political message, for the Anglican liturgy gave no succour to Catholicism, republicanism or the aspirations of United Irishmen.[35]

The stern formality and pomp of Sunday worship under St Vincent's flag gave young Lieutenant Pryce Cumby material for his humour. In a parody of the biblical story of Nebuchadnezzar, Cumby cast his admiral as the Babylonian potentate: having set up an image of blue and gold he required all to bow their heads when he appeared for Sunday divisions, and he had his own peculiarly naval punishment ready for anyone failing to strike headgear at the appropriate moment. This paper had a wide circulation in the Channel Fleet, until with terrible inevitably it reached the admiral's desk. St Vincent sent for the officer and made him read it publicly to the assembled wardroom, and then to universal surprise sent its author home on a fortnight's leave.[36]

Cumby was fortunate to have come across the admiral in a rare moment of jollity. To St Vincent there was nothing light hearted about his purpose. Aware of

---

34 James, *Old Oak*, p. 151. Two chaplains to be discharged were William Hawtayne and Samuel Cole, but neither of their careers suffered; the former continued for long under Gambier, and the other eventually became senior chaplain at Greenwich. Black Book PRO ADM 12/27 C.

35 State prayers in Morning Prayer, *Book of Common Prayer* (1662).

36 James, *Old Oak*, p. 108.

the lower-deck problems, he had one supreme consideration – obedience. Grievances might be settled eventually or not; that was a lesser matter. Thoughtful officers were aware of the challenge to discipline created by the methods of manning, the simmering resentments over impressment, indefinite length of service, restricted shore leave and poor pay. Events in 1797 showed how precarious was the discipline of the fleets upon which England's safety depended.

The Spithead and Nore Mutinies

IN that year, first the Channel Fleet at Spithead and then the North Sea Fleet at the Nore flared into open defiance of authority. Since Britain was facing the combined naval strength of France, Spain and the Netherlands, with Ireland uncertain and threat of invasion only too real, the mutinies came at a time when the safety of the realm was bound up with the dependability of the navy. The Delegates at Spithead resoundingly declared their support for their country – 'we likewise agree in opinion, that we should suffer double the hardships we have hitherto experienced, before we would wish the crown of England to be in the least imposed upon by that of any other power in the world', and they bound themselves to obey their officers should the French put to sea – but the simple fact was that they had defied the authority of their commanders at a time of threatening danger for the country.[37]

The grievances of the lower deck were presented to the Admiralty under the signature of thirty-three Delegates representing sixteen ships of the Channel Fleet. Their demands display astonishing moderation. Priority was given to the fact that their wages were too low. The rates of pay had not been adjusted since Commonwealth days – a pay freeze of a century and a half! Now the seamen complained that they could not properly support their wives and families on 19 shillings a month for an ordinary seaman and twenty-six for an able rate – and this at a time when the basic pay for a soldier was a shilling a day. Nor were the remaining grievances any more extreme, being requests for better provisions, improved care of the sick, continued pay for the wounded and – more controversially – for shore leave.

Essentially the other demands could have been satisfied with money, but not this one. By requesting leave as a right the Spithead sailors were raising more fundamental questions about their status –

---

[37] General accounts of the Mutinies are given in G. E. Manwaring and Bonamy Dobrée, *The Floating Republic: An Account of the Mutinies at Spithead and the Nore in 1797* (1935, new imp. 1966), and James Dugan, *The Great Mutiny* (1966).

which is nowise unreasonable; and that we may be looked upon as a number of men standing in defence of our country; and that we may in somewise have grant and opportunity to taste the sweets of liberty on shore, when in any harbour, and when we have completed the duty of our ship, after our return from sea ... which is a natural request, and congenial to the heart of man, and certainly to us, that you make the boast of being the guardians of the land.[38]

This single petition goes to the root of the navy's problems with manning. In time of peace the navy could be manned entirely with volunteers. Whether appointed by royal commission or Admiralty warrant, only the officers were permanent members of the navy, on full pay if they were actually employed or half-pay if not. The seamen and petty officers who made up the vast bulk of naval manpower were enlisted for a single period of service known as a commission: on conclusion the ship's company was paid off and discharged ashore, free to enlist in another man-of-war or merchant vessel if they chose. In peacetime the naval authorities were not unduly concerned about such a loss of trained and experienced men since they were returning to the national pool of sailors. Both the merchant shipping which carried the nation's trade and the warships which protected it needed prime seamen of the same kind, all drawn from the one maritime community and all seeking their living from employment afloat. In days of peace there were enough sailors to supply both trade and fleet.

Under war conditions the situation altered. As the fleet expanded, it required an ever larger share of the maritime pool until volunteers alone could not possibly suffice. At peak demand the Royal Navy would need five or six times its peacetime strength with experienced able hands and petty officers to give a backbone of skill to newly recruited crews. The problem was exacerbated by the unwillingness of many prime seamen to serve in the fighting fleet. They were not scared of the danger, since all sea-going had its perils, and the risks of injury and death in combat were much less than accident, shipwreck and disease. It would be easy to blame the severity of naval discipline or the harsh life of the lower deck, but merchant ways were pretty tough too. The poor rates of pay were certainly a factor, and basic naval rates lagged way behind wages commonly earned in trade, but the lure of prize money compensated. Successful frigate captains with a reputation for enriching their crews never lacked volunteers. Most sailors, after all, were more gamblers than thrifty savers. Nevertheless wages were an issue, clearly prominent amongst the grievances of the Spithead Mutiny.

At root, however, the comparative unpopularity of the Royal Navy was due

[38] Manwaring and Dobrée, p. 266.

to the loss of personal freedom. Once subject to naval discipline there could be no second thought. Whereas the merchant sailor could forfeit his pay and jump ship if he chose – risky if caught and an offence at law – the same act done by a naval seaman was classed as desertion, a crime against the Crown, for which the punishment was death or flogging round the fleet. Many commanders who had met severe difficulty in getting a crew together in the first place were reluctant to risk losing their men amongst the attractions of harbour life. It was not so much the moral temptations which had to be avoided but the risks of desertion to seek better wages in a merchant vessel. The result for the naval hand was appalling: denied leave to go on shore, he might find himself confined to the same ship and messmates for many months or even years at a stretch. No one could tell how long his service might last, for a wartime commission could be extremely protracted. Furthermore, in their shifts to keep trained men, the Admiralty had made it hard for sailors to receive their accumulated pay at all promptly or even in full unless they made themselves available for further service: there are instances of men being told to claim their earnings aboard a new ship.

It would be wrong to blame this unsatisfactory arrangement entirely upon the obscurantism of the Admiralty or the inhumanity of the officer class. Sailors as a kind contributed to it by their reluctance to make a better system work. Generation after generation, sailors interpreted liberty as the freedom to choose their own ship, which in effect meant the choice to serve under a particular commander with a reputation for fairness or fortune. Until the mid-nineteenth century they were denied the chance of joining the navy for a career, and in truth they had shown no wish for it. A professional naval rating would have to go wherever the drafting office sent him without consulting his wishes: where was the freedom in that?

The French introduced a partially successful *Inscription Maritime* for their navy, with a list of sailors who might be called up for war service, but attempts to create a similar rota on the other side of the Channel were thwarted by reluctance to join. British sailors by and large showed a complete lack of interest in a compulsory system of enlistment for a fixed period, preferring the lottery of impressment. Their thinking is of a piece with the haphazard, reckless habits for which they were famous: they might escape the press-gangs altogether. No one liked the caprices and inefficiency of the old system but at least they were more or less accepted by maritime society.

From the late seventeenth century until the late nineteenth various proposals were made to give the navy an assured reserve of manpower, but nothing proved really workable until the 1850s. Then a trio of reforms altered the whole basis of the argument; out went the old hire and discharge system, and in came the

Continuous Service rating, training ships and the Royal Naval Reserve. Even with these advances, however, it proved desperately hard to man the Crimean War fleets acceptably – either in terms of speed or quality of men. By that stage no Government could contemplate the time-dishonoured method of impressment, but the voluntary principle was stretched to breaking. It collapsed under the demands of the world wars of the twentieth century. Impressment could not be revived for the navy alone, of course, but conscription was used instead – mandatory enlistment for land, sea and air forces, with no opportunity to dodge the draft. Both Parliament and public opinion, so critical of the press-gangs in the past, accepted a much more drastic curtailment of individual liberties. Conscription was perceived as fair because its burden fell alike on all sectors of society.[39]

Britain fought the French Revolutionary and Napoleonic Wars under eighteenth-century ways of manning the fleet. Such an improvised, even chaotic scheme served for armaments and short wars, but it ran into severe difficulties when hostilities extended over many years. As the navy's need for manpower intensified, new sources had to be tried. Normally exempt categories such as watermen were liable to find themselves unlawfully impressed, and once at sea would have scant chance of redress. Inbound merchantmen should have been untouched, but when national defence demanded it they were sometimes taken. Foreigners were never legally subject to compulsory enlistment, but mistakes were sometimes made or the law deliberately circumvented. American seamen were particularly at risk: the popularity of American ships as a haven for English deserters made them a target for attention, while some commanders were only too ready to regard anyone from the Thirteen States as a deserter from the British flag. At first the navy wanted men bred to the sea; at a pinch landmen might be acceptable as idlers and waisters, even though there was scant chance of making prime topmast hands out of them. Such was the thinking behind the Quota Acts of 1795 which demanded a proportion of men from inland districts. Earlier historians blamed this notorious legislation for drafting into the navy the people least esteemed by the county magistrates – amongst them vagrants, misfits and petty criminals – but more recent research has questioned whether the results were so deplorable. And, after a fashion, the system really did work.

It is perhaps too easy to exaggerate the problems which all this posed to the navy, and to heighten the sense of inevitability as 1797 approached. In fact officers and petty officers knew their trade well enough. Without exception they were bred to the sea and knew the dangers and privations of their calling. They appreciated the difference between a happy and an unhappy ship. From teenage years upward

---

[39] Bromley, *Manning Pamphlets, 1693–1873*, relates to this problem.

they had witnessed how authority was exercised and how crews responded. Bearing in mind the salutary experience of peace, when warships competed for prime seamen on equal terms with trade, any officer could see that harsh treatment drove away hands. No sailor disputed the need for clear discipline: it was for his protection as well as that of the ship and the Service. There was a shared understanding amongst seamen, something looser than comradeship, but an unmistakable bond.

It was precisely this quality which was diluted in the 1790s. Impressment strained relationships between officers and men anyway, and refusal to grant shore leave intensified resentment. Then the importation of elements which did not share the brotherhood of the sea undermined the fundamental understanding upon which discipline rested. It could be retrieved as it often was by outstanding leadership. Alternatively authority could invoke the powers of the Articles of War, with their fearsome provisions to bring about obedience and to fashion a united purpose – but based on force rather than consent. It could be done, but at a risk. If sailors' grievances went long unredressed, resentments would fester on the lower deck, where hundreds of men lived at close quarters. Here disorder – and, in desperation, mutiny – might finally kill consent.

Both the Spithead and Nore outbreaks were organised under the noses of the officers with never a hint of its scale suspected by the authorities. Captain Philip Patton reported to the Admiralty that something was afoot, but neither he nor they had any idea of the true seriousness. It is possible that men of education and legal training reached the lower deck by way of the county gaol and the Quota Acts, and that they clothed the sailors' widely felt grievances in telling prose. Somehow the elements of representative government were put in place, and the Delegates put forward the men's demands as their elected spokesmen. Signatures indicated a willingness to accept responsibility which impressed the lower deck, while at the same time the solidarity of the protest conferred a degree of safety upon them.

The demands were presented with a reasonableness which carried conviction even with an exasperated, vacillating and humiliated Admiralty – a dangerous body indeed. The leadership of Valentine Joyce and the other Delegates was quite outstanding; always reasonable and unflinchingly loyal to cause and to Crown, their control over angry men was as remarkable as their courage in the face of a menacing Government. Forced to give way by the simple calculation that no fleet could be run without its sailors, the Admiralty conceded every demand of the Spithead mutineers, including the grant of an unconditional pardon. No less a figure than Earl Howe, the absentee but titular commander-in-chief, had to read the King's Pardon aboard each ship of the line before the Spithead Mutiny ended.

A regatta with much exuberant rejoicing by the seamen demonstrated the essential loyalty and moderation which had marked the event from the first, and had seen it through the most dangerous moments when blood was shed and violence could so easily have become general.

The Nore Mutiny was a more tragic affair. Provoked by news of 'the breeze at Spithead', it began with uncertain aims as a gesture of solidarity, fuelled by fears that the concessions won might not be fully implemented or extended to the other fleets. Once the Spithead affair had been settled the Nore mutineers had a clear choice, either to return to their obedience, trusting in the clemency of their king, or to pursue an agenda of their own. They chose the second course, and advanced a manifesto of eight demands. First they wanted confirmation that Spithead liberties would come to them as well. Again they demanded shore leave, not as a privilege but a right. They asked for anything over six months' arrears of wages to be paid before a ship put to sea. No officer whom the mutineers had turned out of his ship for brutality should be reinstated in the same vessel without the consent of her company. The interests of pressed men were taken up, and an advance of pay was requested so that they could purchase the clothing they needed. Aware of the threat of capital punishment hanging over deserters, they sought indemnity for 'runners' who were now back in His Majesty's service. On finance once again, they wanted a more equitable distribution of prize money, one of the few agreeable prospects of sea service. Finally they sought a revision of the Articles of War to make naval discipline less dependent on terror, thus making the service more attractive for volunteers.

Of themselves the demands were far from unreasonable, but the timing of them was atrocious. Having made the Spithead concessions, the Admiralty dare not give way yet again and so soon, for fear that the whole structure of authority, obedience and national safety might be imperilled. Faced with an unyielding reply, the mutineers became more radical and overtly political, especially when the defiant ships adopted the title of the Floating Republic. Whereas the Spithead leadership had been adamant about their patriotism, a more traitorous turn was given to events at the Nore, when the mutineers – admittedly by then in a state of desperation – threatened to turn over the King's ships to his enemies, the French or Dutch. By now the authorities would accept only unconditional surrender. Starved out by blockade, the mutineers caved in, and the price of their defiance had to be paid in blood. Twenty-nine were hanged, nine were flogged, and scores were gaoled or held in prison hulks.

The two movements were fed by identical grievances but the differing outcomes reflected the circumstances of the two locations. At Spithead the fleet was a coherent force with many sail together. At the Nore the focus was the guardship

Sandwich, an unhappy and transient home for sailors awaiting their draft to sea-going ships. It was less an organised fleet than a collection of vessels on various duties. It is all the more remarkable that a complex movement could have been organised. The eventual leader, Richard Parker, was clever but less balanced and realistic than Joyce, and the aims and methods of the Nore mutineers were not so well defined. All attempts to find the source of the mutiny elsewhere than in the ships of the fleet have so far failed. Despite the most thorough research no historian has yet managed to establish an unequivocal link with Jacobinism, the United Irishmen or even the Corresponding Societies. Individuals may have found their inspiration from any of these sources, but the movement itself appears to have grown without external impulse from the multiple and legitimate grievances of sailors in the fleet.[40]

A most intriguing question arises about the organisation of such a complex happening, especially since traffic between ships was normally in the line of duty or else carefully regulated by their officers. How were plans laid and detailed instructions passed? One supposes a network which could be trusted. We know that Methodists were sent into the navy; occasionally magistrates seem to have done this as a reprisal for their religion. Occasionally unpopular messmates were transferred from one ship to another, on an entirely informal exchange system run by commanding officers. Bo'sun Smith knew of Methodists pressed into the service who had attempted to form prayer groups aboard; sometimes these would be tolerated, sometimes scattered amongst other ships. As a way of reducing the contagion it was, of course, a failure. Men of such conviction sought out their fellows and attracted new members through testimony and conversion. We can be sure of the existence of a tenuous network, then, unknown to authority, but linking men of proven honesty. It can be no more than guesswork, but it is interesting to speculate whether Methodists were used to pass mutinous correspondence, or even that they were instrumental in organising the mutinies.[41]

Bo'sun Smith and Richard Marks knew more about this Christian underworld than anyone, but in their writings neither referred to such a link, even when the mutinies and the war that spawned them had passed deep into history. On the other hand Smith tells of a pious quartermaster, Thomas Doeg, in the *Agamemnon*, who he says was forced to become a Nore Delegate because his colleagues trusted him, and who used his influence on the side of moderation. Whether

[40] Twenty-nine hanged: Manwaring and Dobrée, p. 277; thirty-six according to Dugan, p. 395n.

[41] Smith refers to an incident at Bantry Bay in 1801 when 'pious civilians' took a boat to meet up with 'psalm-singing Methodists' and were allowed aboard a warship; *The New Sailor's Magazine* [hereafter *NSM*], 1828, p. 69.

because of him or not, the thirteen Agamemnons put on trial after the mutiny were pardoned. Doeg went on the run, but only to escape the debaucheries aboard ship, according to Smith, who visited him later. In fact Smith regarded Doeg as one of the influences that brought him to faith.[42]

Undeniably, however, there were religious elements in the mutinies, even though not specifically evangelical. It is noteworthy that the Spithead mutineers used an oath to bind loyalty, a device later turned to advantage by the naval authorities to secure the allegiance of men at enlistment. This was not the only way in which they showed respect for religion. After mutiny had broken out at the Nore, Richard Parker invited the chaplain of the *Sandwich* to take divine service, but if he had hoped to have the blessings of religion for his cause, he was disappointed when the Rev. William Hatherall, with more courage than tact, preached from a text in the book of Job, 'God forbid that I should justify you.'[43] Parker's 'dying declaration' displays some knowledge of scripture with references to atonement, devoted scapegoat and the caprice of the crowd, as shown 'with reverence I write it, in the treatment of Jesus Christ Himself when on earth'. He concludes with a prayer for grace and salvation:

> O pray for me, that in the last scene I may act my part like a man, and that when I am on the point of being offered up, I may be inspired with a charity sufficient to forgive those for whom I am sacrificed. … Parting with life is no more than going to sleep, and God in His mercy grant I may sleep sweetly after my earthly toils, through the merits of my Lord and Saviour Jesus Christ.[44]

To his wife he wrote a tender farewell letter, including a statement of his own faith: 'I trust in Jesus Christ, our blessed Redeemer, that my being cut off is to the glory of God and the salvation of my own soul.'[45] On the morning of his death, moments before the signal for execution was given, Parker prayed on the quarterdeck of the *Sandwich* with her chaplain Hatherall, and asked to recite a penitential psalm with him: 'Have mercy upon me, O God … and cleanse me from my sin.'[46] There seems no way of knowing whether Parker had long held

---

[42] Smith, *NSM*, 1859, pp. 169–71.

[43] Job 27:5. Manwaring and Dobrée, p. 196.

[44] Manwaring and Dobrée, p. 275. Full text of Parker's 'Dying Declaration' in Manwaring and Dobrée, pp. 273–6. It is appended to Minutes of court martial assembled on board HMS *Neptune*, 22–6 June 1797, PRO ADM 1/5339.

[45] Dugan, p. 357.

[46] Psalms 51:1–2.

such convictions, or whether they reflect the reordered priorities of a man under sentence.

The Mutinies induced the Blue Lights to reappraise their aims, in ways to be considered fully in a later chapter. They become less wedded to religious observance and more committed to evangelism and reform. Burn wrote tracts and Gambier distributed them or others like them; teaching, preaching and persuasion became more prominent. Along with public worship went an emphasis on devotion, on the personal ownership and private study of the Scriptures: Saumarez and Pellew were associated with this. More radically, Admiral Duncan and Captain Penrose listened to the grievances of the lower deck and advocated changes which – if implemented sooner – might have stopped the mutinies from happening. But the events of 1797 held lessons for the officer corps generally. Once order had been restored many captains began to look afresh at imaginative ways of promoting discipline, including the value of public worship. Those SPCK minute books provide a barometer of concern.

Religious Literature and Sea Sermons

In 1797 the Society received twenty-three requests for Bibles and Prayer Books. The next year that number rose to thirty-one, and thirty-six the year after, making a total of ninety for the three-year period when consciousness of the great mutinies was at its height. Altogether between 1793 and 1812, with 375 ships supplied with their books, the SPCK was dealing with an average of one request every three weeks until the burden of demand became too great to be handled centrally. Thereafter book depots were set up at the main naval ports so that captains or chaplains could make direct application; bulk figures survive for funds raised and literature issued, but not the names of ships supplied. There was nothing in the society or its methods to upset Evangelical susceptibilities: far from it. Following the lead of Charles Simeon, they supported the parish system; divine service at sea extended the same concept to sailors away from their parish churches. The SPCK was generously supported by Middleton and used by Evangelicals promoting worship afloat. Even Woodward's tract *The Seaman's Monitor* commended itself to them.[47]

In view of its remarkable longevity, with a printing history stretching from 1700 to its twentieth edition in 1812, the tract merits more detailed description. The promise of its subtitle, *Advice to Sea-faring Men, with Reference to their Behaviour before, in and after their Voyage*, was borne out by the fifty-page pamphlet which followed, in which the writer warned of the temptations to which sailors were

---

47 *SPCK Annual Report* 1812, p.188; 1813, pp. 45f.

occupationally prone, and offered spiritual guidance. He dealt at some length with the Gospel promises of mercy to the penitent, assuring his readers of the readiness of Christ to forgive and to bestow the righteousness for which the sinner longs. The 1705 edition (see illus. 5 for title-page) was expanded to include *Queen Anne's Proclamation* against vice and immorality, half a dozen prayers for personal use, a brief sermon entitled *An Address to the Officers and Men in Her Majesty's Royal Navy*, and in conclusion, *A Kind Caution to Prophane Swearers*. The 1723 edition contained a further *Kind Admonition to all Seafaring Persons*, this time *against Mutiny and Pyracy, showing the great Sinfulness as well as Danger thereof*. In this form the *Monitor* went through numerous reissues. In denouncing mutiny, Woodward cited scriptural teaching concerning the duty of Christians to obey lawful government: not only was mutiny a scandal to the heathen and would arouse their contempt for the Faith, but all too readily it would lead on to murder, piracy and the haunting fear of discovery which could prevent a man from ever returning home.

The burden of his message was that sailors should constantly 'maintain the honour of reasonable beings and the good conscience of devoted Christians.' There were not too many of that kind in the navy, but more than enough 'profane swearers'! Was this the kind of book to stir the conscience of a heedless unbeliever? It was certainly realistic about life at sea and pastorally helpful for the struggling soul. In its early years the *Monitor* undoubtedly had a strong appeal, which Rooke, Shovell and Benbow appreciated, but its underlying assumptions had become highly questionable by mid-century, if not well before then. Woodward addressed his readers as men who already made a Christian profession and needed help in living up to their calling – but was he correct to regard them as members of the Church afloat? Many Evangelicals by the last decade of the eighteenth century were contemplating a much more radical approach, as they came to recognise that seamen were, by and large, not Christians at all but a neglected and semi-pagan mission field.

Since the American War evangelicals came to favour their own agency for mission, The Naval and Military Bible Society. It was founded informally in 1779 by two Methodist laymen in London for the benefit of soldiers, sailors and militia. The idea was given immediate and unexpected encouragement by the Gordon Riots which rocked the capital in 1780: many sections of polite society were frightened as much by drunken troops called out to protect their homes as by the rioters themselves. The problem might be lessened if soldiers were given the Bible. Unlike the SPCK, the new society gave away copies of the Scriptures to individual soldiers and sailors, and since it issued Bibles and Testaments without

THE
Seaman's Monitor:

Wherein particular ADVICE
Is given to

Sea-faring MEN,

With reference to their

BEHAVIOUR,

I. Before their ⎫
II. In their   ⎬ Voyage.
III. After their ⎭

With an Addreſs to the Officers and Seamen in Her Majeſty's *Royal Navy.* And ſome PRAYERS for their *Uſe.*

By Joſiah Woodward, *D. D.*
Miniſter of *Popler.*

Publiſhed and Diſtributed by Her Majeſty's Special Command.

LONDON,
Printed for the Author, by *Joſeph Downing* in *Bartholomew-Cloſe* near *Weſt-Smithfield,* 1705.

5 Title-page of *The Seaman's Monitor* by Josiah Woodward, the 1705 edition of a popular and long-running tract, first published in 1700 and reissued for the last time by SPCK in 1813. © British Library Board. All rights reserved. (534.a.36)

note or comment it provided common ground for Anglicans and Dissenters to work together.[48]

Unfortunately the earliest archives of the Society were lost in a disastrous fire in the 1950s. We now have scant chance of putting names to its first supporters, but the *Annual Report* for 1804 survives, and includes some retrospect of the first twenty-five years. It gives an idea of financial income, numbers of Bibles distributed and lists the ships supplied. Members were moved to recall that the *Royal George* had received a large consignment only months before she sank. When news came in the 1820s of the fate of the *Bounty* and the subsequent experience of the mutineers on Pitcairn Island, the Society speculated that the *Bounty* Bible might well have been one of theirs. At the 1839 anniversary meeting, Captain Francis Maude reported that he had been browsing amongst the old papers of the Society, and found that Collingwood had applied for Bibles, along with Sir Alexander Cochrane, and the more obvious names of Saumarez, Gambier and Exmouth.[49]

Middleton had looked forward to the time when religion might again find an honoured place in sea-going routine, with good chaplains appointed, regulations enforced and Christian literature distributed. By the closing years of the eighteenth century those wishes had found glimmers of fulfilment, but all too many ships were still without an effective ministry. Bo'sun Smith claimed that most of Nelson's Copenhagen fleet in 1801 were unenlightened, including the 500 men in his own ship, the *Agamemnon*. 'We had not one man that knew any better; but all were left in this ignorance, and sent out to fight by Christian England! Shame, shame on our country, thus to neglect us! With no Bible or minister to warn us to fell from the wrath to come by a just and righteous God.'[50] And yet undeniably there was a bit more light than in the Seven Years or the American Wars. By 1802, when the Peace of Amiens brought the French Revolutionary War to a close,

---

[48] Foundation of the Naval and Military Bible Society in, Anon., *Appeal on Behalf of the Naval and Military Bible Society* (1834), p. 5 (under British Library Tracts relating to Bible Societies 1816–1872); Introduction to *NMBS Annual Report* 1894; Roald Kverndal, 'The 200th Anniversary of organized Seamen's Missions, 1779–1979', *MM*, LXV (1979), pp. 255–63.

[49] *An Account of the Naval and Military Bible Society from its Institution in 1780 to Lady-Day 1804* (1804), pp. 3–7, 10–16; comment of Capt. The Hon. F. Maude after perusal of Society's papers, *NMBS* 1839, p. 27; report of Capt. Jenkin Jones referring to *Bounty* after his visit to Pitcairn Island, *NMBS* 1843, pp. 21–3; *Royal George*, *NMBS* 1847, p. 19.

[50] Kverndal, 'Memoirs of the Founder of Seamen's Missions in 1801', *MM*, LXII (1976), p. 49.

around eighty ships carried a clergyman; Sunday was more regularly observed as a day of worship, and not only under Jervis; Bibles, prayer books and *Seaman's Monitors* were being issued both for congregational and for individual use. There was more religion about. And yet the Blue Lights had not achieved their aims, for there was little evidence of a revival of faith. It could be argued that this flurry of religion owed little to evangelical fervour, less to mainstream Anglicanism, and most to fear of French atheism. Bo'sun Smith would later denounce all this as 'only reading and prayers, and telling us to be good', but that is unjust.[51] There is no means of knowing how many men found value in the Sunday liturgy, who were encouraged in spirit or found solace in face of death from familiar prayers and texts, but if the surviving sermons are a fair indication they might not have got much out of the preaching.

When assessing sermons the historian has a problem with evidence. The art of preaching is different from writing: the message has to be spoken and heard. There is a hint of stage-craft in effective preaching, as the voice becomes an instrument of varied pace and volume to hold an audience. Words on a page lack expressive emphases and are lifeless in comparison with the warmth and urgency that a good speaker can give them. Probably most good sermons then as now were spiced with humour and topicality which cannot make the journey from that age to this. We have the form and structure but not the essence. Nonetheless our enquiry is not futile. Published sermons gained a circulation because they were admired in their day. They show what some chaplains thought would be good preaching for sailors, but it will be harder work to find what their hearers felt.

Not all shipboard services had sermons. 'Hands to Church' was piped with the captain's permission, and the same authority would determine its format. The normal procedure was for the ship's company to fall in on the quarterdeck in their best uniforms, mustered by divisions, with each group under the immediate supervision of their lieutenant. In bad weather 'church' might be held below decks. Divine worship was preceded by inspection of men and their dress, and the reading of the Articles of War. The presence of captain and officers in dress uniforms, splendid with gold lace and cocked hats, and the marine detachment paraded beside them, gave the occasion stiff formality, relieved to some small extent by the use of signal flags to bedeck an improvised pulpit or lectern. The Prayer Book service of Morning Prayer was read aloud by captain or chaplain, and the crew were expected to join in reading psalms and intercessions – the reason why the SPCK supplied its literature. It was an impressive event which varied routine and would be welcome enough on that score. Even better, after Divine Service would

---

[51] Ibid.

come dinner, perhaps the best of the week, and in some ships a day less arduous than most.

Effective preaching to sailors was not like delivering the sermon in a parish church, but was more akin to the 'field preaching' of the Methodist evangelists. It called for a strong voice to carry in the open air, and sufficient projection of personality to demand attention. For at least some listeners the concept of church was unfamiliar, and made no more attractive through being compulsory. The sea parson needed insight too, a way with sailors and an ability to communicate; if he were wise he would bear in mind that he had a widely disparate audience, from illiterate hands to officers of cultivation. When Ramsay the former surgeon became Admiral Barrington's chaplain in 1779 he gave particular attention to the challenges of preaching for seamen; he published the first naval sermon to have been printed since Queen Anne's reign, and probably the first book of sermons for use in the navy. Claiming that they had been well received when first preached aboard the *Prince of Wales*, he published them for others to use, whether chaplains or more probably captains who might wish to have a sermon as *Regulations* required.[52]

Ramsay's introductory talk highlighted the need for purity, comradeship, humility and service. Through the course of the next eight addresses, he developed themes of morality and service to the community in terms which would have reassured the high command: virtue the foundation of success; the duty of exertion in the country's cause; the sinfulness of mutiny, desertion and drunkenness; and then no less than three sermons against swearing. Only after this did Ramsay move to more specifically spiritual topics for his final six discourses on 'a view of man's duty'. Here the foundation sermon dealt with the value of the soul, after which came talks on duty to God, to ourselves, to our neighbour, to our country, and finally man's duty as laid down in the Gospel. Now at last we are in evangelical territory as Ramsay calls his hearers to repentance and conversion – along with topical warnings against breaches of discipline. Mutiny he castigates as both sinful rebellion against God-given authority and as an ineffective remedy for grievances: the officers, he asserts, will normally want to treat men well in order to secure their prompt and willing obedience. Ramsay addresses topical issues from a quarterdeck perspective. There is guidance for a soul seeking God, but the spiritual message is well mixed with social concerns.

Another volume of sermons was published in 1792 by a would-be chaplain, John Malham, this time attempting to use naval history as a source of modern

---

[52] Rev. James Ramsay, *Sea Sermons, or a Series of Discourses for the Use of the Royal Navy* (1781); Rodger, 'The Naval Chaplain', p. 34.

parables, under the title of *Sixteen Sermons on the most interesting subjects to seamen, comprehending many important events in naval history*. He had apparently been given an opportunity to address a ship's company in Plymouth, and his account illustrates the approach some clergy took. Part of his message concerned the power of a minister to harrow up men's souls: 'let the reader figure ... the preacher ... surrounded by the lower-deck guns of a 74-gun ship, ... his eyes directed to the bulk of the common seamen with a penetrating glow; ... and then conjecture the effects of such an expression, aided as it was by a suitable position and agitation of the fore-finger of the right hand.'[53] Understandably perhaps in view of his strident tone, Malham found no ship to take him.

Any effective sea parson had to bridge the gulf between the educated preacher and his semi-literate unchurched hearers. John Fresselicque's published address celebrating the Glorious First of June demonstrates what could happen when learned pomposity took over. His opening sentence, addressed to the crew of the *Bellerophon*, is cumbersome but comprehensible: 'The natural impulse of gratitude in the mind of men, is never more forcible, or its effects more pleasant, than when the Heart is warmed by the pleasing recollection of the recent benefit.' Thereafter the chaplain's exaltation of language renders him baffling: 'this disposition is always attended with the most agreeable sensations and the spontaneous effusions of the grateful spirit are given and received with equal condescension and favour in proportion as the declaration is made with sincerity.' The chaplain was proud enough of his achievement to have the address printed and published, indicating that his true audience was a fashionable readership rather than a man-of-war's crew.[54]

The published sermons of the Rev. James Stanier Clarke, famous as the founder of *The Naval Chronicle*, although more accessible to sailors' vocabulary and understanding, are further examples of elegant phraseology, almost entirely concerned with moral conduct. *Sermons on the Character and Professional Duties of Seamen* were preached aboard HMS *Impetueux* in the Western Squadron during the blockade of Brest in 1798. If he thought sailors needed conversion, he does not make it apparent: indeed, in a later address to commemorate Trafalgar, he states that their noble character grew out of their religious principles. Jervis knew his men were capable of quite different impulses, and told Morgan to find a sterner message for them. Yet whether 'telling us to be good' was done with Stanier's sentimentality

---

[53] Taylor, p. 191, quoting from Rev. John Malham, *Sixteen Sermons on the most interesting Subjects to Seamen, comprehending many important Events in Naval History* (1792); Rodger, 'The Naval Chaplain', pp. 41,45.

[54] Quoted in David Cordingly, *Billy Ruffian: The Bellerophon and the Downfall of Napoleon* (2003), p. 88.

or Morgan's realism, it was still, in theological terms, preaching law rather than grace. There was nothing here for the broken, fallen man who wanted cleansing, no assurance for the sinner or hope in face of death.[55]

Yet even such a sermon might have social value by sweetening relationships in an overcrowded environment. Approaching these issues in a different way, the menacing Articles of War promoted discipline by forbidding disorder or profanity – but preaching added *moral* arguments. Religion could reach the springs of conduct by addressing grievances and resentments, jealousies and bitterness before they issued in misconduct. Jervis, as we have seen, wanted sermons on benevolence to shipmates and on forgiveness of injuries. Ill-considered words could cause mischief that might sweep through a tightly packed community like a forest fire kindled by a spark; he wanted the chaplain to preach about control of the tongue. Ramsay devoted three of his fourteen addresses to the same subject. Dr Alexander Scott, Nelson's famous chaplain, left notes for a sermon against judging others or destroying character through slander – faults for which men must answer at the throne of God. Such sermons were treating very real problems before they reached the level of indiscipline. At that dangerous point there were remedies, of course, but they were harsh naval ones, not guaranteed to soften men's hearts.[56]

There were some well-known collections of addresses which were used at sea and which did contain a message of conversion. Chief amongst these was George Burder's *Village Sermons*, comprising one hundred talks renowned for their simple directness. Using homely illustrations for humbly educated folk, they were full of Gospel teaching and enjoyed a wide circulation. A prominent Congregational minister from Coventry, and founder of the Religious Tract Society, Burder did some writing specifically for sailors, a volume of *Sea Sermons* to set alongside the village ones. To men long separated from their homes, these simple talks – possibly those with a rural setting above all – made a compelling appeal. They were short and comprehensible, written for the lower deck, whereas Clarke and even Ramsay betrayed their genteel origins. Captains might do a lot worse than read Burder.[57]

---

[55] Rev. James Stanier Clarke, *Naval Sermons Preached on Board His Majesty's Ship the Impetueux, in the Western Squadron, During its Services off Brest* (1798).

[56] NMM MS 53/021: sermon notes on Epistle of James 1:12, dated 26 October 1794. It is not clear whether these are notes of a sermon Scott heard or one which he intended to preach.

[57] Rev. George Burder (1752–1832): his *Village Sermons* (8 vols.) contained 100 addresses, widely used in Britain and America, and translated into several European languages. He also wrote *Sea Sermons, Cottage Sermons* and *Sermons for the*

Some commanders went to considerable trouble over sermon-reading. Philip Broke's copy of Stanier Clarke's sermons survives. He was the hero of the *Shannon's* capture of the *Chesapeake* in 1813, a godfearing and capable officer but hardly a Blue Light. Broke made copious amendments and additions to the printed page to increase its helpfulness to his crew. In the end we can only guess what the effect of such readings might be. Smith's verdict has already been noted, but he was never fortunate in his chaplains. Another caustic comment comes from the pen of Robert Hay, a Scots lad who kept his preference for the Presbyterian way of doing things. He never appreciated the Rev. John Dunsterville as chaplain in the *Culloden*, and was critical of his superior manner. As for his preaching, Hay says scornfully that he was never burdened with having to compose any sermons, but came aboard with two dozen ready prepared.[58]

For a chaplain who did want to prepare his own addresses the difficulties were great. Mangin was exasperated by the ceaseless noise and activity of the gunroom and wardroom alike, and the twilit gloom of his cabin; his private reading was confined to a half-hour period after the normal extinction of lights at ten o'clock at night. As he compiled his sermons he consoled himself with the thought that there would be few critics amongst his listeners. He was almost certainly wrong on that score. Hay, Smith, Marks, Gambier – able seaman, petty officer, lieutenant, admiral – all had strong views on the content of the sermons they heard. They had theological opinions which might have surprised the clergyman.[59]

Even a conscientious minister who carefully prepared his addresses was likely to be culturally remote from the lower deck. It could hardly have been otherwise. The clergyman came of cultivated, educated background, and the kind of topics to please the wardroom might well be incomprehensible to the bulk of his hearers. Take for example the entry in Alexander Scott's diary for May 1803 summarising his sermon to the *Amphion*: 'Eclecticism – prayers and sermon: God who at sundry times and in diverse places.'[60] Nelson was keen to have his men understand the addresses they heard, and he may well have had Scott principally in mind.[61] It needed rare insight to make a sailors' preacher. If the Gospel were to be brought

---

Aged. Congregational minister and founder of the Religious Tract Society, he was a prolific and popular writer, admired by Anglicans as well as Nonconformists and itinerant preachers. Information taken from *BDEB*, 1, pp. 168f.

[58] Peter Padfield, *Broke and the Shannon* (1968), p. 222. M. D. Hay (ed.), *Landsman Hay: Memoirs of Robert Hay, 1789–1847* (1953), pp. 81f.

[59] Thursfield, pp. 11, 13.

[60] Taylor, p. 203.

[61] Knight, *Pursuit of Victory*, p. 240.

home to sailors, talented communicators would have to be found, men who spoke the language of seamen or who could write in their idiom.

Such developments would come more plentifully after the resumption of war in 1803. In the meantime Blue Lights could be grateful for the increase in religious observance that had come in with the war. There was a quickened sense in the naval profession that this was beneficial to the service, good for morale and discipline. The navy was apparently the better for it, but what was being done for the souls of sailors? Men might attend divine worship without any serious engagement of mind and heart. Was it possible to go any further – to encourage personal interest and even perhaps to nurture faith? There was room for a cautious reappraisal of aims and methods.

IV

The Blue Lights during the French Revolutionary War, 1793–1802: A Change of Emphasis

Introduction

THE Blue Lights were individuals, not an organisation. They had no machinery to coin a collective policy, and yet common features do emerge. Initially they focused on religious observance, where they could at least claim the neglected sanction of tradition and regulations. As the French Revolutionary War developed it became increasingly clear to the Blue Lights that this alone would not serve to promote what they called 'vital religion'. So long as the navy could be regarded as a scattered group of worshippers detached from their parish churches, the original aims would suffice, but once the scale of religious ignorance became apparent the Blue Lights had to develop more proactive strategies.

Morality was another common strand in their thinking, and here again they could look back to the lofty aspirations of naval *Regulations*. Whereas the naval code punished indiscipline severely, most captains regarded sailors' moral lapses with a degree of forbearance and even indulgence; the Blue Lights were intent on correcting and establishing the morals of the lower deck, a programme that risked upsetting the stability of shipboard life. If they wanted their beliefs to impinge upon the organisation of a man-of-war, they would have a great deal to prove first. The *Ardent* model might have been appropriate for a stationary guardship, but there was still a question over whether it would serve for a ship's company on active service. Although Middleton and Kempenfelt had persuaded themselves that sailors would welcome a moral and religious programme, this had not yet been proved in experience. Was it either practicable or desirable for warships to become places for preaching and reformation of conduct? And how would the naval profession react?

This chapter considers seven Blue Lights of the French Revolutionary War – a chaplain, a Marine officer, a group of post captains and an admiral. Details of their service in a warlike profession help to establish the basis for their reputation, and hence the good name or notoriety of the faith they professed. In their separate responses to the 1790s, they were fashioning a new consensus about evangelical aims – although they were apparently unaware of it – where persuasion and humanity became at least as prominent as religious observance and issues of conduct.

Horatio and Eugenio, debate the source of true happiness, a discussion which the Christian wins by showing that not only may he enjoy all the rational pleasures of life but that he also has a secure hope in the face of death. This tract ran to a third edition in 1810.[13]

Other writings included a pamphlet on the slave trade in 1792, in which he called for a boycott of West Indian sugar, and a short pamphlet in support of the British and Foreign Bible Society in 1812. It is doubtful whether either of these works, or even the rather learned tracts already described, would have done much to evangelise the ranks of the Royal Marines or the lower deck of the Royal Navy. The approach is altogether too cerebral and cultivated. On the other hand, he wrote a short piece for the Religious Tract Society which was obviously aimed at the conversion of other ranks – *Two Dialogues between a Corporal and a Private Soldier*. As we shall see, Burn was adopting an approach which commended itself to the two greatest exponents of tract-writing for the lower deck – Richard Marks and Bo'sun Smith. The format of dialogue allowed the views of an unbeliever to be first expressed, then modified and finally demolished in response to a growing presentation of Christian teaching. This approach employed a narrative setting to attract and develop interest, with conversations adjourned and resumed. Humour (especially in Smith) and rough woodcut illustrations served to make theology palatable, while the whole debate was set in a context familiar to its audience.

Burn's experience exemplifies many of the traits of the Blue Lights with their strong internal spiritual experience, their love of scripture, and their overwhelming desire to communicate this faith to others. Interestingly enough his journals reveal little point of contact with men of similar stamp. Briefly in 1772 he was shipmates with a Lieutenant RN, Robert Tomlinson, aboard the guardship *Resolution* in Sheerness. Burn, lonely with his new-found faith, recognised a like-minded man who said grace at meals; the two shared times of prayer together and were rapidly stigmatised as religious extremists: 'our new messmate is as great a Methodist as Tomlinson.'[14] His new friend was another writer, but not of tracts: he had written

---

[13] Principal works: *The Christian Officer's Panoply: containing Arguments in favour of Divine Revelation*, by a Marine Officer (1789; 2nd edn 1806), retitled as *The Christian Officer's Complete Armour*; *Who Fares Best, the Christian or the Man of the World? Or the Advantages of a Life of real Piety to a Life of fashionable Dissipation*, by a Marine Officer (1789; 2nd edn 1792; 3rd edn 1810); *Two Dialogues between a Corporal and a Private Soldier*, written by a Lieutenant Colonel of the Army (? date); *The Resurrection of the Two Witnesses exhibited in the Formation and great Success of the British and Foreign Bible Society, being a Paraphrase of the 11th Chapter of the Revelation, in a Letter to a Friend* (1812). Burn also wrote pamphlets against the slave trade in 1792.

[14] Burn, *Memoirs*, I, p. 155 and n.

a pamphlet to show how the fleet might be manned without impressment. His ideas led to a parliamentary bill, for something akin to a naval militia with a fixed term of service and substitution permitted, but it had never had much chance of success and it blighted his prospects for promotion.

Beyond Tomlinson there are no named fellow-believers in his published journals, neither chaplains, officers nor other ranks. We are left with the clear impression that during the American and the French Revolutionary Wars religious convictions like Burn's were extremely rare, exactly as Middleton and Kempenfelt stated, and that no means had yet been found to identify and bind together a supportive fellowship. Burn refers to a man-of-war as 'that dreadful abode for a Christian which I had long inhabited', and a letter to his son-in-law aboard the *Ville de Paris* in 1810 expressed the same fears for a man of faith in a hostile environment: 'it will require great wisdom and much grace … so to act among your superiors as not to give offence by an austere over-scrupulous conduct; at the same time taking care not to grieve the Spirit of God or wound your own conscience by an unwarrantable compliance with any of their foolish and vain customs.'[15]

Like the naval evangelicals, Burn attached importance to public worship but rarely encountered it. In 1773, probably aboard a military transport, he had his first opportunity to lead prayers at sea; in another ship he attended the first service in three years, and felt moved to record in his diary a prayer for faithful pastors to bring the Gospel to the armed forces. His writings confirm the now familiar picture of a fleet starved both of formal religious observance and evangelistic zeal. Through his publications he made an early attempt at a remedy. Where he led as an author others followed. One of the first tract writers for sailors during the Napoleonic War had served for a time in the Marines as an assistant surgeon before moving into the Anglican ministry – Robert Hawker who wrote *The Sailor Pilgrim* in 1806 and 1810, prelude to the much more popular productions of Richard Marks and G. C. Smith.[16]

According to the Burn *Memoirs*, one man brought to faith through reading his writings was Captain James Wilson, simply enough described as a master in the merchant service, but actually with a much more dramatic career behind him, and an influential one ahead. A soldier who had fought at Bunker Hill and in India, he joined the maritime side of the East India Company, and made a fortune by running cargo and carrying intelligence past the French defences. Eventually he

---

[15] Burn, *Memoirs*, I, p. 152; letter to son-in-law, 1810, in II.
[16] Burn, *Memoirs*, I, entry for 11 March 1776. The Rev. Robert Hawker, D.D. (1753–1827), *The Sailor Pilgrim*, Part 1 (1806), Part 2 (1810). For brief details of his life, see *BDEB*, I, pp. 537f.

was captured by the French, escaped (by leaping from a high roof and swimming across an alligator-infested river), and was retaken by Hyder Ali, at whose hands he endured appalling privations, including a 500-mile forced march and months of ill treatment in prison. When eventually released, this adventurer and professed unbeliever returned to England. His spiritual experience was quickened into life through the writings of Burn the soldier, a character for whom he might feel affinity, and finally he was brought to conversion through a sermon heard at Orange Street Chapel in Portsea. By then a master mariner, he became committed to the cause of foreign missions, and conveyed at his own expense the first emissaries of the London Missionary Society to Tahiti and the South Sea islands in the *Duff*, 1796–8. Here is an early link between the Naval Awakening and the global missionary movement of the nineteenth century, a correlation in which the Blue Lights were keen to share.[17]

James Gambier (1756–1833): Captain of a 74

THE best-known Blue Light of the 1790s was Middleton's nephew James Gambier. His name is the one most often linked with the movement, and his career is central to understanding it. His Huguenot great-grandfather had escaped from France at the time of the revocation of the Edict of Nantes. His father was Lieutenant-Governor of the Bahamas, and there he was born in 1756. According to his niece and only biographer, Georgina Lady Chatterton, he was brought up by his aunt Margaret Middleton almost from infancy. In 1767 he entered the navy at the age of eleven aboard his uncle's ship the *Yarmouth*, and at some unknown date he adopted his creed as well: since his parents apparently did not share quite the same beliefs as the Middletons it is a reasonable assumption that he owed his evangelical convictions to his uncle and aunt. Under their influence he became associated with intersecting worlds of navy, politics, Abolition and religion, and the sophisticated subculture of Barham Court. Through Pitt, Wilberforce and the Clapham Sect he was close to the epicentre of political life and (omitting Pitt) to the heart of the new piety. His detractors have commonly stressed the narrowness of his experience, but that is perverse. By the time he came to command a ship of the line in 1793 he was fully fledged in his faith, a personal friend of Wilberforce, an associate of the Abolitionists, a post captain who prayed and evangelised. While his religious views and moral values were certainly narrow in

---

[17] Burn, *Memoirs*, II, p. 94. James Wilson (*c.* 1760–1814): see *BDEB*, II, p. 1207, which refers to J. Griffin, *Memoirs of Captain James Wilson* (1815), and William Wilson, *A Missionary Voyage to the Southern Pacific Ocean in the Years 1796, 1797, 1798, in the Ship Duff, Commanded by Captain James Wilson* (1799). See also Tom Hiney, *On the Missionary Trail* (2000; pbk edn 2001), pp. 11f.

the sense of being strongly held and closely defined, there was enough breadth and sophistication in his background to make him adaptable in varied roles as captain, commander-in-chief, administrator, diplomat and social reformer.[18]

In his first career, the navy, he made unsurprisingly rapid progress, having the powerful patronage of his paternal uncle an admiral, and his maternal uncle a rising captain, while his father too possessed influence especially in the West Indies. He became a lieutenant in February 1777 at the age of twenty, was made master and commander a year later, and was given his first command, the bomb ketch *Thunder* during the American War. He had the misfortune to encounter the Comte d'Estaing's squadron the day after his small vessel had been dismasted in a gale, and was taken prisoner. The experience did no damage to his career, and gave him a lasting friendship with the French officer who captured him, the Marquis de Chabert. Quickly returned to British service, he was made post in October 1778, took command of the frigate *Raleigh*, and was involved in operations to protect Jersey. Ordered to the American theatre, his ship took part in the capture of Charleston (1780), and Gambier served ashore with a landing party sizeable enough to be called a naval brigade. He earned particular praise from Admiral Arbuthnot for operations to secure high ground overlooking the harbour. His frigate captured the 20-gun *General Mifflin*, a smaller American warship in 1781, concluding an active and creditable period of wartime duty.

We know almost nothing about his life in the decade between the American and the French Revolutionary Wars, except that in July 1788 he married Louisa Mathew, daughter of a one-time High Sheriff of Essex. Ten years on half-pay does not prove conclusively that he had planned to leave the sea; even Nelson was five years unemployed and he was nephew of the late Comptroller. On the other hand, few officers could have had better interest than Gambier with his uncle at the Navy Office, and it remains surprising that he did not get a command if he really wanted one. When war broke out afresh he was appointed captain of a 74-gun ship of the line, the *Defence*, the opening of nearly twenty years of controversy. If Gambier was a contentious figure in his own day, he has proved surprisingly uncontroversial since, as historians have all but written him off as a hopeless misfit. His religious views were so sharply etched that they have become his defining characteristic, and any blame or ridicule attaching to him was inevitably passed on

---

[18] For Gambier's life: John Marshall, *Royal Naval Biography*, 7 vols. (1823–30), I, pp. 74–86; Ralfe, II, pp. 82–90; Rev. Edward Ward, *Sermon Preached in the Parish Church of Iver, Bucks. on Sunday April 28th 1833 on the Occasion of the Death of the Rt. Hon. Lord Gambier, Admiral of the Fleet* (1833); Henrietta Georgina, Lady Chatterton, *Memorials Personal and Historical of Admiral Lord Gambier*, 2 vols. (1861). J. K. Laughton wrote a critical entry in *DNB*.

to the religion he professed. From the start he imposed a moral regime in his ship, with swearing punished and unmarried women excluded. Sunday service became routine, and midshipmen were taught the catechism as well as their seamanship. These measures were in line with regulations but unlikely to ingratiate him with the lower deck. 'It was said in the fleet that the *Defence* had too much preaching and praying on board ever to be much of a fighting ship', wrote one of his junior officers in 1794.[19]

Fortunately a detailed portrait of his conduct as captain of the *Defence* survives, in the lively journals of one of his midshipmen, the fourteen-year old William Dillon. His *Narrative of Professional Adventures* was written from a secular standpoint, by an officer who neither understood nor valued Gambier's religion, but did not let it offend him either: he observes it dispassionately as something of a curiosity. These memoirs were written for private circulation a quarter-century later, and are subject to two caveats – Dillon's immaturity (he was a boy of thirteen to fourteen while under Gambier's command), and his self-justification in any case where his honour or professionalism might be questioned.[20]

Dillon's editor, Michael Lewis, stressed Gambier's inexperience, but this should not be exaggerated. Gambier had already commanded a king's ship in time of war. It is true that this was his first appointment to a ship larger than a frigate, and if Dillon's youthful recollections are accurate, Gambier took some time to reacquire his seamanship skills after ten years on the beach and to adjust to the problems of handling a big ship. He unwisely reduced the standing rigging until damage aloft showed the dangers. Along with the first lieutenant and master, the captain appeared indecisive when an onshore gale threatened shipwreck on the Mewstone off the south Devon coast: it was a more junior lieutenant who suggested wearing ship and was allowed by Gambier to give the requisite orders. And yet there are also signs of intrepidity verging on recklessness. Before attempting to tack a ship of the line against a contrary wind through the Needles passage and into the Solent, he deferred to the misgivings of the master and entrusted the pilotage to the experienced master's mate. The *Defence* tacked her way through a restricted

---

[19] Letter from P. Campbell, HMS *America*, Spithead 15 July 1794 to Gambier, his former captain in the *Raleigh* – perhaps Lieut. Patrick Campbell, lieut. 1782, d. 1798 in India in command of HMS *Surprize*. He concludes: 'you have forced the admiration of that very fleet who threw out this reflection. And they are now convinced from you that to serve God and their country are duties entirely compatible, and therefore ought to be inseparable.' Chatterton, I, p. 248f. Dillon makes reference to prayers at sea and consequential ribbing from other ships' companies: *Dillon*, I, pp. 101, 105, 145.

[20] *Dillon*, I, pp. 94–171 *passim*.

channel and so reached Spithead from the west with a contrary wind, a feat of seamanship never apparently accomplished before in a vessel of this size. The credit was given to the master's mate, but there is no doubt who would have been court martialled had the ship been stranded. A few months later and Gambier's seamanship as well as his courage was conspicuously shown at the Glorious First of June, when the *Defence* outsailed the rest of Howe's fleet and broke through the French line.[21]

Until Gambier had proved himself in battle his crew had reason to feel uneasy with him. They chafed under an unfamiliar moral regulation, with more Sunday services and fewer women than usual, and swearing treated as a punishable offence. Rum was served more diluted than in other ships. After a piece of arduous duty Gambier ordered a special issue; when the crew complained that the grog was flat he had the whole consignment poured over the side, a move that Dillon thought unwise. On the other hand, Christmas Day saw an over-liberal supply of rum and most men drunk in the afternoon – potentially hazardous at sea in wartime. Dillon believes that her ship's company were only too ready to desert, but this may have owed something to the better prospects for prize money in frigates.

Dillon gives us a detailed picture of the religious life aboard. First there is the Sunday service regularly held for the whole ship's company, and taken by the chaplain. He describes Gambier taking the prayer book out of the chaplain's hands and reading it himself when he thought a stronger voice was needed. We learn that all officers had to attend, not always with a good grace, and that Gambier made a quick head-count by eye before the service began. Dillon noted some sailors who gave divine worship their rapt attention, but he assumed they were trying to ingratiate themselves with the captain. Gambier held morning and evening prayers each day in his cabin, and expected the young gentlemen to be present; to them he gave personal attention, making their spiritual education his responsibility. When Dillon was late for morning class Gambier told him to repeat the Creed. Later that day Dillon claims to have seen the captain privately, and to have told him that he had not come to sea to learn his prayers, after which he was exempted from attendance. The story as Dillon tells it beggars belief, with a thirteen-year old boy offering such insolence to his commanding officer with apparent impunity – but it almost certainly tells us what many a normal young midshipman of the time would have felt.[22]

Following his uncle's example in the *Ardent*, Gambier was equally determined

---

[21] *Dillon*, I, p. 93, n. 3.

[22] *Dillon*, I, pp. 99f., 103, 108, 129, 140; 96, 97, 101f., 109; 103f., 109f.

to make his ship a pattern of upright conduct, but the maritime community eighteen years on was perhaps still further removed from the influence of a parish ministry, and the lower deck more tainted by unbelief. Furthermore, sailors in wartime experienced long periods of sea-service deprived of the society of women and without the right to shore leave either. Under these sterner circumstances, enforcement of the strict letter of naval *Regulations* would create strong discontent. The *Ardent* had been on harbour duty anyway, so that the maintenance of rudimentary family life had been possible for some married men. The situation of the *Defence* in 1793 was not entirely parallel. Dillon tells how the captain's measures were circumvented by sailors forging marriage lines or even contracting bogus marriages: thus morality prevailed at the cost of forgery and bigamy.[23]

At first Gambier enforced old-fashioned penalties for swearing, including the wearing of a collar weighted with a couple of 32-pound shot. Although this was specified in the *Regulations* it was not normally used elsewhere, but it might have been considered gentler than the flogging that in other ships was sometimes applied as a punishment for blasphemy. The collar was discontinued in the *Defence* when a sailor collapsed under it. Gambier was learning by observation what would work: apparently the old *Regulations* would serve no longer. They belonged to an era when respect for religion and morality was more widely professed, although not necessarily more sincerely followed. Two parallel courses of action were now required. First, the *Regulations* themselves needed revision, and secondly seamen's beliefs cried out for attention: men stood in need of conversion rather than compulsion, of personal religion rather than regulation. The Gospel message might address profounder needs than a disciplinary code.[24]

Gambier's subsequent measures show that he came to see all this. In due time he would make an impact in both areas. How soon did he appreciate the need for evangelism, for a persuasive ministry, for accessible tracts and comprehensible sermons to explain the Christian message? He must have valued his chaplain, the Rev. William Hawtayne, as he retained his services in the *Caledonia* when commander-in-chief 1808–11, but no examples of his preaching have come down to us, nor do we know what addresses he or Gambier read to the ship's company. As Dillon does not refer to tracts at this time, it seems likely that he was still wedded to the original Blue Light concept of regular services and a chaplain's

---

[23] 'Captain's Order Book, HMS *Ardent*', *BP*, I, pp. 39–45; *Dillon*, I, p. 96.

[24] *Dillon*, I, pp. 97, 104; according to Richardson, Captain Whitby of the *Minerva* flogged men for blasphemy: Spencer Childers (ed.), *A Mariner of England: An Account of the Career of William Richardson (1780–1819) as told by Himself* [hereafter *Richardson*] (1908), pp. 105f.

ministry. Command of the *Defence* showed the need for an emphasis on mission, but its implementation was still in the future.

Dillon explains the origin of Gambier's nickname, Preaching Jemmy. It was normal for sailors to visit their friends in other ships when Sunday routine was observed. Boats approaching the *Defence* were liable to be refused access when the ship was at prayer; Dillon implies that the ban on visiting extended to the whole day, but that does not seem likely since the service would not extend longer than an hour or so. The grievance would be that *Defence* crew had shorter time to visit friends; if they went during the working week they would be refused permission to come aboard because other ships' companies would then be at work. So Gambier was labelled a preacher and the *Defence* a praying ship. But would she also be a fighting ship? The answer came on the first of June in 1794.[25]

Gambier conducted himself heroically and won the high regard of his colleagues. Dillon's reminiscences are extremely valuable as a lengthy and highly detailed description of sea warfare, principally focused on the gun batteries but with an occasional glimpse of the upper deck. Since Dillon's action station was in command of three cannon on the lower gun deck in the bows, he had to rely on other eyewitnesses to supplement his own view, restricted unless duty allowed a brief foray to the upper deck. He gives useful evidence about the way the guns were served, the morale and spirit of a ship's company, the treatment of casualties, the steadying influence of the captain and the conduct of her officers: we hear of one lieutenant quick to brandish his sword at his men when he suspected they were reluctant to fight – he was wrong – and another triggering a quarter-deck cannon and causing a potentially lethal fire from the damaged sail canvas draped over the muzzle – he was drunk. There are many vivid touches, such as the way that overheated cannon tended to leap up and endanger the deckhead above, or the taste of the contaminated water in the ready-use containers on the gun-deck, or the sight of two gunports smashed into one by the impact of enemy shot.

During the earlier skirmish on 29 May there was a time when his own battery was completely disengaged and he managed a quick visit to the quarter-deck. Early casualties and damage caused alarm, but Gambier's response was exactly right – first, his own measured coolness, and then the diversion of attention, as he channelled men's fears into activity. This was the first time Dillon had seen a man killed, and he looked to Gambier for reassurance: 'he had on a cocked hat, and kept walking the deck, cheering up the seamen with the greatest coolness.' After being shaken by the wind of a shot, he pulled a biscuit out of his pocket and

[25] The Glorious First of June and the preliminary skirmishing from 28 May are described in detail in *Dillon*, I, pp. 122–39.

'began eating it as if nothing had happened'.[26] When a sailor was smashed by a cannon ball, he went to the casualty, took his hand and pronounced him dead. Soon afterwards a storm of shot caused several casualties and cut the massive main brace. To counter the alarm which immediately set in, Gambier gathered a working party and at once led them in repairing the brace.

When the two fleets engaged on 1 June, the fast-sailing *Defence* carrying upper topgallant sails outstripped the rest of her division and was the first British ship to cut through the French line. Exposed to heavy fire from port and starboard, she had to maintain both batteries in action at once. When both mizzen and mainmast had fallen, men from the tops brought extra hands to work the guns. The British navy had recently introduced flexible rope sponges and rammers which allowed the guns to be reloaded behind lowered gunports: the crew gained considerable extra protection from this. But security was all relative. In a close-quarter gunnery battle, there were bound to be horrific casualties, with men cut down by round shot or mangled by huge wooden splinters. The upper deck where Gambier stood was raked by enemy fire; later in the action, when the fall of the mizzen had brought down the splinter netting across the quarter-deck, making it a kind of cage, Gambier shifted his command position to the even more exposed poop.

Battered and practically unmanœuvrable, the *Defence* faced terminal danger when a French three-decker slowly passed across her stern, threatening a lethal broadside down her complete length. With presence of mind Gambier ordered his company to lie down to minimise risk of casualties – but her antagonist did not fire a full discharge, only isolated shots, enough to bring down her foremast (the only one standing). As soon as the Frenchman ranged alongside her the *Defence* was back in action to return her fire. A memory of that moment of peril passed into naval legend. As the three-decker bore down upon the *Defence* one of her lieutenants expressed himself to Gambier in typical nautical argot: 'Damn my eyes, Sir, but here is a whole mountain coming upon us: what shall we do?' He earned his captain's withering retort: 'How dare you, Sir, at this awful moment, come to me with an oath in your mouth? Go down, Sir, and encourage your men to stand to their guns, like brave British seamen.'[27]

The courageous conduct of the *Defence* was commemorated in a painting by Nicolas Pocock, an eye-witness, showing her dismasted and closely engaged by two assailants (illus. 6), but at one stage she was on her own in a ring of five or

---

[26] *Dillon*, I, p. 125.

[27] Sir John Barrow, *The Life of Richard, Earl Howe* (1838), quoted in Oliver Warner, *The Glorious First of June* (1961), p. 80.

6 HMS *Defence* at the Battle of the Glorious First of June, 1794. The seventy-four-gun ship lies dismasted but defiant. This was the courageous action which made Captain James Gambier's early reputation. The artist was present at the battle. (Oil painting by Nicholas Pocock, 1740–1821) © National Maritime Museum, London BHC0474

six enemies, one result of the speed with which Gambier had entered the action, bravely but perhaps injudiciously refusing to take in sail. Dillon estimated that eventually his ship had exchanged fire with fourteen or fifteen of the French. The battle concluded with seven French taken and one sunk, a highly acclaimed victory for Lord Howe. In the badly mauled and dismasted *Defence* there were many casualties, the 'butcher's bill' being twenty killed and somewhere between thirty-six and eighty wounded, the latter figure so variable because (at Howe's insistence) the slightly injured were not included. As his friend Captain Thomas Pakenham in the *Invincible* surveyed her shattered state, he called across in his Irish tones, 'Jemmy! "Whom the Lord loveth He chasteneth."'[28] It was a tribute to a man who had earned not just the praise of Lord Howe and the award of the King's gold medal, but the admiration of the whole fleet. Dillon was conscious of the changed attitude towards his ship and its captain. 'You were not at prayers on the First of June', he heard – but Gambier had not let Sunday pass entirely unmarked, for he had assembled as many officers as could be spared for pre-battle prayers in his cabin.

As for Gambier personally, his courage had set his career on course for particular distinction because he had gained the good opinion of Lord Howe. 'Look at the *Defence*. See how nobly she is going into action!', he had said to his staff early on, and then, after the close of the battle, acknowledging the cheers of the battered *Defence*, 'if every ship of the fleet had followed Captain Gambier's example, the result of this action would be very different from what it is.'[29] So conscious was Dillon of having taken part in momentous events that he wrote to Gambier each anniversary to congratulate him afresh, 'as his gallant conduct on that day established his reputation in the Navy, and, I may add, with the country' – and he gives a typical reply: 'We both have great reason for praise and thanksgiving for the protection on the day of the fierce combat now six and twenty years past, which we experienced from the hand of the Almighty: which I shall never forget, nor do I think you will.'[30]

We are not yet ready to draw a full character sketch of the man, but Dillon provides elements not easily found elsewhere. He describes him as punctilious and 'extremely neat in his person'; his ship exhibited a good order and cleanliness that reflected her commander and so much impressed a captured French officer. Gambier was open to innovation, adopting the latest gunnery practice of reloading behind closed gunports, and installing an air pump to ventilate the sleeping

---

[28] Thomas Pakenham's son became a leading member of the NMBS.
[29] *Dillon*, I, p. 135.
[30] *Dillon*, I, pp. 148f.

quarters on the lower deck at night, in spite of the disturbance caused to himself by having the cranking mechanism situated just outside his cabin – only a hint of the concern for sailors' welfare which would eventually become predominant. In a funeral tribute, a close friend and former naval chaplain described Gambier as being naturally warm tempered and impatient, until his progress in faith gave him mastery, transforming him into a man renowned for his self-control and kindness. Dillon shows us a younger Gambier still inclined to irritability and anger – apt to rush out of his cabin to rebuke the profanities of the officer of the watch, or sharp to criticise inattentive midshipmen, or impatiently taking the leading of prayers out of the hands of the chaplain – a man of hasty responses. Drawing a parallel with the apparent nervousness of his next captain, Dillon observes that 'if Gambier had not much practical knowledge, he possessed great firmness, which is an essential quality in a chief officer, as everyone then feels confidence in him.'[31] Yet his strictness was not harsh, unless his crusade against profanity and prostitution can be so regarded. In Dillon's eyes he was at times unwise, but only unjust if criticising him; even so he records that Gambier advanced his career in a fair-minded way, and he was glad to regard him as a patron.

There are some staccato entries in Wilberforce's diary for 26 June 1794 when he mingled with the crowds at Spithead, to welcome the victorious fleet, and particularly to congratulate his friend Gambier. The comments reflect a landsman's distaste for lower-deck behaviour, a patrician's sense of kinship with the officer class, a humanitarian's horror at the casualties, and a reformer's sense of the moral and spiritual needs of the maritime world:

> The *Queen* and *Defence*, where pleasing confabulation with Gambier – then *Valiant* Capt. Pringle, where ate – then *Queen*, where dined – sea scene – officers civil – afterwards got off when the ladies did – saw the ship – marine officers and sailors – characteristic manners. Rowed to Haslar hospital, where saw our poor wounded – Gambier well spoken of. Terrible appearance of the men blown up. Home and Gambier's. Portsmouth Point – wickedness and blasphemy abounds – shocking scene.[32]

With Gambier's career in the ascendant, and with his religious views no longer regarded with quite so much contempt, the time was ripe for some of these other concerns to be addressed. There were the 'characteristic manners' of seafarers to reform, as well as the 'wickedness and blasphemy' of sailortown. The time had come for some concentrated evangelism of the naval scene. It is at least

[31] Ward, p. 16; *Dillon*, I, pp. 99, 104, 109; 97f., 168.
[32] Wilberforce, II, p. 57. He also visited the French wounded, p. 58.

possible that some such sentiments were aired at the Gambiers' dinner table that evening.

On Howe's recommendation Captain Gambier joined the Admiralty Board as one of the Lords Commissioners in March 1795, all the more remarkable in view of Howe's earlier spat with Middleton. For the next few years Gambier was closely involved with the direction of the maritime war at its highest level, and his subsequent career is for later consideration. So far as the cause of religion went, he had deliberately looked for ways of promoting it in his own ship, with plenty of services for the whole crew and religious education for the young gentlemen. It was a didactic approach, stronger on compulsion than persuasion. Later events suggest that he was coming to doubt whether this would achieve his hope of evangelising the navy.

James Saumarez (1757–1836): Post Captain and Rear-Admiral

JAMES Saumarez, another officer of acknowledged piety, was making a name for himself in the French Revolutionary War; like Gambier, he would become a commander-in-chief in the struggle against Napoleon. When young James entered the navy at the age of thirteen, he was fortunate to have two distinguished uncles in his pedigree. Philip was educated for a time at Isaac Watts' academy in Southampton; later he sailed round the world with Commodore Anson as his first lieutenant (1740–4); as a captain he won high professional regard for success in a heroic single-ship action (HMS *Nottingham* versus *Mars*, 1747) before being killed in action during Hawke's battle off Cape Finisterre (October 1747). Philip's brother Thomas was accounted a most promising captain before he died of illness. With interest like this and his own undoubted skill, Saumarez rose quickly: as a lieutenant he was in the hard-fought fleet action of the Dogger Bank against the Dutch in 1781. He gained his first small command, a fire-ship, under Kempenfelt, served with him in the successful action against de Guichen off Ushant (1781), and did well enough to be made post captain of a 74-gun ship of the line, the *Russell*, serving under Admiral Rodney in the West Indies. Now twenty-five years old, he fought with distinction in the Battle of the Saints, earning the particular commendation of his admiral for his sound tactical flair in passing through the French line and engaging them from leeward.[33]

---

[33] Saumarez was well served by his former flag lieutenant's two-volume life, Sir John Ross, *Memoirs and Correspondence of Admiral Lord de Saumarez* (1838). Mahan contributed a perceptive chapter in his *Types of Naval Officers* (1902), pp. 382–427, but largely omitted evaluation of the Baltic theatre. That has been admirably provided A. N. Ryan (ed.), *The Saumarez Papers: Selections from the Baltic Correspondence of Vice-Admiral Sir James Saumarez, 1808–1812*, NRS (1968). Recent

He began the French Revolutionary War in command of the 36-gun *Crescent* on independent service, and won the second frigate duel of the war by capturing the *Réunion*, an exploit for which he was knighted. In this action Saumarez showed the skilled seamanship in which he was unsurpassed. He kept the *Crescent* alternately off the port and then starboard quarter of his adversary where no French guns could be brought to bear; as a result she suffered no casualties other than the broken leg of a sailor who stood too close to a recoiling gun.

In 1794 Saumarez in the *Crescent* had two other frigates under his command, the *Druid* (another 36-gunner) and the *Eurydice*, a poor sailer weakly armed with 20 guns. Off the Channel Islands, whose waters he knew so well, he fell in with a considerably superior French squadron of five sail, mounting 192 guns against the British 92. To cover the escape of his weakest ship, the *Crescent* and *Druid* had to hold off two French sail of 54 and two frigates of 36 guns. Skilful manœuvring kept the French at bay while the *Eurydice* got to safety; then Saumarez covered the escape of the *Druid* by closing with the enemy and sailing along their line. By now only the *Crescent* remained to face her antagonists, and capture looked inevitable – but Saumarez still had a trick of seamanship in hand. He steered for the coast, apparently intent on putting his vessel ashore rather than face capture; then tacking in and out of the dangerous shallows of Vason Bay, where the larger French ships dared not follow, he finally sailed inside a rocky reef where they could not pursue. In these operations he was aided by a local pilot who pinpointed the *Crescent*'s position by taking bearings off both his own and Saumarez's house, so close inshore had they come. This feat deserves to be remembered as a gem of seamanship and daring.

He was equally skilled in handling a frigate or a ship of the line. In the *Orion* he took part in the Battle of Cape St Vincent; two Spanish ships struck their flags to him, although one was not secured and managed to make good her escape. Of individual captains, only Commodore Nelson had a more conspicuous part in this victory which earned an earldom for Sir John Jervis. The next year Saumarez was part of Nelson's force sent into the Mediterranean to counter the fleet of Brueys at Toulon. Once again his seamanship was outstanding when, with Captain Ball, he came to the assistance of Nelson after the flagship was dismasted in high winds and seas off Sardinia: Ball earned Nelson's particular gratitude for towing the damaged *Vanguard* away from the rocks, but Saumarez had been there as well. His intrepidity in action was again put to the test when Nelson's ships, having at

studies are by David Greenwood, 'James, Lord de Saumarez, 1757–1836', in Peter Le Fevre and Richard Harding (ed.), *British Admirals of the Napoleonic Wars: The Contemporaries of Nelson* (2005), pp. 245–69, and David Shayer, *James Saumarez: The Life and Achievements of Admiral Lord de Saumarez of Guernsey* (Guerney, 2006).

last found Brueys after a search to the eastern shores of the Mediterranean, sailed into action towards close of day at the mouth of the Nile, on 1 August 1798.

The night battle which followed bears all the marks of Nelson's genius, with its headlong attack, its dependence upon the initiative of his highly trained captains and crews, and his ruthlessness in securing a complete victory. The *Orion* was superbly handled – like all the British 74s. Third in the line, she followed the lead of the *Goliath* and *Zealous* in sailing round the head of the anchored French line and engaging from the shoreward side, tactics which caught Brueys by surprise. Such a hazardous manœuvre required consummate seamanship in handling a ship of the line, sailing her in confined waters and relying on the simple fact that if there was water enough for a French ship to swing at anchor, there must be enough depth for a British ship to sail. A frigate bravely but foolishly attacked the *Orion*: normally by chivalrous convention ships of the line did not engage frigates unless provoked. A single British broadside dismasted her opponent and sank her in shallow water. The real combat was with the French line: the *Orion* anchored opposite her chosen target and opened a fast, controlled cannonade against *Le Peuple Souverain* and *Le Franklin*, fifth and sixth in the French line, and even directed shot against the enormous 120-gun flagship beyond, *L'Orient*. Soon Brueys's hapless fleet at its moorings had enemy to engage on both sides of the line; starting at the van, they gradually succumbed to the terrible British fire. *Orion* anchored at 18.45. *Le Peuple Souverain* cut her cable and drifted out of the line, dismasted and silenced at about 20.30. *Le Franklin* ceased resistance at 22.00. A little before midnight the powder magazines of *L'Orient* detonated with a horrific explosion. Fourteen of her survivors reached the *Orion*, where they were at once given clothing and kindness. During the battle Saumarez was thrown down and badly bruised by a heavy piece of timber which struck him on the thigh. He neither left the deck nor added his name to the list of wounded even though later it was clear that he had been unpleasantly injured. When *Orion* was about to slip her anchor cable and move on down the French line to other targets, it was found that her masts and rigging were too badly damaged to stand the strain.

By now Saumarez had learned that Nelson had been wounded. As senior captain he sent a boat to other captains nearby, urging any who could to slip their cables and assist with the continuing action at the rear of the French line, orders which Captain Miller of the *Theseus* at once put into operation. By dawn the rout of Bonaparte's fleet was complete, and Saumarez had had a distinguished part in one of the most complete victories of the sailing era: eleven French sail of the line and two frigates had been destroyed or taken, while just two battleships and two frigates made their escape under Vice-Admiral Villeneuve – who would later encounter Nelson again at Trafalgar. After the battle Saumarez was tasked with convoying the captured prizes to Gibraltar, a heavy responsibility in view of their damaged state, and with relief he brought his ships to anchor under the Rock, seven British and six ex-French ships of the line.

By seniority Saumarez was second-in-command, and the direction of the fleet would have devolved upon him had Nelson been killed. By a shameful omission which he felt keenly, and for which Nelson is to blame, he was awarded no particular honour, other than the award of the King's gold medal for captains, and he had to wait for almost three years for the baronetcy which should have been his for the Nile. Meanwhile Nelson sailed to Naples to recuperate and to enjoy the honours which his services had earned. Together with the glory, however, went the false glamour of the Sicilian court, and all the controversy aroused by his entanglement there, including his disobedience towards his commander-in-chief, Lord Keith, and his notorious liaison with Emma Hamilton. Nelson's future services to his country were so conspicuous and his brilliance as a fleet commander so unassailable that he soon outstripped Saumarez in the highest exercise of command. A. T. Mahan's judicious assessment rated him as 'the accomplished and resolute corps commander' rather than the most brilliant of fighting admirals. A. N. Ryan, who edited Saumarez's operational correspondence, agrees, but adds, 'to leave it at that would be to judge his professional merit by the most high, and at the same time, most arbitrary, standard. There is also the fact that in an age of strenuous professional competition he outshone most of his contemporaries.'[34]

In character and temperament Saumarez and Nelson were utterly unlike. Saumarez was more aloof and introspective, more cautious, more restrained and morally above reproach. Nelson's ardour, his eagerness to risk everything on an inspired intuition, his panache, recklessness and restless search for glory find no counterpart in Saumarez. During the nerve-wracking chase of Brueys's fleet, beset by the nagging fear that the French might have outwitted them and sailed to threaten Ireland or England, Saumarez admitted in private that he could not have stood the burden of ultimate command. 'Fortunately I only act here *en second*', he wrote, 'but did the chief responsibility rest with me, I fear it would be more than my too irritable nerves would bear. They have already been put to the trial in two or three instances this voyage.'[35] The Channel Islander who had gained the confidence of the much older Jervis never really had the trust of the younger Nelson. There was a coolness between them, possibly owing a little to jealousy. Saumarez was inclined to perceive a slight where perhaps none was intended. After the Battle of Cape St Vincent, for instance, Nelson gave considerable offence by telling Saumarez that

---

34 Mahan, p. 409; Ryan, *Saumarez Papers*, p. xiii.

35 Ross, I, p. 207.

he now believed his claim to have had two ships strike to him since it had been confirmed by a senior Spanish officer: Saumarez resented the idea that his word needed corroboration, and from such a source. Nelson's improper and ungenerous failure to recognise his second after the Nile has already been noted, but there were faults on both sides. Almost immediately after the action, with staggering tactlessness, Saumarez began to question the wisdom of Nelson's manœuvre in bringing the French line between two columns: as a result British gunnery could well have caused injury and damage to their own side. It was a perfectly sound observation in its way, but an extraordinary moment to choose to question Nelson's tactics.

Marked out by the exacting St Vincent for particular responsibility, Saumarez was a good choice to command the inshore squadron of six sail of the line, operating close off the Brittany coast as first line of defence against a French breakout from blockaded Brest. This work had to continue night and day in all weathers, and instead of allowing stormy weather to drive him off watch Saumarez preferred to take shelter in Douarnenez Bay, very close to the French base at Brest. From August to December 1799 he maintained this arduous watch, well past the date previously thought possible for the operation of line ships. St Vincent declared that as long as Saumarez had the inshore squadron he slept as easily as if he had the key of Brest in his possession.

Promoted rear admiral on 1 January 1801 with his flag in the *Caesar* (84), Saumarez had six ships of the line under his direction when he engaged French Admiral Linois's three ships off Algeciras, moored under powerful protective shore batteries. As the action developed, and the heavily pressed French ships were being warped closer inshore, disaster struck. The 74-gun *Hannibal* attempted to go behind the French ships but ran aground. Pounded by the Spanish batteries for an hour and unable to get clear in the light airs, she suffered heavy casualties of seventy-three killed and sixty-four wounded. Without wind to propel them, no British ship could come to her rescue, and the *Hannibal* struck her flag after a stubbornly courageous defence. The rest of Saumarez's squadron had been mauled, and for five successive days and nights of frenzied working they repaired battle damage in Gibraltar. By the time they were ready for sea, Linois's squadron had been reinforced, and Saumarez set sail once more to give battle seriously outnumbered by nine to his own five. The British came up with their opponents in the Gut of Gibraltar, and in a night action off Cadiz won a neat little victory (two Spanish first rates destroyed by fire and a French 74 captured, with Richard Keats the hero of the hour) which restored local command at sea and – in the words of St Vincent – 'put us on velvet'.[36] His next period of service before and after Amiens was less remarkable, involving the local defence of the Channel Islands, but his greatest days in the navy were still to come.

Saumarez illuminates both the public and the private face of the new piety, a man resolute in battle, a stickler for public worship, a commander noted for his humanity and in his personal Christian life a deep man of God with a disciplined life of personal prayer. There is no record in Ross or yet found in his private papers as to how he came to profess the Evangelical faith. Perhaps he grew up with it, having learned it at home – or was there some influence felt from Isaac Watts through his uncle Philip? Did service under Kempenfelt prove decisive? It is not clear, but the reality of his commitment is not in question. It may be seen in his official despatches and his punctilious attendance at public worship, in his personal piety, family letters and private prayer. Through it all there is a humble-minded readiness to ascribe all glory to God and to trust in him through problems and triumphs alike. Amongst the private papers which have been preserved at Shrubland Hall in Suffolk is a manuscript notebook of prayers he composed, mingling public affairs with personal needs.[37] One piece, written on the outbreak of war with France in 1793, shows his concern for the wider good and his belief in the value of Christ's atonement:

> that the Almighty in his tender mercy to the sins of this world may assuage the calamities that now threaten to overwhelm it in war and bloodshed. O thou gracious and benign Being, who of thy tender love to lost mankind did send thy beloved Son to deliver us from everlasting death, I beseech thee to grant that his meritorious death once offered to save all the world from the punishment due to their sins, may be found all sufficient before thee.

There are petitions for his family and household staff, thanksgiving for the birth of a child and a prayer that the boy would 'long live to be an instrument of [God's] glory', prayers for peace and national deliverance, interspersed with ascriptions of worship arising from a rich interior life of devotion: 'in thee I live, blessed Saviour; thou art my Redeemer and kind benefactor. I have on earth none beside thee and desire nothing but the blessed enjoyment of thy presence in heaven.'[38]

The death of his twenty-year-old daughter was a shattering blow to Saumarez which only his faith enabled him to sustain; three days after the news reached him

---

[36] Mahan, p. 421.
[37] Manuscript notebook, undated, preserved at Shrubland Hall, Suffolk.
[38] Ibid.

in his lonely Baltic command in 1812 he wrote to his brother of his 'resignation to the will of an all merciful Being who carries us through this vale of sorrows to make us more perfect for an inheritance in his everlasting Glory'. A little later he could say that that he was largely recovering from the heavy affliction that had bowed down his soul, adding that 'my confidence in the Divine Mercy has never forsaken me and I may truly say that I have never been for a moment deprived of his blessed consolations.'[39]

The inner faith which nourished his soul found plenty of public expression. In his despatches to the Admiralty giving news of success, he, like Nelson, attributed the glory to Almighty God. After the Nile his ship was the first of the fleet to hoist the pennant at the mizzen as a signal for a service of thanksgiving. Before the first attack at Algeciras all ships' companies held divine service; in the opinion of his flag captain, it was a steadying influence in the difficult and arduous days which followed their first reverse. In command of ships he was a stickler for regular Sabbath observance, and he asked the First Lord to make it mandatory for the fleet. He was a great supporter of the Bible Society and a popular speaker at their annual meetings. With his enormous professional standing he was an obvious choice for high office in Evangelical and evangelistic societies, notably the Church Missionary Society and all three Bible Societies – SPCK, Naval and Military, British and Foreign. He spoke openly in testimony to his faith, to the value he had found in the Scriptures, and to the strength he had gained through prayer in testing times – such as between the actions at Algeciras and the Gut of Gibraltar. The NMBS found particular inspiration from his testimony that godly men had proved their reliability and courage in the day of battle.[40]

Contrasting Post Captains: Charles Penrose and Edward Pellew

THE dangerous year of 1797 with the mutinies at Spithead and the Nore had a profound effect on two frigate captains, Charles Penrose (1759–1830) and Edward Pellew (1757–1833). While Penrose's piety is clear, it is uncertain whether Pellew should be accounted a Blue Light at this stage. To Penrose the mutinies proved the critical importance of humanising discipline; to Pellew they showed

---

39 Letters from Sir James Saumarez to his son Richard, from HMS *Victory* in the Baltic, 12 and 18 Oct 1812; Priaulx Library, Guernsey.

40 Despatch to Admiralty, 13 July 1801, Ross, I, pp. 414–17; private letters of same date, ibid. pp. 421, 423. Prayers before Algeciras: Brenton, *Appeal*, p. 79; Sunday observance: letter to Spencer, Ross, I, pp. 318f.; support for Bible Societies: SPCK member since 1789 (in 1811 list), NMBS life member and vice president 1813; quoted in NMBS meeting 1836 (p. 27); address to NMBS 1818 given in 1837 Report, p. 16, with notice of his death.

how precarious authority was and how sternly disorder must be repressed. Eventually Penrose's insights prevailed amongst the Blue Lights, and in due time even Pellew moderated his views.

Penrose, youngest son of the Evangelical vicar of Penryn, Cornwall, was commanding the frigate *Cleopatra* in 1797. Born in the celebrated 'Year of Victories' and with important naval connections in the Trevenen family, it was not a particularly surprising choice for him to go to sea in 1775. He served during the American War of Independence and was made post in 1794. During the French Revolutionary War he ruled his ship with unusual humanity while serving in Pellew's western frigate squadron. His methods proved their worth at the time of the Great Mutinies of 1797 when he was able to rely upon the loyalty of his ship's company. They responded well to his understanding of their needs: all but two returned from leave when a thirteen-week refit was over and she was ordered again to sea. He noted wryly that another frigate had more deserters after being kept in midstream with all her people embarked and armed marines rowing guard around her every night. A further period of service as flag captain to Admiral Lord Hugh Seymour in the West Indies ended when ill health forced his return to England. He enjoyed the unusual distinction of being presented with a written testimonial from the lower deck, expressing their loyalty and thanks on his departure. When the Peace of Amiens brought a breathing space to hostilities he still had to make a name for himself. Even in the next conflict he missed out on the main ways of attaining professional distinction through sharing in a fleet action or holding a frigate command. Nevertheless he had a profound influence as he developed a philosophy of man-management in *The Naval Chronicle*, addressing some of the issues raised by the mutinies.[41]

By contrast, Pellew's response to unrest was after the style of St Vincent: indiscipline had to be crushed, not reasoned with. It would be hard to find a more dashing frigate captain. He entered the navy in 1770 and served ashore in North America as a midshipman during the disastrous Saratoga campaign. As a young man he excelled in feats of daring aloft, such as performing a handstand on a yardarm many feet above deck, or diving from a great height into the sea. No doubt he won the regard of his sailors, tempered by apprehension of what a man without nerves might expect of others. In command of a ship he showed the same kind of reckless courage. He captured the first frigate of the French Revolutionary War, the *Cléopatre*, taken on 19 June 1793 by the *Nymphe* after a sharp action

---

[41] For Penrose's career, see Laughton in *DNB*; Ralfe, III, p. 211; Rev. John Penrose (nephew), *The Lives of Admiral Penrose and Captain Trevenen* (1850), and S. Baring-Gould, *Cornish Characters and Strange Events* (1908; 2nd series 1925).

which cost twenty-three British lives. When commanding the *Indefatigable*, a heavy frigate of 38 guns (cut-down from a 74), Pellew took the French *Virginie* (44) after a fifteen-hour chase on 21 April 1796, this time without British loss. Still commanding the *Indefatigable*, and with another frigate under his orders (*Amazon*), he challenged a French line-of-battle ship, the *Droits de l'Homme* (74) and in heavy seas virtually chased her ashore on the Penmarch rocks off the enemy coast on 13 January 1797: saving his own ship off a wild lee shore demonstrated superlative skill, but the *Amazon* was wrecked with the loss of six lives.[42]

The feat of seamanship of which he was most proud was not an act of war but of rescue. In January 1796 the troopship *Dutton* dragged her anchor in rough weather and ran ashore under Plymouth citadel. Her officers were drunkenly incompetent and, although they got a line ashore, proved unable to set up a breeches buoy. As the hull of the wreck was shifting under the impact of successive waves, the life-saving line needed to be kept properly tensioned, or else those using it would be dragged through the surf at risk of drowning or being battered against rocks. Pellew came on the scene as he was returning home across the Hoe. He tried to shout advice or to get local boatmen to row him out to the wreck but none would do it. Realising that heavy loss of life would result from this threatening disaster, Pellew had himself attached to the shoreward end of the line and pulled out to the wreck, suffering heavy bruising in the process. Then he took command, and organised the seamanlike evacuation of over 500 men, women and children, before leaving to the *Dutton*'s captain and two of her officers the honour of being the last to leave. Pellew carried a child to safety in his own grasp, and was always moved to recall the mother's gratitude. In fact, when raised to the peerage and needing a motto for his coat of arms, he selected the single word '*Dutton*'.[43]

There are other aspects of Pellew's character which are less appealing and attracted notoriety in his own day. Like many naval officers, he had an acquisitive streak in him which might have attracted less notice if he had behaved more sensibly towards his sons, but in combination with an undisguised nepotism it appeared that Pellew was on the make for himself and his family. His tenacity in pursuing the enemies of his country extended into the navy. Faced with mutinous behaviour by a sizeable part the crew of the *Impetueux* at Bantry Bay

[42] See *DNB*, and C. Northcote Parkinson, *Edward Pellew, Viscount Exmouth* (1934). A recent study is Malcolm Rae, 'Sir Edward Pellew, First Viscount Exmouth, 1757–1833', in Le Fevre and Harding, *British Admirals of the Napoleonic Wars*, pp. 271–93. 300 French sailors drowned in the wreck of the *Droits de l'Homme*, evidence for the severity of the winter weather.

[43] Mahan, pp. 425–54; Le Fevre and Harding, *British Admirals of the Napoleonic Wars*, pp. 280f.

in May 1799, Pellew with armed officers and marines put down the rising and applied to his commander-in-chief, Lord Bridport, for a court martial on nine men. His request was refused, for reasons which have less to do with justice than with Bridport's style of command. While the admiral was anxious to restore the calmer relationships between officers and lower deck that had been customary before the Mutinies, Pellew believed the situation was very grave indeed, and that he had nipped in the bud a plot to seize and destroy several ships with the help of Irish insurgents. Pellew would not let the matter rest. He felt that his authority in his own ship had been compromised by the men's defiance in the first instance and then by his admiral's refusal. Keeping the men under arrest, he followed his new orders to join Jervis's flag, and at once applied to him for a court martial. His request was granted: three men were tried and put to death, but even St Vincent seemed to feel reluctance, complaining, 'Why have they made me the hangman of the fleet?'[44] However harsh all this seems to a later age, many of Pellew's contemporaries wholeheartedly endorsed his attitude, as essential for national safety. The penal code afloat was severe, and he operated within it. At a later stage in his career, when his Christian convictions were more prominent, he would become more of a reformer.

Adam Duncan (1731–1804): Admiral and Commander-in-Chief

BORN in Dundee in July 1731, Duncan had first gone to sea in 1746 still short of his fifteenth birthday. The natural dignity of the man, his powerful frame and athleticism would have made him impressive in most contexts but what particularly endeared him to those who served under him was his humanity. Made post in 1761, he became flag captain to Commodore Keppel in the *Valiant* and served with credit at the capture of Belle Isle and of Havana. After a spell on half-pay he was recalled to service during the American War, serving first under Admiral Hardy (with Kempenfelt captain of the fleet) in the inglorious Channel operations in 1779, and then under Rodney at the Moonlight Battle of Cape St Vincent in 1780. In the *Blenheim* he took part in Howe's successful relief of Gibraltar. So far his career was typical of many experienced captains of ships of the line with years of service in peace and war; through seniority he gained his flag but never flew it at sea until called to be commander-in-chief of the North Sea Fleet in 1795. Although now aged sixty-three, he proved ideal for this dangerous posting. Duncan was a natural leader of men with a reputation for personal courage.

---

44 Dugan, pp. 436–8; Rodger, *Command of the Ocean*, p. 451. Rae quotes St Vincent's verdict that Pellew's 'saving the British fleet in Bantry Bay' was his finest service to his country: Le Fevre and Harding, *British Admirals of the Napoleonic Wars*, p. 284.

At this turbulent time he needed more than that to keep the loyalty of his fleet, for the dangerous discontents were building up to mutiny. The problems which his sailors faced were identified by their admiral, and he represented their needs to the Admiralty.[45]

In an important memorandum which Their Lordships would have been wise to have heeded, Duncan urged the necessity for reform. In terms which could almost have provided a blueprint for the Spithead manifesto, he called for drastic improvements in provisioning and pay. Sailors needed better diet – with fresh vegetables and fresh fish which they could catch if provided with lines. Health should be attended to – with a free soap issue, daily lemon juice as an anti-scorbutic and a wine ration for the sick. Pay should be given regularly, even when ships were serving abroad, and the distribution of prize money should be adjusted to give more reward to the lower deck. Turning to the contentious issue of manning, Duncan urged an end to impressment except in dire emergency, and he recommended that all crews should be given shore leave as an entitlement. With years of experience to back him, he was aware of the need for positive incentive and wished that more men should be promoted petty officer with improvements in pay and conditions. He had seen abuses of authority, with men goaded by immature midshipmen and excessive punishments inflicted in the name of justice: he recommended that young gentlemen's powers should be curtailed – and their access to alcohol too – and that the number of lashes awarded by court martial should be limited in the interests of humanity. Turning to the moral and spiritual, he wanted to see swearing curbed and the role of the chaplain extended by giving him responsibility for educating a ship's midshipmen and boys. Duncan's pleas for his seamen were refused by the Admiralty at the time, but what they declined to give at an admiral's bidding was afterwards forced out of them by mutiny.[46]

In order to blockade the Dutch in the Texel more effectively, Duncan's squadron was based at Great Yarmouth, rather closer to the scene of action than the Nore base from which the ships were manned. Duncan believed that active service was a powerful antidote to disorder, and kept his force cruising off the Dutch coast while dissension stirred in the Channel Fleet. When a potentially mutinous

[45] Duncan Papers in NMM: DUN/19 Public and Private Correpondence, 2 vols.; DUN/31 Memorandun Book of Captain Adam Duncan. See R. A. H. P. Duncan, Earl of Camperdown, *Admiral Duncan* (1898), and for a brief modern study, Neil Duncan, *Duncan of Camperdown* (Diss, 1995). The most recent work is J. David Davies, 'Adam, Viscount Duncan, 1731–1804', in Peter Le Fevre and Richard Harding, *British Admirals of the Napoleonic Wars*, pp. 45–65.

[46] Camperdown, p. 167; Manwaring and Dobrée, p. 172; Dugan, p. 125.

7 Admiral Adam Duncan, 1st Viscount Duncan (1731–1804). A portrait which epitomises his reputation as a resolute commander at a particularly dangerous stage of the war. (Oil painting by Henry Pierre Danloux, 1753–1809) © National Portrait Gallery, London NPG 1084

assembly gathered in his flagship the *Venerable* on 30 April 1797 Duncan met the men face to face. According to one account he drew his sword and might have used it but for the chaplain's intervention. Having mastered his fury, he dealt with the protest calmly and reasonably in a way that restored order. It was made easier by the fact that both sides respected each other: Duncan knew how valid their grievances were, and his men knew that he cared. After reassuring them that the Spithead improvements were coming their way, he treated the incident as a trifling local matter which called for understanding rather than repression. When disorder broke out in the *Adamant* he went in person to the ship and addressed her company. Known as he was for his care of his men, Duncan could appeal to their personal loyalty as well as their patriotic duty. One sailor was still disposed to argue but, with superb sense of the moment, Duncan grabbed him and made as if to pitch him over the side to peals of laughter. The admiral's good humour and personality restored a discipline which in his case always depended on an unwritten compact – his known concern for their welfare evoking regard and even affection in return.

That incident was the prelude to further times of testing. Along with the men and provisions sent out to the Yarmouth fleet from the Nore came news of events there, exciting to the lower deck. While another spell of blockade duty off the Texel served to calm ardent spirits for a time, it was not possible to keep the contagion of mutiny permanently at bay. Duncan was caught by surprise the way disorder broke in his own fleet. Ship after ship was taken over by her people who directed a return to port and an abandonment of the blockade, until only the *Venerable* and the *Adamant* with a frigate and light craft remained on watch against fourteen Dutch sail of the line backed by eight frigates and a fleet of transports designed to convey an army of invasion to the shores of England. Duncan faced these odds with daring improvisation. For four days, while the wind was in the dangerous eastern quarter, the Dutch could have sailed out from their anchorage in the protection of the Texel with a fair wind for England and a foul one for their enemies. During that time the *Venerable* remained close inshore, the *Adamant* further off with the frigate beyond, while flag signals were relayed from one to the next, and so apparently to a battlefleet lying below the horizon out of sight of the Dutch. Duncan's bluff worked, and the Dutch never stirred from their moorings when they had such advantage of wind and force.

The Nore Mutiny came and went, with others responsible for crushing it. Thereafter the men-of-war that had been in the hands of Delegates, ships' companies which had been involved in the mutiny, sailors who had been punished for their own part or who had been obliged to execute messmates – these ships and men now had to be restored to useful service. Duncan was the man to inspire their devoted loyalty, for he was known to be just and caring as well as competent. Once again the admiral's influence and his robust belief in the value of sea-keeping proved their worth. Off Camperdown they intercepted the Dutch and, in one of the hardest-fought fleet actions of the war, captured eleven prizes, ending fears of invasion for 1797 and beyond. While honours fell upon Duncan he had one last task to perform as commander-in-chief, to obtain pardon for 180 men still in prison for their part in the Nore uprising. It is doubtful whether any other man contributed so much to the restoration of the navy in that disastrous time.

What was the secret of his success? Supremely it was his humanity, which enabled him to understand the frustrations and grievances of his men. Fundamental to his personality was his open Christian faith. In early years at sea he was known for his Bible-reading habits. At home he was a devoted member of the Presbyterian kirk at Lundie. As an admiral he supported the ministry of an admirable chaplain, the Rev. Alexander Duncan (who may or may not have been a relative). With unforced piety he rebuked his ship's company at a time of incipient mutiny for their swearing, urging them to recognise the Creator's handiwork and then to give Him reverence. Their profane oaths, he was well aware, were 'often without meaning', but 'if there is a God – and everything round us shows it – we ought to pay Him more respect.'[47] As he considered the Mutinies, he believed that God had allowed them as a call to national repentance – 'chastisement … for a warning to mend our ways'.[48] Before clearing for action at Camperdown he prayed with public extempore intercession, and he did not neglect to give God thanks and praise for deliverance and victory at its conclusion. At the age of seventy-three, returning from a visit to the Admiralty in 1804, he felt the onset of death at Coldstream: to his wife he sent his last farewell, assuring her 'that his trust in a Crucify'd Redeemer made him rely for Acceptance with his God and that he was sure he should go to Heaven.'[49] None of the Blue Lights shone brighter than he did, and 'vital religion' had no finer example.

Conclusion

THE Blue Lights in the 1790s were becoming more prominent and controversial in the navy. Gambier's command of the *Defence* had attracted notoriety, and yet his attempts to promote religion had done nothing to frustrate his career: he had Howe's approval, the king's gold medal, a seat on the Admiralty Board and reputedly the offer of a knighthood. Duncan was a national hero. Saumarez and Pellew were amongst the most highly regarded officers of the time. Burn was making a name for himself as a theological writer while continuing to rise in the Marines. Penrose had gained a reputation probably no wider than his own ship, but he had had the experiences which would profoundly affect his thinking over

---

47 Camperdown, p. 106, quoting Ralfe, I, p. 333.
48 Letter to Evan Nepean, 23 May 1797, quoted by Camperdown, p. 122.
49 Quoted in a letter of Lady Duncan, not dated but 1804; NMM DUN/19 vol. 2, MS 9587.

the next decade. Ward had demonstrated what good might be done by a zealous chaplain.

What had happened to the manifesto of Middleton and Kempenfelt? How had it fared and to what extent had it altered? Sir Charles was out of office from 1795 but had not lost his interest in the navy. He was still bombarding Pitt with advice on maritime matters and gathering material for eventual administrative reform, and he had not lost his attachment to Admiralty regulations, public worship, chaplains and literature as the way to christianise sailors. As long as Middleton lived, the manifesto was alive, but it no longer defined the total Blue Light programme. Individual Evangelicals were feeling their way towards a more subtle understanding of religion.

First came the nature of religion itself. If it were a matter of church attendance or moral conduct, people could be made Christian by decree. But the essence of evangelicalism was its emphasis on individual repentance and faith, a process often summarised as conversion. Religion therefore could never truly be a matter of outward conformity but had to become an inward experience. Jervis might order Sabbath observance, and chaplains might read prayers: sermons might call for moral conduct or indulge in theological speculations – but what had any of this to say to a soul seeking for God?

Secondly, Blue Lights had begun to explore ways of moving enquirers from religion to faith. Christianity would have to be explained, not just proclaimed, so that it might be understood and believed. It was good to have the Scriptures made more widely available, but a further stage was required, to clarify, apply and persuade. Tracts might do this, but only if they were read: it became important to have attractive material that sailors could understand – something more appealing in language and approach than the archaic *Monitor*. Gambier had possibly begun to appreciate this, as he became notorious for his tract-distribution in the next war; Burn certainly did so, and was writing booklets to persuade the unconverted. It was the beginning of a trend.

Another developing feature was humanity. It took different forms but its presence amongst the Blue Lights is inescapable. Ward demonstrated it as he ministered to men under sentence of death, and as he reached out to sick, wounded or destitute, and in his pastoral concern for the black population of Jamaica. Saumarez showed it in his prayers for the lost, his concern to retrieve a former mutineer, and his reputation as a considerate commander. Penrose went even further, in the trust he showed his crew, and in the ideas he was beginning to frame for future reform. The most striking example of all is given by Duncan. He represented seamen's legitimate grievances to the Admiralty; he recognised simultaneously the gravity of mutiny and the depths of his seamen's despair, and so – with a gesture that neither St Vincent nor even Nelson could have pulled off – he treated defiance with amazing forbearance, and quelled it with humour and personal appeal. It worked solely because of the man he was and the reputation he had earned for straight dealing and fairness. After the crushing of the Nore Mutiny he gave the North Sea Fleet a fresh chance to prove itself, and used his ascendancy after Camperdown to seek clemency for men still under punishment. Towards his defeated enemy he showed kindness by taking de Winter's hand instead of his sword, and by paying compliments to Dutch valour – gestures that forged a personal friendship between them.

Pellew appears out of step with all this compassion. His determination to have mutiny brought to account reflected the anxious days of 1797; his severity is more apparent than humanity. And yet he was neither cruel nor capricious: he did what he believed had to be done to preserve discipline, within the limits of naval law. There was no kindness that he could see in treating rebellion indulgently. In Rae's opinion his record as a martinet has been exaggerated. In the wreck of the *Dutton* even Pellew stands out as a man of humanity as he risked his life to save others. In the next war Pellew would be responsible for an important check on excessive punishments, another piece of evidence that he too recognised the appeal of humanity.[50]

The Middleton programme would not really work unless seamen were attracted to the Christian message, and that in turn would be unlikely unless religion were made appealing by benevolence. When Gambier made swearers feel the weight of a wooden collar, he was doing more for discipline than religion, but, when Duncan rebuked profanity and pointed men to their Creator, they listened, and when Ward spoke of God's grace to men about to die, they heard him eagerly. It would take another war before these fresh emphases became predominant, but already the Blue Lights were beginning to adopt them, and to make it easier for sailors to link compassion with Christianity.

---

[50] Le Fevre and Harding, *British Admirals of the Napoleonic Wars*, pp. 273, 390 n. 14.

V

Developing the Ethos of the Officer Corps

Naval Religion after Amiens: Holding the Ground Gained

ALTHOUGH religion had long formed part of the navy's constitution, there was no certainty that it would hold its place in a new era of rationalism and revolution. It had featured strongly in the 1731 *Regulations* – surprisingly perhaps, but we have already seen that there were reasons for this. In spite of the theory, the practice of seafaring religion went into decline as the century progressed, only showing signs of revived vitality in the 1790s. Even then it was far from certain what form it might take. There were variations within Protestant Christianity: Anglicanism at its most conservative was a long way from the 'enthusiasm' of Methodism and newly enlivened Dissent. The governing values of the naval profession were those of its officers, and if religion were to have a role in shaping the ethos of the service it would come through them. During the Napoleonic War the issue was settled for the rest of the nineteenth century. Religion retained a footing in the navy's constitution, and became once more an element in developing the values of wardroom and quarterdeck.

For all its minority status, evangelicalism became a major force in this process, through debate and influence, and through direct access to power. Once again Middleton is the central figure: his authority appeared to have ended for good when he resigned in 1795 over a point of principle, a disillusioned critic of the administrations that followed. The extraordinary events of Melville's impeachment and Pitt's search for a replacement brought Middleton back to the Admiralty in 1805 as First Lord, with standing enhanced by his unparalleled grasp both of the minutiae of administration and the sweep of strategy. Besides managing a particularly dangerous part of the war at sea, he also had to handle the revision and reissue of the *Regulations* in which the navy's 'contract with religion' came up for renewal. Given Middleton's creed and political muscle, he was bound to reserve a place for Christianity, but how effective would that prove to be? Perhaps, like the 1731 measures, they would soon be disregarded.

This study will argue that, on the contrary, Middleton's creed made a discernible difference to the ethos of the profession. It was not all his doing, of course. Those principles had to be fleshed out in practice by captains and admirals who took advantage of them to advance the cause of religion. And the way had been prepared beforehand by Jervis and Nelson. When St Vincent insisted on divine service and Nelson gave credit to God for his victories, neither intended a spiritual

Developing the Ethos of the Officer Corps

revival in the fleet, and yet by giving prominence to religion, they made Middleton's measures more palatable. Between them, and working on different agendas, they gave permanence to what had happened in the 1790s.

Two questions are raised by the growth of religion in the Revolutionary War: did it really constitute a spiritual revival, and would it last? Evangelicals were ambivalent in their reply to the first. They were glad enough to see respect paid to God and the Lord's Day honoured, but wary of outward religion that left the heart unmoved. Mere outward conformity, they knew, would never save souls. But might this increased attention to religion perhaps become a dawn of faith? Could any mechanism be found to develop personal faith as well as public worship? Would sailors be willing to read tracts? With more captains looking for chaplains, where were the men for this ministry? There must surely be an opportunity for piety to slip into the fleet along with this new regard for religion.

How much ground had really been gained and how securely could it be held? By 1802 it was no longer eccentric for hands to be piped to prayers; there was more work for the SPCK and more opportunity for chaplains. At one stage Gambier had been mocked for running a praying ship, but all St Vincent's captains had eventually been compelled to do much the same. Religion was becoming more widely practised, officially sanctioned and commanded. Nelson's habit of attributing victory to the blessing of the Almighty no longer seemed out of place. Yet this gain for religion was really quite precarious; it might not survive the passing of the circumstances which had brought it about. For a start, the aggressive atheism of the Jacobin era had gone, and under the Napoleonic state which eventually succeeded it a place was found for religion – a compromised Catholicism perhaps, but no longer a threat to churches and priests. For another, collective worship had been associated with St Vincent and his methods: once his ascendancy was over, his religious policy might pass as well. It had buttressed discipline and morale in its day, but the reforms which followed the mutinies might have made it redundant.

When war resumed in 1803, however, the navy showed no inclination to prefer secularism. The SPCK continued its work with even more energy and support from naval officers as subscribers and committee members. The NMBS supplied more ships than ever before: even Steel's *Navy List* recognised its patriotic work. Clergy filled more of the posts afloat, although there were never enough of them to staff all entitled ships. All three British Trafalgar admirals were supporters of the Bible societies, and could fairly be regarded as friends of religion. Not all this popularity can be attributed to Nelson's influence, but some most certainly can. In his own day he gained an extraordinary ascendancy over his contemporaries, and his death in battle enhanced his aura – well demonstrated when Captain Richard

Keats went into action with a portrait of Nelson displayed in the mizzen shrouds, or Commodore William Hoste inspired his squadron with the signal 'Remember Nelson.' Religious conviction of some kind formed part of his persona, and it was bound to have a profound effect.[1]

Nelson and the Popularisation of Religion

IN later life an embittered St Vincent belittled the private character of Nelson as 'most disgraceful in every sense of the word', but he allowed that his 'animal courage' was a real merit.[2] Truly Nelson's legacy to the fighting navy was unparalleled through tactical innovation, aggression, daring and desire to annihilate the enemy – all qualities which invite comparison with Napoleon on land. But the Nelson bequest was vastly richer than a doctrine of war. He had demonstrated subtleties of command which the naval profession studied and tried to make its own with varying success – communication, delegation, team bonding. The personal style which magnetised every ship he commanded was taken to a higher level in his fleets: in spite of an admiral's state apartments and awesome authority, Nelson found ways of meeting his captains, of passing his thinking to more junior officers, of making personal contact with those of every rank who served him. He could win the regard of almost everyone who served with him; he gave loyal support to his subordinates and won their allegiance in return; he readily trusted his men and took pleasure in lavishing praise on them. Where Wellington could speak contemptuously of his private soldiers, Nelson spoke with warm approval of his sailors and was rewarded with their devotion. 'No man', wrote Codrington, 'was ever afraid of displeasing him but everybody was afraid of not pleasing him.'[3]

Every aspiring officer in the Royal Navy has tried to learn the magic of leadership from Nelson. One essential component was the way he shared the hardships of his men – protracted separation from loved ones, mutilating wounds, the tedium of blockade and the horrifying dangers of battle. Another was his ability to forge unity – by touring the gun decks, dining his officers, communicating with

---

[1] SPCK expansion is chronicled in Minutes Books XXXIII–XXXVI; literature depots set up in dockyards, SPCK *Report of Proceedings 1812*, p. 188; NMBS activities in *Account of the Naval and Military Bible Society, 1804–1810, 1811–1812, 1813, 1814, 1815*; Kealy MS, p. 14, quotes from *Steel's Navy List* for 1 April 1809 (under Miscellaneous). Clergy numbers from Kealy show average of sixty-six serving at sea each year, compared with seventy-five in the French Revolutionary and thirty-four in the American wars. Keats and Hoste in Knight, *Pursuit of Victory*, pp. 539f.

[2] Christopher Hibbert, *Nelson: A Personal History* (1994), p. 388 n.

[3] Le Fevre and Harding, *British Admirals of the Napoleonic Wars*, p. 293.

the fleet. And there was his humanity, a reputation that clung to him despite his severities. As a captain he could be stern, as logged punishments attest; and late in his career, as an admiral, he allowed his flag captain Hardy to make the *Victory* a flogging ship. Towards mutineers and rebels he could be merciless; in Naples his conduct verged on the savage over the execution of Caracciolo and his support for king Ferdinand's bloody reprisals. Even Nelson could refer to the 'Sicilifying of my conscience.'[4] Deep flaws appear in his moral record – his pride and arrogance, his desertion of the devoted Fanny, his notorious liaison with Emma and the laboured deceptions they invented. His father reproved him with a scriptural call to repentance – 'step forth then and save yourself today whilst it is still called today … to recover and preserve your private and publick good. Riches and honour are in one hand, and there are probable means yet left, to secure in the other length of days.'[5] The call went unheeded.

However peerless he was as a fighting commander, Nelson cannot stand as a model of Christian morality. His contemporaries knew less of his flaws than we do, of course, with our massively detailed knowledge of his letters, and he took care to present a public appearance of respectability, but his intimates were aware of his love for Emma, and many others must have suspected it. Hardy, for one, knew what was going on, and disapproved, but still gave unswerving devotion to his admiral. Nelson's legacy to the navy was not affected by his private conduct. The Nelson legend, cultivated first by the man himself, developed by Clarke and McArthur and sanctified by Southey, gave him an enduring reputation for courage and duty, humanity and integrity, morality and religion, which has been modified but not shredded by the modern vogue for destructive revisionism. Despite its limitations, his humanity was genuine, reflected in his endless concern for the health and diet of his ships' companies, a real belief in justice, and a desire to lead men rather than drive them. Some of this no doubt grew out of his need to be loved, but it was not all narcissism: he had a deep sense of what was right – loyalty, truth, honour, human worth – virtues which the Christianity of his upbringing taught. He did not always live up to a lofty moral code, but even his attempts at

---

4 Terry Coleman, *Nelson: The Man and the Legend* (2001), p. 213; Knight, *Pursuit of Victory*, pp. 475f.

5 Coleman, p. 268. Edmund Nelson appears to be alluding to Hebrews 3:13–15: 'Exhort one another daily, while it is called Today; lest any of you be hardened through the deceitfulness of sin. For we are made partakers of Christ, if we hold the beginning of our confidence steadfast unto the end. While it is said, Today, if ye will hear his voice, harden not your hearts, as in the provocation'; and also to Proverbs 3:13, 16: 'Happy is the man that findeth wisdom … Length of days is in her right hand and in her left hand riches and honour' (KJV).

self-justification expressed a conviction that he ought to be doing so. Religion gave him a set of values. So long as he believed he was serving God and his country, he could seek glory: the nobility of the cause made his driving ambition to make a name for himself seem somehow less self-serving. This owed nothing to the new piety, yet paradoxically his sense of religion did much for its standing in the navy. The Nelson legend brought benefits to the Blue Lights.[6]

To outward appearance he was a faithful member of the Church of England, but it is hard to know how orthodox his Christianity really was. Brought up in a Norfolk rectory, he looked to Anglican worship at sea to bolster morale and discipline, and turned to the SPCK for help. Even as he did so, he showed that his driving force was as much political as spiritual. 'I trust that the conduct of the *Agamemnon* and *Vanguard*', he wrote in January 1801, 'has been such as to induce a belief that good to our King and Country may have arisen from the seamen and marines having been taught to respect the Established Religion, and Kings have been shewn that our seamen are religious.'[7] Nelson's flagships *San Josef* and *Victory* were both supplied by the Society at his request, and he noted the beneficial effects of Christian worship on conduct. Religion formed essential stage furniture for the theatre of his life: it was part of shipboard ceremonial; it lent itself to the celebration of his victories with thanksgiving services afloat and with expressions of gratitude to God heading up his despatches. When he wanted to display what he claimed was the purity of his passion for Emma Hamilton, he went with her to Communion at Merton parish church. As his life ebbed away on the *Victory*'s orlop deck, he had his chaplain beside him to give a measure of physical relief along with his prayers. When the nation came to bury its hero, the only setting which would adequately serve was a Christian service in St Paul's Cathedral. But what of his inmost convictions and creed?[8]

As a depressed young midshipman in the *Dolphin* in 1776, he found strength to cope by consciously committing himself to God's care: 'confiding in Providence, I will brave every danger.'[9] More fully he wrote of his faith when commanding the *Agamemnon* in 1793:

[6] James Stanier Clarke and John McArthur published *The Life of Admiral Lord Nelson KB, from His Lordship's Manuscripts* (2 vols.) in 1809, and Robert Southey *The Life of Nelson* in 1831. Roger Knight heads the final section of his magnificent biography 'The Transfiguration', *Pursuit of Victory*, p. 525.

[7] W. O. B. Allen and Edmund McClure, *Two Hundred Years: The History of the Society for Promoting Christian Knowledge, 1698–1898* (1898), p. 456n.

[8] *The Times*, London, no. 6629 (Friday 10 Jan 1806); CD of *The State Funeral of Horatio, Lord Viscount Nelson KB* (Herald AV Publications, 1999).

[9] Warner, *Portrait of Lord Nelson*, p. 16.

> When I lay me down to sleep I recommend myself to the care of Almighty God; when I awake I give myself up to His direction. Amidst all the evils that threaten me I will look up to Him for help, and question not but that He will either avert them or turn them to my advantage. Though I know neither the time nor the manner of my death, I am not at all solicitous about it because I am sure that He knows them both, and that He will not fail to support and comfort me.[10]

In rather similar vein he wrote a further prayer in his private journal just after leaving Emma for the last time:

> May the great God whom I adore enable me to fulfil the expectations of my country; and if it is His good pleasure that I should return, my thanks will never cease being offered up to the Throne of His mercy. If it is His good providence to cut short my days upon earth, I bow with the greatest submission.[11]

Pitted against atheistic and revolutionary France, Nelson perceived himself to be Heaven's warrior, and gave thanks to Almighty God for his victories. He gained inner strength from a sense of God's blessing. It developed his confidence and (it must be added) his self-righteousness. Rather as Cromwell could see the evidence of divine favour in his victories on the battlefield, Nelson found proof that he was an instrument in the hand of the Almighty. Convictions of this kind might easily lead to arrogance, and there was a strong strain of egotism and pride in Nelson. But that is not the whole story. Nelson seems truly to have sensed that God had given victory, and there was something of humility in paying tribute to the Lord. He believed furthermore that success must be the prelude to noble ends – the good of mankind as well as the benefit of Britain, and the attainment of moral goals besides peace and deliverance.

After the Battle of the Nile a service of thanksgiving was held on the quarter-deck of the *Vanguard*, attended by Nelson, head bandaged, as well as most of the ship's surviving company and a group of French prisoners. The culminating prayer was presumably composed by the chaplain, Stephen Comyn, but it reflects sentiments that Nelson espoused:

> O! Almighty God, the sovereign Ruler of all the world, in whose hands is power and might, which thou hast vouchsafed to the fleet of thy servant our Sovereign in distant seas, we offer thee, as we are most bound,

---

[10] Warner, *Portrait of Lord Nelson*, pp. 64f.
[11] Warner, *Portrait of Lord Nelson*, p. 289.

thanks and praise; for of thee alone cometh both counsel and strength for the fight! Thou alone givest victory unto Kings, and deliverest thy servants from the peril of the sword. We beseech thee to give us grace to improve this, and all thy great mercies to thy glory, the advancement of thy Gospel, the honour of our Sovereign and, so far as in us lieth, to the good of all mankind: and keep alive we pray thee, by thy sanctifying spirit in our hearts, such fear of offending thee, such reliance on thy help in time of need, as may daily appear in the conformity of our lives to the doctrine of our Lord and Saviour Jesus Christ; to whom with thee, O Father and thee O Holy Ghost, three persons and one only God, be all honour and glory, world without end. Amen.[12]

Nelson's private life was about to slip out of conformity to the doctrines of Christ, but he retained a deep sense of submission to the sovereignty of God. Such faith led him, as the *Victory* moved towards the Combined Fleet off Trafalgar, to write his famous prayer, for a victory for the benefit of all Europe, for humanity in the aftermath, for his fleet and for himself. Acknowledging God as his Creator he entrusted the issues of life and death into his hands. 'For myself individually I commit my life to Him who made me, and may His blessing light upon my endeavours for serving my Country faithfully. To Him I resign myself and the just cause which is entrusted to me to defend.'[13]

As life ebbed away from the mortally wounded admiral in the cockpit of the *Victory*, his thoughts turned towards God. The main authority for what was said and done around the dying Nelson is the account written by the surgeon William Beatty, who was necessarily called to attend other patients over the three-hour period that followed. He gives us Nelson's closing words of gratitude to God for his duty done. Scott the chaplain was there too, but could not or would not give a full account of his own experiences. Clearly the man was already profoundly distressed by the sights and sounds of that dreadful improvised operating theatre, and the shock of witnessing a desperately wounded officer tear away his bandages to hasten death. Then came his encounter with Nelson, personal friend as well as commander, and Scott was overcome with shock and horror and sorrow. He did not leave while Nelson remained alive, trying to bring what help he could with fan and drink and massage. But Nelson wanted spiritual ministrations too. There is something especially poignant in his appeal, 'Pray for me, Doctor!' as he sought the help and comfort which only religion can give to the dying.[14] According to

---

[12] *NC*, IV (1801), p. 367.

[13] Warner, *Portrait of Lord Nelson*, p. 304.

[14] Taylor, p. 205.

the chaplain no formal prayers could be said: Nelson's pain and Scott's efforts to help 'precluded the reading of prayers to him in the regular form', and it appears to have been Nelson who was prompting Scott to utter intercessions, clipped and confused as they probably were.[15] Perhaps echoing the prayers for the dying – surely Scott cannot have omitted this most basic duty of a priest, whatever his personal sense of loss? – Nelson claimed that he had not been a great sinner. Was he protesting his moral integrity despite the blemishes upon it? Or was he acknowledging that his conduct had been sinful to some degree at least? And was Scott in a fit state to note and record the transactions of a troubled soul as life slipped away? No man can say, but there remains no record of death-bed repentance and conversion of an evangelical kind.[16]

Nelson's faith, though profound, was not the piety of the Blue Lights. Their expressions were often more Christ-centred and they constantly reached out for the grace of God. In contrast, as Sugden has shown, Nelson seems to have believed that exertions in a righteous cause would give a human soul some claim upon God. Recast in theological terms, this would mean that men and women must earn salvation by their conduct – the antithesis of the Gospel of grace beloved by evangelicals. 'Faith and Works' was the rather biblical motto Nelson chose for his coat of arms when raised to the peerage. To the Blue Lights it seemed plain from Scripture that salvation comes from trusting God's forgiving grace, and that such faith would show its authenticity by its deeds. Faith comes first, and actions follow. Is that what Nelson believed, or did he hope for acceptance with God on account of his unparalleled exertions for his country? Some of his utterances might possibly be taken that way, including his last coherent words, 'Thank God I have done my duty.' Even the words already quoted, 'I have not been a great sinner', could mean that he saw no need for contrition and redeeming grace. That he found comfort from religion at the end can hardly be doubted, but whether it was the full Christian hope of the Gospel cannot be known.[17]

Religious sensibilities of a sublime nature were mingled with the death of Nelson, and spilled over into the way the nation perceived and remembered these events. Some sermons, posters and tracts saw the hand of God in giving national deliverance; others found a powerful lesson in Nelson's resignation to the will of the Almighty; a few drew a Christian parallel between the death of the hero and the Saviour who laid down his life for the redemption of mankind. The living

---

[15] Taylor, p. 205.

[16] Carola Oman, *Nelson* (1947; Reprint Soc. edn 1950), pp. 550–7.

[17] Sugden, p. 401; Christopher Lloyd, *St. Vincent and Camperdown* (1963), plate 12, p. 89; Oman, p. 557.

Nelson had given tribute to the God of Battles through his despatches and services of thanksgiving; the tradition was continued with significant differences by Collingwood. His Trafalgar despatch to the Admiralty with first news of the battle, the victory and the death of Nelson was more secular in tone than Nelson's announcement of the triumph at the Nile, but Collingwood attached to it a copy of his general order to the fleet for a service of thanksgiving. When the London press was able to publish the news of Trafalgar on 7 November, the Collingwood despatch was printed with two general orders appended, the first conveying his thanks and admiration to the whole fleet, and the second giving instruction for all ships to hold a day of humiliation before God and thanksgiving for victory. All three documents were dated 22 October on board the *Euryalus* off Cape Trafalgar.[18]

It tells a great deal about Collingwood's priorities that, at this juncture, while mourning the death of a dear friend and managing the shattered fleet in gale-force winds on a lee shore, he saw fit to call his ships' companies to prayer – although realistically, as the survivors were struggling to save their own ships as well as the prizes, he left open the precise date. Here is the text:

> The Almighty God, whose arm is strength, having of his great mercy been pleased to crown the exertion of his Majesty's fleet with success, in giving them a complete victory over their enemies, on 21st of this month: and that all praise and thanksgiving may be offered up to the Throne of Grace for the great benefits to our country and to mankind:
>
> I have thought proper, that a day should be appointed of general humiliation before God, and thanksgiving for this his merciful goodness, imploring forgiveness of sins, a continuation of his divine mercy, and his constant aid to us, in the defence of our country's liberties and laws, without which the utmost efforts of man are nought; and direct, therefore, that …… be appointed for this holy purpose.
>
> Given on board the Euryalus, off Cape Trafalgar, 22nd Oct. 1805
> Signed C. COLLINGWOOD.
> To the respective Captains and Commanders.[19]

When Wilberforce read news of Nelson's death he found himself so overcome that he could not go on reading for tears. He wrote to his friend Lord Muncaster on 25 November 1805:

---

[18] *The Times*, London, no. 6572 (Thursday 7 Nov 1805).
[19] PRO ADM 1/411, Part 5, fol. 568.

> I was delighted with Collingwood's general orders for a day of humiliation and thanksgiving. The latter I had heard of in the case of Lord Duncan's victory and some others, but I do not remember to have ever heard of the mention of imploring pardon for sins, as well as returning thanks for blessings. The former pleased me particularly, for nothing can more magnify goodness than its being unmerited, and that, on the contrary, punishment has been rather deserved.

He went on to express his frustration that the public had not been informed of Nelson's custom to attribute victory to God:

> How abominable it is, that though, as we have recently learned, Lord Nelson and several others have ordered general thanksgivings on shipboard after victories, yet these orders have never till now appeared in the Gazette; and consequently they have not been known, and have not produced their proper effect on the public mind.[20]

Collingwood's signal added an element foreign to Nelson, that the fleet should worship God in a spirit of contrition, seeking forgiveness for sins. This was a startling expression of Collingwood's own deep piety: mention of God's mercy and grace, of human penitence and divine forgiveness were novel concepts in a signal of this kind. It shows how any mood of triumphalism after Trafalgar had been driven out by grief for Nelson's death, a response that gripped the nation. It is also evidence that a new spirit of seriousness about religion had found its way into the navy. After this fleet order it would have been hard for anyone, however senior, to deny a place for piety. The lesson was reinforced by Nelson's funeral in St Paul's which attracted huge public interest: the nation paid tribute in words of Christian hope, beginning with the traditional words from St John's Gospel. 'I am the Resurrection and the Life, saith the Lord; he that believeth in me, though he were dead, yet shall he live.'[21]

The Naval Chronicle published an early sermon on the Trafalgar theme, given on Thursday 5 December 1805, the date fixed by royal proclamation for general national thanksgiving. The preacher was the Rev. James Stanier Clarke. He took his text from 1 Maccabees – whereas Evangelicals invariably eschewed the Apocrypha. His theme was that the victory had been due not just to courage but to Christianity. In developing this idea he swiftly parted company from the Blue Lights. Providence, he claimed, had selected British naval power to keep alive the memory of civil liberty amidst a slavish world, but he understood redemption

---

[20] Wilberforce, III, pp. 241, 243.

[21] St. John's Gospel 11:25.

and salvation in political terms – rescue from chaos rather than deliverance from sin. There followed a panegyric on the 'real and devout character of a British seaman', which he detected in the solemnity and devotion of their shipboard services. In a passage which would have given anguish to Marks, Smith or Gambier, he stated that 'Christianity in its purest state, utterly devoid of hypocrisy, forms the general and leading feature of a seaman's character.' No need for conversion, then! Clarke treated the Christian religion as a sublime moral code, that 'guides him through the perplexed mazes of his duty …; it teaches him humility, patience and obedience – it commands him to suffer long, and to be kind.' He did not speak of where the power to live such a life might be found, nor how failure might find forgiveness. He went on to show that sea-going brought spiritual insights to the seafarer. 'Unto him is given to trace the Creator of the World in the sublimest of its features; he sees him in the ocean, he hears him in the tempest, and looks for his protection amidst the winds and waves!' Clarke believed that these experiences could nurture what he calls a 'religious principle'; this in turn creates in British sailors 'that daring, resistless, but humane spirit which has rendered them the wonder, terror and admiration of our enemies.' He made no link between the God of creation and the God of revelation and redemption; in this sermon he preached no Gospel appeal to repentance and new birth, perhaps because he saw no need for it.

Clarke referred to Collingwood's signal and the surprise it caused enemy prisoners.

> The astonished captive … long since acknowledged the influence of a Duncan's piety, and 'almost was persuaded to be a Christian'. The venerable Sage who now presides over the Councils of the British Navy [Barham] yields not to any one in his zeal for religion; and the lamented Hero of Egypt and Trafalgar … with his last words declared that his Faith as well as his bravery was steadfast. 'Thy will, O God, be done.'[22]

The next issue of *The Naval Chronicle* included another Trafalgar sermon, contributed by the correspondent 'Philo Nauticus'. This one had been preached to soldiers by the rector of Whitburn on 17 November 1805, on receipt of the news of the death of Nelson. It was characteristic of the way in which the event was perceived, that frequently the death of Nelson overshadowed the sense of national rejoicing at the victory gained. The Rev. J. Symons stressed the importance of doing one's duty – especially appropriate for his military audience – and he saw proof of God's Providence in the victory. Turning to Nelson's piety, he showed

---

[22] *NC*, XIV (1805), pp. 487–501.

how he had resigned himself to the divine Disposer of events, by seeking that the will of God should be done. This was an example of the fortitude which religion inspired. The preacher noted that Collingwood had ascribed the victory to God, and had called for thanksgiving to be given to him: his hearers too should look to God for strength. In these events there was a reminder to all, especially soldiers, that they should be 'ready to depart and be with Christ'. At the last, then, we have the authentic note of the evangel, the Gospel call to repentance and faith, missing from Stanier Clarke.[23]

Under St Vincent's baleful glare religion had been restored to something like its traditional place in fleet routine, but Nelson's role had been different. He had shown how religion could inspire. Jervis made it part of discipline, but Nelson merged it with patriotism. Buoyed up by his posthumous reputation, the friends of religion made a more public and confident bid for national attention. A poster preserved in the Nelson Museum at Monmouth may be taken as representative, with its bold assertion, 'Britons! Your Nelson is dead!' (illus. 8). Then it points to the confidence in God displayed by Howe, Duncan and Nelson. While it most strikingly calls for renewed national concern for religion, it lacks the Gospel appeal of the evangelicals. They were not silent, of course. Marks included an essay on Trafalgar in *The Ocean*. Even more poignantly, aged John Newton struggled into the pulpit to preach his last sermon, to raise funds for the widows and orphans of Trafalgar, but the old man lost the thread of his thoughts and had to be gently led by the hand, uncomprehendingly, back to his seat in church. Evangelicals were particularly struck by the tone of Collingwood's order in calling for repentance – the starting point for a biblical understanding of salvation, and thus the stuff of many addresses. Collingwood himself expressed surprise that his order had become the text for a sermon. However these matters are understood, with whatever depth or shallowness, they testify to a newfound willingness of religion to associate itself with nation and navy. Duncan and Howe, in that thanksgiving service in 1797, had led the way, and the Trafalgar effect continued the process, helped in particular by the 'venerable Sage' at the Admiralty.[24]

---

[23] *NC*, xv (1806), pp. 28–32.

[24] Poster printed for and sold by F. Kent (?) and Son, 116 High Holborn. London (1806), preserved in the Nelson Museum, Monmouth. Richard Marks ['Aliquis'], *Nautical Essays, or a Spiritual View of the Ocean and Maritime Affairs, with Reflections on the Battle of Trafalgar and other Events* (1813), reissued as *The Ocean Spiritually Reviewed* [hereafter *Ocean*] (1824); Pollock (1981; pbk edn 1985), p. 181. Oliver Warner, *The Life and Letters of Vice-Admiral Lord Collingwood* (1968), p. 251.

8 'Britons! Your Nelson is dead!' Poster of 1806 calling for repentance and faith in God as the true basis for national security. © Nelson Museum, Monmouth

Middleton and the Revision of Regulations

THE popular religion of Nelson and *The Naval Chronicle* had more of patriotism and duty in it than theology. It had broad appeal as a bulwark of morality. It sanctioned crown and constitution, calling on the powerful to act justly and on the inferior orders to respect authority. Religion like this was rational and temperate, and it had many friends in high places. It was a creed which appealed to Prince William Henry, the future William IV, and to influential clergy such as Stanier Clarke, domestic chaplain to the Prince Regent, and Samuel Cole the navy's senior chaplain after the war. Those who saw religion as the cement of society, promoting good behaviour and suppressing rebelliousness, found it appealing, but it could never satisfy the evangelicals. It was deficient in its theology, for it gave too little space to grace and conversion. It had too much human reasoning about it, not enough Scripture, and it lacked the fire of conviction which was widely called 'enthusiasm'. In some ways it fulfilled the original manifesto of the Blue Lights as they called for Sunday prayers and more chaplains. But by now the new piety was beginning to work on a strategy for evangelising the fleet, addressing concerns that this popular religion ignored. The task was made easier by measures put in place by Middleton. Their importance became apparent later when evangelical activists found how they might be turned to their advantage – how 'establishment religion' could be outflanked by 'enthusiasm'.

When Middleton became First Lord of the Admiralty in 1805, ennobled as Lord Barham – his price for taking up office when little short of eighty – the evangelical agenda had political power behind it, and that 'manifesto' had some chance of implementation. For many years he had planned to revise the long-outdated regulations, and had gathered quantities of material for this purpose, but when he resigned from the Board in 1795 his hopes were seemingly at an end. Now back in power he revived those plans: the eventual volume of *Regulations and Instructions for His Majesty's Service at Sea* became the indispensable handbook of rules and good practice, shaping the naval profession and the ethos of the officer corps for decades to come. Middleton took this opportunity to reaffirm the ancient prominence given to religion, with Sunday prayers and sermon. He staked out new territory for the chaplain. In all this he was doing what he had set out in the memorandum on the duties of captains: 'if good chaplains were appointed ... and the regulations ... enforced ... seamen would be amongst the foremost ... in ... piety and good conduct.'[25] Now Middleton had the power, not just to enforce regulations, but to frame them. For a man of his conviction it was an awesome

---

[25] *RAI* 1806; 'Duty of Captains in the Navy', *BP*, II, pp. 161–5.

responsibility. By the time his work was done, he had made officially sanctioned religion a potential conduit for the new piety.

How was it done? There was no way that even Barham could have skewed the *Regulations* in an obviously evangelical direction. Had he wished to make it a partisan document, it would never have been accepted by Admiralty Board and Privy Council, let alone the navy at large. What he did was both fair-minded and subtle. Conservatively he kept the ancient provisions for Sunday observance and a ban on profanity. He stressed the moral and religious responsibility of commanding officers, and the duty of all officers to safeguard conduct – measures which might have been lost had the wording been more secular. More radically, he gave the chaplains a real stake in the navy by issuing detailed instructions, the rules which set out what they were expected to do, and by corollary what they must be permitted to do. In all this, Barham showed no bias towards evangelicalism, but he left an approach route open for it. Sunday prayers for instance had to be accompanied by a sermon, that means of grace so popular with evangelicals; captains would need to obtain collections of addresses to read to their crews – and the most effective of these were arguably by evangelicals. Or, to take another example, the ban on immoral conduct would allow Blue Lights to tackle the problem of prostitution. Or again, the command that God was to be honoured permitted 'enthusiastic' captains to encourage voluntary prayer groups. Barham's *Regulations* became an enabling instrument: they did not allow the new piety to be expunged or ignored, but the task of exploiting these possibilities was left to successors.[26]

This volume did much to codify good practice by formulating the principles upon which sound governance rested. Part of the strength of Middleton's achievement lies in its distillation of practical wisdom, gathered from a lifetime's observation and reflection. General principles were developed into practical instructions for each rank, with an underlying philosophy that picked up the quasi-spiritual, pastoral responsibilities from the 1731 *Regulations*. There the captain had been made answerable for the conduct of everybody in the ship, and had to set a good example himself; he must hold divine service twice a day (and see that a sermon was provided on Sundays), and he must deal with swearing, blasphemy, cursing and drunkenness with appropriate punishments. The Enlightenment of the eighteenth century with its fashionable Deism might have reduced or removed these overtly religious provisions, but it did not happen. Instead the new *Regulations* preserved a pastoral-spiritual tone. All officers, not just the commander, were to be examples of morality, regularity and good order. No ship was to go to

---

[26] *RAI* 1806, pp. 3, 160 (service and sermon), 247ff. (chaplains); the captain to prevent immorality, p. 160, and not to allow women at sea, p. 244.

sea without a chaplain if one were available, and the captain had to support him. There should be a service and sermon on Sundays. As before, cursing, quarrelling, drunkenness and immorality were to be prevented, and now the lieutenants were specifically charged with curbing these offences. By mentioning public worship, preaching, teaching the boys and visiting the sick bay, the Instructions for the Chaplain defined a role for him and treated him for the first time as an integral part of the navy. It was a momentous development.

The Question of Humanity

IF the Blue Lights were truly beginning to value compassion, surely the *Regulations* appearing under the signatures of both Barham and Gambier would be expected to show it? How about measures to tackle the things modern opinion finds most repellent – flogging and impressment? On the contrary, instead of anything along those lines, the volume does nothing to establish rights for seamen, but upheld the authority of officers and especially captains. Far from wanting to reduce the power of a captain, Middleton hoped to enlist it on the side of morality and religion, for the good of his crew. There is nothing sentimental about the book: it is terse, realistic, detailed, comprehensive – typically Middleton – and yet flashes of humanity can be glimpsed intermittently. Even the compilation of a standard regulation was a protection against the idiosyncratic whims of an autocratic commander. The new measures were not written on a blank sheet, and they need to be set in their context before they can be properly evaluated. That context, of course, was the harsh world of an operational fleet where naval law and justice were constantly, though not always consistently, being interpreted.

For generations the received understanding of naval life has been its brutality. From Dr Johnson's assertion that naval life was effectively like prison with the additional hazard of drowning, there has been a persistent belief that sailors were subject to habitual misgovernment on a sliding scale from neglect to tyranny. The detailed researches of John Byrn, Jr. and the magisterial sweep of N. A. M. Rodger's books have done much to modify previous assumptions and to create a new scholarly consensus. The code under which sailors served was undeniably severe, even draconian and frequently sanguinary, fearfully at odds with modern practice. Press warrants, press gangs, flogging round the fleet, punishments regularly handed out at the gangway, unofficial beatings which passed without record – these things were features of the sailing navy. Yet the inhumanity of it all can easily be exaggerated. With detailed analysis of one remote and potentially disorderly station, Byrn has shown how commanders strove to act within the principles of naval law, rather like JPs afloat. They normally preferred summary measures or courts of enquiry to courts martial, which were difficult to convene and frequently bound to hand out severer sentences. At courts martial legal advice was provided for the accused and for the officers trying the case. He believes that a draconian penal code was administered moderately with a genuine attempt to see justice done – and justice tempered at times by mercy. 'Influenced as they were by the leavening principles of gentility, paternalism and detached justice, His Majesty's captains as a group seem to have exercised the awesome disciplinary powers at their disposal with moderation and restraint.'[27] He calculates that 9 per cent of lower-deck personnel suffered the lash, a figure horrifying enough but falling well short of popular myth and perhaps justified by the circumstances of war service on a station notorious for rum and women.

These conclusions support the principle which Rodger states with reference to the mid-eighteenth century, that 'when brutality occurred, it tended to destroy naval discipline, which rested on unstated consent, not force.'[28] Severe sentences drew attention to the seriousness of the crimes committed, but quite commonly they were not carried out in full. Good order at sea required fairness and rule of law as well as sternness. Byrn's researches have demonstrated that often men who deserted had suffered neither press-gang nor punishment: only 6 per cent of men who ran from their ships had previously been flogged, and 48 per cent were volunteers. Other factors besides brutality provided the impetus for desertion, and often those were economic or social – men seeking better wages in the merchant service or ashore, men who had failed to settle into the community of a new ship's company, or men who wanted to rejoin their families or womenfolk. The grant of shore leave would have helped, but that was a commodity in short supply during the war years. Deserters had real grievances – but they were probably not the discipline or the high-handed methods of manning.[29]

Sailors commonly assessed matters differently from the modern tendency to regard punishment as the test of humanity. They did not value leniency towards

---

[27] John D. Byrn, Jr., *Crime and Punishment in the Royal Navy: Discipline on the Leeward Islands Station, 1784–1812* (Aldershot, 1989), p. 108. He adds the interesting observation that when statistics allow comparison it appears that British officers were probably more lenient than their US counterparts.

[28] Rodger, *Wooden World*, p. 210. Rodger sets naval punishments in the context of law enforcement ashore: 'Eighteenth-century British society made up for the extreme difficulty of catching criminals by theatrically severe punishments, but only a bare minimum were ever carried out. ... A sentence of several hundred lashes was a statement about the severity of the crime, but officers knew that the presiding surgeon would halt the punishment after a hundred lashes or so.' Rodger, *Command of the Ocean*, p. 494.

[29] Byrn, p. 153.

offenders as anything admirable, but they did see needless harshness as oppression. Humanity must be looked for in the maintenance of a fair if strict code of discipline, consistently and justly enforced. But it must also be seen in care for a man's living conditions, his food, pay and health. By such standards the officers of the war period were judged and mostly respected by their crews. Certainly there were some cases of cruel abuse of authority, but not enough to substantiate a case for institutionalised oppression, while those deemed to have behaved with brutality, whether captains, officers or petty officers, were detested by their profession and liable to discipline or dismissal. Given the standards of most officers, capricious tyranny seems to have been rare but possible, because the code was imprecisely drawn. The common law of shore life was replaced by a much vaguer formulary – 'according to the ancient customs of the sea' – but that did not exempt ships from the rule of law. The Articles of War and the *Regulations* of 1731 certainly upheld the authority of captain and officers, for how could any ship sail in safety without it? Nevertheless the armoury of punishment was as formidable in protecting communal living as in maintaining the powers of the officer class: thus theft was always treated with particular sternness at sea, by application of the thieves' cat and sometimes running the gauntlet (or 'gantlope' in naval parlance).

Byrn's belief that 'courts martial enforced the law formally according to the accepted judicial principles and practices of the day' is in contrast to Rodger's opinion that part of the navy's problem with discipline arose from its lack of a developed legal code.[30] Nevertheless both authorities show captains and courts martial attempting to maintain a true rule of law, however imprecise, and doing so with an eye to fairness that was sometimes tinted with compassion. As Rodger stresses, officers came of a background which recognised Christian ethical values including truth, fairness and humanity. So long as crews shared a corpus of moral and professional values, acknowledging the necessary authority of the officers and the needs of their men, the whole system worked well enough, but when wartime recruitment brought an extraneous element into the fleet, the lack of a comprehensive legal structure might create difficulty.[31]

Middleton – and thus by extension evangelicalism – had recognised the need

---

[30] Byrn, p. 5; Rodger, *Wooden World*, p. 218. A.F.Y. in 1813 would have welcomed a system of encouragement and rewards instead of a code of punishment – but a code there had to be; in a later work under his own name, Penrose admitted the difficulties of having a truly uniform system but he suggested guidelines should be issued to officers on first taking up command. *NC*, xxix, p. 400; Sir Charles Penrose, *Observations on Corporal Punishment, Impressment, and Other Matters relative to the Present State of His Majesty's Royal Navy* (Bodmin, 1824), p. 21.

[31] Rodger, *Wooden World*, p. 211.

for institutional reform. He had authoritarian and centralising instincts, and he wanted to see coherence imposed. This process would promote discipline throughout the service and at the same time reduce caprice. This kind of clarification was a feature of Blue Light thinking. Way back in the American War, when he wanted to have the divisional system enforced in all ships, Kempenfelt had been calling for a structural change of high importance. By bringing groups of men under the direct supervision of a lieutenant, he intended to promote health, welfare and good order; once religion had been added, he hoped to see crime and punishment reduced. For his part, Middleton looked to strengthen the role of captains and to spell out their responsibility for their men's moral, spiritual and general welfare.

Accountability gave the Middleton agenda its power: once the *Regulations* had been signed and issued to the fleet, the Admiralty had a benchmark to measure performance. The *Regulations* demanded a level of religious provision from all commanding officers, while the Instructions for the Chaplain spelt out what that should mean. The next phase would involve making some checks on how captains were carrying out the wishes of the Board of Admiralty. The same principle applied to punishments: once the captain was made to authorise all serious punishments, he could be called to account, and the regime of discipline throughout the navy could be monitored and modified if necessary. From 1806 only the captain might order punishment, and never with undeserved severity, while subsequent measures got rid of unofficial beatings. Running the gantlope was abolished in 1806, and starting forbidden in 1809. From 1813 quarterly punishment returns had to be made to the Admiralty. Such moves may rightly be seen as steps towards a more uniform system – although the process would not be complete for another two or three decades, with the eventual introduction of punishment warrants and a standard scale of penalties.[32]

Humanity breaks surface in other parts of the work. Cleanliness is a recurrent theme, as in earlier editions, but the development of medicine is particularly noteworthy. Rules for the cure [care] of sick and hurt were perfunctory in 1731, being mainly concerned with facilities – a room to be provided, attendants to serve night and day, lavatories, cradles, provision of fish where possible – all sensible measures but lacking emphasis on human care. Under the 1806 code,

---

[32] *RAI* 1806, p. 163; *Additional Regulations and Instructions* (1813), p. 3, forbade running the gauntlet, and pp. 3f. required quarterly returns of punishments to be made to the Admiralty by captains. See Rodger, *Command of the Ocean*, p. 492. Also P. K. Kemp, *The British Sailor: A Social History of the Lower Deck* (1970), p. 186. Philip Patton on the Board of Admiralty was an advocate of humane reform; his philosophy may not have been evangelical, but in these matters he shared the Barham–Gambier outlook.

the surgeon is given guidance over the spirit in which his medicine is to be practised:

> It becomes his duty to soothe and cheer ['sooth and chear'] their minds by the most humane attention, to hear with patience all their complaints, and redress whatever they may think grievances by every expression of consolatory kindness, which will naturally inspire them with confidence, exhilarate their spirits and add to their hope of recovery, to which it cannot fail to contribute.[33]

The sick berth was to be placed in the most airy part of the ship, and properly equipped with cradles and buckets. This kind of attention to detail is seen in another health provision, that the cook should clean the coppers and inspect them (for verdigris) before a daily report was given to the lieutenant of the watch. Here were measures to reduce the harshness of sea-going life, and – underlining the fact that enemies were human beings worthy of respect – the *Regulations* demand proper treatment for prisoners of war.

No doubt much of the spirit of the 1806 *Regulations* was common in the navy, where officers recognised benevolence as a virtue and made some attempt to live up to Christian standards, whatever they may have thought of biblical doctrines. Nevertheless the Barham–Gambier board can take credit for making such humane principles explicit, for turning vague expressions of sentiment into detailed instructions, and for making both pastoral and religious measures part of the navy's constitution.

Chaplains – Clarification of Duties

WHEN it came to the evangelisation of the navy, the Blue Lights had little hope that clergy would do the work; nevertheless they were still keen to improve the clerical ministry in the navy. Reforms in 1806 and 1812 defined the chaplains' task and rewarded it properly; a further one in 1820 distinguished between the active list and those whose service days were over. Taken together, that trio of measures marks their coming of age in the navy, with recognised duties and a permanent role. Their obligations were spelt out in Barham's *Regulations and Instructions*, where the chaplain was given his first set of precise obligations and treated for the first time as part of the navy. Hitherto he had done what he felt inclined to do, or what his captain allowed him to do; what the navy might reasonably expect of him had nowhere been defined until now. Hereafter

---

33 *RAI* 1806, p. 159; cook, p. 379. For *RAI* 1731, see Lloyd and Coulter, *Medicine and the Navy*, III, pp. 22f., and Kemp, p. 118.

there was no room for doubt. Although important improvements to his status and remuneration would follow, these were refinements compared with the 1806 measure, which treated him for the first time as a genuine naval officer (albeit as yet without a commission). The new instructions were expanded in 1861, but five of the six paragraphs of 1806 remained in force, practically untouched, until very substantially modified in *Queen's Regulations and Admiralty Instructions* of 1879. Barham's view of the role of the chaplain was therefore highly influential and worth examining in more detail.34

First, a clergyman aboard ship was to remember that he was in the public eye, and that the respect accorded to his holy office would depend upon his conduct and demeanour, which would need to be above reproach. Secondly, his duty was to be as a pastor, counsellor and teacher: he must instruct the young gentlemen and boys in reading and in religion, and he must be prepared to give pastoral help and advice to anyone in the ship. He must carry out the duties of the Lord's Day with appropriate devotion, adapting his discourses 'to the capacity of his hearers ... that his instructions may be intelligible and beneficial.'35 These two articles reveal the underlying Protestantism of Barham's vision of the chaplain: in his pastoral role he was to be a minister of the Word, akin to the 'preacher' of the sixteenth and seventeenth centuries, charged with communicating the truth of God and being available to speak to the spiritually needy. Strikingly omitted from Barham's *Regulations* is any mention of the administration of the sacraments, despite his earlier hopes that flagship chaplains might administer Holy Communion to the ships of the squadron.36

Article IV of the Instructions required the chaplain to supervise the schoolmaster as he taught the ship's boys to read and say the catechism; he must frequently examine their progress himself and submit a report to the captain. He must be ready to attend the sick, to visit any who ask for him, and to prepare for death the dangerously ill, whether or not they send for him. In these two articles are indicated two lines of development, the chaplain as instructor and as associate of the surgeon. Finally came the procedure for drawing his pay. He had to present a certificate signed by the captain that he had not been absent for more than twenty-four hours without proper leave, and a further certificate signed by

34 'For the Chaplain' in *RAI* 1806, pp. 247ff.

35 *RAI* 1806, Section 8, Chapter 1, Articles I–III.

36 *BP*, II, p. 163. Compare the statement of the *aumonier*'s duties in Louis XIV's consolidating code for the French navy, that he must say Mass, offer prayers and catechism, and that he must frequently visit the sick to offer them the consolations of religion; *Ordonnance de Louis XIV pour les armies navales et arcenaux de marine* (Paris, 1689), titre 12 [information supplied by J. S. Bromley].

the captain, first lieutenant and master, that he had carried out his duties properly, had performed divine service whenever so directed, and had led an irreproachable life. Those three signatures show that the chaplain was not just the confidant of the captain; he had wider obligations to the officers, led by the senior lieutenant, and to the ship's company, represented by the master.[37]

His entitlement to pay depended on the faithful fulfilment of his duties. Barham showed his view of the importance of this man: he had a role in the naval service, and he must turn up to fulfil it. One senses the exasperation of St Vincent, who in the 1790s had tried to dismiss chaplains of uncertain commitment: both he and Barham valued the part a dedicated clergyman could play afloat. These new *Regulations* emphasised the chaplain's privileged position as mentor, preacher and sick-berth visitor, and stressed the importance of his example. He was to exercise a recognisably priestly function at sea, in distinction to other routes in which the sea parson might have gone. Some chaplains had been quite obviously the captain's personal friend (as in the Hogarth picture), a role which could easily develop into that of captain's or admiral's secretary (like Ramsay to Barrington and Barham, or Scott for Nelson). Instead the Supply and Secretariat Branch emerged to cover these essential staff functions, combined with the old position of purser. A normal action station for the chaplain was assisting the surgeon, often to give physical assistance with the wounded rather than spiritual comfort to the dying – although in practice there was likely to be much overlap, as with Scott in the *Victory*'s cockpit and his most famous patient. Again, the Medical Branch might make use of the chaplain's service under certain circumstances, but he definitely did not belong to this department as an essential member. Another duty was teaching the midshipmen and ship's boys, sometimes the preserve of the schoolmaster, sometimes the chaplain-schoolmaster, but eventually given to the Instructor Branch. The Barham *Regulations* envisaged the chaplain primarily as a spiritual welfare officer, and in that priestly role the chaplaincy has justified its position of influence and privilege in the navy.[38]

Having a defined role was important, but recruiting enough people to fill it was persistently difficult. Even devoted pastors required a living, and if a clergyman was to be attracted to spend many years in the navy, he needed

[37] Article VI, *RAI* 1806, p. 249.

[38] One chaplain had been a deputy judge advocate, but that is perhaps less incongruous than it sounds. Clergy were often JPs ashore, and clergy afloat might well be more highly educated than many officers. The task of the judge advocate was to aid the administration of justice by advising the court and sometimes the accused on legal matters. This task eventually fell to the Supply and Secretariat Branch instead.

some sense of career development and maybe provision for his old age. Having assured the priest of a role, the Admiralty in 1812 turned to his reward. By then Barham had retired, but his nephew Gambier was prominently carrying on the vision of the Blue Lights, and he commented to the Board on how recruitment might be improved. As a result, the chaplain was given an assured pay scale, additional reward for becoming a schoolmaster, and a pension to look forward to. These clergymen were being paid entirely out of public money (plus any windfall in the form of prize money), and it was time for groats to disappear.

Under the new arrangement all chaplains were to receive an annual salary of £150 plus an allowance for a servant, with additional remuneration for educational duties for those who chose to instruct the young gentlemen. Three years sea-service brought a pension of 2 shillings a day, rising to 5 shillings after eight years. It was not an over-generous scale, but it compared reasonably well with the pay for army chaplains, which began at £115 per annum for a garrison padre, and rose to £292, a major's rate, for a brigade chaplain on foreign service. The First Lord had proposed paying £265 for a chaplain-schoolmaster, but such glittering rewards remained a distant prospect.[39]

Then came the question of how the chaplains should be organised. In the days when a chaplain's appointment was virtually a private contract with a captain, there was no need for centralised administration, but once they ceased to be the 'property' of a commanding officer, they belonged presumably to the naval service, and might expect to be posted and controlled like any other officer. It seemed logical for the Admiralty to group them into a recognised branch under a newly appointed Chaplain General. The idea was an excellent one, ahead of its time, but it was practically bound to fail when an army man was given the post. Archdeacon John Owen had done well as head of the military padres, and he had been under fire in the Peninsular War. He had sufficient sympathy with evangelicalism to reassure the Blue Lights, but he had no acquaintance with the special problems of service afloat. On the other hand, he was a capable administrator who somehow managed to combine directing army padres and naval chaplains simultaneously; he owed no particular favours to captains or chaplains, and did his best to administer their affairs with impartiality. The experiment did not thrive, and

[39] Taylor, p. 233. For Admiralty Board discussion see Owen to Yorke, 28 Dec 1811, PRO ADM 3/174, and Admiral Domett's note appended to Yorke's minute for consideration by the Board with the superfluous warning, 'take care that his salary does not amount to more than that of the Captain', 7 Dec 1811. For the Commons' debates, see William Cobbett, *Parliamentary Debates*, 1st Series, XXI [7 Jan – 16 Mar 1812] (1812), p. 885.

soon the chaplains were organised in traditionally haphazard fashion, not by a Chaplain General or an archdeacon, but by the senior chaplain of Greenwich Hospital.[40]

The crucial reforms owed much to the vision of the Blue Lights. The instructions came in with Barham and his nephew, and the pay scale owed something to Gambier, supported by the Claphamite Spencer Perceval and his administration. The next step was to organise the chaplains into a permanent part of the naval profession, with prospect of a full-time career. Entry requirements, with qualifications properly scrutinised, supervised service with appropriate means of monitoring, a recognised role in a fighting service and a pension after it – these changes followed naturally enough in the 1820s and beyond. Eventually the thorny question of status had to be faced: from 1843 the chaplain was appointed by commission and was therefore an officer, but he held no rank and wore only the simplest of uniform. The hope was that he might seem to take the rank of whoever he was counselling, whether admiral or ordinary seaman. His learning and commission inevitably set him apart from the lower deck, but the vision was a sound one: to be of real use to sailors he must be identified with them. That, after all, is the practical outworking of incarnational theology!

Penrose and Professional Debate

AT BEST the 1806 handbook was an enabling document that laid out general principles of good governance and codified regulations. While reaffirming existing structures of authority, it emphasised the paternalistic responsibilities which went with them. It recognised the special role that chaplains could play. Of itself, it was powerless to spread the Gospel, but it left channels open for it, principally through captains reading prayers and chaplains preaching sermons. It helped to mould the ethos of the officer corps during a period when different values were competing for the soul of the naval profession.

There was a strongly conservative, authoritarian faction that had learned nothing from the enlightened ways of Duncan, Nelson and Collingwood, and precious little from the mutinies of 1797. It favoured control by command backed by punishment. In point of numbers it was probably a very small group, but there were always officers to be found without finesse or management skills, and with an inclination to severity or even brutality; if in command of a ship's company they were a menace. By contrast the great majority of the profession, including the Blue Lights, accepted the responsibilities that went with rank, and attended to the welfare of their divisions and crews. Blue Lights tended to draw attention

---

[40] Taylor, pp. 235–8; Snape, p. 94.

9 Admiral Sir Charles Vinicombe Penrose (1759–1830). An influential thinker and naval reformer who earned a wartime reputation for operations in support of Wellington's army in the Peninsula and became peacetime Commander-in-Chief of the Mediterranean fleet. (Oil painting by W. Sharp) © Royal Naval Museum, Portsmouth

to themselves by rather enthusiastically promoting religion and attacking vice – a process which unwisely handled could also provoke unrest.

Another force of growing power went unrecognised in *Regulations* – the concept of citizens' rights. Tainted as this seemed to be with Jacobinism and rebellion, it made little immediate appeal to the evangelicals nor the rest of the officer corps. The Blue Lights generally favoured reform, but the means of achieving it was by working on the attitudes of their fellow officers, in line with the principle that if they were taught Christian ways, they would act with mercy and justice: according to this view, the navy would reform itself from within by its own actions. In sharp antithesis the Radicals believed that the navy was too conservatively entrenched behind outdated ideas of rank and privilege to be willing to change, and to force reform they used the argument from human rights. Pressure of this kind came predominantly from politicians and journalists outside the navy, encouraged by a few maverick officers like Cochrane and Thomas Hodgskin. A three-way struggle between unreasoning conservatism, paternalistic reform, and radical agitation set the context for the further evolution of the ideals of the naval profession. The Blue Light Sir Charles Penrose stands out prominently in this process, as an officer who stirred up debate, a controversialist whose ideas constituted an agenda for change. He had a tolerant view of captains' authority but hated tyranny. He supported compulsory collective worship but wanted to see more voluntary gatherings. Where his colleagues were apt to see shore leave as an indulgence, a reward for good behaviour, he began to talk of it as a right. He expressed opinions on punishments and shipboard prostitution, and he had views of how the chaplains could usefully develop their ministry. Any attempt to understand naval evangelicalism and its impact must include this man.[41]

After the Amiens truce collapsed in 1803 Penrose's war service continued, first for six years in charge of the Padstow Sea Fencibles, a maritime militia, then to Gibraltar as commodore with his pennant in the guard-ship *San Juan* from 1810 to 1813, and finally in command of the small boats and light naval craft supporting Wellington's military operations on the coasts of Spain and France. His Padstow years had given him experience unusual for a post captain, of small vessels and estuary waters; he became expert in conveying troops and their equipment, with cavalry horses and field guns, across swiftly flowing rivers, sometimes under

[41] Penrose, *The Lives of Vice-Admiral Sir Charles Penrose and Captain J. Trevenen*. Penrose wrote a manuscript biography of his brother-in-law, who was commissioned lieutenant in October 1780, served in RN until Dec 1787, and then entered the Russian navy: R. C. Anderson and C. Lloyd (eds.), *A Memoir of James Trevenen, 1760–1790*, NRS (1959).

fire, or else he could make his sailors improvise a bridge of boats complete with protective boom, as he did for the crossing of the Adour river. An understanding of seamanship and of military campaigning enabled him to give close inshore gun support. He helped to reduce French batteries around Bordeaux, forced the passage of the Gironde and destroyed quantities of enemy shipping in the river. By the time his war ended, he had earned Wellington's gratitude. Public recognition followed, with a flag, a knighthood and appointment to the Mediterranean as commander-in-chief from 1814 to 1819.

On the face of it, Penrose's career, though arduous, was scarcely outstanding in comparison with many of his contemporaries, and this was perhaps the reason why the Admiralty selected Pellew instead of him to have charge of operations against Algiers in 1816. Yet it was Penrose who put his stamp on the post-war navy by drawing up workable proposals for reform and by attempting to educate the opinion of his profession. He saw more clearly than most that change was required and that the attitudes of the officer corps needed mending just as surely as the morals of the men needed reshaping. His means of communication were the letters he wrote for *The Naval Chronicle* under a pseudonym during the Napoleonic War.[42]

This periodical was founded in 1799 by the Rev. James Stanier Clarke, the erstwhile naval chaplain and now a society preacher, later the friend and domestic chaplain of the Prince Regent, and edited by him in collaboration with John McArthur, former purser, prize agent and writer. The journal was well produced and illustrated, and appeared every six months between 1799 and 1818. It was widely read by serving officers, who contributed a good deal of the material, including autobiographical pieces from both Nelson and Collingwood. Its correspondence section opened up a number of professional topics, and allowed for the development of informed public debate over controversial issues. At this time there was no staff college or official academy for the training of officers where naval doctrine could be formulated (the Portsmouth Naval Academy was really a private school). This is why patronage, the gathering of young aspirants around a captain or admiral, was so important: it was the means whereby the arcane knowledge and customs of the profession were taught. *The Naval Chronicle* provided something new, a platform where ideas could be debated amongst professionals: it pointed

[42] Taylor speculates that Penrose was passed over because of his known evangelicalism and the fear that beliefs of this kind were incompatible with aggressive warfare, p. 239. The argument is considered in the next chapter. Whatever the reason for choosing Pellew, the Admiralty's failure to keep Penrose in the picture was reprehensible: C. Northcote Parkinson, *Britannia Rules: The Classic Age of Naval History, 1793–1815* (1977), p. 173.

the need, as yet indistinctly felt, for some forum where ideas could be refined and best practice applauded.[43]

This was the medium which Penrose used to publish his thinking, knowing that in this way he would reach the most thoughtful officers of his generation. Like most contributors he used a pseudonym, and the fourteen letters of 'A.F.Y.' under the general title of 'The present management and discipline of the Navy' stimulated combative replies from 'Albion', 'Aeolus' and 'Nestor' during the period 1808 to 1809. Since he was writing for a professional rather than ecclesiastical readership, his arguments were not couched in religious terminology, except when evidently appropriate – as for example, when discussing the role of chaplains. Nevertheless his other writings reveal the inner spring of his ideas. *A Short Address to the Unlearned on the Advantage of Possessing the Holy Scriptures, and the Best Use to be Made of that Possession* (1820) clearly sets out his Evangelical faith, while *The Danger of the Church Considered* (1829) from the pen of 'An Old Member of the Establishment' shows that he had not lost his essential Anglicanism. Penrose, then, was a Blue Light, but of an unusual kind – a publicist and pamphleteer.[44]

The ideas he published in *The Naval Chronicle* proved to be the forerunners of informed debate in the profession; they contained principles which, when widely adopted, transformed naval discipline. Fundamental to his view was that 'the spirits of freemen must be ruled by a system of confidence', and he extended its implications into recruitment, discipline, leave and rewards.[45] He had come to

43 *The Naval Chronicle*, 40 vols. (1799–1818). 'The present management and discipline of the navy': letters of A.F.Y. in *The Naval Chronicle*, XIX (1808): Letter 1, p. 196; 2, p. 286; 3, p. 289; 4, pp. 382–4; 5, p. 460; XX (1808): 6, p. 23; 7, p. 115; 8, pp. 202–5; 9, pp. 296–8; XXI (1809): 10, p. 28; 11, pp. 109–12; 12, pp. 199–202; 13, p. 473; 14, pp. 464–6. Other letters of A.F.Y.: XXIX (1813), p. 390 – Admiralty administration; pp. 399–402 – punishments; pp. 475–7 – chaplains; XXX (1813): pp. 51f. – chaplains; pp. 130, 136–8 – Admiralty matters; pp. 310–12 – maritime rights; pp. 405–6 – abuse of authority (response to Hodgskin – see p. 157 n. 30 above); pp. 480–4 – professional thinking; XXXI (1814): p. 36 – administrative matters.

44 Pamphlets: C. V. Penrose, *A Short Address to the Unlearned on the Advantage of Possessing the Holy Scriptures, and the Best Use to be Made of that Possession* (Bodmin, 1820); 'A Real Friend to British Seamen' [C. V. Penrose], *A Friendly Address to the Seamen of the British Navy* (Bodmin, 1820); C. V. Penrose, *Observations on Corporal Punishment, Impressment and Other Matters* (Bodmin, 1824); 'An old Member of the Establishment' [C. V. Penrose], *The Danger of the Church Considered* (1829); C. V. Penrose, *Observations on the Impressment of Seamen, on the Means of Manning the Navy generally, and the Means whereby Desertion and Discontent may be Best Obviated* (Bodmin, 1824).

45 *NC*, XX (1808), p. 23.

believe that time-honoured methods had to change, partly because the character of sailors had changed as well. Now (1808) they were better educated than their predecessors of a generation earlier, and much more inclined to debate the rights and wrongs of all measures; it would be possible to appeal more often to their minds, for the sailor constantly demanded to be 'treated like a man'. Thus led, happy ships' companies would respond loyally, whereas discontented men had to be driven.[46]

An appealingly recurrent feature of Penrose's philosophy is the need for mutual respect. Every member of the crew must be able to look to his commanding officer for just treatment and active kindness. This did not mean that a captain should court popularity by lax discipline, but he should seek to earn the loyal regard of his men. 'I am so far fond of popularity', he wrote, 'that I could not for a moment feel easy if I thought any man under my command could with justice accuse me of having acted injuriously or unkindly towards him.'[47] At each stage of his career, before gaining promotion from midshipman, lieutenant or commander, an officer should have adequate experience of leading men, learning how to get the best from them, and recognising the difference between strict and harsh discipline. Lieutenants must learn how to command by first learning to obey orders cheerfully. Officers generally must be careful not to speak disrespectfully of their seniors: their flimsy canvas cabins are not castles, and comments spoken apparently in private will assuredly find their way onto the lower deck. But the same spirit of courtesy must work from senior to junior – and in his first letter he took a swipe at the tone of correspondence which had begun to emanate from the Admiralty itself: 'I fancy it must have been under the administration of a naval earl, that it became a custom to write such letters or orders to admirals and captains as would not have been seemly if coming from a boatswain's mate to a sweeper.'[48]

In his second letter he addressed the question of shore leave. The accepted view of quarterdeck officers (as we have seen) was that to give men shore leave was to invite them to disappear; in consequence sailors were sometimes confined between the planks of their own ship for months and even years at a stretch – away from home and loved ones, and denied the pleasures of the shore. Like Duncan, Penrose felt deeply the injustice of this – as had the Spithead mutineers. Leave should be an entitlement; sailors thus treated would respond with loyalty – and he could quote his experience with the *Cleopatra* to prove it.[49]

[46] *NC*, XIX (1808), p. 384.
[47] *NC*, XXI (1809), p. 109.
[48] *NC*, XIX (1808), p. 196.
[49] *NC*, XIX (1808), p. 286.

It was not simply that sailors did not know when they might be allowed leave: they did not have any idea how long their total service might be. Penrose favoured a system of limited service which would tell the sailor how long he had to serve, and would let the naval authorities know how many men they had. In this way the 'ever hateful, however unfortunately necessary tyranny of the impress' could be ended.[50] Duncan had said much the same thing privately to the Admiralty, but now in 1809 Penrose was bringing the matter into public debate. He proposed that increased pay and advantages should be awarded after seven years' service, with pensions payable to all who survived to the end of the war.

Somehow the navy had to be made more attractive to real seamen who were invariably good hands when enlisted. Penrose warned that it would be disastrous to revert to the disgraceful manning methods of the Quota Acts, when the 'off-scourings of jails and the refuse of the parishes' (as he described them) were forced into the fleet.[51] He reverted to the same topic in 1824, when he lamented the failure of the registry proposals to attract enough interest and called for an enquiry to establish a better system of manning. Amongst his writings there is an insistent note that sailors' rights should be respected: in the Royal Navy seamen should continue to be allowed to choose their own ship and commander; in the merchant service, he believed it was wrong for crews to be discharged when ships came into port to unload, with prime seamen simply put on the beach unwanted and unprovided for. In the high Victorian era the navy found the nearest it came to a solution, with the introduction of the Continuous Service contract – general service ratings who went where they were sent. That ended the old 'hire and discharge' pattern for the fleet. Penrose had not foreseen the career RN bluejacket, but he had recognised the injustice and inefficiency of making sailors unemployed at the end of a voyage – when they became easy prey for the crimps and land sharks.[52]

One of his most important contributions to the manning debate was his emphasis on what the navy had to do to make itself attractive. He believed that the great mutinies had been caused by unnecessary harshness: well-handled crews had no objection to the strictness of discipline required afloat. Several of his letters highlighted the need for humane treatment. No man, he urged, should be flogged for a first offence. When faced with someone who was not an habitual offender, captains should make wider use of a free pardon or a conditional

---

[50] *NC*, XXI (1809), pp. 199–201 (Letter 12).
[51] Ibid. Probably an unfair judgement.
[52] Ibid.; Penrose, *Observations*, p. 34.

again. Any concern for human welfare should include the spiritual. This is familiar Blue Light territory, but Penrose moved strongly towards a fresh understanding of evangelism. He was working out how to appeal to the unchurched. He wanted to see minds educated to consider the demands of Christianity, through 'rational' enquiry into biblical faith. Unlike Kempenfelt, he did not treat religion as the way to make men moral, but as something owed to men because they had immortal souls. His proposals assumed that human beings are capable of moral behaviour because moral consciousness is part of being man. The navy owed its men better treatment because that was just, and not because it would improve their conduct or make them religious.

Two more recommendations show the drift of his thinking about spiritual matters. First, the chaplain should be given choice of cabin, so that he may position himself where anyone, officer or foremast hand, could most readily approach him. Penrose wanted to give the chaplain the role of a confidential pastor and counsellor, a welfare officer accessible to all, a view completely at variance with the concept of the captain's friend. In fact, this is the way in which the chaplain's branch evolved – and the 1868 *Regulations* about cabins as interpreted in an Admiralty Circular of 1870, practically used Penrose's wording as well as his idea. Secondly, he warned against compelling attendance at too many services, but advocated more voluntary gatherings.[58]

He was not suggesting that compulsory worship should be abandoned: quite the contrary. There should be an obligatory service every Sunday, and on Christmas Day and Good Friday; there should be daily prayers in the sick berth, and twice daily in the gunroom (where the young gentlemen berthed). Penrose was calling for no less than the existing *Regulations* demanded. For many decades to come, the navy would use compulsory religion to affirm group values. Public services based on the Book of Common Prayer took Anglican beliefs for granted, making no concessions for Catholics, dissenters, Jews, or adherents of other religions, and used inclusive wording for collective prayers ('Our Father …', 'O Lord, we beseech Thee …'). Effective sermons also aimed for general acceptance by drawing in their hearers. With this in mind, Broke of the *Shannon* made manuscript

[58] The chaplain's cabin should be placed 'so that he may have free intercourse with any of the ship's company who may wish to consult him or request his prayers or advice on particular occasions': *NC*, xx (1808), p. 298. Cf. Admiralty letter dated 24 Feb 1871, referring to Circular of 21 October 1870: 'as the object of giving the chaplain the first choice of cabin after the Senior Executive and Navigating Officers is that he may select that best suited for enabling the Ship's company to consult him without being exposed to unnecessary publicity, this principle is … to govern the selection of those cabins.' Kealy, p. 19.

amendments to Stanier Clarke's addresses, replacing the pointed 'you' and 'your' with the more welcoming and inclusive 'we' and 'our'.[59]

The new note that Penrose strikes is his suggestion for voluntary gatherings beyond the routine for 'those who can and choose to attend'.[60] He was thinking of optional daily prayers and Sunday afternoon meetings where more good might be achieved than by any amount of compulsion. In a voluntary gathering a chaplain might raise more direct and challenging personal issues, and could answer doubts and questions. This was a promising vehicle for evangelism and for nurturing discipleship – as Lieutenant Marks was discovering in the *Conqueror*.

Whereas the Blue Lights had once looked on the navy as the Church maritime, they were coming to see the true situation – that committed believers were scattered through a fleet which was effectively an unevangelised mission field. Penrose had come to appreciate the limitations of the old Blue Light approach and had taken the first steps towards voluntarism. By stimulating discussion over the place of religion and the rationale of reform he contributed to the evolving ethos of both the Blue Lights and the wider naval profession.

---

[59] Padfield, *Broke and the Shannon*, p. 222 and photo following p. 62.

[60] *NC*, xx (1808), p. 298.

VI

The Impact of Evangelical Enthusiasm on Fighting Determination: Quarter-Deck or Organ Loft

Questioning the Professional Competence of the Blue Lights

IN his authoritative history *The Sea Chaplains*, Gordon Taylor states that 'Evangelical enthusiasm sometimes caused an officer's fighting determination to be questioned', and to support this view he quotes from an article published in *The Gentleman's Magazine*, applauding the dismissal of certain officers who were 'more fitted for the organ-loft than the quarter-deck'.[1] Since Blue Lights held senior positions on active service in wartime, the issue needs careful examination, as failure in this regard would have cost them the respect of their profession.

Duncan's hour of glory had come in the French Revolutionary War, but he was too elderly for further service when the peace broke down. The fighting reputation of the Blue Lights passed to others during the Napoleonic War, when three held fleet commands – Saumarez, Pellew and Gambier – and at least three more were captains well known for their combat record. If Taylor is right – and we must return to that question later – was the supposed hostility to evangelicals based on fact or prejudice? Much of the controversy focuses on one man, Gambier, and one action, the Basque Roads (1809), but it would be unjust to pass over the services of his fellow-religionists, beginning with the most distinguished of them – James, Lord de Saumarez, Admiral of the Red and the first Guernseyman to be raised to the peerage.[2]

Sir James Saumarez as Commander-in-Chief

WHEN war resumed, Sir James Saumarez as a rear admiral had responsibility for the sea-borne defence of his native Channel Islands, with a small squadron to protect British trade, intercept French commerce, and raid possible enemy invasion forces in Saint-Malo and Granville harbours. In 1807 St Vincent asked for him to become his second-in-command, but by this time the aged earl was not well enough to serve at sea, so the daily responsibility for the Channel Fleet devolved upon Saumarez, with his vice-admiral's flag flying first in the *San*

---

[1] Taylor, p. 239, quoting from *The Gentleman's Magazine*, 1830, II, pp. 242f.

[2] For Saumarez's details, see p. 124 n. 33 above.

Josef and then in the *Prince of Wales* (Captain William Bedford), blockading Brest. These were waters he knew well, and he showed his usual skills of seamanship in the dangerous tidal conditions around the Channel Islands and off the coast of Brittany. Then came the senior appointment which was the climax of his naval career.

In 1808 he was appointed commander-in-chief in the Baltic. For the next four years, when spring brought clear water and renewed trade, he sailed through the Skagerrak, with his flag in the *Victory*, and took up anchorage at Vinga Sound off Gothenburg. It was a strange calling for a fighting admiral, for he was now to be more diplomat than warrior. He was the ideal choice; bilingual in French and English, never given to precipitate words or actions, restrained, dignified and known for his integrity, Saumarez piloted his course through the murky intricacies of Baltic politics with as much skill as he managed his extended floating command. National interest was now focused on the Peninsula, where Wellington was making a name for himself and his army. Baltic affairs appeared peripheral to the great events in central Europe, where Napoleon by turns was master or fighting off challenges to his hegemony. In fact this unglamorous and now largely forgotten posting was central to Britain's survival.

After Trafalgar the Emperor had been forced to admit the truth of what his admirals had long been telling him. Despite the arithmetic, which added up the ships of France, Spain, Holland and Denmark, and made the total superior to Britain's tally, Napoleon's naval power was inferior. When he found that he could not break the British blockade, his strategy turned from invasion plans to economics. If he could bring about the ruination of British business, there would be two effects: an English economy drained of money would be unable to finance European coalitions against France, and trading interests shorn of profits would demand peace on Napoleon's terms. In the Emperor's mind it had become a plan to use the power of the land to win at sea: his soldiers and diplomats would secure the closure of all Europe's ports to British trade. This was the Continental System, enforced by the Milan and Berlin Decrees. The British Government countered by Orders in Council which prohibited neutral traffic with any port closed to English ships. Blockade and System together brought hardship to the people of Europe, and gave both sides opportunity for diplomatic leverage.

In 1807, fearing that Napoleon would seize the Danish fleet, the British Government made a pre-emptive attack on neutral Copenhagen. It succeeded in acquiring those ships, but at the cost of Denmark's open hostility. Moreover Russian pride and fears were kindled, making it all the easier for Napoleon to bring Tsar Alexander into the Treaty of Tilsit, which closed Russian harbours to British trade. On the other hand, the austerities forced upon trading communities by the

10 Vice-Admiral James Saumarez (1757–1836). An accomplished captain of both frigates and ships of the line, he achieved particular distinction as commander-in-chief of the Baltic theatre 1808–12, and was the first Guernseyman to be raised to the peerage. (Oil painting by Edwin Williams)   © National Maritime Museum, London BHC3010

Napoleonic System were always resented by European merchants, and Britain tried to exploit such grievances. When Napoleon tried to enforce his Decrees upon Portugal, Lisbon revived its ancient friendship with Britain, and Napoleon's efforts to control the whole Iberian peninsula ignited a popular insurgency and guerrilla struggle which he never overcame.

The Baltic was a crucially important area. Its naval stores were essential to Britain – timber (other than English-grown oak), hemp for cordage, flax for canvas, Stockholm pitch and tar. In return it was a market for British products, and a mutually important and lucrative trade existed with Russia, Prussia, Sweden and Denmark. The Napoleonic System threatened British trade and prosperity: by 1812 prices of bread in Britain had reached almost famine levels. But in the process the livelihood of many of Napoleon's reluctant subjects was gravely injured, and, despite the penalties, they were strongly tempted to break his trade embargo. Napoleon had decreed that Europe's ports should be sealed against English goods: Saumarez was sent to the Baltic to see whether he could prise them open. It needed more than simple force: it required diplomatic gifts of a high order, combined with endless patience and unsleeping vigilance. He had to be prepared to see below the surface of events, to distinguish between words or actions to pacify the Emperor and those designed to harm Britain.

His exercise of the Baltic command from 1808 to 1812 is a textbook example of the pressure which seapower could exert in the days of sail. It was a war of small ships, with coastal traffic to be interrupted and prizes to be taken. There were British and allied merchantmen to be protected from privateers and enemy cruisers. Always the battlefleet had to be there to shelter the light forces from interference by enemy major units. This year's friend might be next year's foe, and *vice versa*. By turns the Swedes, Prussians and Russians were enemies and allies. Britain's force in the Baltic was visible proof of her commitment to the powers of the Third and Fourth Coalition against Napoleon, and the route whereby treasure or supplies could be sent to her allies. When Sweden was forced into a show of belligerence, Saumarez wisely held his hand – and so enabled Bernadotte to join the anti-Napoleonic league in due course. For three years Sweden was technically at war with Britain, but by maintaining personal contact with Stockholm and refraining from provocative action, Saumarez preserved peaceful relations and kept the essential Baltic trade flowing. Later the Swedes described Saumarez as their country's guardian angel: if he had fired a shot against the Swedish flag they could never have switched sides so deftly.[3]

It was Sweden which particularly esteemed the Channel Islander and rewarded

---

[3] Baron Platen to Saumarez, (probably) Nov 1812, Ross, II, p. 293.

him with one of their country's highest honours, but Russia should rightly have recognised him too. It was the presence of the British fleet in the Baltic year by year, gathering a huge flock of merchant ships for escorted convoy to British markets, which gave Russian traders their opportunity to break free of Napoleon's restrictions, and it therefore played a part in Alexander's decision to break with the French alliance in 1812. This was the pivotal moment for Napoleon: once he pitched the *grande armée* against Russia with all her resources of manpower, distances and weather, his System was doomed. It took time for the Napoleonic Empire to crumble, but the process was irreversible thereafter. Saumarez eased the path for Russian defection, together with Swedish and Prussian desertion of the French cause. Although he had returned home to Guernsey by the time Ney's rearguard was crossing the River Beresina and Napoleon's Russian campaign ended in disaster, Saumarez's great work had been accomplished.

It was not a spectacular theatre of war for the navy, and he had to wait until 1830 before his services were recognised with a peerage. It is possible that the long delay in awarding him a barony represented some official disapproval of his religious scruples, as his biographer surmised. The given reason was that his flag had not been flying when peace came, but that seems less plausible than Ross's further explanation – that he had no political ambitions and would have given no support to Lord Liverpool's ministry at Westminster, unlike Sir Edward Pellew, who was given preference. There might have been a further consideration: the name of Saumarez was linked with the greatest British maritime disaster of the French Revolutionary and Napoleonic Wars, the loss of three capital ships and 2,000 lives. HM Ships *St George*, *Defence* and *Hero* were wrecked in atrocious weather conditions on Christmas Eve 1811 while returning from the Baltic under the direction of Saumarez. Even though the personal judgement and conduct of the commander-in-chief could not seriously be challenged by those fully acquainted with the details, his association with the catastrophe made it easier for his services to be overlooked when peacetime honours were distributed. His subsequent post as commander-in-chief at Plymouth was largely honorary, and his rank as general of marines entirely so – the Admiralty's way of rewarding particularly distinguished service.[4]

Enough has been said already to show that his outward serenity was won in conflict with other, more turbulent emotions. The touchiness, the over-sensitivity to matters of honour, the ambition for recognition are seen as blemishes on his character, but they were perfectly well understood in his own day, and regarded as

---

[4] Ross, II, pp. 299–302, 306f., 310; A. N. Ryan, 'The Melancholy Fate of the Baltic Ships in 1811', *MM*, L (1964), pp. 123–34.

admirable rather than reprehensible in the officer corps. Whatever struggles he may have had in his own soul, his subordinates saw the public display of a man at peace with himself. Officers who had served with him in times of stress found him a man of rock-like confidence. Yet they also observed a man of extraordinary gentleness. They remembered how he had worked hard and successfully to rehabilitate a former mutineer, and they knew that he had encouraged his chaplain to act as a welfare officer for the lower deck, welcome to speak in favour of defaulters. His family recalled his efforts to pacify a pair of duellists, and his composure when his jewelled insignia of the Bath was lost through a servant's carelessness. He was keen to bring the Christian message to sailors and to the whole unevangelised world: it was natural that he should become a generous supporter of missions, both SPG and CMS. To the NMBS he was perhaps the beau ideal of the Christian warrior, untainted by failings in character or professional performance.[5]

The biographer Ross, once his flag lieutenant in the Baltic, claimed that Saumarez had been in more actions than any other officer during thirty years at sea. The statement would be hard to prove, but he had certainly achieved an extraordinary record. To have commanded a ship of the line in three major battles, the Saints, St Vincent and the Nile; to have taken an enemy frigate without suffering loss; to have handled the inshore squadron with unfailing skill; to have gained success as an admiral in the battles off Gibraltar, and finally to have served with skill verging on brilliance in the troubled Baltic – these are remarkable services. Here, in one man's career, is adequate rebuttal of the 'organ-loft' canard.[6]

Sir Edward Pellew (1757–1833) as Commander-in-Chief

IN 1804 Pellew became an admiral and was sent as commander-in-chief to the East Indies for five years, a vast and complex responsibility, with British trade to safeguard against French raiders and Chinese pirates, operations to secure Dutch possessions and even a sideshow to conduct in Chinese waters. English politics added to the complications, when Addington demanded a lucrative position to reward Admiral Troubridge for his loyalty to St Vincent, and as a consequence Pellew's command was split for reasons that made no operational sense. Pellew was enraged at the folly of it and resisted handing over the designated share to Troubridge, whose fury in turn seems to have badly distorted his professional

---

[5] Brief contemporary memoirs of Saumarez in *NC*, VI (1801) pp. 85–116, and *The United Service Journal* [hereafter *USJ*] (1836), pp. 524–30. Kindness to mutineer, *NC*, VI, p. 102; Ross, II, pp. 317, 320–30. Anon., 'Memoir of the late Lord de Saumarez', *Guernsey and Jersey Magazine*, Nov 1836, pp. 298–324. References amongst family papers in Priaulx Library, Guernsey.

[6] Ross, I, p. 6.

judgement. When at last the home Government saw sense and recalled Troubridge to the Cape he impulsively and imprudently set sail for his new command in a dangerously unseaworthy ship, which sank with all hands on passage to Cape Town. Pellew's career continued to prosper. Under his direction British ships crushed Dutch resistance at Batavia and captured Java in 1807. He made a fortune out of prize money, for a C-in-C was entitled to a cut of every vessel taken and sold. Money meant a lot to Pellew, perhaps reflecting the insecurities of his youth, when at the age of eight he had lost his father. It is difficult to know whether he was avaricious, as opposed to properly ambitious for fortune and family. Certainly he looked out for his brother and his two sons, who were advanced with scandalous speed under their father's patronage. Both were lieutenants before their sixteenth birthdays; Pownall was made post at age nineteen, Fleetwood when still eighteen. Although the times he lived in recognised the justice of interest, these are instances of sheer nepotism which conferred rank before responsibility had been properly learned: Pownall never really shone, and the Admiralty had to remove Fleetwood after he crushed a mutiny with excessive severity.[7]

After returning from the East Sir Edward Pellew was allowed a year ashore before being appointed to the Mediterranean command 1811–14, where he displayed his characteristic grip on operations by keeping the Toulon fleet bottled up – and by exchanging gunfire in the last fleet manœuvres of the war, as the French contrived to slip a new warship into port in February 1814. It was fitting that he should have ended the war a commander-in-chief, for he had captured the first French prize taken in a frigate action way back in 1793. When Napoleon abdicated and peace returned, he was raised to the peerage as Lord Exmouth, a distinction well earned by his many years of service, but a source of anguish for Saumarez, who was already smarting with indignation at the Government's failure to honour him. This elevation of a more junior admiral only emphasised the injustice. Some discerning officers shared this view, and Byam Martin expressed that opinion in a letter to Saumarez on 10 May 1814:

> Sir Edward Pellew is most deservedly esteemed as an active, zealous, intrepid seaman, but his pretensions on the score of battles fought bear no comparison with those who, like yourself, were conspicuous in the great

---

[7] For details of Pellew's career, see p. 132 n. 42 above. His father was master of a Post Office packet. Account of *Dutton* rescue in Mahan, pp. 452–4. Pownoll Bastard Pellew: b. 1 Jul 1786; lieut. 9 Apr 1802, cdr. 1804, post 22 Jan 1806; assumed title as 2nd Viscount 1833; died 2 Dec 1833. Fleetwood Pellew: b. 13 Dec 1789; entered RN Mar 1799, lieut. 8 Sep 1805, cdr. 1807, post 14 Oct 1808, rear adm. 1846, CB 1815, KCH 1836; d. 28 Jul 1861.

actions of the 12th of April, 14th of February, the Nile, at Algeciras ... In short it has been Sir Edward's misfortune never to be in action in a ship of the line. If he had none would have been more distinguished.[8]

Herein lies the awkwardness between the two admirals, and the explanation for the coldness noted by Northcote Parkinson: Exmouth can hardly be blamed for accepting an honour from the Government, and if Saumarez's jealousy kept them apart, it still owed more to his perception of injustice than to personal rancour. Ross records how the two men met at Plymouth, apparently in a gesture of personal rapprochement, when Saumarez succeeded Exmouth as Port Admiral in 1824.[9]

Fairly justifiably, critics accused Pellew of greed and nepotism, but more doubtfully of over-severity on the basis of his handling of the Bantry Bay affair in 1799 – already noted. As commander-in-chief of the East Indies Fleet, however, he was responsible for one of the most progressive reforms of his time, by requiring every captain to submit a quarterly return of all serious punishments: by these means he monitored the way his ships were disciplined, and could check abuses of authority. The Admiralty was quick to appreciate the potential here for wise regulation, and extended the practice to every ship, with returns to be made to the Board. It then became possible to compare ship with ship, and to shame the over-harsh into gentler methods of control.[10]

While in the East Indies Pellew was responsible for having 700 copies of the Scriptures supplied by the NMBS, of whom he became a strong supporter. Later he became a Vice-President and, like Saumarez, a speaker at their annual meeting. He gave opportunity to his civilian secretary, Edward Hawke Locker, to exercise a lay ministry in the flagship by giving voluntary lectures on Bible and liturgy in the gunroom, a further example of the way in which the new piety was spreading through informal off-duty gatherings. In a private letter of 1807 Pellew described his faith to a friend: 'God has been merciful to a miserable sinner; in shame I say it, I have been a wicked fellow – more by constitution than in heart, I hope; long have I repented, although I dare not look up with one atom of confidence but through the mediation of my blessed Saviour whose blood has been shed for the propitiation of all our sins.'[11] There it stands, the same faith of the Blue Lights,

[8] Martin to Saumarez, 10 May 1814, Ipswich Records HA 93 6/1/2450.

[9] Parkinson, *Edward Pellew*, p. 411; Ross, II, p. 309.

[10] Laughton in *DNB* noted the importance of punishment returns.

[11] Pellew to Alexander Broughton, Madras 22 Jul 1807, in Parkinson, *Edward Pellew*, p. 376. Bibles for Pellew's East Indies fleet, *NMBS* 1808, p. 21, 1809, p. 21; subscriber of 20 guineas, 1809, NMBS vice president 1815, life member 1817; quoted at 1836 anniversary meeting, p. 27.

with assurance of peace with God through the substitutionary and atoning death of Christ, the only hope for sinful mankind.

When did he come to adopt such a clear faith? As early as September 1793 he had asked the SPCK for a supply of literature for his frigate *La Nymphe*, and received the usual scale for a complement of 260 men – a large Bible, prayer book and eighty psalters for use in public worship, with a further twelve small Bibles and eighty *Seaman's Monitors*, possibly for distribution amongst the messes. So far, there is little to distinguish his religion from that of many of his fellow commanding officers. His biographer states that he was probably a High Churchman who became friendly with the Evangelical vicar of Charles Church, Plymouth, Dr Robert Hawker (1753–1827). Pellew and his wife had been dining with him on the evening of the *Dutton* exploit. It is easy to see why the two men might have been drawn together, for Hawker had naval links: he was married to the daughter of a naval commander, and before his ordination he had served as an assistant surgeon in the Marines for three years. Since 1797 he had been deputy chaplain to the military garrison of Plymouth. His interest in the evangelisation of servicemen drew him later into writing tracts for sailors. Whether or not Hawker was instrumental in awakening Pellew's 'vital faith', his Christianity becomes more prominent from this period, as witnessed by his membership of the NMBS, his Bible distribution to the East Indies Fleet, and the freedom he gave his secretary to develop lay ministry to seamen.[12]

Although war against Napoleon ended at Waterloo, Pellew's skill in fighting had a final demonstration in 1816. Reappointed commander-in-chief in the Mediterranean, he was charged with the bombardment of Algiers, the destruction of the Algerine corsair ships and gun batteries, and the liberation of 3,000 Christian slaves. The operation did not call for the ship-handling skills for which he was famous, but it required careful placing of the bombarding vessels with a high degree of determination and courage on the part of all participants from the admiral down: he was just as much at personal risk as any sailor in the fleet. He deserved his viscountcy.

---

[12] SPCK Minutes, XXXI, p. 176. Although a renowned Calvinist theologian, Hawker upset the Clapham Evangelicals by refusing to preach the need for holiness of life. Wilberforce regarded his doctrines as poisonous [*BDEB*, I, pp. 537f.]. William Hawke Locker was a civilian layman, private secretary to Pellew, and staunch supporter of the new piety in the navy, even if technically not an Evangelical: he expressed misgivings to his fiancée about her views, which he feared were becoming 'Huntingdonian': Locker-Lampson Papers, Lewes Records III 49 (1), letter dated 13 Aug 1823. Locker gave lectures on the Bible and theology to the ship's company of Pellew's flagship *Culloden*.

Pellew was perhaps a less complex man than either Saumarez or Gambier, more obviously the warlike sailor and less the deep thinker. While not so well known as a Blue Light, he showed himself, like them, a friend to Bible distribution, to lower-deck religion and to disciplinary reforms. His faith did not cancel out his professionalism nor did it diminish his standing in a fighting service. The same might be said of several officers, less conspicuous perhaps but still with a high reputation – men like Brenton, Hillyar and Austen. Even quite open piety was no automatic bar to advancement if accompanied by evident competence.

Captain Jahleel Brenton (1770–1844)

JAHLEEL Brenton, brother of the historian Edward, was born in Rhode Island in 1770, the son of a loyalist admiral whose property was sequestrated during the American Revolution. It was not until his thirties that he could confidently align himself with an evangelical faith. He entered the navy as a midshipman in 1781, during the American War, and then served for a while in the Swedish navy. Commissioned lieutenant in 1790, he was in the *Barfleur* at the Battle of Cape St Vincent and was promoted commander in 1799. In the brig *Speedy* (later to be made famous by Lord Cochrane) he made a name for himself by saving his own ship and the one he was escorting when attacked by twelve Spanish gunboats off Gibraltar, a feat which earned Nelson's praise and post rank in April 1800. High points of his career included serving in the *Caesar* as flag captain to Saumarez at Algeciras in 1801. After the initial reverse in which the *Hannibal* had been lost and the squadron damaged in an unsuccessful operation close inshore, Saumarez withdrew to Gibraltar to refit. His ship appeared too damaged to remain as squadron flagship, but Brenton inspired quite extraordinary exertions from her crew and dockyard staff working in continuous shifts day and night to get her ready. So when Saumarez sailed five days after his original defeat to take on the much larger Franco-Spanish fleet, the *Caesar* was still his flagship and Brenton his flag captain. Two years later he experienced defeat (but not disgrace) when his frigate *La Minerve* ran aground in fog under the gun batteries off Cherbourg and surrendered after a spirited ten-hour defence.[13]

As a senior captain he had considerable responsibility for British prisoners of war, first on their march to captivity and then in the prison fortresses of north-eastern France. On the journey he usually travelled a day ahead of the main party to make arrangements for their accommodation, or else a day behind caring for

---

[13] Although the *Speedy* was made famous by Lord Cochrane, it should be noted that when he took command of her in May 1800 he inherited from Brenton a well-trained and enterprising crew already used to performing exploits.

the stragglers and the sick. At Brenton's request, the Rev. Robert Wolfe was sent to Givet, where his ministry sustained morale and discipline to a remarkable degree. We shall consider later what impact this had on lower-deck religion, but for Brenton himself during this period of captivity the effects were life-changing. Ever since serving with Saumarez he had taken religion seriously, but now, with Wolfe's instruction and time to reflect on it, he developed evangelical convictions. The frustrations of two and a half years in captivity ended when he was exchanged for a nephew of Marshal Massena.

Back in the navy, he was given a fresh command, the new frigate *Spartan* (38). He collaborated with Cochrane in the *Impérieuse* to devise several daring onshore raids in the Languedoc area, to destroy French military facilities such as barracks and signal post, and so to disrupt enemy coastal traffic. A hard-fought action off Naples in May 1810 earned him a baronetcy for seeing off two frigates, two small brigs and a pack of gunboats, with heavy damage and the loss of a brig on the French side. Brenton was wounded badly enough to be lame for the rest of his life. He became commissioner at Port Mahon in 1813 and then spent eight years at the Cape, before becoming lieutenant governor at Greenwich in 1831.

In his personal life Brenton had experienced difficulty and loss which deepened his sympathy with sufferers. He lost his first wife and son within a short time of each other. His smashed hip gave him a lifelong battle with pain. The failure of his agent and loss of prize claims led to a spell of bankruptcy. He supported his brother Edward – naval captain and historian – in a charitable scheme to settle homeless boys in South Africa, but it was inadequately financed and collapsed amidst allegations of scandal. Through it all his faith grew stronger, and gave him an appreciation of life's burdens for the disadvantaged. He was particularly concerned for shipwrecked and destitute sailors, for juvenile delinquents, for victims of the slave trade, and for emancipated but still impoverished Africans. During his time at the Cape, he became aware of the spiritual needs of the Hottentot peoples and urged the Church of England to evangelise them.[14]

---

[14] Rev. Henry Raikes (ed.), *Memoir of the Life and Services of Vice-Admiral Sir Jahleel Brenton* (1846), abridged by his son Sir Charles Brenton (1855). See also Michael A. Lewis, *Napoleon and his British Captives* (1962), and *Dillon*, II, pp. 38–56 *passim*. Edward Pelham Brenton: b. 1774, entered RN 1788, lieut. 1795, cdr. 1802, post Dec 1808; author of *Naval History of Great Britain from 1783–1822*, 2 vols. (1823), and *The Life and Correspondence of John, Earl of St Vincent* (1838); d. 1839. Jahleel wrote *The Memoir of Captain Edward Pelham Brenton* in 1842 to defend his brother's reputation.

Amidst all his other concerns, sailors figured prominently, and he became an effective advocate for their welfare. *An Appeal to the British Nation on Behalf of her Sailors* combined a sympathetic character sketch with insight into the deprivations many suffered. In *The Hope of the Navy* he looked to Christianity as the best influence for reforming men and their communal life. In the naval profession these views gained authority from his reputation for compassion and courage, but their credibility would have lessened if his 'fighting determination' had ever been in doubt.[15]

Captains James Hillyar (1769–1843) and Francis Austen (1774–1865)

ANOTHER well-known frigate captain was James Hillyar. He joined the navy in 1779, being first taken to sea by his father, a surgeon, after the early death of his mother. Hillyar served in the American War, and was commissioned lieutenant in 1794. He fought at Toulon and in the Battle of the Glorious First of June. He earned post rank for his work in the Egyptian campaign of 1801, when he played a notably courageous part in the boat operations to put the British land forces ashore under fire. Lacking personal means to support the dignity of a post captain he declined to advance beyond commander's rank until 1804; thereafter he saw more war service in the Baltic, East Indies, Java and Mauritius. Appointed to command of the frigate *Phoebe* by Saumarez in 1809, he was still with her in 1813 when sent to the Pacific to prevent American raiding against British whale fisheries. Engaging the US frigate *Essex* (Captain David Porter) off Valparaiso, he captured her after a gallant action. One of his midshipmen, Allen Francis Gardiner (1794–1851), helped to bring the prize into port, and subsequently earned tragic fame for himself as a pioneer missionary to Tierra del Fuego. Hillyar's career prospered in the slightly patchy style typical of the post-war era, when post captains were plentiful but ships scarce. He commanded ships of the line, was knighted twice and gained his flag in 1837.[16]

It is not clear when Hillyar's faith developed, but he appears to have been a practising Evangelical by the time he took command of the *Phoebe*. At the NMBS anniversary in 1837 the newly promoted admiral described how the long pursuit of the *Essex* (6,000 miles of the Pacific after rounding Cape Horn) was turned to

---

[15] Published 1838 and 1839, when he was Lt-Governor at Greenwich Hospital.

[16] See *DNB*; W. O'Byrne, *A Naval Biographical Dictionary* (1849), p. 516, and *USJ*, 1842, Part 3, pp. 271–85. Rodger, *Command of the Ocean*, p. 519, mentions Hillyar as an example of an officer who declined promotion because he could not risk being unemployed in a higher rank. Eldest son of a naval surgeon, he lacked financial means, and was supporting his mother and sisters out of his pay; otherwise he could have been made post in 1803.

advantage. He invited his sailors to improve themselves. Men who could not read were given elementary literacy classes with letters formed from sand on the deck. Sixty men could not say the Lord's Prayer, and presumably they were given the chance to learn, but there seems no way of knowing if instruction was voluntary. Capable men were encouraged to learn navigation, with the result that one man earned promotion to master on returning to England, and three others obtained their own commands. Hillyar believed that these schemes of religious and general education had helped morale and improved the conduct of the crew; on the strength of his experiences he ventured to suggest that a man-of-war might be the best school of reform in existence. Presumably with his approval, a group of sailors met regularly for prayer under the leadership of a marine, generating a further wholesome influence on the lower deck as membership grew to about twenty. Nonetheless Hillyar was aware that all these gains for religion and morality could be snatched away by a fortnight's stay in a British port. This was fast becoming evangelical territory after the war. The disciplined environment of a warship could produce upright conduct so long as it was in place, but no work of reformation could last in isolation: more than just the navy had to change. There was no logical place to rest until the whole seaport culture had been healed of its vices.[17]

In a gesture reminiscent of Duncan and Saumarez, Hillyar called on his men to unite in prayer before battle. Like other Blue Lights he was a staunch supporter and eventually committee member of the NMBS, appealing to his colleagues to give the Word of God to seamen: 'why should not they be taught how they might be accepted of God through Jesus Christ, the Saviour of the World?', he was asking in 1837.[18] Again in line with other Evangelicals he would rebuke profanity. He was a greatly loved commander with a high reputation for humanity, according to the obituary published in the *United Service Journal*, which noted his reluctance to order flogging (quite an issue by 1842) and how keen he was to support institutions that relieved suffering. In personality he was warm tempered, but never one to nurse his anger; he was a conciliator who followed the biblical principle of not allowing the sun to go down on his wrath. The man's religious conviction was evident as 'the main spring – the actuating principle that moved him – the foundation on which all his virtues were built'. And as for the content of his faith, that was equally clear: 'on the merits of Christ his Saviour alone did he rest for salvation; and in prayer through Him to the throne of grace did he close his days on earth.'[19]

[17] *NMBS* 1837, pp. 20f.; 1840, p. 22.
[18] *NMBS* 1837, p. 20.
[19] *USJ*, 1842, Part 3, pp. 271–85.

Another Blue Light was Francis Austen (1774–1865), whose sister was making a name for herself as a novelist. Commissioned in 1792, he was made post in 1800 as reward for a spirited action in the Mediterranean when his sloop the *Peterel* chased and captured the French brig *La Ligurienne* with no British casualties. His first service in this rank was as flag captain to Gambier, who was rather distantly related to him by marriage. Was the appointment made because of the family link or on the basis of shared convictions? Alternatively, perhaps this was the period when his evangelicalism developed. As flag captain to Rear Admiral Louis in the *Canopus*, Austen took part in Nelson's pursuit of Villeneuve to the West Indies and in the subsequent blockade of Cadiz. To his lasting regret, the Battle of Trafalgar took place while he and the rest of Louis's squadron were away replenishing stores. The next year however he had his part in a fleet action, when Duckworth's action off San Domingo in 1806 eliminated Leissègues's squadron and resulted in three prizes brought home and two ships of the line destroyed. Thereafter he commanded the *St Albans* (64) and was employed several times on convoy escort duties between 1807 and 1810, before becoming flag captain once again to Gambier in the *Caledonia* (December 1810 to May 1811). When Gambier hauled down his flag, Austen became captain of the 74-gun *Elephant* serving in the Baltic. The end of the war brought him thirty years of life ashore until appointed commander-in-chief of the West Indies and North American station in 1845 for a final three years afloat. Longevity finally raised him to the rank of Admiral of the Fleet in 1863, with a GCB and the honorary appointment of Vice Admiral of the United Kingdom, but these distinctions rewarded his age rather than his services.

For one of Nelson's captains who had fought in a major sea battle of the war, there was something a little lack-lustre about Austen's career. A recent writer has suggested that he suffered from being linked with the unpopular Gambier, and that is why he was appointed to a rather unglamorous 64-gun ship in 1807. This seems implausible, since his patron was in high credit with the administration at the time. Perhaps more to the point was Austen's relative lack of experience in independent command of a capital ship: as flag captain he had been directly under the eye of admirals Gambier and Louis. When he did obtain his own 74-gun ship, his performance gained critical notice from his admiral, Sir George Hope, and from the Admiralty on account of the high number of floggings. The matter calls for closer scrutiny.

If we had only his time in command of the *St Albans* (64) to go on, Austen would be reckoned a mild and humane commander: according to the log book, the punishment grating was rigged on just eight occasions in the course of a whole year, with thirty floggings amassing a total of 510 lashes. For seven of the twelve months there were no logged punishments at all. But when he captained the *Elephant* (74) in 1812–13 the picture changed startlingly. Two periods have been closely examined, a stretch of ten months and two more later by way of comparison: over these twelve months there were 180 floggings and a total of 3,050 lashes, plus one crew member sentenced by court martial to be flogged round the fleet collecting an additional 280 lashes. He had not abandoned his confidence in religion, for nineteen Sundays were marked by divine service, and there were a further sixteen musters when perhaps more or less perfunctory prayers might have featured. What had changed the character of his command and management style so completely, leading to unfavourable notice from his commander-in-chief and from the Admiralty?

In his own defence he explained that two sizeable bodies of men had been drafted into the *Elephant* with no opportunity to develop fresh communal values before the ship deployed on active service. He claimed that there were already endemic problems of drunkenness amongst the new hands. His case is plausible: with 180 men transferred from the *Formidable* and ninety from the *Tigre*, merging with over 300 of the existing crew, Austen confronted three large factions with repeated opportunity for unhealthy rivalry. Furthermore, men drafted from one ship to another were likely to be profoundly resentful, for such methods of manning undermined their traditional rights. Sailors expected to be discharged at the end of a commission with wages in their pocket and time to spend them ashore. The navy's insatiable need for manpower had changed all this. By drafting men to a new ship, the Admiralty took away sailors' customary freedom to choose where they would serve, and it had probably been done without honouring their expectations of leave and full wages. The resultant morale problems would have taxed the ablest commander. Austen strenuously denied that he had acted from caprice or cruelty or that any punishment had been excessive.

The log shows that the ship was beset by offences which were typically punished by flogging – disobedience, insolence, neglect of duty, drunkenness, quarrelling and fighting – and that the sentences awarded of one or two dozen lashes and an occasional thirty-six were in line with the norm. Now and then a single month in the *Elephant* exceeded the annual punishment tally in the *St Albans*. Here was a ship's company with probably years of protracted service behind them and no ready prospect of being paid off, clashing with an equally war-weary captain without (one imagines) enough ingenuity or sense of humour to calm their frustrations. While Austen's record does not prove him a tyrant or an incompetent, it suggests an unimaginative commander without the magnetism of Saumarez or the inspiration of Duncan. Once checked by the Admiralty, Austen gradually reduced those dire figures, suggesting that the ship's company had learned their lesson or that the captain had learned his.[20]

Austen was raised in a country vicarage; although his father was not Evangelical, an uncle was. Maybe this was the source of his own religious leaning, unless perhaps it owed more to Gambier's influence. Father Austen felt close enough to Gambier to importune him on behalf of his sons when Gambier was at the Admiralty in 1798, and Austen acknowledged the debt he owed to the admiral's kindness when writing to Cochrane many years later. By 1803 his piety had attracted attention ashore, and when he obtained his own command he promoted religious observance. In the *St Albans* he used to read sermons at Sunday service, usually from Burder's collection beloved of evangelicals. Prayers were held in the sick bay, and the boys were taught the catechism. On Sunday evening a second service was held, probably a voluntary one for any who cared to attend. The captain's clerk regularly placed fresh supplies of tracts on the messdecks, presumably at Austen's instigation. The disciplinary record suggests a happy ship's company, and after his experience in the *Elephant* he must have looked back on his earlier time in the *St Albans*, not as a frustrating and ignominious period but as a golden period of his naval career. In old age he became one of the founding members of Parry's Naval Prayer Union and a committee member of the Loo Choo Naval Mission; he thus becomes one of the tangible links between the wartime Blue Lights and the mid-century flowering of their influence.[21]

Given Austen's length of service during the war, his three spells as a flag captain and his two ship commands, he cannot be cited as proof that evangelicals were kept from senior appointments. He survived the criticism of his discipline, remaining as captain of a 74 for almost three years, and there is no evidence that he was considered lacking in fighting resolve. The suggestion that evangelicals were prevented from commanding ships or squadrons during the war simply on account of their religion cannot be sustained. When the combat

[20] Captain's log: PRO ADM 51/1826 *St Albans*, 1808; ADM 51/2344 *Elephant*, 1812–13; David Southam, *Jane Austen and the Navy* (2000; pbk edn 2005), pp. 288ff.

[21] George Charles Smith, *Windsor* (1828), pp. 65–71. J. H. and Edith C. Hubback, *Jane Austen's Sailor Brothers* (1906), p. 114. His brother Charles, although less clearly identified with the Blue Lights, unfailingly read the daily Bible lessons in the Anglican lectionary. In 1812, when captain of the *Namur*, he applied to SPCK for Bibles and prayer books for public worship, together with spelling books for sixty boys and girls who received schooling aboard during her fitting-out at Sheerness. In 1852, dying of fever when naval C-in-C during the second Burmese War, he recorded writing to his wife and holding his daily Bible reading on his last full day of life.

records of Duncan, Saumarez, Pellew and other Blue Lights are considered, any argument that fighting qualities were disabled by their beliefs becomes untenable. It was stated during the war, however, under extraordinary circumstances by two angry officers, and the object of their wrath was Lord Gambier, the prince of Blue Lights. The outcome was two courts martial which will need consideration in detail. It is time to look at the career of this most enigmatic of admirals.

Gambier's Reputation

MIDSHIPMAN Dillon was exasperated to find how much religious instruction featured in the *Defence* under Captain Gambier. Fifteen years on, when Gambier was a commander-in-chief Sir Eliab Harvey made a similar allegation – that his religious concerns were interfering with his warlike duties, and that he was unfit to hold command. Lord Cochrane made equally strident criticisms when he encountered Gambier in 1809 and even more damagingly in his memoirs.[22]

This view was presented humorously but with withering sarcasm in a cartoon of August 1809 (by Williams and Fores): it is entitled 'Sternhold and Hopkins at sea', in reference to an edition of metrical Psalms (illus. 11). Gambier sits in his great cabin intoning a verse, 'Moab my washpot is, my shoe o'er Edom I will throw', ignoring Cochrane and (probably) Harvey who are trying to tell him about the tactical situation. Harvey in dismay comments 'Your shoe won't do for the French Fleet. I think we had better throw some shells, your Honor', while Cochrane with drawn sword adds, 'Why Admiral! D – n their eyes! They'll escape if we don't make haste.' Gambier's disdainful insouciance is partnered by the shocked response of his chaplain: 'Oh the wicked dog! He has put us quite out; he is insensible of the beauties of divine poetry.' Discarded on the cabin floor lie telescope, log book and a batch of Congreve rockets; on his desk is a large edition of Sternhold and Hopkins, and on the bulkhead no nautical chart but a map of the Holy Land.[23]

Gambier's religion was viewed in his own day as misplaced at sea and a distraction from his proper concern, the business of war. By and large historians have

[22] *Dillon*, I, p. 110; Earl of Dundonald, *Autobiography of a Seaman*, 2 vols. (1860), I, pp. 357f.; references which follow are to the more accessible one-volume Woodman edition, *The Autobiography of a Seaman, by Admiral Lord Cochrane*, ed. Richard Woodman [hereafter Cochrane] (2000), pp. 216–19;. Lord Cochrane became 10th Earl of Dundonald in 1831.

[23] Cartoon reproduced in Richard Woodman, *The Victory of Seapower: Winning the Napoleonic War, 1806–1814* (1998), p. 47.

11 'Sternhold and Hopkins at Sea or a Stave out of Tune'. This satirical etching of August 1809 encapsulates the popular view of Gambier, his mind devoted to religion and neglecting his responsibility for a fleet at war. (Original by C. Williams)

© National Maritime Museum, London px8601

echoed this opinion, and generally backing the views of Harvey and Cochrane have oscillated between the regretfully disappointed (Laughton), the dismissive (Lewis) and the harshly critical (Lambert). What then is the case against him? While it is not restricted to the Aix Roads action of 1809 – usually described as a fiasco – Gambier's apparent failure there has attracted such harsh notice, from contemporary London newspapers, William James's *Naval History of Great Britain* (1847) and Dundonald's memoirs onwards, that it becomes quite hard to see his virtues in other contexts.

Take Laughton's entry in the *DNB*:

> 'Gambier's long connection with the board of admiralty, his command at Copenhagen, and the scandal of the Basque Roads have given his name a distinction not altogether glorious. His conduct on 1 June 1794 prevents any imputation of personal cowardice, but emphasises the miserable failure in April 1809, which certainly suggests that he was out of place in command of a fleet.'

Editing the *Dillon Papers*, Lewis noted that 'Preaching Jemmy' was a unique officer 'whose running of a capital ship in wartime is an almost unbelievable tragi-comedy'. Woodman's introduction to a modern reissue of the Dundonald autobiography contains this sentence: '"Dismal Jimmy" Gambier was a religious tractarian much given to sanctimonious pronouncements and the urging of his commanders to exhort their seamen to Christian rather than martial endeavour.' In a biographical essay on Cornwallis, Lambert is even more scathing of Gambier, 'who lacked sea-experience, toadied his political masters at the Board, and made a public display of all the least endearing aspects of his evangelical beliefs', and he alleges that Gambier may have sought to frustrate Cornwallis 'through professional jealousy, political malice or personal spite. Lord Cochrane was not the only officer in the service to consider him "a canting and hypocritical Methodist" who owed his position to the fact that he was related to both Pitt and Middleton'. Alongside such moral deficiencies Parkinson's dismissal of him as 'an old woman' seems mildly generous – harmless and ineffectual, well meaning perhaps, but evidently not the man to hold a naval command. Taylor's *Sea Chaplains* takes a similar line: here was a man egregiously misplaced, a religiously minded officer who should have found a different outlet for his zeal. Lewis, too, exonerates him of over-much moral blame:

> Gambier was not a bad man; indeed in one sense almost too good. His weakness was that, in attempting to run an eighteenth-century ship of the line like a convent school, he lacked not only a sense of proportion and tact,

but also of elementary humour; all of which stemmed, perhaps, from lack of experience.[24]

We seem to know Gambier so well – and yet there are features which demand reappraisal. For one thing, had the man of sublime courage at the Glorious First of June really lost his nerve in the Basque Roads? It is of course quite possible, for the valour required of a fleet commander may be different from that of a captain in the stress of battle – but he had only recently shown a capacity for decisive action at Copenhagen. And his career was spent swimming against the tide of accepted behaviour, not just an isolated brave deed but a whole life-style of moral courage. It is worth taking another look at the notorious action of 1809. Then again, some of the hostility in his own day was based on malice peppered with inaccuracies, as with Cochrane, or misunderstanding, as Harvey. Some of the criticisms of the famous Gambier court martial (packed, partial, obstinately closed to proper handling of evidence) are convincing if Cochrane is true, but less so if his statements are misleading: the existing records at least deserve a fresh look. Furthermore, if Gambier really was quite so hesitant, inept or even cowardly as critics assert, why was he backed by Admiralty, Parliament and the senior officers who sat on his court martial? Political interest might account for some of this, of course, but surely not all. And if they are right who assert that he was a despised and unpopular admiral whom the Admiralty had decided to sideline and remove, why did they not get rid of him – as they did Orde, Calder, Thompson, Harvey and Cochrane – without allowing him to serve out his three-year term? It is often asserted that he was not employed again when he hauled down his flag – but that is only true of a sea-going command. He was given the task of revising the system of signals which was closely linked to tactical doctrine – far too important to entrust to an operational incompetent. His appointment as British plenipotentiary for the peace negotiations with the USA at Ghent was, of course, well supported by the diplomats and lawyers who worked on the detailed provisions behind the scenes, but it hardly points to his being out of good odour with the Government.

The main criticisms of Gambier relate to his record as an operational commander, and while it is entirely proper for a wartime admiral to be assessed on that basis, it is not the only valid perspective. Navies need administration, and what have come to be known as human resources. Contributions in these areas may be unglamorous, but are not to be discounted. Historians have rightly been

[24] *Dillon*, I, p. xxxii; Cochrane, p. xvi; Andrew Lambert, 'Sir William Cornwallis', in Le Fevre and Harding, *Precursors of Nelson*, p. 367; Parkinson, *Britannia Rules*, p. 152; Taylor, pp. 239f.; *Dillon*, I, p. 63.

keen to give Cochrane his day in court, and have understandably tried to correct what they perceive as a rogue verdict in the Gambier court martial; they have been less confident to exonerate him of blame in his later trial for fraud. Few writers have tried to assess Gambier against what he was trying to achieve. Even his sole biographer, Lady Chatterton, largely failed to provide this perspective: she did not really understand the navy or the significance of the reform movement. Some of her best material concerns the court martial, but her cogent arguments are obscured by rambling text and irrelevant family letters. Gambier left no memoirs and no descendants to guard a body of correspondence; his writings are scattered in various collections and Admiralty archives. As a broad generalisation, it may be said that naval historians focus on tracts and the Basque Roads, but neglect his special contribution to the Sailors' Cause (which linked evangelism with social reform – much broader than shipboard services and tract distribution), while Church historians treat him as an associate of the Clapham Sect by courtesy of his famous uncle, but show little interest in the intricacies of his naval career. Neither viewpoint gives the full picture. At the very least he deserves a biography that takes him seriously as a man not of cant but of conviction.

Modern secularism finds him hard to appreciate, as he apparently tried to force his religious opinions on the lower deck. Tract distribution is the evidence – but in fact it proves something else. Tracts were persuasive, an appeal to reason: they treated sailors as men with minds, with consciences, with souls of eternal worth. No one was compelled to read, much less to believe. Recipients had a choice – to read or discard; readers had another choice – to believe or to reject. A more educated and sophisticated audience would probably find the tone patronising, but the offer of such a moral and spiritual challenge was ennobling. This voluntary appeal is different from St Vincent's manipulation of religion: in his hands it was an engine of compulsion, an aspect of discipline, which made a contribution to morale and morality but never saw sailors as immortal souls. To those who saw religion as social cement, Gambier's appeal to the mind was dangerous, for it encouraged men to think for themselves. To people content to confine religion to church on Sundays or to private thought, Gambier's wish to let Christianity pervade all aspects of life was profoundly disturbing, in a way that Nelson's invocation of God was not. Piety of this new kind would shape values and moderate conduct. Far from being innocuous pap, this was intoxicating stuff, and the movement that purveyed it was highly suspect.

And so we come to our paradox. Gambier is often perceived as eccentric, irrelevant and ineffectual, utterly misplaced as a fleet commander, someone who should have been a bishop, not an admiral. Yet if we take a longer view and see him as a figure of the nineteenth century, Gambier appears no longer old-fashioned but far-sighted. And might something else be true? Maybe he was not just clinging to eighteenth-century values when they were anachronistic; nor should he be viewed as a proto-Victorian, embarrassingly premature in an Evangelicalism that had still to become popular. Could it be that he was himself one of the forces that shaped those emergent values and gave them maritime currency? So many later trails can be tracked back to Gambier. He distributed Bibles: within two decades the Admiralty issued one to every man. He circulated tracts: Victorian sailors could pick up fresh ones regularly on their messdecks. He tried to restrict prostitution many years before the navy would even admit that it was a problem. Victorian sailors had Sunday services, daily prayers and voluntary gatherings – the very things that brought such scorn on Gambier. The expansion of the chaplains' branch could hardly have happened without the measures he had pushed for in 1812. The whole concept of welfare involving sailors' families and life ashore became prominent in nineteenth-century reforms, just as they had featured strongly in Gambier's thinking. Although Middleton was the predominant force behind the *Regulations and Instructions* of 1806, his nephew shared in their compilation and consequent influence that would stretch forward seventy-five years.

When the evidence has been weighed, Gambier may still be regarded as eccentric, misguided or misfit, but he cannot be written off as a nonentity. And if his kind of values came to sway the future, how was that done? Was this a species of *léger de main*, administrative trickery, accomplished by ideological hijacking of the Admiralty when the navy was properly focused on the war against Napoleon? In short, if the man were so ineffectual, how did he become so influential? Had evangelicalism managed to gain access to levers of power through clever networking or political jobbery? Surely we need an explanation more subtle than the family interest of Barham and Gambier – even when harnessed to the Pitt and Melville political machinery. With the new piety temporarily ascendant at the Admiralty, it still had to take effect where captains and admirals held local authority. If evangelicals were so few in the navy and so despised by the salt-water fleet, their religion would make little impact. The mechanism of value-transfer needs examination.

Gambier's career and the role of the Blue Lights are interrelated – but how precisely? When they are mentioned, it is often in the context of this man. When methods of evangelism afloat are referred to, they are often described as 'Gambierism'. For good or ill, here is the archetypal Blue Light by whom the whole movement tends to be judged. Because of his centrality to the development of naval evangelicalism it is necessary to devote a seemingly disproportionate amount of space to an evaluation of him and his career. Only restricted attention will be given here to the reform movement (the 'Sailors' Cause') which featured so prominently in the post-war period and his later career.

Gambier the Naval Administrator

CAPTAIN Gambier joined the Admiralty Board in March 1795, and a year after the Glorious First of June was promoted rear admiral. The First Lord was the political head of the navy, a cabinet minister responsible to Parliament; he and his three sea officers, of whom Gambier was one, comprised the Lords Commissioners of the Admiralty, responsible for strategy, ship deployment, appointments, regulations and anything that could not be delegated to the Navy Board. During these years, therefore, Gambier was closely involved with the direction of the maritime war at its highest level, giving advice to the First Lord, the initially inexperienced Lord Spencer.

The strategic direction of the war was in the hands of Pitt the Younger, Henry Dundas the Secretary of War, and Spencer. To be of much help, Gambier had to develop an understanding of complex issues – trade and its protection, blockade and coastal defence, the role of sea power in the War of the Second Coalition, the consequences of British evacuation of the Mediterranean, the effects of Spanish hostility; the threat from the Dutch, Nelson's foray into the Mediterranean again in 1798 and its triumphant effects, how to deal with Denmark and the Baltic league. Fundamental to every consideration was the protection of the British Isles – including Ireland – against invasion. The role of the navy was indisputably to provide the first line of defence at home and for Britain's overseas possessions. And during Gambier's term of office the loyalty of the fleet collapsed for a time as the mutinies at Spithead and the Nore seemed to put national survival into jeopardy. As one of the responsible Commissioners, Gambier was forced to reflect on problems of manning, morale, discipline and conditions. The fruit of his thinking would be seen years later in his support for the reform movement.

His usefulness to Government and his fair-mindedness in a partly political role led to three periods of service to successive administrations. While Laughton disparaged his long service at Whitehall, and Lambert found evidence of discreditable subservience to ministers, there was nothing inherently dishonourable about ensuring that the First Lord and hence the Cabinet understood naval technicalities. From May 1795 until February 1801 he served the younger Pitt's Tory administration (in conjunction with Portland and his Whigs), with Lord Spencer at the Admiralty. When Addington became First Lord of the Treasury in 1801, the Whig-inclined St Vincent took over the Admiralty and Gambier lost his seat at the Board. He was recalled to the Admiralty in May 1804 to serve under Lord

12 James, Lord Gambier (1756–1833). The most controversial of the Blue Lights. His part in the Aix Roads action of 1809 is remembered, and his tireless commitment to the Sailors' Cause forgotten. (Oil painting by Sir William Beechey, 1753–1839)

© National Maritime Museum, London PU4696

Melville (formerly Henry Dundas – a distant relative) when Pitt was Prime Minister once more. During this administration Melville was forced to resign over financial irregularities, and Gambier's uncle Charles Middleton was appointed First Lord in May 1805 with the title of Lord Barham. With Pitt's death and the change of administration in February 1806, both uncle and nephew lost their seats at the Board, but not for long in Gambier's case. For the third time he became an Admiralty commissioner, this time in Portland's administration with Lord Mulgrave at the Admiralty from April 1807 for a year. In the summer of 1808 he embarked on a three-year appointment as commander-in-chief of the Channel Fleet.[25]

Between his first and second spells at the Admiralty Gambier was at sea for a few months as third-in-command of the Channel Fleet (with his flag in the *Neptune* (98) from February 1801) before going to Newfoundland as governor and commander-in-chief. His three-year term is remembered there for his measures to improve education, agriculture and public health. At the Admiralty his particular interests lay in ship design and signalling; he also helped advance the status of chaplains. He was largely responsible for the experimental *Triton*, which tested the practicality of using a lot of straight timber, an important trial in view of the shortage of compass (shaped) timbers during the war. Another of his projects was the *Plantagenet* design for a 74 which dispensed with a poop, as a way of disguising the real power of the ship so that she might the more effectively oppose frigates. Always interested in signals, he implemented an idea first proposed by Howe, of giving each ship in the Navy List an individual recognition number; after leaving the Board and his fleet command he chaired a committee to revise the code, and recommended that Home Popham's telegraphic system should supplement Howe's numerical flags. Although his signature appears with Barham, Garlies and Patton on the revised *Regulations and Instructions for His Majesty's Service at Sea* when published in 1806, this massive work owed most to Middleton, but Gambier heartily endorsed his uncle's view of the central importance of religious

---

[25] Administrations and First Lords:

	Administration	First Lords
Dec 1783 – 1794	Pitt the Younger	Howe, Chatham (from Jul 88)
Jul 1794 – 1801	Pitt with Portland Whigs	Spencer
Feb 1801 – 1804	Addington	St Vincent
1804–6	Pitt's second administration	Melville, Barham (from May 1805)
1806–7	Grenville – 'Talents'	Grey (Ld. Howicke), Grenville
1807–9	Portland	Mulgrave
1809–12	Perceval	Mulgrave, Yorke (from Apr 1810)
Jun 1812–27	Liverpool	Melville

observance and moral values; he played his own part in this a few years later by promoting adequate remuneration for chaplains.[26]

For years, then, Gambier was more a civil servant than a warrior. He spent his days with documents and memoranda, with officers in search of sea-going appointments, with politicians and parliamentarians. He was a public servant able to turn his hand from the running of the navy to governing a province, and even – briefly – to diplomacy. Did all this desk-work disqualify him from high command at sea? Not in the eyes of his political masters who entrusted him with a strategically sensitive mission against neutral Denmark in 1807, and then appointed him to the premier position afloat in charge of the Channel Fleet from 1808 to 1811. In comparison with many other senior officers, his sea-time was derisory – two years as a captain of a 74, and something under five years as admiral. Much of his war service had been spent in Whitehall, amidst anxious uncertainties, but a far cry from the dangers of close blockade. Portland wanted a politically skilled admiral to deal with the Danish problem of 1807; the gratitude of Government was shown first by the award of a peerage and then by a plum appointment. It may have been unwise to invite him to command the Channel Fleet, so very senior a position with such seasoned officers under him, but if so the blame lies primarily with Portland and Mulgrave. It seems unnecessary to suppose that Gambier manœuvred himself improperly into this appointment, but his paucity of shared experiences of hardship and danger created a gulf between him and – for example – his second-in-command Sir Eliab Harvey, and (following Lambert's findings) Sir William Cornwallis. There were ambitious officers who regarded his elevation with jealousy, and would be quick to denounce failure. More than the Government's reputation was bound up with Gambier's fortunes, for he had made religion a part of his persona both private and public.

Moral controversy surrounds the Danish expedition, while questions of competence were aroused by his action – or inaction – at Aix Roads. The issues have reverberated from that day to this, with Gambier getting much the worse of the argument. Critics of the new piety found their misgivings confirmed, but that did not spell the demise of 'Gambierism'. Instead its influence grew, as naval evangelicalism adapted to change.

---

[26] Smith, *The Navy and its Chaplains*, pp. 186f. Correspondence of the Chaplain General, John Owen, including minutes of the Admiralty Board concerning the status of chaplains, PRO ADM 3/174. Tunstall, *Naval Warfare*, pp. 227, 264.

Commander-in-Chief at Copenhagen, 1807

In 1807 Denmark declared its intention of siding with Napoleon in an armed neutrality, designed to limit Britain's trade with continental Europe. In truth there was little else that Denmark could do in face of French preponderant force. To the British Government it created a worrying situation. Other countries, notably Russia, were lining up behind Denmark as Napoleon's economic policy began to tell. If the Danish navy came under French operational direction, it could block the Sound and cut Britain off from the essential Baltic supplies of timber, hemp, flax, tar and iron. Sea power in Nelson's hands had overcome a hostile Denmark once before in 1801, and now Portland's Government resolved on a fresh demonstration of force to drive Denmark out of her mistaken policy, or if that should fail, to seize the fleet. Lord Cathcart was in command of the operations overall, with Sir Arthur Wellesley assisting on the military side. Gambier was entrusted with the maritime part.[27]

The operation was controversial in its own day, and has remained a moral conundrum ever since. In the event, Britain took belligerent action against a neutral country in an operation that involved setting fire to a largely wood-built city, with hundreds of civilian casualties. In return, Britain acquired a war fleet from Denmark, but at the cost of her bitter enmity and henceforward willing support for Napoleon. And since Gambier – moral and God-fearing – was the agent of such suffering, critics of his religion found the word hypocrisy minted for them. In truth, of course, he was bound to obey his orders or else resign his commission: he was not the architect of anti-Danish policy, but neither was he uneasy about his mission. To understand how this could be, it is necessary to recall the Government's dilemma.

They knew of Napoleon's ascendancy following his victory over the Third Coalition. Austria had been forced to make peace after her catastrophic defeat at Ulm and Austerlitz; Prussian hostility to Napoleon led in turn to her devastating loss at Jena and the French occupation of Berlin (October 1806). The states of Germany fell under French suzerainty. With no immediate prospect of recovery in southern Europe – Naples was a broken reed – and with northern Europe collapsing too, Anglo-Russian collaboration was all the more important. Alexander, however, was no match militarily or diplomatically for Bonapartist ruthlessness. Damaged at Eylau and beaten at Friedland (June 1807), the Tsar was cajoled and compelled to join Napoleon's schemes when the two men met face to face at Tilsit

---

[27] A. N. Ryan (ed.), 'Documents relating to the Copenhagen Operation, 1807', *The Naval Miscellany*, v, ed. N. A. M. Rodger, NRS (1984), pp. 297–329.

in July 1807. Here Alexander made his peace, promising collaboration hereafter in the reconstruction of Europe according to the French blueprint. That vision included driving British trade out of the ports and harbours of the Continent. The British Government knew all this – and more, for secret intelligence indicated that Denmark and Sweden would be forced to join Napoleon's imperial system.

The results would be critical for Britain. With no reliable ally of military significance, she was isolated, and if she were now to be cut off from the Baltic trade in the shipbuilding supplies essential to her maritime effort, the economic consequences would be grave. And there was a further threat that could prove fatal. With the Danish fleet under French control, Napoleon might revive invasion plans. Portland's Government resolved to act in a way that would reduce the risk: they must secure the Danish ships before the French could seize them. A fleet and army of overwhelming strength were dispatched to Copenhagen in August 1807 to overawe the Danes and force a bloodless and honourable surrender, before Napoleon could make any counter-move. Unable to disclose their intelligence and hence its source, the British Government was judged not by its reasons but by its actions – aggressive, immoral, brutal – and the bombardment of Copenhagen after refusal of terms seemed a war crime of truly Napoleonic proportions. In fact Portland's cabinet had about as much choice in this matter as Churchill in 1940, when he called on France to immobilise her capital ships or sail them to British ports to prevent their use by Nazi Germany. And Gambier had as little freedom as Somerville, when at Oran he carried out his profoundly distasteful task of opening fire on neutral sailors who had recently been allies. In both cases Britain was fighting for her life, and had made a request which seemed reasonable to her leaders under the stresses of war, but the consequential violence cannot have been anything other than deeply regrettable. What would actually have happened had Napoleon taken the Danish fleet intact can only be a topic for speculation, but it is hard to see how Britain could have kept open the Baltic trade route – with all the implication that this eventually had for the frustrating of the Continental System and for precipitating Napoleon's disastrous invasion of Russia. Had Portland allowed the moment for action to pass, French hegemony over Europe with Britain included might have followed.

Gambier did his part skilfully and decisively with his 27 of the line and attendant bomb vessels. Once the British terms were rejected, troops were landed and the naval bombardment began. Danish defence was brave but futile, heroic folly when faced with overwhelming force. Some 2,000 civilians died, as well as 250 combatants – tragically and needlessly, because General Peyman, the Danish governor, refused the proffered opportunity to evacuate the city before the bombardment began. On the third day the Danes were ready to surrender, and immediately Copenhagen dockyard was taken over by Gambier's men. Danish warships were manned and sailed to England – eighteen of the line and fifteen smaller vessels – and the valuable naval stores became cargo for shipment to British yards, all accomplished within six weeks – 20,000 tons in ninety-two cargoes. Once he knew of the issues involved, even scrupulous Wilberforce was convinced that the attack on Denmark was justified, but he felt that the Danish fleet should have been interned, as originally promised, and held on trust for return at the end of the war: he believed that to use these ships for British interests was morally wrong – but here again the blame must attach to Government rather than Gambier. Evangelical opinion concurred, and messages of congratulation arrived from Bishop Porteus and Hannah More. Grateful ministers awarded him a peerage, but, mindful of the cost in human life, he declined a pension.[28]

Commander-in-Chief at Aix Roads, 1809

From 1808 until 1811 Lord Gambier was commander-in-chief of the Channel Fleet. The immediate danger of invasion had passed. Prospects for a fleet action were not good. For the navy, these years were for the most part spent in monotonous, exacting, dangerous work of maintaining close blockade of the enemy's coast, whatever the season and whatever the weather. It was the vital but uninspiring exercise of sea control, in an economic war of attrition. There was still prize money to be made, of course, but little out of the French. There were too few craft at sea under the tricolour, whether man-of-war or merchantman, to provide many rich pickings for the fleet. On the other hand, neutrals who refused to trade with Britain but bestowed their favours on Napoleon's ports became legitimate prizes – in British eyes, at least. For the frigate crews, the sloops and cutters, there was still great prospect for enrichment. While every commander-in-chief would share in the takings anywhere in his area, there was nothing for the officers and men of the third rates, the line of battle ships upon whom the blockade depended. They must do their duty, thrashing to and fro in sometimes dangerous waters, with no end to the war in sight, no exhilaration of battle and no prospect of prize money. Frustration was bound to set in. A commander-in-chief had to have as much concern for morale and discipline as for tactics.

To Gambier these circumstances suggested a spiritual opportunity. Chaplains were welfare officers of an unusual kind; church services, while not quite entertainment, were a change from routine. While his fleet was performing

---

[28] Woodman, p. 118; Ralfe, II, pp. 82–90; Wilberforce III, p. 347; Kverndal, *Seamen's Missions*, p. 662 n. 119.

its military function, its moral and spiritual temper could be improved. Bibles and Christian literature would provide interest and instruction together. Away from the temptations of shore, sailors might be expected to be more responsive. Alcohol consumption would be controlled by naval discipline; the problem of women could be practically ignored; religious observance could be made obligatory by the admiral's decree – and beneficial results might be anticipated. No thinking observer could deny that there was a potential problem with seamen's conduct, their licentiousness and irresponsibility – but was this the time to do anything about that, and was a war zone the right environment? Some believed that warlike spirit might be put at risk if sailors were affected by religious sensibilities.

As to how widely services were held, the log for Gambier's flagship shows that divine service took place almost every Sunday as required by regulation. This record may have been unusual, but it can hardly be regarded as excessive. It would be good to know more about the titles and quantities of tracts distributed: presumably they were made available for dog-watch recreational reading. In his *Autobiography of a Seaman* (1860) Lord Cochrane states that, when he joined Gambier's flag in the Basque Roads, he found the fleet divided over tract distribution and, it must be presumed, the evangelistic purpose that lay behind them. Opposition was focused in the person of Rear Admiral Sir Eliab Harvey, Gambier's second-in-command. Although boastful and not popular, he was already famous as the captain of the *Téméraire* at Trafalgar, the ship that had plunged into the French line immediately astern of the *Victory* and had given much needed support to the flagship in her duel with the *Redoutable*. Courageous and impetuous, he had little patience with Gambier and had come to attribute the coolness between them to their different religious convictions. It may be true: Harvey was not a Blue Light, but neither were many other officers whose careers prospered nonetheless. It seems likely that Harvey's real frustration arose from the tension between the relentless tedium of blockade and his thirst for laurels won in combat – but he must speak for himself at the proper time.[29]

Cochrane alleges that the fleet was divided into factions over the religious issue. No doubt this is true to a degree, but its significance is easily exaggerated. Certainly many of Gambier's officers regarded his religious zeal as quaint and superfluous, maybe even offensive, but how many seriously regarded a Sunday service and the circulation of reading material as corrosive of fighting efficiency? What little evidence there is shows that renewed attention to religion was not unwelcome on the lower deck, where a weekly sermon helped morale, and to be given

[29] Cochrane, pp. 219f.

orders without being cursed at the same time was a refreshing novelty. Commenting on his experience in the *Caesar*, when part of Gambier's Channel Fleet, warrant officer William Richardson recalls the ship's company being receptive and even devout when Sunday prayers were held for the first time, and a sermon preached by the new chaplain; some officers customarily regarded swearing as a normal concomitant of seafaring until Admiral Stopford gave a different lead when he made the *Caesar* his flagship. In the gunner's memoirs, *Caesar*'s captain Charles Richardson appears embarrassed during the first service and uncomfortably unsure of when to stand or sit – while the admiral knelt for prayers. Perhaps he was genuinely critical of the whole christianisation programme; more likely he simply did not know what was expected of him.[30]

With indiscretion tinged with arrogance Cochrane chose to get involved by sending a few tracts to Cobbett for his more public and inflammatory comment. Why did he choose to dabble in a matter largely irrelevant to him and to the mission on which he had been sent? Gambier's privileged background, patrician ways and evangelical religion offended Cochrane's radicalism, but stirring up mutual distaste made a close working relationship hard. Cochrane's testimony is evidence of a body of support for Gambier's literature crusade. When he alleges that 'the fleet was in a state of great disorganisation on account of the orders given to various officers for the distribution of tracts', we are in the realm of hyperbole. His intervention pitted him against the religious reformers, whom he describes in political terms as 'the tractarian faction, consisting for the most part of officers appointed by Tory influence or favour of the Admiral', and also against the critics of religion, who feared that he would arouse 'the irreconcilable displeasure of Lord Gambier'. Interestingly Cochrane's own account shows that he was more severely treated by his ideological allies, who 'lost no opportunity of denouncing me as a concocter of novel devices to advance my own interests at the expense of my seniors in the service.'[31] In other words, dress up the controversy as he may, Cochrane shows that he was the problem – his presence, his ambitions, his contentious spirit. It suited his overall design in his autobiography to portray himself as the leader of enlightened opinion against an incompetent commander-in-chief, but if we follow Cochrane uncritically we shall do Gambier an injustice.

Cochrane had a genius for war, and particularly for unconventional operations. His courage was matched by astonishing resourcefulness. He also possessed a talent for self-advertisement. Although doubts persist as to whether he was corrupt

---

[30] *Richardson*, p. 234.

[31] Cochrane, p. 220.

or merely naïve over the alleged stock-market fraud that led to his dismissal from the navy, it is clear enough that he could be manipulative and untruthful. But he was also persuasive, a man of action with a gift for words. He had an amazing story to tell in his autobiography, with a barely concealed subtext of self-justification combined with a settling of scores against the social and political establishment which had expelled him. His strictures against Gambier need cautious handling, not least because several strands become wound together. Harvey's outburst, although apparently linked with the tract controversy, is found on inspection to be separate; Gambier's deficiencies in handling the Aix Roads action are a different issue; the Admiralty's arrangements for the Gambier court martial need to be distinguished from allegations of false evidence or even perjury made against Gambier himself. And there as a backdrop is Cochrane's urgent desire to rehabilitate his reputation. The case against Gambier must be considered item by item, with Admiral Harvey appearing as witness for the prosecution once the scene of controversy has been set.[32]

In the spring of 1809 the war off the French coast quite suddenly assumed a more threatening aspect. Eight sail of the line under Admiral Willaumez (soon to be superseded by Allemand) eluded Gambier's force blockading Brest and took shelter in Aix Roads amongst the islands, reefs and shallows, in preparation (as we know now) for a raid on the West Indies. The French improved their position by guarding the seaward approach with a massive boom, itself protected by gun batteries. It seemed to the Admiralty a rare opportunity at this stage in the war for a stab at a French fleet, away from its regular defensive base. Their Lordships favoured the idea of an attack by fire-ships, but Gambier, thinking of a conventional tight blockade, was far from enthusiastic. The Board now turned to an officer of enterprise and genius. Lord Cochrane had made a name for himself as commander of a brig and then a frigate, and he had achieved legendary success. Not only was he a most courageous and inspiring leader, but he was also fascinated by novel and unconventional means of warfare. The fact that he was a member of the Commons and heir to an earldom gave him political leverage, but his radical leanings perturbed the Government. In the eyes of Lord Mulgrave, the First Lord, Cochrane was the very man for a hazardous operation which could bring great credit to the administration and might even tame his restless spirit. In modern warfare Cochrane would have been an obvious choice to lead elite forces on commando raids. In 1809 he was eager to use explosive vessels, fire-ships and

[32] Cochrane's career was favourably assessed by Christopher Lloyd, *Lord Cochrane* (1947). More balanced modern studies include Brian Vale, *The Audacious Admiral Cochrane* (2004). Cochrane gave his views on administrative reforms in *Observations on Naval Affairs* (1847).

Colonel Congreve's new and dangerously unpredictable rockets to dislodge the French and make them targets for British guns.[33]

The operation as originally planned was distasteful to Gambier. Responding to a suggestion that fire-ships might be used, Gambier admitted to Mulgrave on 11 March that the French ships lay exposed to an attack of this kind. 'It is a horrible mode of warfare', he added, out of a compassionate mind's revulsion at the terrors induced by fire at sea.[34] Even the much more secular-minded 'Jack Nastyface' found the concept appalling: mistakenly assuming that the proposal to use fire-ships had been Gambier's, he blames him for his lack of principle, an interesting commentary on how this form of warfare was regarded: 'though it was an enemy, yet the thought is shuddering, that nearly ten thousand men, whilst they were harmlessly asleep in their cots and hammocks, might be roasted to death and perhaps without a moment's time to say, "Lord have mercy on me!"'[35] If these were Gambier's scruples, they do credit to his humanity, but raise more sharply the question of why he had used fire against civilian homes in Copenhagen as a weapon of war. On that occasion he may have supposed that people would have had a chance to escape, but once the city had fallen it was only too obvious what a terrible price in human blood had been paid; was he now more reluctant to take life in flames? Did he wish even his enemies to have time for repentance? It may be so – it would represent a laudable wish to preserve humane values which war so often stifles.

Fire-ships were regarded as the outer limit of acceptable methods of war, with the result that crews were liable to be shot if they fell into enemy hands, as Nastyface explains: 'every man taken on such an expedition by the enemy is liable to be dealt with in a similar manner as a spy, and put to death. It is a mode of warfare dreadful to resort to and should not be practised by a civilised nation.'[36] That volunteers could be found was never in doubt, but Gambier was reluctant to hazard brave men's lives needlessly. When Cochrane pressed for an immediate attack the admiral refused to sanction what he thought would be unnecessary

---

33 Sources for the Basque Roads action and the court martial which followed are: [W. B. Gurney], *Minutes of a Court Martial Taken in Shorthand by Mr. W. B. Gurney* (Portsmouth, 1809); *NC* XXII (1809), pp. 107–30, 215–42; Chatterton, II, pp. 95–170; Edward Pelham Brenton, *The Naval History of Great Britain from 1783 to 1836*, 2 vols. (1837), II, pp. 278–83, 331f.; William James, *The Naval History of Great Britain from 1793 to the Accession of King George IV*, 6 vols. (1847), V, pp. 99–130; Cochrane, pp. 202–68.

34 Chatterton, II, p. 95; Cochrane, p. 205.

35 Henry Baynham, *From the Lower Deck: The Old Navy, 1780–1840* (1969), p. 50.

36 Baynham, *From the Lower Deck*, p. 51.

sacrifice of British lives, with the risk of the fire-ships being boarded and their crews murdered: 'it was his duty to take care of the lives of others, and he would not place the crews of the fire-ships in palpable danger.'[37]

Reluctant as he was to inflict unnecessary sufferings on the enemy or needless losses on his own men, Gambier was in the end a servant of Government. If ministers believed such an operation of last resort was justified, he would have to obey or resign his commission. 'It is a horrible mode of warfare', he wrote to Mulgrave, 'and the attempt very hazardous, if not desperate.' Having made known his personal views, he added his professional opinion as to how the venture might be approached: 'if you mean to do anything of the kind it should be done with secrecy and quickly.' He advised that no less than a dozen purpose-built fire-ships should be used, together with smaller craft, and he was sure that there would be volunteers in plenty to man them.[38] Critics have discerned that the admiral had no liking for the scheme, and was from the start distancing himself from it. But is this a correct interpretation? Cochrane interestingly provides a different view. He told Mulgrave he agreed with Gambier that an attack with fire-ships alone would not succeed, as French boats under oars would be able to tow them aside. On the other hand he had a variant which would turn a highly desperate venture into one that could hardly fail – explosion vessels to accompany fire-ships. Once one of these had exploded, the French guard boats would treat them all as potential bombs, and the fleet they were supposed to protect would have to slip their moorings to escape. Did Gambier disengage himself from this enhanced version of the fire-ship plan? Apparently not, for Cochrane allows himself some gentle mockery of the inconsistency of the admiral's religious scruples: 'Lord Gambier had to incur the bitter sarcasm of the fleet – that when the Admiralty wanted to attack the enemy with fire-ships, he had denounced the operation as a "horrible and anti-Christian mode of warfare"; but that now that he saw my plan of explosion vessels, in addition to fire-ships, was likely to be crowned with success, he no longer regarded it in the same light.'[39]

The way Cochrane presents Gambier's letter to Mulgrave is significant, for he has corrupted the admiral's 'horrible and hazardous' into 'horrible and anti-Christian'. As a believer, Gambier had faced the fundamental issue of conscience over whether he could bear arms and take life. He had shown a desire that war should be fought with as much regard for humanity as possible, but he had not condemned operations with fire-ships as impossible for a Christian. In due

---

[37] Cochrane, p. 226.

[38] Chatterton, II, p. 95; Cochrane, p. 205.

[39] Cochrane, p. 220.

course, as we shall see, Cochrane wanted to show Gambier as an observer or at best a reluctant participant in the action that followed. Was it cowardice, caution or conscience that inhibited him? Everyone knew that religion drove him, and surely here might be found explanation enough of his pusillanimity – the man was wrestling with a moral dilemma. But that is to give his words a weight they will not bear.

Mulgrave wanted the attack to go ahead and sent Cochrane to lead it. The choice was bound to upset eager spirits in the Channel Fleet who felt they had been passed over. Knowing of the projected attack, and believing that Gambier had called for Cochrane, Harvey assumed his commander-in-chief doubted the abilities of his own officers. Enraged to the point where judgement evaporated, Harvey came aboard the *Caledonia*, Gambier's flagship in Basque Roads, expressly to volunteer to lead an attack on the French, and with a list of officers who would happily join him. To his anger he found Cochrane aboard, already sent from the Admiralty to carry out the very operation – as though officers of his seniority and daring could not be trusted to bring it off. He announced his intention of striking his flag and returning to England. Publicly on the flagship's quarterdeck, he denounced his commander-in-chief, pouring out his frustrations, his fury, his doubts about the religious programme, and his general dissatisfaction with the conduct of the fleet. Whatever his arguments, this was not the way to air them, and the result was foregone. Such insubordination was dealt with by court martial; the verdict went against him and the fire-eating Harvey was not employed afloat again. The crucial words he spoke demand attention.

In Cochrane's presence, in the flag captain's cabin, Harvey said he had never seen anyone so unfit for command of a fleet as Gambier. Instead of sending boats to take soundings and prepare an attack on the French, he had busied himself with mustering ships' companies – presumably for prayers. As he went back to his waiting boat he shouted, 'This is not the first time I have been lightly treated … because I am no canting Methodist, no hypocrite, no psalm-singer and do not cheat old women out of their estates by hypocrisy and canting.'[40] The words of an angry man they may have been, but they highlight one of the problems which would always be associated with a service where interest counted for so much. Any senior officer expected to gather around him the people he knew, the men he could trust, the staff with whom he felt comfortable. Those excluded from the circle were also likely to lose out on promotions, honours and the opportunity to have *their* adherents advanced in the profession. In fact there is no evidence that Gambier was favouring Blue Lights: while his flag captain, Bedford, was certainly

[40] Cochrane, p. 217.

sympathetic to his religious views, and so was Admiral Stopford, none of the other commanding officers appear in obviously evangelical circles such as subscription lists or membership of the Bible Society. Harvey was furious that his own scheme for winkling Allemand's fleet out of Aix Roads had not been accepted, and to find a junior captain given the opportunity for winning glory was unendurable.[41]

If the charge of religious favouritism was probably unfair, the allegation of rapacity was certainly so. Presumably Harvey was referring to a passage in St Mark's Gospel where Jesus condemned the outrageous contrast between the religiosity of the scribes and their actual conduct: 'they devour widows' houses and for the sake of appearance say long prayers.'[42] Gambier's sincerity was transparently evident, however unacceptable his views; as for his possessions, according to his niece, he owned no estate but 'a small copyhold house and garden with a field at the back of it'.[43] Yet in highlighting religious issues Harvey had a point, however imprudently expressed: the business of the battlefleet was war, and its commander owed it to his country to be expert in that. Of course there was no reason why Gambier's evangelistic programme should not have gone on simultaneously with the active prosecution of hostilities. He cannot seriously have meant that a few minutes of prayer at daily divisions hindered operations, but he did mean that Gambier's mind was not wholly given to the war.

If Harvey was correct that no proper reconnaissance had been ordered, the charge would have been grave indeed. Cochrane was keen to prove that he knew the state of the French anchorage and that Gambier did not – it became a crucial plank in his platform of self-justification – but was it true? Cochrane liked to think he had been opposed by a conspiracy of senior captains and admirals, and that the commander-in-chief's advisers had plotted to frustrate his success by disguising from Gambier the true state of affairs – depth of water and breadth of channel in particular. Cochrane, who knew these waters from of old, made a close reconnaissance of the Île d'Aix, and noted that its fort was less formidable than supposed: he reported his findings to the First Lord but – incredibly – did not inform Gambier for fear of contradicting his opinion. Not only did Cochrane claim to have better and more accurate knowledge than the admiral's advisers – correctly, we may assume – but he also asserted, as Harvey had done, that proper

---

[41] Harvey had a plan for a dual attack on the Île d'Aix and on Aix Roads: while an assault force backed by half the fleet was to disable the batteries, the remaining ships would engage the French squadron in their anchorage; Baynham, *From the Lower Deck*, p. 50. A landing under fire posed enormous hazards, and insufficient military forces were to hand.

[42] St Mark's Gospel 12:38–40.

[43] Chatterton, II, p. 115.

soundings had not been taken. Here he was being less than just, as others too appreciated the value of accurate intelligence. Stokes, the *Caledonia*'s master, had sounded and surveyed the anchorage within the Île d'Aix and the space between the Boyart and Palles shoals. The operational decisions made by Gambier were based on what he believed was good evidence: if Cochrane had better information which he felt unable to disclose at the planning stage he must bear some of the blame for what happened later.[44]

It seems clear that Gambier, for all his earlier heroism and his uprightness of character, failed to create that sense of comradeship in arms for which Nelson was legendary. Personally he was courteous: Cochrane noted with surprise that, unwelcome as he was to the Channel Fleet, Gambier and those closest to him (Stopford and Neale) were the only ones who treated him with consideration. Nevertheless he appears reserved, dignified and even aloof, a difficult man to know personally. In command he suffered from having spent too long at the Admiralty, removed from the sea-going environment which created such strong bonds of comradeship and loyalty. The much younger Cochrane – still a teenager when Gambier had won his reputation at the Glorious First of June – neither won his trust nor really respected him.[45]

Rightly or not, the Gambier connection afloat was perceived as a religious link, rather different from the usual clientage of interest which gathered round anyone with patronage to bestow. Was opposition to Gambier due to his overt Christianity or was it created by some difficulty in building team spirit? Probably a bit of both. He was not as his best in handling people. When appointed to command naval operations against Copenhagen, for instance, he chose the unsuitable Home Popham to be captain of the fleet. They shared a fascination with signalling, and Gambier's cumbersome fleet dispositions called for some sophisticated means of communication, but the disadvantages of the appointment were more obvious. Not only had Sir Home Popham been censured shortly before this for his irresponsible attack on Buenos Aires, but he was junior to some very deserving captains like Byam Martin and Keats, and adding insult to injury, Martin was obliged to give up his ship and quarters to the man, and his personal belongings for Gambier's use. An admiral with more awareness might have ordered things better. Saumarez, another Blue Light, managed to combine his perfectly well-known Christian convictions with a courteous consideration which won deep

---

44 Cochrane to Mulgrave, 3 April; Cochrane, pp. 221–3. On failure to take proper soundings, ibid., pp. 218f.: Cochrane was inclined to blame the masters rather than Gambier.

45 Cochrane, p. 220.

loyalty and spread throughout the ships under his flag: 'the spirit, the love, the enthusiastic kind of attachment formed between our officers and ships' companies is one of the most interesting things I ever witnessed', wrote Byam Martin of the Baltic Fleet in 1808.[46] Such bonds were not easily created, and they were the result of inspired leadership beyond the reach of most commanders, including Gambier. And his skills were about to be sternly challenged.

After Harvey's precipitate return to his ship, the attack on Aix Roads still had to go ahead, and Cochrane was the officer appointed to lead it under the general direction of the C-in-C. Cochrane's account and those modelled on it tend to overlook Gambier's role in the whole affair: after all, he and his staff drew up the operational plan with diversions and support, as well as the actual preparation of the pyrotechnic force. Cochrane was never sent to command the fleet! His task was the extremely dangerous one of leading the fire-ships, which he did with his customary skill and daring. At night on 11 April, with a strong current flowing and an onshore wind, he released the explosive vessels, which broke the boom and opened the way for more incendiary ships to sail down onto the anchored French. They slipped their cables but had insufficient room to get under way, and ship after ship stranded on the shallows. After personally conning one of the explosive vessels into Aix Roads, Cochrane returned to his frigate *Impérieuse* and sailed into the anchorage next morning. He found eventually eleven of the enemy ashore and was understandably desperate for the big ships to finish them off before the rising tide could refloat them. Cochrane tried to goad his C-in-C into action by a series of signals but Gambier was not to be drawn into committing the battlefleet at this stage. The tide was in the last quarter of the ebb; by the time the ships had weighed and entered Aix Roads they would be borne in with a full spring tide, and there was considerable risk that they would be trapped in the confined waters or stranded on the shallows. When he judged it safe Gambier ordered in four of his capital ships, enough to help Cochrane appreciably but not sufficient for annihilation – three battleships burned, a heavily armed troopship destroyed, a frigate lost.

Cochrane was far from satisfied, and he was eager to resume action on the 13th, before the French could refloat all their stranded ships. Yet Gambier was

[46] Tunstall, *Naval Warfare*, p. 262; R. Vesey Hamilton (ed.), *Journals and Letters of Admiral of the Fleet Sir Thomas Byam Martin, 1773–1854*, NRS, 3 vols. (1898–1903), II, p. 48. It is noteworthy that, for all the warmth and camaraderie in the Baltic Fleet, Martin took exception to Saumarez's comments over the risks he had run in a successful action and demanded a court martial on his own conduct. Harmony was eventually restored without one. See Alan McGowan, 'The First HMS *Implacable*', *MM*, XCI (2005), p. 298.

unwilling to commit more than light forces, with frigates and bombs; before they could complete the work of destruction, the French were able to salvage their remaining ships and drag them across the mudbanks into the safety of the Charente, having reduced their draught by jettisoning guns and stores. In fact the enemy had suffered grievously, and the whole idea of a voyage to the West Indies had to be completely written off. In related operations, for which Gambier could claim no personal credit, Stopford had destroyed three more large frigates off Sables d'Olonne on 24 February, and the 74-gun *Jean Bart* had been lost on the Palles shoal while entering Aix Roads two days later. Gambier had effectively presided over the demise of the French West Indies fleet, and with it their last hope of retaining Guadeloupe and Martinique. Not only had the French suffered grievous material losses, but the fighting spirit had been knocked out of them, as an officer in the flagship *L'Ocean* sadly noted:

> It is first necessary to inspire our sailors with that spirit with which they were animated before this unfortunate affair, and which the greatest part are so discouraged at as no longer to possess. Every day I hear them lamenting their situation and speaking in praise of our enemy's. This is, in my opinion, the greatest injury the English have done us.[47]

The Government which had been so alarmed by the escape of Willaumez from Brest in February was vastly relieved by the outcome, and proposed to convey the thanks of Parliament to Gambier and his fleet. Cochrane, smarting from what he perceived to have been the admiral's lack of support, was far from mollified by the praises he received in Gambier's immediate despatch:

> I cannot speak in sufficient terms of admiration and applause of the vigorous and gallant attack made by Lord Cochrane upon the French line-of-battle ships which were on shore, as well as of his judicious manner of approaching them, and placing his ship in a position most advantageous to annoy the enemy and preserve his own ship, which could not be exceeded by any feat of valour hitherto achieved by the Royal Navy.[48]

From Cochrane's perspective it had been a profound disappointment. He believed that a decisive intervention by the main fleet would have spelt the destruction of the whole French force: in the true spirit of Nelson he was aiming at the enemy's annihilation. Although Gambier had praised the captain of the *Impérieuse*, the admiration was not reciprocated – and Captain Lord Cochrane in

---

[47] Hamilton, *Journals and Letters of ... Sir Thomas Byam Martin*, III, p. 327.
[48] Cochrane, p. 247.

the form of Thomas Cochrane MP announced his intention of opposing any vote of thanks to Gambier in Parliament. His criticisms were public and pointed, leaving Gambier with little choice but to demand a court martial on his own conduct as the only way to clear his professional reputation.

In this he was supported by the Admiralty for more than one reason. Of course, Gambier was their appointee, and the Board naturally would have felt some sense of loyalty to him, but there was more involved. Parliamentary tributes were customarily paid to a commander and the force operating under him: that was the convention. Gambier's praise for Cochrane won him the red ribbon of the Bath, a coveted distinction, and there was even a suggestion that Cochrane's name might be coupled with Gambier's in the wording of the thanks of Parliament. Cochrane's fury at the outcome of the battle was turning into an onslaught against the admiral, vindictive and disproportionate, which would have had the effect of denying public affirmation to the fleet he had commanded. The interests of the navy were not served by this kind of protest, which raised the question of Cochrane's loyalty to his own service. His opposition was perceived as malicious and subversive of discipline: a demonstration of Their Lordships' support for the commander-in-chief was necessary for the maintenance of proper subordination.

Again, Cochrane had chosen to side with the Radicals in the Commons, Burdett and Cobbett, apparently out of a complex set of motives. Love of liberty was one, however difficult to define; a desire for reform was another, but tied up with his personal grievances against Admiralty prize courts; and undoubtedly he enjoyed baiting the Establishment. In a strange way his character needed adversity: such pugnacity made him formidable in conflict, where his courage, resilience and inventiveness could find full scope. The same temperament regularly pitted him against authority, and his restless career was marked by a whole succession of conflicts – with St Vincent, Keith, Gambier of course, Admiralty lawyers and their courts, successive Governments in Britain, his masters abroad in foreign service. Having the ruling classes against him exhilarated him; it allowed him to feel he was somehow helping the underprivileged, and ennobled his self-interested crusade for recognition and justification.

Even after Gambier's acquittal Cochrane would not let matters rest. Having pitched his own word and judgement so emphatically against his admiral's, he could neither accept the court martial decision nor acquiesce in the vote of thanks to Gambier. He continued to pursue the matter, demanding that the published minutes of the court martial be laid before Parliament, and reiterating his criticisms. By now Mulgrave wished to be clear of the matter, and offered Cochrane command of a squadron of frigates and a regiment of soldiers to carry out his own plan for coastal harassment: Cochrane chose to interpret this as a bribe to buy off his opposition. As Lords and Commons wanted to put the whole issue behind them, he judged that he was now isolated from all except the independent members who were themselves disorganised and deceived by ministers. He felt himself opposed by persecuting factions, by the Government-controlled press and its 'jackal howl', and by 'the organised masses in power' or those eager to replace them. The debate over the Aix Roads affair had, he believed, seriously damaged the Tory party – 'and that party ever afterwards made me a mark for their revenge. In this brief sentence may my whole subsequent history be comprised.'[49] The frustrating of his hopes of high command, his disgrace and dismissal, his self-imposed exile and his struggle to exonerate himself, all coloured his views of the Gambier court martial – naturally enough – and influenced his autobiography. A recent biography of Cochrane sheds fresh light on his character, including his recurrent assumption that the world was conspiring against him, and his readiness to distort facts in his own defence. Through his own writings Cochrane appealed to the judgement of posterity, which has generally supported him (as James, Laughton, Lloyd, Woodman), effectively reversing the court martial opinion and arraigning Gambier (defended by Brenton and Chatterton practically alone).[50]

Since Gambier's evangelicalism has always been perceived as part of the essence of the man, no assessment of the Blue Lights can fail to revisit the court martial.

The Commander-in-Chief on Trial

AT HIS own request Gambier faced a court martial for his handling of the fleet at Aix Roads, on the specific charge 'that Admiral the Right Hon Lord Gambier, on 12 April, the enemy's ships being then on shore, and the signal having been made that they could be destroyed, did, for a considerable time, neglect or delay taking effectual measures for destroying them.' Although the charge was obviously based on Cochrane's allegations, he was not the accuser in the court room, and he was not given the opportunity he would have liked to cross-question the admiral. The charge was answered to the court's satisfaction by Gambier and his witnesses – professional officers, captains of line ships (unlike Cochrane), and by no means all drawn from his circle. The question was whether the commander-in-chief could have done more to secure a more glorious outcome. Should he have

---

[49] Cochrane, p. 268.

[50] Gurney's minutes were published soon afterwards, and the *Naval Chronicle* offered a digest. Near contemporary comment appears in Chatterton and Brenton (both favourable) and James (critical).

sent his heavy ships into Aix Roads as soon as Cochrane signalled that the French ships were aground? A detachment was sent eventually, but ought they to have moved in sooner?

Any responsible answer had to take into account sea conditions, depth, wind direction, current and state of the tide. There was obvious danger in committing two- or three-deckers to the confined waters between the Île d'Aix and the shoals beyond, where they would come under fire from gun batteries on the island. When the wind was off-shore, say from due east through to south west, a damaged ship with enough water under her keel might expect to be brought out safely, particularly on the ebb tide. A strong incoming tide with a westerly breeze would give more depth of water and less risk of running aground, but the same conditions would be hazardous for a ship of restricted manœuvrability as she would be trapped against a lee shore or the treacherous Boyart shoal. Fairfax, the master of the fleet and chief expert on pilotage and navigation, believed that the width of the channel was barely more than a mile. Although Cochrane gave evidence that it was actually twice that breadth, the court had to concern itself with what Gambier knew or believed at the time of the action. The master of the *Caledonia* and others had taken soundings and advised the admiral accordingly; Cochrane knew the approaches to Rochefort well from earlier service, and he made a thorough reconnaissance himself – he was brilliant at survey work in a boat with lead, line and compass – and his own conviction that there was a two-mile channel was confirmed by a Neptune Français chart captured during operations. With such a breadth of water the big ships could have given the Aix gun batteries a wider berth and so greatly reduced the danger from red-hot shot. Almost certainly therefore we are right to conclude that Gambier could have taken bolder risks without jeopardising the fleet, but at the time, given the knowledge he had, his caution was neither unseamanlike nor cowardly.

Rear-Admiral Stopford was asked whether he would have considered it prudent to send or lead the battlefleet into Aix Roads when the *Impérieuse* signalled that the enemy were on shore. His reply assisted Gambier:

> In my opinion the dislodgement of the enemy's ships by fire-ships removed but a small part of the obstacles. With the wind as it then was (strong from the north-west), and the broadsides of the enemy's ships still commanding the approaches, we should have been so crippled in going into and in working out of the passage a little more than a mile in breadth, that I think I should not have risked the ships, had they been under my command.[51]

[51] Parkinson, *Britannia Rules*, p. 151.

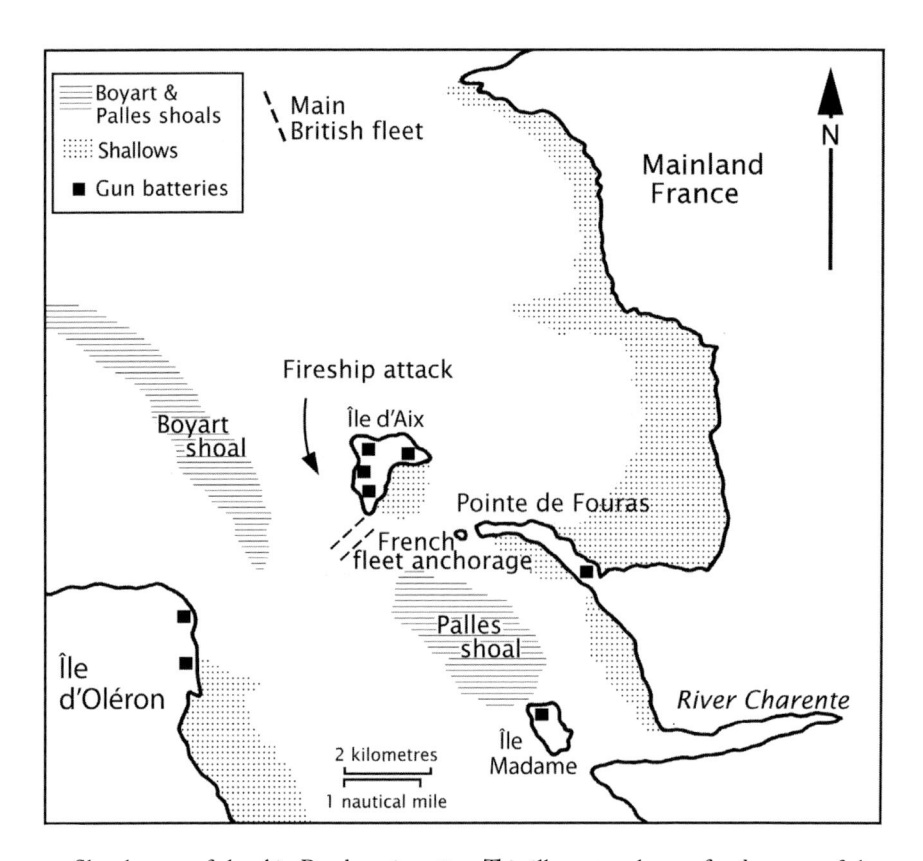

13 Sketch map of the Aix Roads action 1809. This illustrates the confined waters of the French anchorage, and the fairly narrow channel down which the big ships had to sail to the westward of the Ile d'Aix. Both the flood tide and wind direction were generally from the north west. Gambier saw the dangers of committing his capital ships to such restricted waters under fire from French gun batteries, with wind and current driving onto a lee shore. Once the tide began to ebb, a damaged ship would have more chance of coming out safely, and Gambier resolved to hold back the ships of the line until the tide turned.

Captain Pulteney Malcolm gave a more ambiguous reply – that if the *only* way to destroy the stranded ships had been by sending in the main fleet, then it should have been tried. Of course he and the court knew that frigates, bomb ketches and other light craft had been sent in to exploit the opportunity, and so the heavy ships were not the only way. He concluded that in the whole operation there had not been more than half or three-quarters of an hour which could have been called delay. Captain Broughton believed it would have been advantageous had the heavy units gone in at half-flood, between 11 and 12 o'clock instead of three hours later – but at risk to the fleet.

With wind and tide both heading directly into the French anchorage from 8 a.m. for another seven hours, Gambier considered that the right time for the battle ships to intervene would be when the tide turned at around 3 in the afternoon. At that stage, the onshore wind would have been offset by the ebbing tide with its offshore current, and the 74s could justifiably be committed. That was the time when the *Revenge* (Captain Kerr) opened fire, with *Theseus* (Beresford) and *Valiant* (Bligh) in company. As John Beresford said in evidence, 'the proper time for sending ships in was at the time of tide that would insure their coming out in case of accident.'[52] Now we have the reason for Gambier's apparent lethargy when Cochrane signalled that the French were on shore: he had no intention of committing the 74s to the battle until he believed the risks were acceptable – in other words, when the change of tide would give them a decent chance of getting out if they had been crippled by enemy shot. Gambier, Stopford and the captains of the ships of the line recognised this perfectly well, and their testimony was coherent, consistent and seamanlike.

Cochrane scoffed at the danger from enemy gun batteries. His reconnaissance convinced him that the fort on Île d'Aix was being reconstructed and therefore not so formidable – and events proved him right. Nonetheless, as recently as 5 April he had reported to Neale (captain of the fleet) that he had seen five furnaces for heating shot, and it was right for the commander-in-chief to give due weight to that intelligence. After his experience of sailing past this point, first in an explosion vessel and then in the *Impérieuse*, Cochrane derided the risks of red-hot shot – but his passing at night conferred more safety than ships of the line might encounter in daylight. There is evidence garnered by Chatterton but too often ignored by later writers concerning Gambier's intentions: Stopford and Broughton said that he had originally planned to take in the *Caledonia* (his flagship) and the *Caesar* (Stopford's) to engage the batteries, but decided to hold back when the pilotage specialists warned of insufficient depth for three-deckers. While he was holding the two flagships in reserve, the scattering of the French fleet after the fire-ship attack relieved him of the immediate need to hazard his capital units. Now we have a reason why he ordered the battle ships to prepare for action with springs on their cables and then committed only four of them to Aix Roads. It is reasonable to see Gambier weighing risk against possible advantage, and deciding that prudence should prevail. None of the captains of his line of battle ships criticised Gambier's handling of affairs, and even George Seymour of the frigate *Pallas*, who had supported Cochrane's *Impérieuse* in close-quarter combat, said in evidence, 'I have my doubts whether line-of-battle ships would

[52] Chatterton, II, pp. 158f.

have succeeded by going in.'[53] He added that there would have been sufficient depth of water for them at 11 o'clock – but that is not a contested issue. Over whether the ships ought to have been committed then, the admiral had to use his discretion.

Following Cochrane, British historians have reflected bitterly over the wasted opportunity of Aix Roads: by his valour and skill Cochrane had presented Gambier with a unique and brilliant opportunity which the commander-in-chief threw away. It is hard to imagine Nelson or Hawke reacting so cautiously, and by their standards Gambier failed. But the Government which looked to him to defeat its enemies also relied on him to protect its chief war asset, an incomparable fleet. Brenton's summary is judicious:

> It should not be forgotten that the situations of Lord Gambier and Lord Cochrane on the 11th and 12th April were essentially different; the first having responsibility, the second none. Had Lord Cochrane lost the Impérieuse on the Boyart Shoal, his character would, if possible, have received a higher lustre. Had Lord Gambier so committed the fleet under his command as either to have run the ships on shore or exposed them to conflagration in a narrow anchorage, the nation might have felt the effects of his imprudence, and his character would have suffered in the eyes of the world. The object in view, the total destruction of the enemy's fleet, was not to be obtained by the risk of the Channel fleet, the main support of the empire.[54]

The arguments have much the same resonance as those over Jutland, but Jellicoe has been more fortunate in finding defenders of his cautious tactics. At the time of the court martial naval opinion was more generous to Gambier. His second-in-command and the captains of his fleet – Stopford, Bedford, Bligh, Seymour, Broughton, all competent officers – exonerated him. They pointed out to the court the dangers of hazarding the big ships in confined waters of uncertain depth, in variable and light breezes, in range of enemy artillery. One admiral and nine captains gave evidence, and none was openly critical of Gambier: most of them unequivocally asserted that no blame could be imputed to him. They knew the risks that had been taken with the 74s and appreciated the danger. Three of them took the ground for a while in the Aix Roads: the *Revenge* suffered casualties when she came under fire while stranded, and Stopford's *Caesar* was only brought off after considerable exertion under cover of darkness. Gambier's caution deserves more credit for its seamanlike calculation than it usually receives

---

53 Chatterton, II, p. 141. Cf. critical interpretation: Cochrane, p. 257.
54 Brenton, *Naval History*, II, p. 284.

– and yet the disappointment remains. He showed little dynamism in support of Cochrane or liking for this kind of warfare, so unlike the majestic deployment of fleets for which he was better suited. He could feel satisfied with the outcome of operations which had eliminated a whole squadron of the French navy for many months at least and had rendered their projected expedition completely abortive. The cost to Britain in blood was trifling as these things go – ten dead and thirty-five wounded. Gambier was great enough to acknowledge that this was truly Cochrane's triumph, and he made no move to steal his laurels. Besides a frigate, the French had lost three ships of the line and the 56-gun *Calcutta*, laden with ammunition and military stores, the logistical heart of the projected West Indies expedition. Four Spanish prizes taken in 1797 had won an earldom for Jervis, but that was before Nelson had raised the nation's expectations.[55]

In 1809 the court martial cleared Gambier of blame, and paved the way for a parliamentary vote of thanks. Cochrane would not accept the verdict as valid. He criticised the composition of the court martial, the conduct of the trial, the fact that he was not allowed to cross-question Gambier, and the veracity of the evidence. He condemned the admiral and those who had advised him, sensing a conspiracy everywhere to deprive him of his just rewards. He alleged falsified charts, doctored minutes and even perjury. In his autobiography he referred to having seen the chart used in Gambier's defence, and could then see why the court martial had cleared him; at this point he had to allege that the chart had been falsified. Yet we now know that the master's chart of the *Impérieuse* bore later additions, that there were errors in the reckoning of his own position, and a grotesque exaggeration of Gambier's remoteness from the scene of conflict. On such a dubious foundation he impugned not just Gambier's decisions – partly at least a matter of judgement – but his honour, honesty and integrity. While few writers have been so partisan, many have concluded that Gambier was out of place in command of a fleet. On the back of that, some have drawn the further implication that Gambier's religion was the heart of the problem. On this basis the Blue Lights were an eccentric group whose agenda was not in the navy's best interests: these further implications of the court martial call for reappraisal. And Gambier himself, so frequently written off at this stage as an irrelevance to the navy, was on the brink of some of his most important work for sailors. He too will need reassessment in due time.[56]

[55] *Richardson*, p. 248.
[56] '... the openly avowed object of the court martial was the suppression and invalidation of my evidence by any means that could be brought to bear'; 'Lord Gambier's defence was contradicted by itself ... and by his own witnesses; many of whom as to essential facts, were at variance with themselves and with each

For Lord Cochrane the Gambier court martial was a grave setback, even something of a personal tragedy. He was a Radical with a strong sense of irreverence verging on insubordination. He had challenged the Establishment, the Admiralty and the whole concept of respect for rank. In a hierarchical service it was hard to find a place for the likes of him, even though at Aix Roads his skill at war had shone in all its brilliance. His reconnaissance had been the most thorough yet; using his knowledge of these waters he had discovered much valuable intelligence – depth, breadth of channel, state of the fortifications and the existence of the boom. His tactics were bold and innovative, with explosion vessels to break the boom and fire-ships to panic the enemy. Once action began, his presence was an inspiration and his conduct fearless, first in conning one of the two explosion vessels, then commanding his own frigate to force his way into the anchorage, and finally in harrying the enemy ships on the shoals. How desperately he needed good relations with the commander-in-chief, instead of allowing his predilection for controversy to sabotage trust. His vindictive conduct rendered him unemployable, an irreparable loss to navy and country but largely self-inflicted. Gambier, as he acknowledged, had been personally considerate and had secured a knighthood for him. It was Cochrane himself, not Gambier, who deprived the navy of its most talented captain. Involvement in an alleged stock exchange fraud in 1814 led to his dismissal from the navy and the Commons, together with expulsion from the Order of the Bath – but he was reinstated in 1832 after a career of restless brilliance in the navies of Chile, Brazil and Greece. Eventually Cochrane – by then the Tenth Earl of Dundonald – was allowed to fly his flag in command of British ships as admiral on the American and West Indian station, but he had to wait until 1848.

Historians have tended to support Cochrane rather than Gambier over the Basque Roads affair. Not unnaturally, in the wake of Camperdown, Nile and Trafalgar, press and public had begun to expect the elimination of enemy fleets, and disappointment was expressed early on, for instance by the London *Times*.

> other'; 'the chart of the 12th of April was in a most material point false – and in every respect a fabrication'; 'charts made up for the purpose of proving imaginary dangers'; Cochrane, pp. 254, 259, 267f.; Lloyd, *Cochrane*, p. 62. Southam, p. 319, quotes a letter from Austen in favour of Cochrane and alleging that he was not properly supported because of 'Lord Gambier's being influenced by persons about him who would have been ready to sacrifice the honour of their country to the gratification of personal dislike to yourself.' But Austen had not been present, and was writing fifty years later on reading Cochrane's autobiography: as he had no direct personal knowledge he was echoing what he had just been reading. It proves nothing.

Then and subsequently, Cochrane stated his continuing sense of grievance with eloquent power from a parliamentary pulpit and through a well-handled press. Gambier's side of the argument has not always been given due weight, not least because he neither spoke nor wrote publicly to defend himself after the court martial had given its verdict. Napoleon's apparently even-handed condemnation of the competence of his own admiral and the showing of his antagonist is often quoted as authoritative, even by historians who are critical of the emperor's understanding of basic maritime matters. James's history leans heavily towards Cochrane, but the caveats of the earlier Edward Brenton deserve a hearing, as do the comments of Georgina Chatterton – sharp but almost lost in the byways of her rambling biography. Nowadays we have come to be more critical of Cochrane's veracity at various points in his self-advertising and self-justifying autobiography, and are now less ready to accept his own evaluation. Gambier deserves his day in court – once again.

Gambier's silence might be seen as an admission of guilt, or as patrician arrogance in disdaining to enter the lists against a Radical like Cochrane and his friends. Alternatively it may show certain traits of character that are not necessarily to be despised. Those who knew him best had no wish to see him disgraced, and with the support of his senior subordinates he was exonerated at the court martial. He lacked the Nelson touch, of course, and his caution was too pronounced, but for all that, he had served his country capably in war. On the face if it, these proceedings are about operational matters and have nothing to do with Gambier's religion. It was first Harvey and then Cochrane who turned the spotlight onto the 'Methodist' question. But there was a sequel. A couple of year after these events Admiral Harvey became a generous subscriber to the SPCK in its work of distributing Bibles and prayer books to sailors. Perhaps he had been reassured about this Society by finding that Archdeacon Owen, the navy's chaplain general and a staunch supporter, favoured a little tract entitled *Against Enthusiasm*, or maybe he had come to recognise after all that sailors were much improved for a little more religion![57]

The Seaman's Friend

As a fleet commander Gambier lacked originality or flair, but he acted with cautious wisdom. He could claim some credit for neutralising two perils – the threat of the Danish fleet in hostile hands, and the danger from a French expedition to succour Martinique. As a spiritual leader, however, he displayed flexibility, innovative vision and a remarkable capacity to respond to developing

---

57 *SPCK Report of Proceedings*, 1811.

challenges. In his early years and in the heyday of his influence in the navy, he was heir to the vision of Kempenfelt and Middleton. Like them he believed that sailors must be recalled to their Christian faith and conduct. They needed facilities for worship and a decent ministry at sea, just as they might have expected on land. Some degree of compulsion was required, reflecting the fact that England was a Christian country, the navy was a Christian service and they were – more or less – lapsed Christians. So the early policy of the Blue Lights, and Gambier amongst them, was to insist on a proper observance of the *Regulations* which clearly laid down these principles.

Wartime showed how little this view corresponded with reality. There had always been an evangelistic element to the Blue Light programme and the work of the Bible Societies. In the French Revolutionary War this persuasive component becomes more evident. As the Blue Lights became increasingly committed to evangelism, new tactics were required. There was no need to abandon public worship; indeed, that requirement was more desperately needed than ever, but it would not of itself make disciples. In this new era, more proactive outreach was needed. In Gambier's case this took the form of encouraging Gospel preaching and tract distribution – 'canting Methodism' to Admiral Harvey, proselytism or 'Gambierism' to historians. To people principally involved in spreading Christianity on the lower deck, any serious programme of evangelism required 'sailor missionaries', men who would witness to their colleagues in any number of off-duty conversations and who would maintain their faith by mutual fellowship. To this spontaneous movement of lower-deck religion Lord Gambier could contribute nothing: his rank and status meant that he could at best be an enabler of others, through new measures at Admiralty level.

Now a new age of evangelistic witness was arising. Naval seamen, as we have often noted, came from the maritime pool, itself largely unreached by the churches, and all too often a reef of vice on which many a youthful life was wrecked. Far-sighted sections of the post-war Church deliberately attempted to evangelise the total marine community. Wider issues were involved than simply preaching to sailors: they were forced to deal with social and legal matters, the whole dark world of sailortown's abuses. The Seaman's Cause became the new frontier for these pioneer missionaries and social reformers. Mere zeal was not enough. The issues needed airing in press and Parliament; money had to be raised, ventures set afoot, pressure groups formed, public attitudes altered.

To this new cause Admiral Gambier lent his weight. At the height of the Basque Roads controversy in 1809, there was a striking reference to him in *The*

Naval Chronicle as 'the Seaman's Friend'.[58] He was quick to understand what Bo'sun Smith was trying to achieve, and he was glad to give him his personal support. At a time when the Establishment was highly critical of Smith, Gambier became first president of his British and Foreign Seaman's Friend Society and Bethel Union in 1820, and would often take the chair at annual meetings. This movement was to encourage evangelistic and fellowship meetings aboard merchant ships in the River Thames. Just as ships of the navy had flown their church pennant as a sign of divine service being held, so trading vessels would welcome their own and other crews to public worship under the Bethel flag. Part of Smith's genius was his instinctive understanding of what would appeal to seamen, and he was quick to appreciate their reluctance to mingle with well-heeled shoreward congregations. He opened for them, first a mariners' church and then a floating chapel in the Thames, both of which became highly popular. Gambier gave the ventures his backing and the dignity attaching to his high social and service rank.

It did not matter to him that these schemes were largely initiated by Nonconformists, for, as he said, 'whoever supports this cause is not a dissenter from the cause of Christ.'[59] Nevertheless his Anglican loyalties remained strong, and he keenly backed a scheme to set up an Episcopal Floating Church Society, becoming vice-president in 1825. His enthusiasm for spreading the Gospel led him to become first president of the Church Missionary Society. He was vice-president of the Naval Charitable Society and the Marine Society that Hanway had founded. He was a supporter of the Lock Hospital (for women), the destitute seamen's asylum, the Benevolent Institution, and – reflecting his abiding interest in the Abolition movement – the African Institution. His personal generosity towards needy sailors was well known – especially wounded men needing more help than official funds allowed. Although his sympathies and interests were wide, seamen remained particularly close to the heart of this man who, through longevity, eventually became Admiral of the Fleet in July 1830. He was a welcome speaker at meetings of the NMBS and a publicist for maritime charities. From the circle of young officers who had come under his influence at sea came a good number of half-pay lieutenants and captains to staff the new peacetime ventures. His nephew, George Cornish Gambier, together with the retired commander Robert James Elliot, brought into reality Smith's idea of a Sailor's Home. With his example and practical support a new era of marine evangelisation was launched;

[58] Letter from 'J.C.', *NC*, XXII (1809), pp. 102–4.
[59] Kverndal, *Seamen's Missions*, p. 209.

without his standing and collaboration the task would have been immeasurably harder.[60]

In this battle there were no honours to be won from the public, no addresses of thanks from Parliament, no gold-hilted swords from patriotic societies. Gambier was not in pursuit of such transient trifles when he took up the Seaman's Cause, but was consciously seeking a heavenly reward. The epitaph on his tomb is one he would have cherished. In Iver churchyard, Buckinghamshire, there stands a memorial shaped like an open Bible and with the following inscription:

>Sacred to the memory of
>ADMIRAL LORD GAMBIER
>of Iver
>His name adorns the annals of his country
>As one of her undaunted defenders
>But his chiefest record is on high
>As a humble and lowly follower of the Lamb.

[60] Kverndal, *Seamen's Missions*, p. 210.

VII

Evangelical Activity on the Lower Deck: The Psalm-Singers

Introduction: The Origin of Lower-Deck Praying Groups

WHILE the Blue Lights were developing a strategy for bringing Christianity to the navy, they were joined by allies of whose existence they initially knew very little. At one level the officers were concentrating on how to make the whole community more Christian. On another level were lower-deck hands struggling to keep their own faith alive in a sternly testing environment. Theirs was the harder task. An officer's religious eccentricity might become the stuff of lower-deck ribaldry behind his back, but naval discipline was always there to protect his person and authority; by contrast, a known Christian on the messdecks was exposed to mockery or potential harassment. Always under scrutiny, he could never escape abuse if his words or actions failed to match his professed beliefs. It was an obvious measure for men of faith to look out for fellow-believers, and if possible to mess together. And so was born the shipboard prayer group that powered the third phase of evangelicalism afloat. They were not called into being by captains or chaplains, still less by Admiralty regulations, but evolved as a self-help device for spiritual survival on the lower deck.

These gatherings appear as if from nowhere in the later years of the French Revolutionary War. Most likely they had existed in unstructured and extemporised form before that, a pair here and a group there, coming together as occasion allowed, dissolving and reforming under the demands of war service, undocumented and hence undiscoverable. There was no strategy behind their formation, and no organisation needed to sustain them. The earliest example so far unearthed is from 1798. It began when a young woman became concerned for her brother, then serving in the second rate *Barfleur*. She asked her minister, the Rev. John Campbell of Kingsland Chapel, London, to write to him about spiritual matters. The sailor showed Campbell's letter to a friend and, as a result, eight men wrote back asking if they too could receive some regular Christian instruction. They formed a circle which eventually numbered two dozen. As Campbell was a Scottish Dissenter it is possible that the unnamed seaman was a Scot who mistrusted Anglican clergy: it is worth noting that the *Barfleur*'s chaplain was the Rev. William Hawtayne, who enjoyed the particular approval of James Gambier –

surely, therefore, a man of Evangelical sympathies, but not (it seems) one to whom a lower-deck seaman readily turned.[1]

Campbell recalled hearing of groups like this in a couple of other men-of-war before the Peace of Amiens in 1802. In later years Bo'sun Smith claimed to have knowledge of a group of thirteen meeting aboard one of the ships that fought at the Nile: the name is not given, but the *Orion* with her Blue Light commander Saumarez seems possible. This gathering began when one sailor shared his testimony with another.[2] That simple statement explains the dynamic of spiritual growth on the lower deck. An individual telling his personal story of lostness, repentance, conversion and salvation, might convey hope and faith to a troubled colleague. Such a testimony would have to be authenticated by the life he lived at sea: if he claimed to know God, what difference did it make? In a context of danger, privation and moral testings of various kinds, did his faith seem durable and worthwhile? The pressures that made it hard to live the Christian life gave plenty of opportunity for its utility to be shown and its quality to shine. Once a group formed it had potential for growth, so long as it could prove its credentials of sincerity and consistency. Unlike the preaching of a chaplain, disregarded perhaps when he withdrew to gunroom or quarterdeck, or the message of a tract forgotten as soon as read, this form of evangelism had lasting potency: it was embodied by a shipmate exposed to the same temptations as his colleagues, someone who could be challenged, questioned, watched and evaluated. A handful of individuals who met to pray or read their Bibles might still be ignored by the uninterested, but a group that sang psalms or hymns and confidently shared their testimonies would certainly attract wider attention. Some of the reactions were hostile, of course; yet even controversy would ensure wide currency for their message. This process of personal evangelism gave an entirely new perspective to the concept of christianising the navy. It had almost no connection with Sunday observance or the recruitment of chaplains: it was about 'soul-winning' (to use a familiar nineteenth-century expression). While the Blue Lights were devising a strategy to promote religion, the 'psalm-singers' on the lower deck were by-passing those means and finding their own culturally authentic ways of spreading the Christian message.

These groups grew in number after war resumed in 1803, but it is not easy to

---

[1] Campbell's letter, *NMBS* 1812, pp. 63f.; Smith to Fuller, and 'TMH' to Smith, *NSM*, 1827, pp. 386f.; *NSM*, 1831, pp. 133–4; George Charles Smith, *Portsmouth* (1858), p. 26. Campbell (1766–1840) was a Dissenter formerly associated with the Haldane brothers, nephews of Duncan and well-known evangelists.

[2] Kverndal, *Seamen's Missions*, 1986, gives *The Sailors Magazine* (ed. Smith), 1820, pp. 14–15, as authority for the Nile group.

account for the increase. Kverndal believes that the interval of peace provides the key: as warships paid off in 1802, thousands of officers and men were discharged ashore amid 'mushrooming religious societies and a general spirit of revival in the land', a view which echoes Heasman's earlier *Evangelicals in Action*.3 Both authorities suggest that the expanded navy of 1803 drew men from this newly enlightened community ashore, but, given the constant uptake of manpower in the previous decade, there had already been a stream of recruits from this source. What had changed? Might both Heasman and Kverndal be mistaken? Could it be that what happened in the Napoleonic War was that certain officers began to catch sight of an elusive lower deck phenomenon that had kept itself unseen all through the 1790s? And yet there is a new factor too, in the confidence of the cells, their willingness to become visible (for example during dog-watch recreational time), their active evangelism and their growing numbers. Can all this be attributed to the growing spiritual sense of the population ashore? Surely not. More probably we are seeing the cumulative effect of the new piety afloat: this will require more detailed analysis later, but for now a tentative conclusion is offered.

In the climate of the Napoleonic period religion itself had become more acceptable following in the wake of Jervis and Nelson. Once religious values had been given new prominence by Barham's *Regulations*, officers affected by the new piety discovered fresh boldness in sharing their faith. Meanwhile the lower deck had become more receptive to the Christian message; reasons for this include the circulation of Bibles and tracts, the increased encouragement of religion at a high level, some improvement in chaplains and preaching, and the developing witness of the cells. All this reflects not so much larger numbers of active evangelicals and Methodists recruited, but higher levels of Christian activity once they came aboard. Men who might once have kept their religion out of sight now identified themselves with 'psalm singers' at sea, and sailors with these convictions drew enquirers to join them. Once the movement began, it gathered momentum. The main reason why Christian life developed in the Napoleonic period should be sought in what was happening in the navy, not in what was going on in the churches ashore. Evangelism afloat rather than recruitment from the land is the more convincing explanation of growth.

The navy too had changed since the earlier war. Dread of combinations and conspiracies peaked in 1797. Although St Vincent never lost a hint of paranoia, and continued to see plotting or corruption at every level, the collective wisdom of the officer corps concluded otherwise. Most officers had learned from the mutinies

---

3 Kverndal, *Seamen's Missions*, p. 103; Kathleen Heasman, *Evangelicals in Action* (1962), pp. 246–54.

that their crews could be trusted, and that even pressed men, though they might try to jump ship, were not the natural allies of anarchy, revolution or Napoleon. Duncan and Nelson had shown what prodigies of endurance and valour could be shown by ships' companies in blockade and battle, and a host of captains and admirals had demonstrated the same. Within limits, seamen could be trusted. Small groups gathering below decks off watch might once have conjured up fears of sedition, but in the aftermath of Camperdown and Nelson's victories they were more likely to be tolerated. In this more favourable climate prayer groups began to appear. How they were treated in their own ships depended on a number of factors, predominantly the attitude of the captain, but including the collective feeling of the lower deck, and no doubt the personalities of the psalm-singers themselves. As we shall see, the fortunes of any one ship's group might ebb and flow, flourishing at one stage but suppressed at another, but in the fleet as a whole the movement grew.[4]

The existence of the prayer groups is known from the post-war writings of an ex-sailor and Baptist minister, the Rev. George Charles Smith, and a former lieutenant and Anglican clergyman, the Rev. Richard Marks. Although the rambling anecdotal publications of Bo'sun Smith contain much relevant material, the truth would have remained obscure in the lantern-light of reminiscence and conjecture but for Marks. While Smith learned from others what was happening afloat, Marks was a participant, the prime mover behind one of the most successful cell groups. As an officer and an accomplished writer, he was uniquely placed to record what was happening and assess its significance. As an associate of Bo'sun Smith, he had access to the extra anecdotal information accumulated during and after the war. In Marks's judgement the spiritual stirrings in the navy became clearly discernible after hostilities resumed in 1803. During his naval service from 1797 to 1810 he saw 'something of the manner, of the coarseness and immorality of what is called the old school … before the Scriptures were circulated or God's name known and revered.' For more than three years he claims to have seen no Bible nor to have met a single character who 'ever pretended to fear or love God', but in his later period of service he saw 'the beginning of better times'.[5]

The lower-deck gatherings initially owed nothing to their officers. They developed independently of the Blue Lights – but they were incontestably another aspect of the new piety. With or without officer interest the groups would have

---

[4] Eighty ships is the figure given by both Smith and Marks: *NSM*, 1831, p. 133; Marks, *Ocean*, p. 255, *Retrospect*, p. 275.

[5] *NMBS* 1820, pp. 39–46, for full text of Marks's address.

appeared in some localised form as believers struggled for spiritual survival. Unforeseen and unplanned was the eventual confluence of these two streams, as officers and men came to recognise one another as allies in the christianisation programme. The precise relationship between the lower deck and quarterdeck will take some teasing out, but a fairly crude model will serve as an introduction at this stage. At one level there were 'enablers', the remote authorities who encouraged religious observance and a clerical ministry through revised *Regulations*, while the Church ashore provided clergy and literature. Ships' officers were encouragers and mentors, but the true activists were on the messdecks. Christian instruction was a beginning, but if it were truly to find acceptance it needed explaining in terms that seamen could understand. It had to apply on the lower deck – where the cell groups operated.

Methodists Afloat

SAILORS who professed 'vital religion' were invariably known amongst their shipmates as Methodists. Amongst Cornishmen particularly there must have been a good many followers of Wesley, but it would be unwise to look for precision in the use of the name. Any religiously inclined sailor was liable to be called a Methodist or even more mockingly, a 'psalm-singer'. A seaman given to reading his Bible or known for personal habits of prayer might be given the label, and it was readily applied to anyone careful of his language, especially if inclined to rebuke others for theirs. As Richard Marks put it: '"Methodists" [was] a term which in their vocabulary comprised individuals of all sects, parties, ranks and ages, who feared God and endeavoured to work righteousness.'[6]

Besides the normal deprivations of naval service and horrors of warfare, 'Methodists' faced added problems. High moral standards were profoundly difficult to keep in such an alien environment. The daily rum ration, even when diluted into grog, was far from innocuous, and as a result drunkenness was not uncommon. In harbour Jack was famed for his thirst and the general abandonment which accompanied it. Every port was well provided with its taverns and brothels, and a sordid underworld of ale-house keepers, loose women, thieves and crimps who conspired to help him spend his pay. 'The populous town of [Plymouth] Dock', wrote the physician Thomas Trotter in 1802, 'was apparently converted into a huge brothel.'[7] Another surgeon estimated that 20,000 prostitutes had plied their trade in the Portsmouth and Gosport area during the Napoleonic War. If the demands

---

[6] Marks, *Retrospect*, p. 168.

[7] Dr Thomas Trotter, in Christopher Lloyd (ed.), *The Health of Seamen*, NRS (1965), p. 248.

of hostilities denied the sailor leave to go ashore, naval custom allowed women and drink to come aboard. One officer who had been captain of the *Bellerophon* described a typical scene aboard the lower deck of a 74-gun ship on the night of her arrival in port, with 500 men herded together with 300 or 400 women and 'giving way to every excess of debauchery that the grossest passions of human nature can lead them to', scenes characterised as 'open, undisguised, unblushing concubinage'. One of the *Dreadnought*'s seamen of 1809 or thereabouts reckoned that she had embarked enough women to match every member of the ship's company with thirteen to spare – and scarcely fifty being wives.[8]

Andrew Burn had described a man-of-war as a 'dreadful abode for a Christian' when he had the social privileges and relative privacy that accompanied commissioned rank; on the messdecks where every man was exposed to the unremitting pressure of communal living, where scarcely a word or action, day or night, could pass without scrutiny, any attempt to live according to the Gospel might meet with ridicule or harassment.[9] Coarseness and casual profanity were woven into the conversation of many a sailor, and the crudities of seaport life – abundant alcohol and loose women – formed the pleasures of life ashore and the substance of dreams at sea. It was an environment perpetually at odds with the Christian's calling to live a life of purity and self-control. No doubt there were some who chose the easier way of conforming to the prevailing culture of the messdeck, shunning the grosser sins perhaps, but avoiding any appearance of being religious. Others remained committed to their faith and were prepared to run the taunts and opposition of their colleagues. Whenever an isolated Christian found a kindred spirit it was natural for fellowship to develop – and in the context of their faith that meant praying together, and talking of the biblical truths so dear to them but despised by their shipmates.

'Church' rigged on the upper deck with service read by captain or chaplain could not meet the needs of their souls. They might have appreciated a good sermon, but were often disappointed in this. What they longed for was 'fellowship', the opportunity to talk of their faith with other believers, to discuss the Scriptures and their application to daily life, and to pray together. For this the Methodist 'class' provided a perfect model, and people from that kind of background sought one another's company. If sufficiently numerous they could apply to form their own mess, the basic unit of lower-deck society, grouped around one of the great

[8] Anon., *An Address to the Officers of His Majesty's Navy, by an Old Naval Surgeon* (Dublin, 1824), p. 28n; Anon. [Capt. (later Adm.) Edward Hawker], *Statement of Certain Immoral Practices Prevailing in His Majesty's Navy* (2nd edn 1822), p. 25; Stokes in Baynham, *From the Lower Deck*, p. 130.

[9] Burn, *Memoirs*, I, p. 152.

guns. Here they slung their hammocks, ate their meals, kept their sea chests with all their belongings, and spent their leisure. It was as near to a home afloat as they could get. Duties were given out and rations were served to each mess in turn. It was a traditional right of sailors to make up their own mess, which naturally acquired its own character, attracting or repelling different types of men. A known pious mess would inevitably attract attention. The same structure was a haven to its members and a target for outsiders. According to a member of the *Victory*'s crew before Trafalgar, there had been 'a set of fellows called Methodists on board' who formed their own mess and used to meet together to sing hymns; although a rather isolated group who did not mix easily with others, they were regarded with respect because of their competence as seamen. A midshipman in the *Repulse* remembered that the so-called Methodists associated with the chaplain William Terrot were a definable group, although he does not say they formed a distinct mess; he claimed that they were recognised as outstandingly good seamen who never needed punishment.[10]

When we talk about the navy's underclass of pressed men on the lower deck, we are not dealing with articulate and educated men, accustomed to keep diaries or record the events of their lives. We cannot expect to find much evidence of that kind. What we do have in surprising profusion are the recollections and anecdotal snippets given to Bo'sun Smith in a long lifetime of service to sailors. There is work still to be done in gathering out all the scraps of information he provides about these groups, scattered through the pages of his periodicals, especially *The Sailors' Magazine*. In spite of their fragmentary form, they give a coherent and understandable picture of the life that known Christians had to face, with mockery and rough humour from their shipmates.[11]

The great revival ashore had been born in song, and Methodism without music

[10] Stuart Andrews, *Methodism and Society* (Harlow, 1970), pp. 123f. (quoting Robert Ingram, *Causes of the Increase of Methodism and Dissension*, 1808); Pakenham in *NMBS* 1836, p. 24.

[11] Rev. George Charles Smith edited *The New Sailor's Magazine* from 1827 until his death in 1863. Its first title was *The New Sailor's Magazine and Naval Chronicle*. Reflecting Smith's changing priorities and altered alliances it reappeared from time to time under different names, such as *The Mariners' Church Society Magazine and Naval Chronicle* (from 1833), *The Mariners' Church Soldiers and Sailors Magazine* (from 1836), and *The Mariners' Church Temperance Soldiers' and Sailors' Magazine* (from 1839). Related periodicals include *The Sailor's Magazine and Naval Miscellany* of 1820, edited until 1827 by Smith under the auspices of the British and Foreign Seamen's Friend Society and Bethel Union, *The Asylum*, and *The Pilot*. Volume numbering is similarly idiosyncratic. See BL Catalogue, and Kverndal, *Seamen's Missions*, pp. 841, 847. For examples of opposition, see *NSM*, 1827, pp. 124f., 163.

is scarcely worthy of the name. In those times, hymn singing and church going were by no means linked. The Church of England recognised psalms both chanted and metrical, but other Christian poetry and song had no place in parish worship until the 1820s. Inspired first by Isaac Watts, Dissenters had been singing hymns for decades, and the Methodists were quick to follow with the songs of Charles Wesley, prince of hymn writers. In the opinion of the lower deck, seamen who sang religious songs identified themselves as Dissenters of some kind. Further definition was superfluous: they were labelled 'Methodists'. Ironically, their other derisory title of 'psalm singers' was quite the wrong expression, as that would have made them Anglicans! But as with all such expressions, precision was not the purpose.

'Bo'sun' George Charles Smith (1782–1863)

SMITH first heard that shipboard prayer groups existed when he was minister of the Baptist chapel in Penzance in 1809. Because of his previous experiences afloat he was immediately interested, and looked for ways to get in touch. Back in 1796, having taken up an apprenticeship in an American schooner, he had been pressed into the *Scipio* (74) off Surinam, before being transferred to the *Agamemnon* in the North Sea Fleet the next year. Grim highlights of his career included the Nore Mutiny, the Battle of Camperdown and the Battle of Copenhagen. He served as able seaman, midshipman and boatswain's mate, but never held the rank by which he is best known. Once ashore, he came to hear and believe the Christian Gospel and turned from sea-faring to preaching. He trained for the Baptist ministry under the Rev. Isaiah Birt of Devonport and became the accredited minister of the Octagon chapel in Penzance – but it took an apparently fortuitous event to make him renew links with seafarers.

In 1809 the revenue cutter *Dolphin* found refuge from stormy weather in Mounts Bay, and some of her people asked Smith as a local minister and former sailor to come aboard and lead a service of thanksgiving for their survival. As Smith was being rowed ashore after the impromptu service, the stroke oarsman mentioned that he knew some people of his 'Methodie religion' in the fleet. Intrigued, Smith pressed for details, and with one name and one ship he had enough to start with. To this stranger aboard the *St George* Smith wrote words of Christian encouragement – much as Campbell had done some nine years before. The sailor replied, suggesting some like-minded men who would, he was sure, appreciate a letter. In this way, with one correspondent giving another name or two to follow up, Smith contacted the *Royal George, Royal Oak, Zealous, Elizabeth, Ganges, Tonnant, Repulse* and *Conqueror*, all ships of the line, with a further set of contacts aboard frigates and smaller warships. His floating readership was held together by a postal network of some complexity – and expense.[12]

'It will be highly interesting and important to the future historian of Maritime Christianity', wrote Smith in the *New Sailor's Magazine* in 1827, 'to have documents and dates to which he can refer.' He then quotes a letter sent by Midshipman WBB from the *Conqueror* off Toulon, addressed to the Rev. Andrew Fuller, secretary of the Baptist Missionary Society, and dated 19 August 1810. It describes how there had been a religious society under Lieutenant Marks, discountenanced by the captain and now abolished. It consisted of ten to twelve men, with two lieutenants and three midshipmen, including the writer. He mentioned the existence of a society aboard the *Repulse* led by the chaplain (William Terrot) and the captain's clerk. Smith comments that 'in a place so vile as a man of war, there are a few who dare openly to avow their faith and dependence on a crucified Redeemer.'[13] There follows a letter from Smith to Fuller with the germ of an idea for structured pastoral support:

> I served in the navy six years. Ever since my conversion my soul has agonized in secret for poor seamen. Nothing has ever been done for them. The Naval Bible Society is partially useful, with the very few chaplains – scarcely one of them morally decent. Mr Greathead of Newton Pagnell is here, with whom I have consulted about the project of some nautical society, specially for the promotion of Christianity in the navy. He greets the project, and said, if only I could interest you in it, much might be done.[14]

---

[12] Bo'sun Smith's career may be followed from details scattered through his many pamphlets and magazines. Kverndal has edited several of the most important autobiographical sections; 'Memoirs of the Founder of Seamen's Missions in 1801', pp. 47–51. His son wrote a brief prospectus for a full biography never written: Theophilus Ahijah Smith, *The Great Moral Reformation of Sailors: Prospectus* (1874). Smith's conversion, in Kverndal, *Seamen's Missions*, pp. 117f., quotes from G. C. Smith, *The Boatswain's Mate*, Part VI, pp. 15–34, and *NSM*, 1861, p. 309f.; his encounter with the Revenue cutter and call to maritime ministry, Kverndal, *Seamen's Missions*, pp. 120–2, and *NSM*, 1832, p. 273, *NSM*, 1859, p. 430, *NSM*, 1857, p. 89; the establishment of the 'Naval Correspondence Mission', Kverndal, *Seamen's Missions*, pp. 122–6 (quoting *NSM*, 1832, pp. 273f.). Smith, in *Portsmouth*, p. 26, gave the name *St George* as the first ship he wrote to.

[13] *NSM*, 1827, p. 385.

[14] Ibid. Rev. Andrew Fuller (1754–1815), Baptist theologian and first sec. of BMS; Rev. Samuel Greatheed [*sic*] (d. 1823), pastor of an independent chapel at Woburn, was a director of the LMS, which he helped to found; Rev. William Terrot served one commission 1806–7 in HMS *Repulse*.

Samuel Greathead was particularly interested in servicemen, for he had been a captain in the artillery before becoming a Baptist pastor. Smith proposed to write to clergy and dissenting ministers in naval ports, to find from them 'every fresh appearance of piety in a naval officer or seaman.' One reply came from the Anglican minister of St John's at Devonport, the Rev. Thomas Hitchins, in December 1810. He said he had a supply of Bibles from the British and Foreign Bible Society but only soldiers, not sailors, were asking for them; he believed that there was a real need for more tracts specifically written for seamen. Meanwhile he rejoiced to learn of Smith's growing correspondence with believers in the navy, evidence that 'there are some aboard so many ships who love our Lord Jesus Christ.' He was acquainted with only a few naval officers who made a profession of religion. There was Captain H. of the *Christian VII*, and Captain Vansittart of the *Fortunée* frigate, 'who is, I believe, a good man.' He knew of Lieutenant Marks now ashore. A midshipman of the *Repulse* (actually Pakenham) spoke of being led to the Lord by the preaching of the chaplain Mr Terrot, whose ministry had been blessed to the conversion of seven or eight men. Meetings for reading the Scriptures and for prayer had continued even after the chaplain had left the ship as Captain Halliday had no objection. Hitchins was aware that some of this intelligence was a year old, and he had lost his chief informant, Pakenham, when war service took him to the Mediterranean.[15]

With the perspective only possible years later, Smith identified 1807 as perhaps the pivotal year in which 'a very powerful attention to evangelical religion was produced in several ships of His Majesty's Navy.' He identified the chief figures as Richard Marks, the Rev. William Terrot, chaplain of the *Repulse*, and Hugh Roberts, sailmaker in the *Tonnant*, but to close the list at that point does an injustice to a larger group.[16] Smith probably had little knowledge of what Barham and Gambier had achieved at the most senior levels in the Service, nor of the impact certain captains were having in their ships – notably Hillyar, Brenton and Austen. His principal interest was in the lower-deck meetings, but even in that restricted field John Hubback – master's mate and lay pastor – deserves a mention. And what of the influence of the Rev. Robert Wolfe amongst captives in France, and Lieutenant John Cox faithfully distributing tracts to newly pressed

---

[15] *NSM*, 1827, pp. 388f.; Captain Pakenham to NMBS meeting, *NMBS* 1836, p. 24. John Pakenham: b. 1790, son of Adm. Sir Thomas Pakenham (1757–1836), who had commanded HMS *Invincible* at the Glorious First of June; entered RN Apr 1804 as Vol. First Class in *Repulse*; lieut. Jul 1811, cdr. Jun 1814, post captain 26 Aug 1826, RA retd. 1854, adm. June 1864; by his first marriage was son-in-law of Adm. Sir Home Popham; d.1876.

[16] *NSM*, 1831, p. 133.

men in his manning tender? The spiritual stirrings afloat were widespread and varied: cumulatively they were bringing the Gospel to a wider section of the seafaring population than before, with accessible literature and people on hand to explain the message personally. As Smith was always eager to acknowledge, the missionary work in the navy could never be attributed to one man's endeavour or even the visionary work of a handful. Something of more than human contrivance seemed to be happening here: he believed it was nothing less than the activity of Almighty God.

Smith's idea of a correspondence link revived Campbell's 1798 model, whether consciously or not. His object was to nurture existing faith. It was not direct evangelism, for that could only be done by active Christians at sea. Smith's energy in locating and pastoring his 'virtual congregation' was unceasing, and its costs rapidly amassed. The Naval Correspondence Mission, as he called it, was a burden he could not carry alone. He rarely had much money and never had a head for finance, a fault which even put his marriage under some strain. Penniless sailors could hardly afford the stamp, and were anyway unwilling to have their letters franked aboard, as this would indicate that they were writing to a minister of religion. Smith was therefore obliged to cover the costs of both incoming as well as outgoing mail. The project was rescued by the wealthy Claphamite banker William Henry Hoare, fortunately resident in Penzance, and he met the postage charges, no trifling sum when Smith was writing some fourteen letters a day. From this huge correspondence Smith quoted widely in his various periodicals, giving a view that was patchy and anecdotal, but full of authentic detail and the flavour of the sea service which he knew so well. By the end of the Napoleonic War he claimed to know of groups scattered throughout the fleet.[17]

Although Smith was the most prolific, he was not the only one engaged in supporting such groups from ashore. Indeed, he listed others doing much the same – Fuller, Greathead, Lieutenant Francis Collins of the Religious Tract Society and a few more. It is no coincidence that most of them except Hoare were Dissenters, since the main thrust of Anglican outreach was now through the revitalised chaplaincy and 'Gambierite' officers. There is hint of a social and ecclesiastical divide here, with the Church of England attending to the officers, while Dissenters reached out to the lower deck, but that is only partially true. The full picture is in fact more complex and considerably more revolutionary, for these informal groups provided common ground for all denominations and – intriguingly – for

[17] William Henry Hoare (1776–1819), evangelical and CMS committee member, belonged to the respected family bank Samuel Hoare & Co.

officers and men together. From the testimony of both Smith and Marks it is clear that the cell structure of the 'Naval Awakening' was essentially unplanned. Probably there were individuals or groups who were never drawn into this correspondence network: their existence would have remained unknown. As both Marks and Smith aver, the work seemed to grow up spontaneously, without deliberate intention or much human organisation. Here was proof of its divine authorship, as Marks claimed a few years later:

> Do you ask when and where and how the Lord began this work? He began it on the bosom of the ocean on board of a few ships of war, where neither chaplain nor spiritual guide was found! ... Here a poor sinful seaman, and there a stern and profane officer ... Their custom was to assemble a few of their shipmates in some retired part of the ship where, screened round with a few old hammocks or a piece of worn-out canvas, they read their Bibles, and in their unadorned but earnest manner, discoursed of heaven and of hell – of death and of judgement – of the sins of men, and of the merits, the sufferings, the love and death of Christ. Thus did the Lord begin to attack the power and reign of Satan.[18]

Marks concluded with an estimate of the extent of the Naval Awakening, giving an astonishingly high number which is corroborated by Bo'sun Smith: 'at the conclusion of the war we had a band of praying officers or seamen on board of about fourscore ships of the Royal Navy.'[19] The occasion was the third anniversary of the British and Foreign Seamen's Christian Friend Society and Bethel Union, an organisation to which Marks attributed much of the recent 'rapid growth which religion has made amongst seamen'.[20] Although a supporter and collaborator of Bo'sun Smith, Marks would not claim for him, or even for himself, the authorship of the naval movement: he felt they had been only part of a wider activity of God. Smith was going to prove indispensable to the post-war revival of religious interest amongst merchant sailors. The origins of this movement lay in the wartime fleet, where men thrown together by the demands of hostilities, forced by their circumstances to face issues of life and death, had begun of their own accord to seek religious explanations. In this quest they might turn to the New Testaments that had been widely distributed by the Bible societies. To their work Marks attributed the beginnings of the spiritual movement on the lower

---

[18] Address by Marks preached at St Bride's Church, Fleet Street in October 1821, and included in *Ocean*, p. 255.

[19] Ibid. For number of ships involved, see n. 4 above.

[20] Ibid.

deck and amongst merchant seamen. He stated as much at the anniversary meeting of the NMBS in 1820:

> It is this Society which must be considered as the parent, in the hand of God, in planting the seed that now begins to spread its branches over the river – of commencing in the Royal Navy that Christian work which is carrying on by and so much influencing the conduct of the mercantile seamen in the river Thames in this season of peace.[21]

Opposition to 'Methodists' and Cell Groups

How were the lower-deck prayer groups regarded by their colleagues? In a fighting service, comradeship is more than a sweetener for communal life: it is its essence, the bond which inspires self-sacrifice and gives assurance of support when lives are at stake. Discipline will forge unity, of course: it was the virtue every officer prized. On the lower deck it was comradeship that counted, loyalty to one's fellows – and that was something which worked at a deeper level altogether. The psalm singers fell foul of this basic serviceman's creed. They were putting personal convictions ahead of group loyalty, the collective solidarity which had been the key to success at Spithead. Worse than that, these Christian believers, with their talk of conversion, implied a criticism of their colleagues. They were uncomfortable shipmates, always unpopular. In officers' eyes, the 'psalm-singers' might put good order at risk in at least two ways: first, there might be something subversive about private gatherings below decks (insofar as privacy of any kind was attainable there), and in the second place any irritant to social harmony was to be deplored.

From Smith we learn how they were treated. Verbal abuse was apparently common, directed at 'the religious mob, the sanctified sect, the psalm-singing methodist club'.[22] At times there seems to have been a more menacing edge to the mockery, with threats of violence. Occasionally they were roughly handled. When the *Barfleur* was at Spithead in 1798, a drunken lout, with the noisy encouragement of a group of prostitutes, disrupted a prayer meeting. Writing in 1823 of the 'religious groups in the King's ships in the last war', Smith described how they would meet every evening for prayer between the guns on the main deck 'while

---

[21] *NMBS* 1820, p. 46. The Thames Revival is the term used by Kverndal to describe the rapid growth of prayer meetings and church services aboard merchant vessels in the river and port of London. Smith contributed to it with his floating chapel and mariners' church. Kverndal discerns its origins in the wartime naval developments. See pp. 274–5 below.

[22] Contemptuous expression attributed to an officer in the *Barfleur*: *NSM*, 1828, p. 124.

their enemies sent in prostitutes to interrupt them, threw various things at them, and rolled shot in among them.'[23] Sailors might be moved from one ship to another or their meetings might be broken up by authority. There is no evidence of real persecution – such as befell two corporals at Gibraltar in 1803, sentenced to 200 lashes for attending a Methodist meeting in the home of a civilian in the town.[24] In general, pious sailors could expect mockery rather than violence, benefiting from the broad generosity of spirit which seafaring life engendered.

The 'psalm-singers' often managed to win a grudging regard, as in the *Victory* and the *Repulse*: they were respected by their officers as men who needed no punishment and by the lower deck as prime hands. This was the boast which Smith was keen to record. Far from being a liability, they were as skilful and daring as their colleagues, but added rarer qualities of steadiness and sobriety. Under a sympathetic captain they might be allowed considerable liberty – to meet for Bible study and prayer, or to learn reading and writing, or to form a music group. These were harmless ways of filling hours off watch which offered constructive benefits to the ship's company. Occasionally there was abuse of the privilege. Ross recalls a bogus group in the *Prince of Wales*, allowed a private berth for their devotions, who used it as a hideaway for stolen goods.[25]

It was no doubt for reasons like this that most commanders preferred any group to be led by an officer, a chaplain, or a trusted petty officer. In the *Elizabeth* the master's mate John Hubback organised a regular gathering for prayer, singing and spiritual discourse on three evenings a week until warned to stop by the captain; then, according to Smith, the meetings continued, but in a less obvious manner and without any singing to give them away. Hubback had been mate of a merchant vessel when impressed in 1807, and he reached the rank of master three years later – a steady, reliable man able to give mature leadership to his group and to head off confrontation with authority. In the *Ganges* the captain approved of the new piety and sanctioned a large lower-deck gathering of two dozen men without an officer in charge. The directing 'pastor' was a seaman named John Clark, who had been converted at Tahiti, and was running the work very effectively as two Methodist classes when Marks encountered it in 1809. Something comparable went on in the *Phoebe* with a Methodist marine under a Blue Light captain. To be effective, these gatherings did not require officer leadership; after a fashion they could function without official approval, but a captain's encouragement lent protection to their

[23] George Charles Smith, *Minehead and Watchet Officers and the Bethel Flag* (Bristol, 1823), p. 19.

[24] B. D. Crofts, A. K. Stanley and P. Jefferies, *Upon this Rock* (Gibraltar, 1969), p. 9.

[25] Ross, II, p. 93.

activities and hindered opposition to their evangelising tendencies. As increasing numbers of Blue Lights attained commissioned rank and command the cell groups grew in size and number.[26]

Multiplying Cell Groups

THE mutinies had shown how capable lower-deck leadership and organisation could be, with enough ingenuity to hold their clandestine meetings. The psalm-singers possessed the same qualities. At its simplest, it only needed two like-minded men to find a few moments to pray together. If they showed any propensity to share their beliefs, to 'witness' to their faith, they would attract others, both the idly curious and the genuinely seeking. The process of expansion, involving individual testimony, was inevitably slow and undramatic. It was normally confined to one ship and it left only haphazard evidence of its happening, in the testimonies gathered by Bo'sun Smith.

The Blue Lights had rekindled an interest in religion, a stress on its importance and value: with their rank they had given a fresh impetus to wardroom discussion. They had made religion topical and respectable. Individual captains felt obliged to look out for volumes of suitable sermons to read aloud on Sundays – an embarrassing task for some. A fortunate commander might find he had a lieutenant eager to take the service – exactly the process whereby Lieutenant Marks was instructed by Captain Israel Pellew to lead divine worship for the crew of the *Conqueror*. In his case, the opportunity for Sunday prayers led on to more, and he was permitted to hold a Bible study group for the men. As the impulse towards regular public worship gathered momentum, it gave encouragement to this informal movement below decks. If the tiny prayer groups were to grow beyond a handful of men, they needed the protection of an officer's authority to give the lie to any suspicion of a subversive gathering. As more officers of this persuasion made their appearance in the fleet, so more of the lower-deck gatherings became visible, numbers attending grew and the cells proliferated. They could exist without officer leadership, and would have continued anyway because they exactly met the needs of the hour. The enlarged numbers meeting together and the remarkable proliferation of the phenomenon is explained by the linking of the lower-deck groups with spiritually minded officers. Strikingly, and only a few years after the Great Mutinies, 'vital religion' was bringing together officers and men in shared Christian fellowship where ideas were discussed and prayer offered.

[26] Kverndal, *Seamen's Missions*, p. 109. John Hubback (1774–1810), drowned Nov. 1810 while serving as master. Kverndal, p. 667 nn. 212–16, gives important references as evidence for lower-deck groups: *The Sailors Magazine*, 1820, pp. 113–17, 154–60, and *The Evangelical Magazine*, 1817, pp. 168–72.

An example of how powerful a captain's attitude could be in giving endorsement and respectability to a cell group comes from the frigate *Phoebe*. A marine (William M) joined the ship in 1806; in civilian life a Methodist lay preacher, he earned notoriety by trying to divert his shipmates from vice to true religion, but the arrival of Hillyar in command encouraged shipboard services and evangelism. Interest in Christianity grew, there were some notable conversions, and eventually the 'Methodist Parson' was leading a group of twenty men. Without Hillyar's endorsement the group might have struggled, but without an active pastor on the lower deck the captain's efforts might have remained ephemeral. The marine's earlier and unfruitful attempts to evangelise his shipmates proved that evangelicalism was not simply a quarter-deck fad or a means of social control.[27]

Two eyewitness accounts give a glimpse of religious groups in named ships at the height of the Napoleonic War. First, in Austen's *St. Albans*, 'abreast of the pumps on the larboard side we find the pious John Cavanaugh, with his little society, singing the praises of God, reading and expounding the Word of God, joining in mutual prayer ... and praising the name of God.'[28] While all this was in progress, officers and men gathered to listen. Once Austen had been superseded by a captain of a different temper in 1810, these open religious activities ended, confirming that officer-encouragement had real impact.

A particularly valuable picture of a cell in operation is presented in the letters of Private William Wheeler of the 51st Regiment of Foot. In 1809, while on passage in HMS *L'Impetueux* for the Walcheren expedition, he formed a highly critical view of the navy, principally on account of the ferocious floggings he witnessed. In January 1811 the regimental headquarters and five companies of troops embarked in the troopship *Revenge* as reinforcements for Wellington in Portugal. His opinion of the navy was totally altered. The relevant extract from his letters is worth quoting *in extenso* for its detailed picture of religious observance at sea. Incidentally it portrays a pious commander beloved of his crew – James Nash – and a ship where religious observance was an accepted, even perhaps welcome, part of routine.

> When on board the *l'Impetueux* I had formed a very unfavourable opinion of the Navy. A short time on board this ship has in great measure corrected

[27] Kverndal, *Seamen's Missions*, p. 109.

[28] Smith, *Windsor*, p. 69. John Cavanagh was an Irish-born officer (but not commissioned) who became interested in Christianity in the 1790s through one of the Bibles supplied to his ship. Accused of 'Methodism', he determined to find out what that meant, and joined the Portsmouth Society; Kverndal, *Seamen's Missions*, p. 668, n. 222.

that opinion. The Captain goes by the name of 'Father'. Cursing and swearing is not allowed. The good feeling existing between the Captain and sailors was fully displayed last Sunday morning, when the ship's company assembled for the Captain's inspection. It was truly pleasing to see the good old man, their 'Father' as the men have justly named him, walking through the ranks of sailors, who all appeared as clean as possible, with health and contentment glowing on their faces. As he past the men he seemed to impart to each a portion of his own good nature. After the sailors, our inspection came on. The good old man accompanied the Colonel through our ranks, his affectionate looks and smiles gained all our hearts.

There follows a description of 'Church' at sea and the occupations of Sunday, with a glimpse of a religious group at their devotions, together with some evidence on the question of literacy:

After inspection all hands were piped to church. The place set apart for Divine service is the quarter deck, which is sheltered from the wind or sun by hanging out different colours. This day the spirit of the fourth Commandment was put into force far beyond anything I could have expected, nothing was done but what was absolutely necessary, the sailors neat and clean employing themselves agreeable to the bent of their own inclinations. In one place might be seen a sailor sitting on a gun reading to his shipmates, others reading to themselves, in another place a party could be listening to the hair breadths escapes and wonderous deeds of some well fought battle, while others less careless would assemble in some sequestered spot, offering up prayers and singing Hymns of praise to their Creator and Redeemer. Amongst each party of sailors might be seen a good sprinkling of red jackets, this gave life to the scene. I viewed it with delight, and I might truly say I never passed a day in my life so completely happy.

Wheeler's picture of shipboard routine shows a soldier's mind fascinated by all he saw. Sailors might have noticed more the monotony, and yet it is clear that a happy ship's company found ways to enliven their leisure. Again we note that the prayer group makes a mid-week appearance.

Through the week all is bustle, every hand is employed, the same cheerfulness prevailed, no cursing or swearing or rope's ends is brought into practice. The word of command or Boatswain's pipes is sufficient to set this mighty living machine in motion. Two evenings each week is devoted to amusement, then the Boatswain's mates with their pipes summon 'All hands to play'. In a moment the scene is truly animating. The crews

For 500 men and boys he organised schools in which literacy and elementary seamanship were taught by the better educated sailors. He established a choir and orchestra, important ways of filling leisure when apathy and disintegration of society could have set in so easily. The value of his contribution was recognised by the Admiralty, who regarded him as an unofficial naval chaplain and paid him accordingly (and the *détenu* clergyman who succeeded him). When transferred from Givet after more than five years, he left behind a community largely transformed: where formerly their word could not be trusted, now 200 were allowed out on parole. Defection to the French was reduced. Instead of apathy and crime there was a flourishing educational system and organised recreation; according to the reminiscences of John Wetherell, a seaman from HMS *Hussar*, the French referred to Givet prison as 'a repository of Arts and Sciences'.[33] All church services were voluntary, and out of 1,500 prisoners, over 200 regularly attended worship. Significantly, Wolfe noted that many of them had never been in church before; of these he baptised several. In his view the responsiveness of sailors might be measured by the reverent and even tearful way in which the first fourteen communicants received the Sacrament, or by the attendance of a full hundred men gathered for an early service in the damp and cold of a winter morning, but he was realistic enough to acknowledge that the faith of quite a few was still shaky. Nonetheless he was sure that by the time he left Givet there were men of practical piety in every mess, and the work continued under his successor.

An awakening of a similar kind was going on amongst other seamen prisoners. At Cambrai there was a society of forty-six members 'agreeable to the Word of God'. They were led by John Taylor, presumably a sailor, and their meetings often attracted sixty or seventy in attendance. They met for prayer and hymn-singing each day, with a 45-minute meeting morning and evening, and their leader preached a sermon every Sunday. Evening prayer meetings were held to 'exercise' members. They knew of similar blessings experienced at Valenciennes, Verdun and Longwy. Again it is noteworthy that sailors with neither officer nor chaplain proved perfectly able to organise meetings for worship and for religious instruction. The evidence for all this activity is extensive, including the reminiscences of Wolfe and Brenton, the reports which Bo'sun Smith collected and published, and the account of an escape by Captain Boys – in addition to Wetherell's journal. Captain Boys and two midshipmen escaped from Valenciennes: one of them included a prayer book with his kit, and the party read the service of morning

---

[33] C. S. Forester (ed.), The *Adventures of John Wetherell* (1954), p. 177.

prayer from it together while hiding in woods when the sound of church bells reminded them it was a Sunday.34

In later years Smith reckoned that almost 800 men had been converted during this period, but such a figure is beyond verification. Incontestably many sailors had been touched by the work amongst prisoners, and the effects were felt after the war, when most of them had found their way into the merchant marine. Evangelistic work amongst Thames shipping in 1816 discovered an unexpected willingness of seafarers to gather for prayer. The response was so great that Kverndal, the historian of maritime missiology, has called it the Thames Revival: he believes that men who had served a spiritual apprenticeship in the French prison fortresses were ready to play their part as evangelists, helpers and lay shipboard pastors to their messmates. As we shall see, some features of this movement replicated wartime gatherings afloat, with lay leadership, prayer groups, Bible reading and hymn singing. The ground had been well prepared.35

Lieutenant the Reverend Richard Marks and The Retrospect

WHEN Blue Lights were admirals and captains they became enablers of more junior figures who in turn took advantage of the improving climate for religion. Senior officers could promote respect for Christian observance and could provide opportunity for worship and witness, but they were too far removed from wardroom and messdecks to have much personal impact. *Regulations* might encourage better chaplains or more regular Sunday observance, but the work of arousing interest and of nurturing personal faith required closer engagement with people. The dynamics of the movement can be studied through the experience of a junior officer, Richard Marks. He wrote his reminiscences, not as autobiography nor a history of naval religion, but as a collection of homilies for private use. Close friends from his parish ministry were curious about his sea-going past, and for them he composed a few papers to illustrate biblical texts from his experiences. Drawing upon some dramatic events and reflecting upon them with theological insight and a pastor's heart, Marks could find sermons in snatches of autobi-

---

34 *NSM*, 1828, pp. 217–19; Forester, pp. 149, 177; *NSM*, 1827, pp. 52, 217–19; Commander Edward Boys, *Narrative of a Captivity and Adventures in France and Flanders between the Years 1803 and 1809* (1827; 2nd edn 1831), pp. 138f.; Michael R. Bruce, 'The Escape of Midshipman Thomas Blakiston, RN', *MM*, XLIX (1973), pp. 209–17, 335–52.

35 Kverndal quotes the figure of nearly 800 converts from *NSM*, 1834, pp. 189–91, 227. Lewis comments on officers' detention at Verdun, together with critical observations concerning Brenton's over-scrupulous interpretation of his role as senior officer: *Dillon*, pp. 40–5.

ography. He was best known for his spiritual memoirs *The Retrospect*, first published in 1816 but much extended in later editions, and a collection of essays *The Ocean Spiritually Reviewed*, another publishing success which appeared first in 1813 as *Nautical Essays*. His purpose was didactic but his style was warm, persuasive, encouraging. Nothing was included for the sake of a good narrative but to illustrate the Christian message in ways that readers could apply to their own circumstances.[36]

The second chapter is headed with a verse from the Psalms: 'Bless the Lord, O my soul, and forget not all his benefits.' There follows an account of the wreck of the *Prosperpine* in 1799, with reflections on his shameful ingratitude to God after rescue, and a call to his readers to praise the Lord for his blessings. The next brief chapter is headed 'One shall be taken and the other left.' Again the focus is on the survivors of that shipwreck off the ice-bound mouth of the Elbe; one apparently strong woman died in the cold while a seemingly delicate newly delivered mother survived. Marks meditates on the reason: 'we must look beyond natural causes and effects, even unto the will of Him whose ever-watchful and over-ruling providence numbers the hairs on our heads, and suffers not a sparrow to fall to the ground without his permission.' The human mind can give no answers to the problem of suffering, but must trust itself to the righteous judgement of a merciful God. A later chapter takes the theme of God's over-ruling once again, but this time it is a reflection of how the blessing of God may turn apparently trivial actions or words into something of eternal significance. The Christian's task is to sow good seed – a familiar New Testament image – and God may well turn it to someone's blessing a good time later: 'Cast your bread upon the waters, for thou shalt find it after many days.'[37] Here Marks recollects a letter sent, a book loaned, a few words spoken and forgotten by him, but influential in changing the thinking and conduct of someone at sea.

The anecdotes he uses are deftly drawn, and they become parables to explain how the Christian life should be lived. The style would be too flowery for modern taste but was evidently well appreciated in the early and mid-nineteenth century. The first readers of the papers valued them enough to pass them to others and to

---

36 Rev. Richard Marks (1778–1844): admitted sizar at Magdalene College, Cambridge, 12 Apr 1813; ordained deacon at Norwich, 20 Dec 1812; ordained priest, 27 Jun 1813 (Venn); vicar of Great Missenden, 1820–44; retired through ill health; died 22 May 1847 after long illness. Richard Marks [as 'Aliquis'], *Nautical Essays* (1813), reissued as *The Ocean Spiritually Reviewed* (1824; 7th edn 1848); *The Retrospect* (1816; 20th edn 1842). See also the Rev. J. B. Marsden, *Two Sermons on the Life, Ministry and Death of the Late Rev. Richard Marks* (1847).

37 *Retrospect*, p. 21. 'Cast your bread upon the waters': Ecclesiastes 11:1.

ask for them to be published. The demand for further editions encouraged Marks to expand the collection, and *The Retrospect* became highly popular. By 1842 it had reached twenty-one chapters and a twentieth edition, with an additional chapter entitled 'An especial address to Naval Officers' concluding an octavo work of 346 pages. Marks had become a best-selling author. *The Ocean, Spiritually Reviewed and compared to passing scenes on the land* was another work which used his nautical experiences to illuminate practical theology: it was into its sixth edition by 1840. *Familiar Questions* for junior classes of Sunday Schools had reached 27,000 in print by the same date, while various tracts had gone to multiple editions, fourth, eleventh, eighteenth and so on. It has been estimated that his nautical tracts alone attained a circulation of a million.[38]

Using didactic autobiography as evidence about the state of naval religion calls for caution. It was written neither as history nor as a connected narrative but there are nevertheless reassuring features. The first edition was published in 1816, reasonably close to his wartime experiences, and the author had apparently kept a few records from those times – personal diaries, letters and copies of outgoing correspondence. Furthermore, his motives for going to press were unconnected with vanity. Marks was a self-effacing author. He wrote under the revealing pseudonym Aliquis – 'anyone' – with the subtitle 'Formerly a Lieutenant in the Royal Navy and now a Minister in the Established Church.' The ships he served in are identified by initial capitals only, P, N, D, C, and individuals are camouflaged as 'Macarius', 'Eugenius' or in a late footnote 'Sir G.H.' His text in *The Retrospect* does not betray even the name of the parish or county in which he ministered. Anonymity suggests that he was not writing for personal glorification. But he did have a good story to tell, and, where verification is possible, his details are clearly authentic. It is time to let him relate his experiences.

His glimpses of naval life are all the more telling because they appear like details in an illuminated manuscript, incidental to the main purpose but sharp and colourful. The pathetic band of survivors from the *Proserpine* struggling against wind and ice to find shelter; boat work close inshore when moonlight made his cutter a target for infantry fire, and Marks had to stand in the stern-sheets to con her out of danger with the loss of one man killed; life-saving treatment in the naval hospital at Malta; off-duty rambles in the hills around Port Mahon; the comradeship and stimulus of wardroom life, where officers display breadth of reading and even erudition. He confirms how sparse religious observance was in most ships: in eleven years' service the *Conqueror* went almost eight without a Sunday service, 'nor was this by any means an uncommon thing in the navy.' It would

[38] Kverndal, *Seamen's Missions*, p. 108.

have been true for two-thirds of battle ships and nine-tenths of smaller ships and vessels.

> The distinction between Sunday and other days at sea consisted, in the writer's time, of setting aside the more laborious and dirty work, mustering the crew in their best clothes, examining and taking an account of their wearing apparel, reading the Articles of War every fourth week, and giving liberty for the purchase of an extra and unnecessary portion of rum from the shore when in port.[39]

The main outlines of his career can be teased out from *The Retrospect*, supplemented by reference to the Navy List and records in the National Archives. Born on 31 December 1778, he was brought up by an aunt following the death of his mother. In childhood his adventurous temperament attracted him to water, boisterous sports and exploits with gunpowder, while his reading conjured up romantic dreams of seafaring. He therefore enlisted as a landsman in February 1797, apparently without significant interest to promote his career. In the *Expedition* he survived hard wartime service in the Mediterranean, apparently including operations in Egypt in 1801. His life was imperilled by enemy action, and by near-fatal fever at Malta. Twice he had a brush with fire aboard ship, and on one occasion he found and dealt with the danger single-handed while in port. Further service took him to the North Sea. In wild winter weather he survived the wreck of the *Proserpine* (Captain J. Wallis) on the island of Baltrum at the mouth of the Elbe in February 1799. Fifteen lives were lost, but the survivors struggled across ice and waded through near-freezing water to eventual safety in Cuxhaven. According to *The Naval Chronicle* the miraculous escape of so many should be attributed to Providence.[40] As master's mate he endured a second shipwreck in one year, when the *Nassau* was lost off the Dutch coast on 14 October.

By now recognised in his profession as tough and capable, he did duty as an acting lieutenant in a small ship before joining the 74-gun *Defence* (Captain George Hope) in June 1803. The next month he passed the examination for lieutenant, but without a vacancy to occupy, reverted to his substantive rank of master's mate with further responsibilities as leader of the fire-fighting team and heading a boarding party. In her he took part in the blockade of Cadiz and the Battle of Trafalgar. The *Defence* was close to the rear of Collingwood's division, but there was still hard fighting to be done by the time she was fully engaged. She did battle with both the French *Berwick* and a Spanish ship of the line, taking the

---

[39] *Retrospect*, p. 110n.

[40] *NC*, I, p. 334.

surrender of the *San Ildefonso* late in that afternoon of carnage, but her losses of seven killed and twenty-nine wounded were relatively light. As part of the prize crew, Marks shared in a desperate struggle to save her from the subsequent storm and bring her safely into Gibraltar. In the promotions which followed victory, Marks received his lieutenant's commission in November 1805, and was selected to accompany Captain Hope into the *Conqueror* (74) for further operations off the Spanish coast.

Hope was succeeded by Sir Israel Pellew, and again Marks was fortunate in his commanding officer. A post captain since 1793, he had experienced loss of ship (the *Amphion*, destroyed by accidental explosion), mutiny (his crew in the *Greyhound* had put him ashore in the 1797 disturbances) and fleet action (in command of the *Dreadnought* at Trafalgar, where he received the surrender of the French admiral Villeneuve). Pellew's spiritual convictions eventually paralleled his brother's. Although he does not appear as a supporter of the NMBS, the favoured tool of naval evangelism, he gave vital encouragement to the *Conqueror*'s group. Like his brother he was influenced by Hawker his parish priest, and he closed his life with the apostle Paul's affirmation of faith, 'I know in Whom I have believed.'[41]

Pellew invited Marks to read Sunday service for the ship's company, thus beginning a varied ministry of formal worship and voluntary gatherings for Bible teaching, branching out into literacy classes, music groups and a lending library. For two or three years this work continued, until terminated by a new captain. By now Marks was beginning to consider a vocation ashore. He had served pretty well continuously for twelve years at sea and had begun to suffer from rheumatism. Although he had a powerful friend to advance his naval career, for Sir George Hope had become an admiral and was on the Board of Admiralty, Marks had developed another ambition. His heart was set on a parish ministry where his preaching and teaching gifts could be given free rein. His application to go ashore was allowed in 1810. At an hour's notice he was ordered home in the *Royal Sovereign*, having served four years in the *Conqueror*; when he landed at Portsmouth it seemed that all naval links would be severed. He entered Cambridge university to train in theology. Then came a seven-year curacy in the village of 'W..ch' (perhaps Whitchurch), before appointment to the living of Great Missenden, Buckinghamshire, where he ministered for more than twenty years. At his own request he came off the Navy List and forfeited half-pay because he had no intention of leaving church work in order to serve at sea again.

---

[41] Mahan, p. 476. Rev. Robert Hawker, DD (1753–1827), controversial vicar of Charles from 1784 and deputy chaplain of the Plymouth garrison, wrote *The Sailor Pilgrim*, Part 1 in 1806, and Part 2 in 1810; *BDEB*, I, pp. 537f., and p. 182 n. 12 above.

Although vicar of an inland parish Marks could not completely disentangle himself from his sea-going past. In 1813 he published his first book, reflecting on nautical themes, followed three years later by his pseudonymous memoirs. The authorship was probably clear enough to Francis Collins, for he had shared in some of the same operations as Marks, and he was on the lookout for someone who could write effectively for sailors. A former lieutenant in the frigate *Dolphin*, Collins had often been on service in the Mediterranean in company with the *Expedition*, and may well have become acquainted with Marks during this period; he had been promoted lieutenant in 1800, but a promising career ended in Egypt with a wound which carried him out of active service. After the navy he had found a new career with the Religious Tract Society; he knew how seamen derided any literature that misused nautical terms, and he believed Marks was just the man to create Gospel tracts that sailors would treat with respect. This was the impetus that drew Marks back to maritime evangelism, with the first of his seven RTS tracts, *Conversation in a Boat*, published in 1816. His success as a writer was stunning. Within ten years half a million of his tracts were in circulation, a figure eventually doubled. From his inland vicarage Marks now began to reach, not just one ship's company, but thousands of seamen in the fleet and the merchant marine. If his tracts became the ready-use ammunition for the activists who pushed forward the Thames Revival, his books stirred shore-going supporters to pray and give money to fund this evangelism. His self-assessment of the achievement was modest, but Marks must surely be linked with Bo'sun Smith and Gambier as the chief post-war advocates of the Seamen's Cause.[42]

Marks's Spiritual Development

THE *Retrospect* demonstrates how one individual came to possess the faith of the Blue Lights, and how that set of beliefs affected naval service. There seems to have been nothing particularly religious about Marks's upbringing, and nothing to shock him when he encountered unrefined sea-going life. For a time he had a conscience about 'the horrid and prevalent practice of swearing', but within a few months he was blaspheming like his colleagues. He read 'vile and infamous writings' (as he later came to regard them), and copied out extracts. Once he tried to find a Bible, but solely to parody its literary style for the amusement of his fellow midshipmen. Not even his first experience of shipwreck produced any concern for his soul; instead he and his fellow survivors celebrated their narrow escape from death with 'drunkenness, oaths and profane songs'.[43]

[42] *Retrospect*, pp. 59f.; Kverndal, *Seamen's Missions*, p. 167.
[43] *Retrospect*, p. 34.

Drafted next into the *Nassau* for blockade duties off the Dutch coast, Marks had joined an unhappy ship with a captain given to drunkenness and an incompetent sailing master; the crew had not been together long, and lacked the easy comradeship of much shared experience. The lieutenants were gentlemanly enough, but appeared to dislike the ship. Blasphemy abounded, and Marks detected more of the characteristics of 'a hell afloat' than any other ship he knew. 'What this vessel might have become had she floated for a few years longer, time only could show; but God would not permit the experiment to be tried.'[44] Marks continued his self-education aboard her, and began to write verse. Occasionally he explored exalted moral themes, as in his poem 'The Sailor's Prayer', disparagingly described by its author as a few petitions to the Ruler of the Universe for wisdom and courage under all conditions of seafaring life. And, of course, sea-going was beset by frequent danger.

Interestingly, Marks believed that the experience of combat was too fast moving to produce the kind of fear which turned a man to his Creator; shipwreck was another matter.

> In the heat of battle it is not only possible, but easy, to forget death and cease to shrink; but in the cool and protracted hours of a shipwreck, where there is often nothing to engage the mind but the recollection of tried and unsuccessful labours, and the sight of unavoidable and increasing harbingers of destruction, it is not so easy to forget ourselves or a future state.[45]

The *Retrospect* contains a detailed account of the loss of the *Nassau*. In high seas and poor visibility, with a strong on-shore wind, the captain was convinced that a fixed light marking a shoal was a distant ship. Soon after midnight the ship ran aground.

> We dashed upon the fatal bank with such violence that those on deck were thrown off their feet, and those below were instantly roused from their slumbers to hear the doleful report, 'The ship is on shore! The ship is on shore!' All was confusion and alarm; the crew were seen on deck, some half-dressed and others just as they leaped out of bed. The long-boat was hoisted out, and instantly filled, and was dashed to pieces alongside; signal-guns of distress were fired every minute; blue lights were burnt; and measures taken to prevent the ship from falling over on her side. The chain-pumps were set to work, but our leaks defied all such resistance. The ship bilged, the sand worked through the bottom, and long before dawn the well was choked up,

---

[44] *Retrospect*, p. 37.
[45] *Retrospect*, pp. 45f.

and the lower part of the vessel filled. A raft was now made with our spare top-masts and other available materials, should any means of using it be afforded. This done, nothing remained for us to do but to wait the return of day.[46]

The ship was stranded seven or eight miles from shore. The raft was swamped before it could be used to save lives. Around noon the weather moderated and a British brig anchored nearby to give help. Marks volunteered for a boat's crew to attempt to reach her, but he was ordered out in favour of a stronger man. A few moments later a wave smashed the boat against the wreck, destroying the oars on one side, and rendering it vulnerable to the next surge which capsized it, taking the lives of all its occupants. Despite all perils, 200 men had been safely transferred to the brig by nightfall, leaving the remaining survivors with another anxious night aboard a ship which was breaking up in the pounding seas. Marks got off in one of the two last boats of the day, choosing his moment to jump in the gathering darkness and succeeding where many failed. Next day the disintegrating wreck was cleared of its remaining crew, but sixty men had perished.

For Marks as he looked back, his rescue from the *Nassau* was an amazing demonstration of God's grace to him, inexplicable, and certainly owing nothing to the pathetic bargain he had tried to make – as many must have done before and since in such a desperate situation – offering God his allegiance if He would save his life. Once safe, the deal was forgotten, until death came close again. This time it was illness that threatened, a fever apparently contracted from the French garrison at Genoa after their surrender. After many days of delirium in hospital at Minorca, Marks had time and strength to review his past life. Although he believed in the justice of God and the reality of life beyond death, he had no assurance of salvation. He knew he was not guiltless but hoped he might be good enough for God. He read through the Prayer Book services for the sick and dying, but still remained ignorant of 'salvation by grace through faith in a crucified Redeemer.' Marks still assumed that he must try in some way to deserve God's favour. 'I still conceived of the Almighty as a being unamiable, austere, and full of terror. I saw nothing, I knew nothing of him as a God who delighteth in mercy.'[47]

When he returned to the *Expedition* he was still ignorant concerning faith, but reckoned he had become more aware of his conscience and more teachable. Help came from reading. The captain thought well of Marks, and treated him as a friend; Marks was with him when he died of an illness, and valued as a keepsake his two volumes of Burder's *Village Sermons*. They had not been read by the

[46] *Retrospect*, pp. 38f.
[47] *Retrospect*, p. 53.

captain, but they were eagerly studied by the master's mate. In particular Marks was struck by a sermon about the Roman jailer at Philippi, who asked what he must do to be saved, and was told to 'believe on the Lord Jesus Christ.' When close to death in hospital Marks had wanted an answer to the same question. At last he was beginning to see that the Christian message was about faith not conduct, about grace not deserving, about receiving not doing. He began to appreciate the need for a peacemaker between God and his own soul, and realised that the Son of God had become just such a mediator. Hope was dawning along with his understanding.

Marks read the sermons and followed them with Bible readings. He stopped deriding religion and tried to clean up his language. He read *Pilgrim's Progress* and felt he was hearing not the words of Bunyan but the voice of God. Yet true faith eluded him. The change was still a matter of behaviour, not a personal relationship with God. Not even the improved conduct lasted. He was now concerned about honour and how to merit it. Marks tells us darkly that angry passions drove him on. Trafalgar brought promotion but his soul was not satisfied with success. When he moved into the *Conqueror* he was still questioning, still seeking. By now he had begun to doubt that the Bible could be the only guide and he explored Deism. No peace of mind came from his philosophical studies. He knelt beside the cannon in his cabin and prayed that God would show him where truth lay. He returned to Bible reading but found that undisciplined thoughts hindered any serious study.

Another brush with death forced deeper questionings. As a group of young officers was returning from a shooting party ashore, one of them made Marks a target for a pebble fired from his gun, mistakenly convinced that it would harmlessly disintegrate into powder. The shot put a hole in his hat, and lent urgency to his quest for spiritual certainty. He went to service on Sunday at Old Stoke parish church. There he heard an address which explained the grace of God. Marks went back repeatedly for public worship and private counselling until he was sure that the death of Christ had atoned for his sins. With his life now reorientated he looked for opportunity to serve God. His reluctance to return to sea was settled by the minister's challenging question, 'Who knows but that the Lord may make you serviceable in the ship?'[48]

Marks's Mission at Sea

MARKS provides a detailed picture of how he interpreted his spiritual mission at sea. It is clear that religious cells formed aboard a number of ships but how they operated is less evident. His account of one group's life cycle

---

[48] *Retrospect*, p. 85.

from inception, through heyday and on to eventual closure is particularly valuable as it illuminates a number of issues. Groups, as we have seen, could function as autonomous lower-deck affairs, but the account in *The Retrospect* shows the process might work differently. In the *Conqueror* it was Marks who called a religious group into being, the culmination of a process which began at Pellew's dinner table.

On one occasion the conversation revolved around religion. The general view was that particular belief was less important than sincerity, and all creeds might be considered equally acceptable before God. Pellew suggested a rationale for a less inclusive view: if Scripture had any authority, then surely men were not free to form their own creed? Marks promptly supported his captain with some further comments on man's inability to save himself by his own efforts. His intervention went down well with Pellew if no one else. 'You preach very well, Marks', he said 'and you shall read prayers next Sunday if you will.' Marks asked permission to read a short discourse from a book of published addresses in addition to reading the formal liturgy. So began the first divine worship held in five years.[49]

Marks gives a picture of the scene. Rigging church involved clearing a space where the whole crew could assemble and fitting it up for worship. 'This is done sometimes between decks, and sometimes on the quarter or upper deck. Stools are placed and flags of different colours suspended round the sides and over-head, so as to form an enclosed space, and to produce a pleasing effect.'[50] That first service proved a testing occasion for a young lieutenant, sure of the captain's support, but conscious that his wardroom colleagues would determine his social happiness for a long time to come. And how would the ship's company respond to the unfamiliar service? For a time at least the variation to routine was welcome, and some curiosity surrounded Marks and his proposal to hold voluntary evening prayers later in the day.

> The day was remarkably fine. No public duty intervened. … The church was rigged, the bell rang, and the captain, officers and entire crew soon took their seats according to that order and discipline which prevails in ships of war. Much as I had longed for, and pleased and rejoiced as I certainly was at the sight, yet it confounded me. More than 600 bare heads and attentive looks, all directed to myself, as I advanced to my stand, were more terrible than the muzzles of so many frowning cannons had ever been. A nervous feverish heat actually dried up my tongue and nearly prevented articulation, which of course much increased my confusion; in short, this proved

[49] *Retrospect*, p. 90.
[50] *Retrospect*, p. 90n.

one of the most formidable undertakings I had ever embarked in. I literally trembled while I read through the prayers, and more so, if possible, when I came to the sermon. At length I got through the service and retired to my cabin, full of confusion and self-reproach in that I had not looked up to God with sufficient earnestness for a realising sense of his presence, as the only thing that could deliver me from this snare – this fear of man.[51]

During the tedious blockade of Brest the *Conqueror* spent many Sundays at anchor, when church was rigged and service read. Pellew gave permission for voluntary evening prayers with a sermon to be held below decks, attended by some 200 men.

To enliven Sunday worship Marks instigated a music group comprising a choir of up to a dozen members accompanied by a band of 'two clarionets and a bass'. There were two additional benefits in this activity; first the involvement of several more than Marks in the preparation and leading of divine service, and secondly the provision of a dog-watch interest for men off-duty. There was apparently an upsurge of interest in Christianity, aided by a supply of sixty-four Bibles obtained in Gibraltar from the NMBS and tracts from the Religious Tract Society. At least one copy of the Scriptures was to be found in each mess. Some crew members bought their own prayer books so that they could follow and share in public worship.

The next step followed logically. If sailors were to read and understand the Bible they must be given opportunity to learn their letters. Marks soon found himself with a programme of adult education. Under his direction, literacy classes were provided, chiefly for the ship's boys. Marks loved his teaching role; he extended it when he became a clergyman by instituting a village school for his parish. He refers to the *Conqueror*'s boys as 'poor', and it is not difficult to infer that he was developing that 'bias to the poor' which some theologians find implicit in the Gospel. When moving into the ministry he deliberately chose to work in a village parish where his acquired learning could serve a school and his untutored medical skills – mostly gained from experience as a patient – enabled him to set up a dispensary for folk who could never afford a physician. A number of his tracts were clearly intended for uneducated villagers and lower-deck seamen; for both categories he had enough sympathetic insight to be able to write tellingly. Not everyone from the ranks of property agreed with the philosophy of educating the poor, to read who knew what, and to develop opinions leading who knew where. The captain put an end to the project, on the grounds that it was 'a mistaken idea

---

[51] *Retrospect*, pp. 90f.

... to forward the happiness of the poor by giving them an education.'[52] On the other hand he may have had wider misgivings too, to be examined in due course.

Marks deserves credit for another reform aboard the *Conqueror*, the introduction of a lending library. He was less interested in general education than in the promotion of the Christian faith, and so the titles were restricted in their scope. Nevertheless this was an innovation of considerable importance to morale as well as evangelism. In his memoirs Bechervaise describes the thirst for reading material on the lower deck:

> The establishment of libraries in the Royal Navy has more powerfully tended to improve the minds of seamen than can be supposed. For many years that I served as a petty officer before libraries were given, a book of any kind on the lower deck was a great rarity; and in any of the messes that had one, it was read and re-read and lent from man to man, until it became difficult to tell the original colour; and even these were of a kind that frequently injured rather than improved the morals of the men. ...
>
> How different it is now; every one can get a book and read for himself. He can go to the library, take out a volume from a well-selected stock of books, and one day with another at sea, can have three hours to read and improve his mind.
>
> We have men now in the service, and I could name more than twenty from one ship, who, on their entering into her did not know one letter in the book; and now within five years, have learnt to read, write and cipher merely at their spare time.[53]

The Marks scheme worked on a subscription of 4 shillings, which allowed a borrower to have one volume out at any time, and to change titles whenever he chose. On leaving the ship he could keep at least one book for himself. 150 men joined the lending library, and two-thirds of the stock of 200 volumes was always in circulation. A few books were stored in a chest in the maintop, so that sailors not involved in tending the sails might read. He records how one man, so blasphemous that he had been flogged for his language, found Doddridge's classic *Rise and Progress of Religion in the Soul* and began to read. He took ten minutes for dinner at noon, left his grog for someone else and rushed aloft to finish his reading. Deeply stirred, Robert A. joined the 'wingers' (as Marks's group were known,

---

[52] *Retrospect*, p. 101.

[53] Baynham, *Before the Mast: Naval Ratings of the Nineteenth Century* (1971), p. 54, quoting John Bechervaise, *A Farewell to my old Shipmates and Messmates, by the Old Quarter Master* (Portsea, 1847), pp. 34f.

from the part of ship where they assembled) and in time became 'a patient meek and humble Christian', proof that sailors could read such works with interest and understanding.[54]

Marks's efforts were having some influence in the ship's company, and they began to shape the future pattern of his life. On Sundays he was leading a regular Sunday service to the ship's company and reading a sermon as part of it; he would take a further voluntary service below decks in the evening. At the music practice he would read something scriptural. The boys' school gave him another opportunity. Whenever something needed explanation or expansion Marks gave his own comments. This was both an apprenticeship as a preacher and an initiation into pastoral ministry as he grappled with the problems of the group and its mixed membership. Some proved insincere or gave up in face of harassment; others created dissension and had to be curbed, such as the Methodist whose ideas of sinless perfection disturbed the gathering to such an extent that he had to be excluded. The clarity of Marks's descriptions in *The Retrospect* and his ability to apply doctrines practically suggest that he was an enthralling teacher. Men listened and learned from him. He prayed and they prayed. He taught and they began to express their spiritual experiences too. One sailor might bring a friend, while others joined to see what was going on. The cell was becoming self-propagating. And Marks was beginning to see a role for himself in parish ministry ashore.

Not all this work was well received. Initially the bulk of the crew was sceptical rather than hostile, but all was about to change. So long as Marks exercised direct supervision, the twice-weekly evening sessions of reading, teaching and prayer were regarded tolerantly enough. On occasion when duty prevented his attendance, the cell group began to function on its own. A few lower-deck sailors read and prayed, giving rise to the assumption that preaching was going on. Rumours of Methodism began to fly, stirring enmity amongst the sailors and alarm amongst the officers. To Marks all this seemed like prejudice against his faith, but it is possible that more justified fears were at work. After all, groups of seamen meeting in seclusion on the lower deck might be a cover for crime, for gambling or sedition. The troubles of 1797 were no distant memory, when mutiny had been organised under the noses of ships' officers with scarcely a hint of the coming storm discernible. The *Conqueror*'s first lieutenant, carrying particular responsibility for the good order of the crew, was eager to crush these meetings,

---

54 Philip Doddridge (1702–51), Independent theologian, writer and educator, wrote in 1745 *The Rise and Progress of Religion in the Soul*, the book that led to the conversion of Wilberforce.

however innocuous their intention might have been. His opportunity came when Pellew was succeeded by Captain Thomas Fellowes in July 1808, a commander less sympathetic to Marks and his mission. The sequence of events thereafter shows how a captain's attitude could nurture or stifle a prayer group.

Marks tells how the watch on duty after dark would commonly talk and sing to keep themselves awake when not engaged in working the ship: his 'wingers' often took the opportunity to sing hymns or talk of serious spiritual issues. One night the captain was irritated to hear psalm-singing from men on duty and forbade it henceforward. When the first lieutenant told him of the regular dog-watch gatherings, they too were banned. To Marks this was evidence of religious discrimination, and clearly enough it emanated from someone unsympathetic to his brand of fervour. It is noteworthy that a further ban was placed on officers reading religious books to sailors, and on midshipmen meeting with an officer in his cabin except on duty: one might reasonably deduce that the captain was concerned about discipline, and feared the creation of cliques which at best might engender jealousies and at worst could disguise crime or subversion. It is possible the gatherings were crushed because the captain and first lieutenant were jealous of Marks's following. Although Fellowes tried to dissuade his midshipmen followers from attending the group, three out of six became regular 'wingers' – until officers' cabins were put off limits for them and their religious gathering was stopped.[55]

According to Marks, the suppression of his ministry afloat was largely accomplished over succeeding months. As the ship's logs show, Sunday worship continued, but it was in truncated form, with sermons suspended after two more occasions, music gradually eliminated by pressure of other duties, and divine service reduced to the simple reading of prayers. He suspected that his group of followers were subjected to petty injustices, while ships' officers were told to check living spaces each evening and to report any informal religious gathering. Nonetheless Marks's influence could not simply be effaced. Several colleagues went out of their way to show personal regard for him, and two or three officers continued to gather for Bible reading or serious discussion in one or another's cabin. Nothing could stop individual seamen from responding to questions about their beliefs, such as the Irish barber Jerry, whose cheery faith attracted comment from officers and sailors, or Robert A, who endured ridicule and ostracism without giving way. Such men were better suited to lower-deck evangelism than any officer. To Marks, however, the situation was bitterly disappointing after his many months of ministry afloat. A new ambition had been kindled during his sea service, to have the 'cure of souls', as an evangelist and pastor, and this quite naturally led him towards

[55] *Retrospect*, pp. 104–7.

parish work ashore – if he could procure the appropriate training and ecclesiastical acceptance. When he returned to England in 1810 he thought he was finished with the navy for good, whereas in fact a new stage of usefulness was about to begin. As he left the *Conqueror* he must have reflected on what had been achieved. The ship's logs allow some objective evaluation to be made.

The Evidence of the Conqueror's Logs

Captain's and master's logs preserved in the National Archives at Kew corroborate aspects of Marks's account. Confirmation that he really was aboard her at the time he claims is easily established from the pay ledger, while the log gives a cross-check on certain details mentioned in *The Retrospect*.[56] For example, Marks states that after a couple of brigs had been captured off Sardinia, he was charged with taking the two prizes to Gibraltar. The log records that the *Conqueror* was involved in taking a French privateer, the *Constant* of Genoa, and in recapturing her prize, the merchantman *Clipper* of London; on 13 January 1809 the master recorded, 'Received ten prisoners of war and sent Lieutenant Marks and ten men on board to take charge of her with twenty-one days' provision for fifteen men and took her in tow (the *Clipper*).' On 23 February his return from Gibraltar is noted.[57] Marks refers to the passage of Admiral Berkeley to Lisbon: the log shows that he hoisted his flag on 24 December 1808 and shifted it to the *Ganges* in the Tagus river on 3 February. He states that he met two officers of the *Ville de Paris* at Port Mahon a year before he left the ship, and sure enough the record proves that the *Conqueror* was there at around the right time.[58]

Another corroborative detail concerns a punishment: Marks states that a seaman 'Robert A' whose oaths and profanities 'went beyond all bounds of order and decency' was flogged for breach of the second Article of War, but later professed conversion and lived such a changed life that even lower deck derision was silenced. The log for 13 July 1809 records that Richard Anderson and Robert Edwards were punished 'for blasphemy'. Since Anderson was soon back in trouble,

---

[56] *Conqueror* Ship's Logs (PRO):
ADM 51/1585 Captain's log 1 Jan 1806 – 30 Apr 1807
ADM 51/1734 Captain's log 1 May 1807 – 18 Jul 1808
ADM 51/1979 Captain's log 19 Jul 1808 – 31 Jul 1809
ADM 51/2219 Master's log 28 Dec 1808 – 28 Dec 1809
ADM 51/2220 Master's log 29 Dec 1809 – 31 Mar 1820 (but not used in this study beyond 31 Jan 1811)
ADM 35/2150 *Conqueror* pay ledger

[57] *Retrospect*, p. 165; PRO ADM 51/2219.

[58] *Retrospect*, pp. 207f.; PRO ADM 51/1979.

being punished for theft on 30 January 1809, it seems unlikely that he was the converted blasphemer; if Robert Edwards really was the man, Marks mistook the capital letter of his surname – a trivial error years later, when the point was not to identify an individual but to recall an event.[59]

Moving on from confirmation of minor details, what can the logs tell about Marks's assessment of the effects of church services and other Christian activities? He was careful not to claim too much. He did not speak of many conversions or massive change in the conduct of the crew, but of a slowly growing influence for good. 'It was my privileged lot', he wrote later, 'to take a small part in that day of small things when the power of God began to be known in the conversion of several, and in the awakening of many more in our fleets to a sense of the value of their souls.'[60] Like all Blue Lights, he felt that religious observance would improve any assembly of people, and in this ship there was so much more than Sunday prayers and sermons. There were school classes and voluntary gatherings, and a beneficial influence spreading out to wardroom and lower deck. If anything significant was really going on it would be reasonable to look for improvements in the record of punishment.

Log entries are not infallible, but the wealth of detail given – name, status, crime, number of lashes and approximate time of punishment – shows how meticulously floggings were normally logged. It is fair to use them to show changing levels of punishment, and as a rough barometer of the conduct that gave rise to them. Statistical findings have been presented in eight successive periods of thirty weeks; to give some idea of how much religion featured during the same time spans, numbers of church services have been added.

Time span	Men punished	Total lashes	Services held
Sun 19 Apr 06 – Sat 14 Nov 06	84	1,284	0
Sun 15 Nov 06 – Sat 13 Jun 07	63	972	0
Sun 14 Jun 07 – Sat 9 Jan 08	55	902	18
Sun 10 Jan 08 – Sat 8 Aug 08	45	670	16
Sun 9 Aug 08 – Sat 4 Mar 09	23	565	7
Sun 5 Mar 09 – Sat 30 Sep 09	72	1,034	21
Sun 1 Oct 09 – Sat 28 Apr 10	89	1,475	10
Sun 29 Apr 10 – Sat 24 Nov 10	80	1,336	2

[59] *Retrospect*, pp. 137–40; PRO ADM 51/1734 entry for 13 July 1808; names in ADM 35/2150; entry for 30 Jan 1809 ADM 51/1734.

[60] *Retrospect*, p. 275.

Evangelical Activity on the Lower Deck 261

Some of the steep rise in punishments from March 1809 can be accounted for by the different style of Fellowes and his first lieutenant George Fitzmaurice, who handed out floggings for offences that do not appear under Pellew – nine lashes for 'skulking', six for 'not pulling his strength at the fall', twelve for losing clothes, fifteen for having ragged clothes, and six for letting out a reef without orders.[61] Clearly there was a turbulent element who were much given to drunkenness, quarrelling and fighting, and men with a defiant streak often described as 'insolence and disobedience'. Prince amongst them was Patrick Gorman, whose varied and repeated offences attracted 18 dozen lashes in rather less than two years between September 1806 and July 1808. The deteriorating discipline in 1809–10 may also reflect the frustration of a ship's company penned up for years at a stretch without sight of home. Well-led men would have been difficult to handle under such demands, but it is hard to resist the feeling engendered by the logs that they were being treated harshly and perhaps unreasonably.[62]

It fits with Marks's picture of the Fellowes regime. The singing group stopped; there was to be no orchestra for services and no more reading class. With apparent spite to match the folly, Fellowes cut out of his crew's routine the very things that brought variety, culture and opportunity for self-improvement. No more sermons were allowed to make their appeal to men as moral beings, with immortal

---

[61] Master's log, entries for Feb 1809, May 1810, Mar 1810, 8 Sep 1810, May 1810, 14 Dec 1809; PRO ADM 51/2219.

[62] Captain's log for 11 Sep 1806 records Gorman's insolence and neglect of duty, and the next day 12 Sep insolence and disobedience; 13 Jan 1807 riotous behaviour; 3 Apr 1807 rioting; PRO ADM 51/1585. Captain's log entries for 20 Jun 1807 insolence and neglect of duty; 1 Feb 1808 rioting; 18 Jun 1808 insolence; 1 Jul 1808 neglect of duty ADM 51/1734. He was apparently uncowed by so much correction, and received another two dozen later on: Master's log entry for 8 Sep 1810, ADM 51/2219.

A five-year span has been examined; captain's logs cover the period from 1 January 1806 to 31 July 1809, and master's logs extend from 28 December 1808 to 31 January 1811 (and beyond). Where the two accounts overlap, from January to July 1809, the master's log has noted a heavier punishment rate than the captain – sixteen men receiving 275 lashes in March 1809 instead of five men and 72, or – even more striking – a discrepancy in June between the captain's nine men and 123 lashes, and the master's thirty-eight and 741. In nine instances where the severity of the punishment has not been recorded I have assumed a fairly standard one dozen lashes. On 15 September 1807 the entry reads, 'punished several men for drunkenness', but for lack of further detail I have been unable to add them to this record. On 19 January 1809 the master's log states 'punish'd', but no name, crime or sentence follows, and the captain's log offers no help. Twice no reason for punishment has been recorded. Marks began taking services on 14 June 1807. Sir Israel Pellew was superseded in command by Captain Edward Fellowes on 18 July 1808.

souls and responsibility for their choices. As these motivators were withdrawn and Marks's influence diminished, the captain had no management resources more subtle than punishment, but the statistics reveal what a poor substitute the lash made. Of course, the records also show that divine service was held quite regularly until the last occasion on Sunday 13 May 1810 – possibly marking the end of Marks's time in the ship. In the sixth period, when the number of men punished more than trebled, and the overall tally of lashes nearly doubled, there was a service every two Sundays out of three. This evidence calls into question one of the foundation tenets of the Blue Lights, namely that merely holding prayers would reduce crime and punishment. It did not do so in the *Conqueror* in 1809–10, or in Austen's *Elephant* in 1812–13. Were the earlier hopes misplaced, or were there other factors at work here?

At an earlier stage in the war, when there were prospects of battle to focus thoughts and energies, and when there was reasonable hope of returning home in some imaginable time frame, morale was sustained more readily. Divine service played the part already considered – the novelty, the change in routine, the lofty moral sentiments, and all the dignity of worship. But by 1810, as the strain on ships' companies intensified, something profounder than palliative gestures was required. There seemed scant chance of home leave while war continued and there was no end in sight. Blockading fleets could maintain themselves with a high degree of efficiency on a foreign station and had no great need to return to a British home port: when the *Conqueror* finally paid off and was laid up in a British dockyard she had been in commission for eleven years, according to Marks.[63] Sailors felt far from home and loved ones, neglected by an uncaring Government. If religion merely endorsed the *status quo* and invoked heaven's blessing on the injustices of war and the pain of long separation, it would itself become an aggravation. To an Admiralty official a sailor might be no more than a name on a list, but to Marks he was a soul of infinite value in the eyes of God. To address deep psychological needs, religion would have to minister assurance of God's love and of the value of each individual. Meaningful worship and pastorally sensitive preaching could convey all this, whereas liturgical repetition faced more of a problem.

Once Sunday worship in the *Conqueror* had been reduced to the saying of a few prayers, shorn of the appeal of a Burder sermon, and once the singers with their accompanists had gone, it ceased to be participatory and inclusive. Marks was mistrustful of the purpose behind the services that Fellowes allowed: 'as to religion he seemed to have no other idea of it, but as being useful to keep the

[63] *Retrospect*, p. 110n.

lower orders in subjection.'[64] There was nothing in all this to uplift the soul, while the sense of what had been lost added to the discontent. The Marks era showed what really could be achieved by sensitive use of religious appeal, but the Fellowes period underlined its limitations as a force for social cohesion. The impact that Marks had when encouraged by Pellew and when relatively unhindered by Fellowes was extraordinary. When formal worship was enlivened by music and sermons, and when off-duty classes and prayer groups were spreading Christian influence on the lower deck, there was an unmistakeable reduction in misconduct and punishment rates. During 'early Pellew', when collective religion had no place, and 'later Fellowes' the numbers of men flogged and the severity of punishments are comparable, but in the couple of years when Marks was most active, the *Conqueror* had a period of relative happiness. Might other ships expect the same benefits from a religious movement?

A spreading Influence

It is unlikely that Marks in his naval days ever had a strategy for the wider evangelisation of the navy. The original challenge to his new-found faith had been to find ways of serving God aboard his ship. Had he envisaged any fleet-wide programme, he would have stayed in uniform, or else, like Bo'sun Smith, focused his energies upon the seafaring community. Instead he left the sea behind him, pursued his studies at university, and found an inland curacy. He imagined that he had finished with the navy, but his influence afloat was far from spent.

For a start there were a few converted through his personal evangelism who could spread the message further. He mentions a chaplain taking passage in the *Conqueror* (apparently the Rev. John Turner) who was at first offended by Marks's directness, but then inspired to study Scripture more closely until he acquired evangelical beliefs.[65] The ship's surgeon seemed a hopeless case at the time, but, after pondering what Marks said, he eventually came to faith. Although Marks knew of a few sailors converted through the witness of his circle, they were not many. He makes no claim of large numbers joining the psalm-singers – twenty to thirty over a three-year span, he reckoned. No large-scale revival broke out aboard the *Conqueror*, and yet something influential had begun. If Marks is right, the tone of the wardroom improved, and blasphemous expressions went out of favour.

[64] *Retrospect*, p. 99.

[65] Marks records that during 1808 the *Conqueror* conveyed from Spithead to Lisbon Admiral B--- and his entourage including the chaplain Rev. Mr. T---. This is presumably the Rev. John Turner, whom Kealy's list shows as serving in the *Leopard* (1806–8), the *Conqueror* (1808–9) and the *Barfleur* (1809), Admiral George Berkeley's flagship. *Retrospect*, p. 207.

Officers began to direct the crew with much less profanity and abuse, and general conduct throughout the ship reflected a new wholesomeness.[66] It offered a pattern for others to follow.

The ripples spread beyond this one ship. A year before his coming ashore for good, Marks met up with two rising young lieutenants in the commander-in-chief's entourage aboard the *Ville de Paris* at Mahon. He identifies them by the pseudonyms Macarius and Eugenius, but the details provided show that they were Richard Coote and Ashley Maude, experienced officers awaiting vacancies for command. It seems likely that these two serious and upright men wanted clarification on matters of faith, and were led to Marks because of his reputation. He sent them Wilberforce's *View of Christianity*, and followed this with other books and letters. Both men found faith and then wanted to know how it should impact on sea-going life. The three lieutenants met to talk and pray in the hills around Port Mahon, exhilarating in the freedom to discuss privately and in the enjoyment of fellowship unusual at sea.[67]

Maude, a lieutenant of four years' standing, volunteered for a boat operation at the end of October 1809, in which seven French transports with a light naval escort were attacked by night under the gun batteries of Rosas Bay. It was a highly successful action, completing the rout of Ganteaume's effort to reinforce Barcelona, and it resulted in four vessels brought off as captures and the rest destroyed, despite the formidable defences. Collingwood with the main fleet out at sea witnessed the flames arising from Rosas Bay and the return of the successful raiders. Maude was lightly wounded and marked for early promotion. In October 1810 he obtained commander's rank and was made post in March 1814 at the age of twenty-seven. His naval career continued in peace time, and he commanded the 50-gun *Glasgow* at the Battle of Navarino in 1827. When he died aged fifty-five in 1841 he had not attained flag rank, but he held British and foreign knighthoods and was a CB. His Christian faith, fanned into flame by Marks, continued strongly for the rest of his life.[68]

Once Maude had left the flagship, Coote felt his isolation keenly, and kept up a correspondence with his mentor, Marks. He did not leave for England when

---

[66] *NMBS* 1829, p. 20; *Retrospect*, p. 97.

[67] Richard Coote (1782–1814): entered RN 1796, lieut. 1804, cdr. 1810, post Jun 1814; awarded CB for operations against USA; drowned when his ship *Peacock* foundered off South Carolina. The Hon. James Ashley Maude (1786–1841), son of Viscount Hawarden: entered RN 1798, lieut. Mar 1805, cdr. 1810, post Mar 1814; commanded *Glasgow* at battle of Navarino and awarded CB 1827; knighted 1836.

[68] Joseph Allen, *Battles of the British Navy*, 2 vols. (1852), II, pp. 299–301; Warner, *Collingwood*, p. 224; *NMBS* 1839, p. 27; *Retrospect*, p. 163.

the dying Collingwood was ordered home in the *Ville de Paris* in 1810, but was transferred to another ship of the line. He was delighted when the captain began to take Sunday services. Following Marks's example, Coote invited small groups of officers to discuss serious topics in his cabin; from this circle there were at least two conversions amongst the lieutenants. At Gibraltar fifty New Testaments and tracts were obtained for distribution to seamen and marines. By permission of the captain, Coote began to take Sunday prayers in the sick bay, often using one of Burder's sermons. The tracts, Testaments and sermons were widely read on the lower deck, he claimed.

Coote reached commander's rank in 1810 and was appointed to the brig *Borer*. Here he made a name for himself as a humane and judicious captain, eager to promote the welfare of his crew and the education of his midshipmen, and as a proficient officer on a war station. The *Borer* was not particularly fast, but she had great success against US merchant shipping off the North American coast in winter. The diligence of her captain was particularly noted – allegedly going three weeks without proper sleep, surviving on little more than occasional half-hour naps. In spite of the demands of the service and severities of the wintry weather Coote held prayers twice daily. He was selected to command a flotilla of six boats for a raid on the Connecticut River on 7 April 1814, an operation marked by the destruction of seven privateers, twelve merchant ships and ten coasting vessels off Pettipague Point. His rewards were the CB and a post captaincy in a larger vessel, the 18-gun sloop *Peacock*, which had been known as the *Wasp* until her capture from the Americans. In her, Coote and all his crew were drowned in stormy seas off South Carolina in August 1814.[69]

It was a sad loss for the Blue Lights and the cause of naval evangelisation. Marks had looked to him to play an influential part in his own profession and as a philanthropist:

> We fondly hoped that for this very end the Lord had raised him up, and that many years would be added to his days, and much fruit borne to the honour of religion and the glory of God. But herein our thoughts were not as the Lord's thoughts. ... This is one of those events which compel us to exclaim, 'Touching the Almighty, we cannot find him out!'[70]

And yet in retrospect we may see that Coote's influence did continue in the navy. One junior officer came under his command for the Connecticut River operation, Lieutenant William Parry of the *La Hogue*. He apparently valued the

[69] Allen, II, 456; Robert Gardiner (ed.), *The Naval War of 1812* (1998), pp. 45, 140; *Retrospect*, pp. 159f.

[70] *Retrospect*, p. 160.

Christian example he witnessed then, and Coote was remembered in the tributes paid years later after Parry's death when he in his turn had become the leading Blue Light of another generation.[71] Marks gives an intriguing postscript to his meditation on the career of Richard Coote. 'Henceforth thy duty as a citizen shall no more wound thy benevolent heart by calling on thee to distress or cut off thy fellow creatures.'[72] Almost certainly Marks is here echoing earlier discussions about the legitimacy of war, where a follower of the Prince of Peace might find himself under orders to kill. While still a naval officer Marks had become something of a pastoral counsellor: he mentions other moral dilemmas – the existence of evil, the inconsistencies of the good, the sorrows of illness and separation, the anguish of recognising personal failure. In a church-based ministry those interests and counselling skills had room to develop outside the navy, and yet he did not lose his earlier concerns. In his new career he became one of the outstanding writers for seafarers and a powerful advocate for sailors' causes.

As an author Marks became influential in two ways. First, he managed to communicate the needs of sailors to the church ashore, the Christian community who provided the prayer support essential for any spiritual work of God, and who also contributed the necessary finance for evangelists and literature. Secondly, in ways that only Smith could rival, he wrote the tracts which explained the Gospel message to sailors who still stood outside the ministry of the churches. Attention has already been given to the sheer volume of written matter which appeared under his authorship. Even more striking is the testimony to its effectiveness. One of the most courageous and diligent distributors of tracts on the River Thames was Thomas Phillips, who was particularly careful in his choice of reading material. He found Marks's leaflets were admirably effective in engaging the attention of sailors, and in breaking through their emotional reserve. He witnessed occasions when rough colliermen from the east coast coal trade broke down in tears after reading these tracts, and he sometimes gathered numbers to evangelistic meetings by promising them further supplies of Marks's writings. Phillips wrote: 'For such as will neither enter a place of worship nor read the scriptures, Religious Tracts, freely distributed, appear to be the only way to get at their consciences: these they will accept and read.'[73] Marks knew how to pass on the Christian message in a way that invited not mockery but faith.

Before Marks there were few tracts written expressly for seafarers. By the

---

[71] Rev. Edward Parry, *A Brief Memoir of Rear-Admiral Sir Edward Parry* (King's Lynn, 1857), p. 7.

[72] *Retrospect*, p. 162.

[73] Quoted in Kverndal, *Seamen's Missions*, p. 167 – referring to the Thames Revival.

Napoleonic period Burn's sophisticated and intellectual rebuttals of Deism were no more suited to wide distribution on the lower deck than Woodward's archaic *Monitor*. Robert Hawker produced *The Sailor Pilgrim* in two parts, published in 1806 and 1810. Mass circulation of popular titles had to wait for Bo'sun Smith, whose first tract, *The Boatswain's Mate* appeared 1811. Other titles were *The Sailors on Shore*, *Jack Tars at Plymouth* and *Torbay – or the Fleet at Anchor*. Writings perhaps deliberately aimed at naval personnel were *The Quarter Master*, *The Dreadnought* and *The Royal George*.[74] This nautical Bunyan, the inventor of characters such as Sampson Sailabout, wrote tracts of evangelistic appeal, semi-autobiographical, and filled with the maritime jargon and dramatic incident which succeeded in winning a large naval audience. They were cheap and simply illustrated, designed to attract the unconcerned and to awaken a sense of spiritual need. Marks, a better writer who understood sailors equally well, developed the genre further with titles produced for the Bristol Tract Society, *Conversation in a Boat*, *The Two Shipmates*, *The Seaman's Friend*, *The Smugglers* and *The Wreckers*. They proved outstandingly successful and achieved massive circulation, establishing Marks as Smith's only rival in communicating to seafarers. Through his books he helped to stir the church ashore to take up the sailors' cause.

Thanks to Marks we have some understanding of the dynamics of the new piety, how it operated through shipboard gatherings and replicated itself through personal evangelism. This movement could work to a restricted level even without official approval, but where commanders allowed it to function or even gave it their known support – as Hillyar and Austen did – it could thrive. While numbers of committed adherents remained small, even a few zealous Christians had a moderating influence on a ship's company, and by the war's end they were to be found widely spread through the fleet. When linked with the revival amongst prisoners-of-war in France, evangelicalism can be seen to have had an impact on both the wartime navy and on the national pool of seamen. By circulating literature – Bibles, tracts and lending libraries – the movement was making an appeal to men's minds and hearts. The lesson was reinforced by the growing custom of Sunday worship, and by the promotion of improved chaplains and better preaching. These were the ways in which the salt and light of the new movement were spread. Yet the most potent model of growth was the self-replicating cell, and the best evangelists were seamen and officers ministering to their own fraternity by life and testimony.

74 Tracts by 'A Naval Officer' [the Rev. George Charles Smith]: *The Boatswain's Mate*, *The Quarter Master*, *The Sailors on Shore*, *Jack Tars at Plymouth*, *The Dreadnought*, *The Royal George*, *Torbay – or the Fleet at Anchor* (n.d. [1811]). Marks's tracts are listed in Marsden: see p. 246 n. 36 above.

VIII

Evangelicalism at the End of the Napoleonic War: A Flare in the Darkness?

Surviving the End of Hostilities

WARTIME evangelicalism never claimed to be more than a minority movement. Blue Light officers, pious Christians on the lower deck and Evangelical chaplains made up a small proportion of each category. Much of their influence initially came from Middleton's power at the centre of naval administration; it spread widely through the navy as increasing numbers of officers were prepared to see what religion could contribute to the management of men. But that was during hostilities. So much changed with the coming of peace that naval evangelicalism faced extinction.

As the great wartime fleets were paid off, their crews took with them into civilian life the religious stirrings which had sustained morale during hostilities. The tolerant acquiescence of the officer corps, never really enthusiastic, steadily evaporated, for what concern was needed now with issues on the periphery of the navy's *raison d'être*? With volunteer crews and shorter commissions there were fewer manning issues anyway; the events of 1797 were but a memory, and peacetime sailors in the fleet could expect living conditions appropriate for a select and willing service, with better rations, clothing and pay, more generous leave and a slightly more considerate code of discipline. There was less need for religion either to help personal morale or to unite a ship's company.

The great figures of the wartime movement disappeared. Duncan had died long ago, followed by Barham in 1813 and Burn a year later. Gambier and Saumarez hauled down their flags before the war's end; Brenton was now too lame for active service; Austen became a country gentleman before resuming his naval career as an admiral and commander-in-chief thirty years on. Hawker discovered a new vocation as a press correspondent and pamphleteering controversialist. Marks buried himself in an inland parish, while Smith busied himself with a string of worthy causes that stretched from erstwhile smugglers in the Scillies to domestic servants in London's back alleys. The Church ashore diverted funding from the Naval and Military to the British and Foreign Bible Society, and much of its energies from servicemen to foreign missions. The evangelical cause afloat was maintained by the notable trio of Pellew, soon to be a national hero after the bombardment of Algiers, by Penrose, who succeeded him as C-in-C

Mediterranean, and by Hillyar, but this was a depleted group of senior officers. The cell groups disappeared; the 'Naval Correspondence Mission' closed down; the prison congregations came home from France; few clergy opted for a naval life. The great days of wartime religion came to an end, and the Blue Lights might have fizzled out like the night-time flares from which they took their name.[1]

This movement had travelled far since Middleton and Kempenfelt had sharpened one another's ideas about the place of religion. Now, its mission accomplished, it might reasonably have disbanded along with the regiments and fleets of wartime. The reinstatement of Sunday worship, which had seemed so distant a prospect in 1780 and so controversial in the 1790s, had become widespread by 1815. Decent chaplains with a preaching ministry, so rare in the American War, were now more common, and Bibles or tracts might be found on any messdeck. Surely all this is proof that the original 'manifesto' of the Blue Lights had been fulfilled by the time of Napoleon's defeat? To some degree that is so, of course, but evangelicalism was powered by a creed of restless dynamism that tried to transform the national church and then began to evangelise the globe. In its naval form the new piety was about to acquire fresh energy, widening into pioneering evangelism and social reform that would have a lasting impact on the maritime subculture, the merchant fleet and even world mission. Yet for all its growing diversity, this movement had identifiable adherents and a definable body of beliefs.

The Blue Lights and their Creed

THE Blue Lights were officers of the Royal Navy and members of the Church of England. As they did not constitute a society with a defined membership and subscription list, there may be some doubt as to who truly qualify for inclusion. Blue Lights supported public worship – but many who did the same would have recoiled from the title. Not every captain who punished profanity was a Blue Light, even though this was one characteristic associated with them. Evangelicals disliked drunkenness and prostitution on the lower deck, but they were not unique in that. They were devoted to the spreading of Scripture but not all who distributed Bibles could usefully be described as Blue Lights. Then again there were certain prominent officers like Lord Northesk, William Bedford or Robert Stopford who were closely associated with their practices and may

[1] Sir Edward Pellew (1757–1833): C-in-C Mediterranean 1815–16; bombardment of Algiers 1816; viscount Exmouth; later C-in-C Plymouth. Sir Charles Penrose (1759–1830): C-in-C Mediterranean 1814–15, 1816–19. Sir James Hillyar (1769–1843), capt. *Revenge* 1830, *Caledonia* 1832; rear adm. 1837.

14 Bible-reading on board a British frigate, *c.* 1830. This picture of lay-directed piety expresses a cardinal aim of the Blue Lights, fulfilled at last after the Napoleonic War.

© National Maritime Museum, London BHC1119

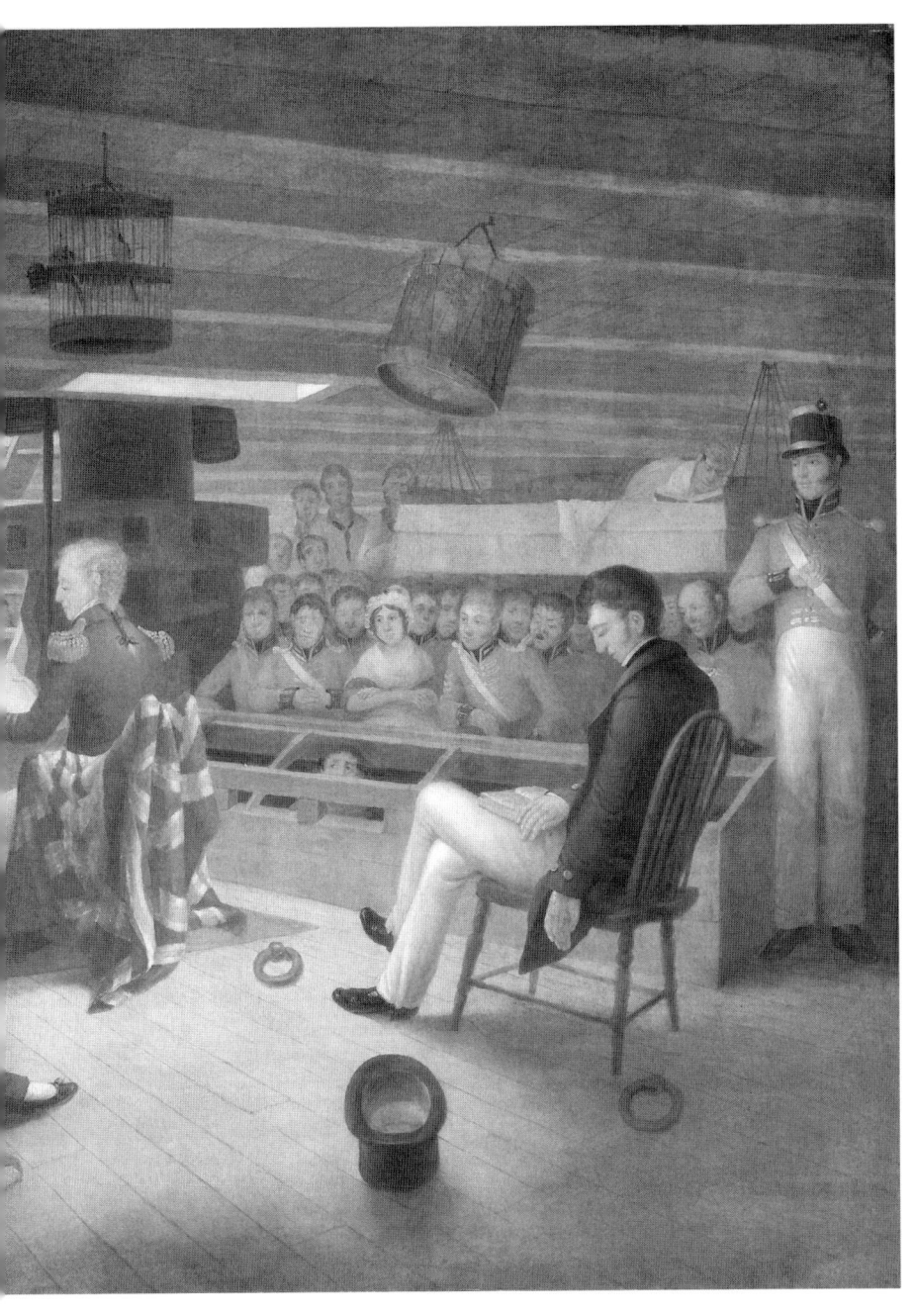

Oil painting by Augustus Earle, 1793–1838. In 1820 Earle sailed in HMS *Hyperion* under the command of Captain Thomas Searle; this painting is believed to be a record of a church service conducted by the captain during the voyage from Callao to Rio de Janiero.

well have deserved inclusion but whose personal convictions are less readily discerned than those of Middleton, Kempenfelt, Duncan, Saumarez and Gambier, the definitive Blue Lights.

The movement really has to be understood in theological terms. First – a characteristic not confined to them – they were deeply concerned for the honour of God. This explains their unresting concern that respect should be shown for God's Name and the Lord's Day. When, for example, Duncan restored the *Ardent's* people to obedience and then told them to mind their language, he appealed to their sense of what was owing to their Creator. Or, to take another instance, as the ships of the Gibraltar squadron mustered for Sunday service before battle off Algeciras, Saumarez was rendering to the Almighty what he believed was due to Him. In Gambier's fleet, religious observance became a part of routine because he believed that there was an overarching obligation due to God from all His creatures. When Captain Michael Seymour had won a notable frigate action, Gambier sent him a reminder:

> We must not forget Who it is that gives us the ability to contend with our enemies and gives the victory. I therefore hope if you have not already done so, that you will take the earliest opportunity when all your people return on board to assemble them, and read the Thanksgiving after a Victory.[2]

That was typically Gambier, and an authentic Blue Light reaction.

Secondly and crucially, they believed in the need for conversion. They understood from the Bible, their authority in all matters of belief and conduct, that human nature was irretrievably estranged from God, and that this alienation was demonstrated by moral failure in thought and deed. To remedy mankind's lost condition God had sent His Son to live as a man amongst men, to teach the truth about God and men, and to die as a substitutionary sacrifice to atone for all sin. 'In the Old Testament', Penrose explained, '… some atonement for sin was always deemed requisite; … at the appointed time the great atonement made by the sacrifice of the death of Christ will be known to all mankind.'[3] To benefit from God's grace, the sinner had to turn to Christ, receive his forgiveness, and prove the reality of this conversion by a changed life. Then he might with full confidence anticipate eternity in the presence of God. Thus, as his life ebbed away, Duncan

---

[2] Quoted in Tom Wareham, *The Star Captains: Frigate Command in the Napoleonic Wars* (2001), p. 186. The action was the capture of French *Thetis* by HMS *Amethyst*, Nov 1808.

[3] Penrose, *A Short Address*, p. 13.

passed word to his wife that his trust in the Redeemer gave assurance of God's acceptance and of a heavenly destiny beyond death.[4]

Thirdly, they based their beliefs upon the Bible. They entertained no doubts as to its truth or authority, and they were keen to promote its reading, understanding and possession. These were cardinal Evangelical tenets, held as firmly by sea as by land. A fourth feature of their religion was an emphasis on the need for public worship – but in this they shared the outlook of increasing numbers of their contemporaries.

While their doctrine did not change, the interpretation of their mission did, as it developed through three phases spread over forty years. No part of the original programme was dropped, but a new commitment added in response to changing perceptions of need. Although they were as conservative socially as they were in theology, they improvised and innovated in an effort to apply the Christian message to changing times. Some of the implications of their programme were strikingly radical. Where shipboard gatherings were led by an officer, they fitted the accepted pattern of subordination in a hierarchic service, but what novel dynamics were suggested by times of prayer when men of all ranks might lead the group? Again, since literacy was the key to understanding the Bible, surely basic education should be seen as an entitlement for everyone? And if salvation was the most important distinction between people, it offered a status that had no link with birth or wealth or rank. Where might such egalitarianism lead? Eventually it brought about a set of reforming initiatives outside the navy that became known as the Sailors' Cause: this fourth phase directly improved conditions for merchant seamen and therefore indirectly for the navy as well, since it was in competition for volunteer crews.[5]

Let us summarise the distinctive emphases of the three initial phases. During the **first phase**, the 1780s and 1790s, the insights of Kempenfelt and Middleton predominated. The navy was perceived as a floating parish, a part of the national Church but neglectful of its religious duties. The remedy lay in fulfilling what was laid down in the *Regulations*: captains must hold prayers and sign on suitable chaplains. Then sailors would behave more like the Christians they purported to be, to the great gain of discipline.

The **second phase** began with the French Revolutionary War and extended until the coming of peace in 1815. The Blue Lights had come to recognise that

---

[4] See p. 137 above. The reference is to a letter of Lady Duncan to a friend; Duncan Papers in NMM: DUN/19 MS 9587.

[5] Kverndal, *Seamen's Missions* is the magisterial work on the subject, published by the William Carey Library, Passadena, California. See pp. 129, 315–50, etc.

the Kempenfelt programme failed to match the realities of the swollen navy of the 1790s. They continued to draw attention to the neglect of public worship, and they were in the vanguard of efforts to revive regular Sunday observance. Now an additional plank was added to the platform – evangelistic activity. For the attainment of the first objective the SPCK was admirable, and its grants of appropriate books for public worship powerfully aided shipboard services. But for evangelism, the spreading of the Gospel to the spiritually unawakened, other approaches were needed – Bibles for personal distribution, tracts to explain the Christian message, preaching to persuade and convert. The Naval and Military Bible Society and the Religious Tract Society were the new sources of literature, and a reinvigorated supply of chaplains was sought.

The **third phase** featured voluntary, informal gatherings which began tentatively in the late 1790s and grew apace during the Napoleonic War. The emphasis now shifted to particular ships, where isolated groups of believers were meeting to nourish their own faith and to communicate its comforts to their colleagues. Public worship, chaplains' ministry, Bible distribution and tract circulation still preoccupied senior Blue Lights. On the mess decks, however, in gunrooms and in officers' wardrooms another force had appeared: voluntary gatherings, informal and sometimes without official sanction, where prayer and Bible reading were shared. While these groups were entirely autonomous, they showed a tendency to link up with Christian ministers ashore, and there may have been tenuous links between ships.

Those who pastored the shipboard cells were scared of what would happen to these tender young believers when they were paid off from their ships and reverted to the life of sailortown with its ready drink and women for hire. It would take a man of superhuman resolve to lead a life of Christian purity. Much needed to be done to provide an alternative subculture with decent lodgings and supportive fellowship. A massive challenge was perceived, nothing less than the moral transformation of the maritime world ashore, hitherto neglected by the Church. In time this became the aim of a **fourth phase**, initially outside the navy, but influencing the employment pool from which the fleet was manned.[6]

Far from dying out in 1815, naval evangelicalism underwent another of its creative metamorphoses, so extensive and far-reaching that only the most cursory review is possible now. Even a brief sketch will show how its influence continued to gain momentum. Sailors converted in the French prison camps or in RN cell groups at sea found their way into the merchant fleet in peacetime. Some

---

[6] Much of this work was associated with Bo'sun Smith. See Kverndal, *passim*, and Smith.

Christian sailors in the Pool of London sought the kind of prayer fellowship that had meant so much to them in wartime, and from such an insignificant beginning there arose a spiritual movement powerful and lasting enough to be called the Thames Revival. As a lay movement for prayer and spiritual encouragement it was like the naval awakening, but its chief difference was that it drew together men from several ships while they were waiting to put to sea. To signal when a service was being held the famous Bethel flag was devised. Within a few years the movement was given shape – largely by the irrepressible Bo'sun Smith – with a mariners' church and a floating chapel. A hostel for destitute seamen was the precursor to a diverse array of welfare schemes, giving support to sailors and their dependants, this whole movement of social betterment deserving its title of the Sailors' Cause. The free churches led the way and the Anglicans followed, until Missions to Seamen, floating churches and seafarers' homes became typical of major ports throughout the world.

Although this phase focused on merchant seamen it was closely related to the RN. Some of those converted through the ministry of Smith or William Scoresby or the Sailors Home of Commander Elliot and Captain Gambier found their way into the Royal Navy to boost the Christian presence on the lower deck. The numerous societies and institutions that embodied the Sailors' Cause were staffed by half-pay officers and ex-wartime ratings, while retired admirals and captains were thickly represented amongst the trustees and benefactors. The Thames Revival and the Sailors' Cause cannot be understood without reference to the wartime awakening.[7]

Far from confining itself to the private sphere, the new piety grew into a multifaceted movement encompassing Admiralty policy, chaplains, literature, humanitarian reform, unofficial prayer groups and much else. Is it fair to treat it as a single movement at all? The answer is definitely yes, for all these elements belong to the same theological outlook, rooted in Scripture and pressing for 'conversion'. By this, evangelicals understood an experience that included conduct change but was more radical than moral improvement alone: instead, it meant a switch in the value system that an individual professed. The old reference points had to be replaced by new, as God became real to a person's perception. Evangelicals often

---

[7] For the Thames Revival see Kverndal, *Seamen's Missions*, pp. 151–93. A brief chronology of these events would include: Bethel flag 1817; floating chapel at Rotherhithe 1818; Mariners' Church, Wellclose Square 1825; Destitute Seaman's Asylum; Sailors' Home (later Red Ensign Club) 1828; first Episcopal Floating Chapel with the Rev. William Scoresby as Anglican clergyman, London 1829; Cdr. R. J. Elliot and Capt. G. C. Cornish assumed direction of Smith's asylum 1828, and developed into the well known Sailors' Home in 1835; Anglican Missions to Seamen 1856.

spoke of an encounter with Christ – a profoundly life-altering crisis, immediately distinguishing those who had experienced it from everyone else.

The Psychology of Conversion

SURVIVING autobiographical material allows the phenomenon of seafaring conversion to be investigated – but with care. Rodger warns that such writers exaggerate the depravity of life before conversion, and adds that 'naval life was not really as depraved as the convention of this sort of story requires.'[8] The caution is just, but calls for a further caveat. Evangelical piety identified unbelief as sin: it follows that anyone describing their unregenerate days would be remorseful about lapses of conduct and conviction, however trivial they might seem to an outsider. The genre requires peculiar sensitivity in interpretation, so that we avoid drawing exaggerated conclusions about the prevalence of vice in the navy – while giving proper weight to the felt burden of moral alienation. This load of guilt was inescapable in evangelical experience, for how could one be forgiven without repentance, and how could one repent unless troubled by a sense of failure?

Those who wrote of their experiences had an unusual capacity to order (and possibly tidy) their recollections of impulses deeply felt. Perhaps there were others who acquired 'vital religion' but along pathways less easily defined. Nevertheless the exercise is worth conducting, for common elements emerge to give an insight into this experience so important to the Blue Lights.

George Charles Smith and Richard Marks showed certain similarities. Smith vividly described his state of mind before the attack on Copenhagen in 1801. Already he knew what a naval battle was like from his experiences at Camperdown, but this time there was a vital difference. Then there had been a tempestuous rush to engage and a flow of adrenalin to combat fear, but now by contrast the deliberate preparation for action, spread over days, left time for dread to rise.

> O, what pale, agitated countenances I saw among the crowd of men on our forecastle, among the greatest drunkards, blasphemers, whoremongers … Not a man but trembled, all ready for battle – yet not one soul ready for eternity! I was like the rest, only, having been a Sunday School boy … and with a pious father and mother … I knew more about sin and hell, and shuddered with horror, so that the officers' cry for 'King and country – fighting for king and country' could not quell the risings of conscience, and the prospects of death and judgement.[9]

---

[8] Rodger, *Command of the Ocean*, p. 492.
[9] Kverndal, *Seamen's Missions*, p. 616, reproducing material from *NSM*, 1852, pp. 417–23; 1858, pp. 321–7.

Fear of dying with an uneasy conscience robbed Smith of his peace, and led him to find a place of privacy for prayer – the foretop of his ship, the *Agamemnon*. He asked for God's protection and vowed in return to live a righteous life. The prayer once answered, the promise was neglected, and Smith's religious feelings passed. It took another life-threatening crisis to bring him to true repentance. On 19 March 1803, his twenty-first birthday, he was taken violently ill with a virulent fever while visiting a former shipmate in Reading; despairing of recovery, he clutched at the words of the nurse who treated him, 'He does not despise prayer, sir … The Lord can save your soul.' He sought counselling from the minister of a nearby chapel, and was led to trust in Christ as the only one who could save him, and had died on the cross to prove it. Ever afterwards Smith honoured that anniversary as both his natural and spiritual birthday.[10]

Fear of death and a lost eternity caused Smith to call upon God, but his conversion followed repeated crises, time for reflection and spiritual instruction which enabled him to make sense of childhood teachings, conscience and Gospel promises. He had a godly mother who gave him a copy of Newton's autobiography and encouraged him to attend nonconformist chapels where the Gospel was preached. He possessed a reasonable knowledge of Christian teaching, but needed some crisis to make him claim these truths as his own. This kind of faith, often described by evangelicals as 'saving faith', is closely related to hopelessness: it most often seems to come when a soul recognises its helpless inability to improve or to atone for wrongdoing, and cries out to God for mercy. Despairing of life and fearing to meet his Maker, Smith prayed for forgiveness through Christ. Then followed assurance of salvation and a changed life.

As with Marks, the navy had brought him face to face with death, but in both cases there was a stepped response – a first prayer for physical deliverance which turned afterwards into a plea for moral cleansing, for forgiveness and for the grace of a changed life. In this process, both men needed the aid of experienced ministers of religion, and they followed up their new profession of faith

---

[10] Smith was visiting his *Agamemnon* friend John Lovegrove in Reading, to avoid the risk of being taken up by the press in London when hostilities resumed. After becoming ill at the Jack o' Newbury inn he had to transfer to sick lodgings off the London road. His nurse asked for prayer from the local Baptist minister Rev. Weller, who visited Smith and counselled him about salvation. After recovering, Smith took a job in Bath, where he attracted the attention of Opie Smith, merchant and Baptist deacon, who suggested he should enter the ministry, paid for training from Dr Isaiah Birt of Plymouth, and helped him obtain the post of minister at the Octagon Baptist chapel in Penzance in October 1807. Kverndal, *Seamen's Missions*, pp. 113–29.

with detailed study of the Scriptures. Their later course of life was evidence of altered values in both present conduct and future aspirations. These were true conversions.

A lower deck parallel is provided by the reminiscences of Samuel Stokes, covering thirty-three years of seafaring. He gives a lurid account of his time in the *Dreadnought* (98), exaggerated perhaps in his recollection and coloured by his subsequent convictions:

> I am now in a ship where I can give full scope to every sinfull practise, for if ever there was anything on earth that deserve to be called a hell, this ship was one, but she was just what suited me. ... The sins of this ship was equal to the sin of Sodom, especially on the day we was paid, for we had on board thirteen women more than the number of our ship's company, and not fifty of them married women. Our ship's company I think was very near eight hundred men.[11]

On that terrible Christmas Eve of 1811, when three ships of the line were wrecked, the *Dreadnought* narrowly escaped disaster in the same storm, but Stokes had his own – probably fairly typical – way of dealing with fear and guilt.[12] 'When I was struck with a sense of sin I always got drunk to drive away what I then called Dull Thoughts; and this was the case on 23 December. I got drunk for joy, instead of giving God thanks for such a deliverance.'[13] Over the succeeding months he showed no wish to turn to God, but he was unable to assuage a guilty conscience. After the war, God and his past caught up with him. While serving in a merchant ship in 1816, he fell from foretop to deck, and broke his thigh. The prospect of dying unreconciled to God opened his mind to some Christian counselling, and his growing spiritual interest was nurtured through private reading of the Bible during hours off watch at sea. With responsibilities as a second mate, he started to pray in earnest during a perilous voyage to Quebec in 1817, and he began to attend church whenever sea-going allowed. Gradually he became convinced that good intentions would not suffice, but there was hope for a sinner like him, and a way to God through the death of the Redeemer. Stokes's values so changed from his early days afloat that he left seafaring to become clerk of St Peter's church, Ipswich.[14]

---

[11] Samuel Stokes, quoted in Baynham, *From the Lower Deck*, p. 130.

[12] For loss of the Baltic ships, see p. 178 above.

[13] Baynham, *From the Lower Deck*, p. 136.

[14] Baynham, *From the Lower Deck*, pp. 139, 142. Further details from transcript of full MS, 'The Life of Samuel Stokes written by Himself', on loan to H. F. W. Baynham.

Sir Jahleel Brenton (1770–1844) was no drunken profligate but an officer of upright character. He thought deeply on spiritual issues, especially (he says) once he had become flag captain to Saumarez. Nevertheless, he felt in retrospect that his Christianity had been little more than a scheme of moral behaviour, and it took a prolonged period of reflection to bring him to spiritual commitment. This crisis came during his time as a prisoner in France. Under the ministry of the Rev. Robert Wolfe his Christian understanding developed to the point where he believed he had found 'vital religion', the saving faith for which evangelicals looked. If his conversion was not strictly a response to a crisis – except in the sense that his two and a half years in detention constituted one – it was the result of a prolonged period of testing and frustration. In after years he supported charitable and evangelistic ventures for seamen, a Blue Light turned social reformer.[15]

Lieutenant William Rhind (1794–1863) was another exemplary character who yet came to feel the need for conversion. He was never a Blue Light in his naval days, but his experience underlines the need which many felt for a sense of moral cleansing, despite their upright conduct. The son of a master RN and a godly mother, he entered the navy aged twelve, with a Bible in his sea-chest and exhortations to follow the ways of God. As a midshipman in the *Macedonian*, he knew the terrors of a bloody action and the bitterness of defeat when his frigate was forced to surrender to the *United States*, and he was detained for seven months a prisoner-of-war. During battle, when his ship suffered heavy casualties with thirty-six killed and sixty-eight wounded, he knelt briefly beside a cannon and prayed that God would spare his life. He returned home with prayer forgotten and Bible unread, and yet with some vague respect for divine things which kept him from ridiculing religion. Later, when a half-pay lieutenant, he happened to attend a church in Plymouth where the preacher spoke from the text, 'Behold the Lamb of God which taketh away the sin of the world!' It was the invitation he needed to find peace for a guilty conscience. Thereafter Rhind's life's work became itinerant evangelism. In this role he went aboard HMS *Genoa* in Devonport before

---

[15] Brenton's career with details of conversion from the biography compiled by the Rev. Henry Raikes (1846) and abridged by his son Sir Charles Brenton, *Memoir of the Life and Services of Vice-Admiral Sir Jahleel Brenton* (1855), p. 163. High regard for Brenton is shown in an enthusiastic letter to Saumarez from his nephew Richard, who served under him in the action off Naples; Richard Saumarez to Vice-Admiral Sir James Saumarez, HMS *Spartan*, Malta, 9 Jun 1810. I am grateful to Captain P. L. Saumarez RN for kindly drawing my attention to this letter. See also W. Rolleston (ed.), 'Some Letters of Mrs Richard Saumarez', *Transactions of the Société Guernesiase*, XI (1933), pp. 319–47.

she left for the Mediterranean and the Battle of Navarino; he sold a few Bibles and felt he had been well received by her company.[16]

Another *Macedonian* conversion made its way into print. Samuel Leech served on the lower deck, was captured by the *United States*, and then deserted to the USA. His memoirs are critical of the Royal Navy, its system of discipline, its overuse of flogging, and the petty tyrannies exercised by midshipmen. He found the debaucheries of lower deck life abhorrent – but then he had to excuse to himself and his readers his desertion to a country at war with his own. It may have been a part of this exercise which brought him into the Methodist Church in the USA, and allowed him to conclude the story of his life with a fittingly pious tailpiece: 'though I have not gained all that is desirable and that is offered in an abundant gospel, yet I have been trying to stem the torrent of my iniquity, which runs through the earth, and striving to make my way to the path of Glory.' Once again it was a felt need for moral cleansing that brought him to conversion, but more as a process than a crisis.[17]

The examples of Maude and Coote show two serious-minded men of impeccable character: no 'torrent of iniquity' here, but a wish to learn more from Marks. He guided their thinking through books and letters, with studious reflection once again a more powerful driver than emotion. It also predominated in the experience of Robert Wauchope, who, like Maude and Coote, was made post in 1814. As a captain he was obliged to serve on a court martial in 1818, and found himself listening to evidence of an ordained schoolmaster, Patrick Pounder, who claimed to be indwelt by the Holy Spirit and who led a small cell group aboard HMS *Favorite*. There had been an incident in which Pounder had been in dispute with the ship's surgeon, then the first lieutenant and finally the captain, Hercules Robinson. When he found that a respected captain like Robinson appeared to believe at least some of these Trinitarian ideas, Wauchope resolved to study the New Testament for himself. He began with Matthew's Gospel, 'and by the time I got to the end of Revelation', he wrote, 'I was a true believer, born again of the Holy Spirit.'[18]

[16] Details of Rhind's conversion from funeral tribute: Anon. [J.B.I.], *Faithful unto Death, a Memoir of William Graeme Rhind, RN* (1863). Rhind surrendered his commission, studied for the Anglican ministry under Charels Simeon at Cambridge, but became an itinerant Nonconformist evangelist instead: F. Roy Coad, *A History of the Brethren Movement* (Exeter, 1968), p. 73. Visit to HMS *Genoa* noted *NMBS* 1828, p. 28.

[17] Samuel Leech, in Baynham, *From the Lower Deck*, p. 92.

[18] Wauchope, pp. 82–5. Minutes of court martial of Rev. P. Pounder in PRO ADM 1/5499, 24–8 Dec 1818.

If our sources are typical, we are led to the conclusion that conversion was more often associated with reflective thought than dramatic episode. Sea-going life and war combined to create a lively awareness of mortality. In some instances a moment of danger forced a despairing cry to God, but that act did not of itself constitute a life-changing conversion. In the lower deck memoirs of George Watson, the author describes how he lost his footing aloft and was about to fall to almost certain death, when he gasped a momentary 'prayer to Him that is alone able to save' – and found a rope swing close enough for him to grasp, yet his memoirs do not suggest a life of faith thereafter. On the other hand, Wauchope knew of a lieutenant whose faith awakened as a direct result of a brush with death. In his struggles to get clear of a foundering craft he framed the Lord's Prayer before he began to sink, apparently for good; in that instant, a grating released from the wreck came up exactly underneath him and saved his life. The officer was convinced that God hears the cry of the desperate, and entered thereafter into a Christian faith which lasted a lifetime.[19]

Andrew Burn's journey into faith has already been described. Like many others he was raised in a generally God-fearing culture, but drifted from it in manhood. He found himself in a harsh world of warfare and moral pressure, where conscience easily hardened and where God might be neglected. Yet he could not find soul-satisfaction in secular culture, philosophy or self-indulgence. He craved something dependable to give meaning to life and hope beyond death. He found it eventually in the message of the New Testament. In his case, as with Marks and Newton, Smith and Rhind, there came a dawning of understanding that they all attributed to divine revelation. This growing awareness was a process, and not a steady one either. Most of the characters under discussion slipped back a few times into the darkness before they were sure of the light. Burn found particular help from a dream – of struggling to find his way under a door, and having to leave his fine clothes outside. It was an almost tangible experience of the abandonment described by the hymn-writer Toplady:

> Nothing in my hand I bring; simply to Thy Cross I cling.
> Naked come to Thee for dress.[20]

There was, then, nothing about naval life which led inexorably to the vital religion of the Blue Lights, but there were features about it which constantly raised issues of eternity. To many, perhaps the majority, the resultant 'Dull Thoughts'

---

[19] Watson in Baynham, *From the Lower Deck*, p. 115; Wauchope, pp. 47f.

[20] Burn's conversion, see pp. 109–10 above; Burn, *Memoirs*, I, p. 79; dream, I, pp. 129f.; hymn 'Rock of Ages' by Augustus Montague Toplady (1740–78).

needed exorcising in the spirit of 'Eat, drink and be merry, for tomorrow we die.' Yet, paradoxically, even dissipation could become fertile soil for the good seed of the Gospel: sailors trapped in grosser sins than many who lived sheltered lives might long for a clean conscience as a result. This was true of John Newton (1725–1807), ex-midshipman and able seaman of the Georgian navy, ex-slaver turned Abolitionist, 'the old African blasphemer' (as he called himself): the dreadfulness of his offences bred an intensity of repentance and commitment. Although once a midshipman, he was not a Blue Light; nevertheless Newton touched the lives of some who were, notably Middleton, and his influence was so pervasive throughout Evangelicalism that he must be regarded as a major force within the movement. He was a particular encouragement to Burn who met him around 1773, and his widely read autobiography, often used as an evangelistic tract, illuminates the phenomenon of conversion in the context of seafaring.[21]

As a child Newton attended a dissenting church with a godly minister. His mother died when he was seven, and thereafter he lost touch with systematic Christian teaching. He went to sea in his father's ship from the age of eleven. Religious impulses came and went, sometimes with gloomy intensity, and always with a sense of divine disapproval upon his lifestyle. 'I saw the necessity of religion as a means of escaping hell, but I loved sin and was unwilling to forsake it.'[22] At best his religion was a scheme of self-discipline to keep him away from wrongdoing – Law rather than Grace – but he could never keep it going beyond a few months or two years. Morose morality was succeeded by Shaftesbury's deistic philosophy – happier at one level but conscience-deadening. Newton was challenged by a dream he had in Venice, of a precious ring that he was tempted to hand over to a fiend who then threw it into the sea; it was retrieved for him by a heavenly figure who promised to keep it safely for him. For a while Newton clung to the Gospel teaching that he could never keep himself pure without God's help, and that only the Lord could give him salvation and hold his life secure. Although he soon let the message grow dim in his mind, he never altogether forgot it.

[21] Newton's conversion in his autobiography, *An Authentic Narrative of some remarkable and interesting Particulars in the Life of [John Newton]*, first published as letters to Rev. T. Haweis, 1764, and reissued as *Out of the Depths* (Chicago, c. 1965), pp. 15–115 (Letters ii–xiii); and in Richard Cecil, *Memoirs of the Rev. John Newton* (1808), updated as *The Life of John Newton*, ed. Marylynn Rouse (Fearn, Ross-shire, 2000), *passim*, esp. pp. 17f., 23–9, 43–56, 60–95. Also Pollock, *Amazing Grace*, pp. 69–128. Newton's autobiography was a help to Bo'sun Smith.

[22] Newton, *Out of the Depths*, p. 20; Newton's dream of the ring, ibid., pp. 27–9.

For the present, however, he found more immediate pleasures and concerns that effaced religious impressions.

Gradually his sea-going brought him into increasing depravity of conduct, but he was rescued from total abandonment by falling in love with Mary Catlett, the girl he eventually married. 'When I later made shipwreck of faith, hope and conscience, my love to this person was the only remaining principle which in any degree took their place. The bare possibility of seeing her again was the only means of restraining me from the most horrid designs against myself and others.'[23] In 1744 Newton was pressed aboard HMS *Harwich* and soon rated midshipman. In love with Mary, he twice broke his leave to see her; for the first offence he lost his privileged status, and for the second he was flogged and reduced to the lower deck. By now Newton had earned a reputation for recalcitrance, and his captain was pleased to get rid of him by transferring him into a slaving ship in return for a prime seaman.

In the slave trade his initial hopes of advancing himself were dashed when he fell under the power of an unscrupulous master who virtually enslaved him. Two years later he had the chance of returning to England in the ship *Greyhound*, but a wild Atlantic storm in March 1748 nearly caused her to founder, and Newton, at last confronting the possibility of imminent death, called upon God to have mercy upon him. He recognised that he would have to give account of his immoral life, and knew that he desperately needed God's forgiving grace. Afterwards he commemorated the day of deliverance, 21 March, as marking not quite his conversion, but the time when he 'began to know that there is a God who hears and answers prayer.'[24] He explains that his faith was still gravely deficient: he had learned of his need to be forgiven for the offences he had committed, but he had not yet discovered that his whole character needed to be renewed, and that he could find assurance of future forgiveness and the gift of spiritual strength through Christ.

> I sensed my more enormous sins, but I was little aware of the innate evil of my heart. ... The hidden life of a Christian, that of communion with God by Jesus Christ, and dependence on Him for hourly supplies of wisdom, strength and comfort, was a mystery of which I had as yet no knowledge. I acknowledged the Lord's mercy in pardoning what was past, but depended chiefly upon my own resolution to do better for the time to come.[25]

[23] Ibid., pp. 24f.
[24] Ibid., p. 79.
[25] Ibid., p. 83.

He needed deeper understanding of Scripture and further experience of his own shortcomings before he found peace of mind. On an island off Sierra Leone, and afflicted with a dangerous fever, he 'cast [himself] before the Lord' and 'was enabled to hope and believe in a crucified Saviour.'[26]

After his experience of God in the *Greyhound*, Newton continued in the slave trade, and had four voyages as master of his own vessel. Only gradually did his conscience awake to the enormity of what he was doing, and the inconsistency of professing to love God while oppressing his fellow creatures. In 1755 he suffered a seizure, left the sea, and settled down as the surveyor of tides at Liverpool. Ashore at last and happily married, he developed links with the evangelical movement, and extended his theological studies. In 1764, aged almost forty, Newton was ordained in the Church of England, and began his new career as pastor, preacher, author and hymn-writer at Olney and then (from 1780) at St Mary's Woolnoth in London. Having left the sea, he was deeply convicted of guilt over his involvement in the slave trade. He became an ardent Abolitionist, supported Wilberforce, gave damning evidence before the Privy Council, and published his own tract denouncing the trade in 1788. Late in life, widowed, almost blind, with health deteriorating and his mind rambling, he would not abandon preaching, on the grounds that he could never cease to pay tribute to the amazing grace that had saved him.[27]

Newton, like Marks and Burn, came to faith as result of a lengthy process, with setbacks as well as moments of illumination. Evangelicals often spoke as though conversion was a sudden decision, a moment's resolve to abandon self and to trust in Christ for salvation. Whether or not that ever happened, the examples of leading evangelicals suggest that it would have been exceptional. More usually there was a gradual appreciation of moral guilt before God. Fear of hell was certainly a feature, but perhaps it figured less prominently than a desire for cleansing of soul, to be rid of the burden of sin, and to feel right with God. In each case the realisation that everything needful for salvation had already been done was overwhelming. Since Christ had died for every sin, all that the sinner could do was to accept forgiveness and new life as gifts of God.

The foundations of faith were often laid in childhood, when a pious mother taught her child of the love of God. This was so in the experience of Newton, Smith and Rhind. In early manhood there may have been a period of unbelief

[26] Ibid., p. 92.
[27] 'I hope it will always be a subject of humiliating reflection to me that I was once an active instrument in a business at which my heart now shudders'; Cecil, ed. Rouse, p. 75, quoting Rev. John Newton, *Thoughts upon the African Slave Trade* (1788).

like Burn, of ignorance and heedlessness like Marks, or of rank immorality like Newton. A crisis, or perhaps a series of them, brought a sharp sense that life was fragile, and that one day every human soul must face its Maker. Instead of denying this, or despairing of finding any remedy for wrong-doing, these individuals all turned towards God. From their reading or childhood memories or from listening to a sermon, they had been led to believe that a loving God would receive one who repented and sought his grace. The crucial factor was that a person came to long for a right relationship with God, and came into it by throwing themselves upon the grace of Christ. Faith of this kind was normally accompanied by a great outpouring of joy and a deep sense of peace and assurance.

It might be expressed by Charles Wesley:

> Amazing love! How can it be
> That Thou, my God, should'st die for me? …
> Long my imprisoned spirit lay
> Fast bound in sin and nature's night.
> Thine eye diffused a quickening ray:
> I woke. The dungeon flamed with light.
> May chains fell off. My heart was free!
> I rose, went forth, and followed Thee.

Or by John Newton:

> Amazing grace – how sweet the sound –
> That saved a wretch like me!
> I once was lost but now am found,
> Was blind but now I see.[28]

Common to each one was the need for careful thought and sometimes deep study; for this, the overcrowded and routine-ridden life of a messdeck was far from ideal, and not infrequently the final act of Christian commitment took place ashore. Although Marks, Smith, Brenton and Newton were all led to take a decisive step of faith under the ministry of a godly pastor, the essential part of their spiritual awakening had taken place already during their time at sea.

---

[28] Hymn by Charles Wesley (1707–88), 'And can it be …'; hymn by John Newton, 'Amazing grace', from *Olney Hymns* (1779).

A Lasting Contribution to the Ethos of the Post-War Navy

FEWER evangelicals were to be found in commissioned ranks after the war, reflecting in part the much reduced number of sea-going appointments. It is possible that Admiralty prejudice hindered evangelical careers once the powerful patronage of Barham and Gambier ceased to operate: there is a certain amount of anecdotal evidence to suggest that as a type they were a bit awkward to employ – apt to be rather stuffy morally, a bit censorious, perhaps a disturbing element in a wardroom – a risk which did not have to be taken when there were so many more qualified officers than vacancies. Beyond doubt, when all chaplains were brought under the supervision of Dr Samuel Cole at Greenwich, they were subject to a clergyman who had no sympathy with either Evangelical Anglicans or dissenters. With the support of the Duke of Clarence when Lord High Admiral, he tried to stop their kind of tracts from reaching the lower deck. Sir Thomas Hardy as professional head of the navy showed a marked disinclination to allow the avowed evangelical Wauchope to serve at sea as a flag captain, lest he cause disorder by his strict notions of morality. Certainly the question had become contentious within the navy by this time, but, while Wauchope felt that his faith was a barrier to professional preferment, his own prickliness may have been as much of a problem. Evangelicals caused a stir with their propensity to write pamphlets on controversial issues, of which the pre-eminent example was Edward Hawker's anonymous *Statement concerning Certain Immoral Practices* in 1821, which condemned the admission of prostitutes to ships of war in harbour, and triggered a fierce debate. Blue Lights were not always comfortable to accommodate.[29]

Nevertheless, at almost the exact time when Hawker was creating controversy, another Evangelical was sailing into high favour. Edward Parry so impressed John Barrow, the dominating second secretary at the Admiralty, that he was marked down for promotion, honours and the opportunity to lead another three Arctic ventures. Eventually Parry, a serving admiral with a knighthood and high credit in his profession, became the doyen of a new generation of Blue Lights. Under his leadership the movement adopted two influential developments: the Naval Prayer

---

[29] Rev. Samuel Cole DD: entered RN, 1790; involved in Spithead Mutiny in HMS *London*, where he intervened to save Adm. Colpoys, and was put ashore by mutineers; served in *Monarch* at Camperdown; senior chaplain at Greenwich Hospital, 1821–38; domestic chaplain to Duke of Clarence for thirty years. Opposed by Smith over tracts: *NSM*, 1827, pp. 290f., and Smith, *Windsor*. See also E. L. Waldo Smith, *The Navy Chaplain and his Parish* (Ottawa, 1967), pp. 12f. Wauchope's interview with Hardy was in 1834, and is described in his privately published memoirs: Wauchope, pp. 98–105; Hawker, *Statement of Certain Immoral Practices*.

Union for officers and Scripture Readers to reach the lower deck. By that stage – around 1850 – several younger evangelical officers were reaching senior rank, often through distinguished service in suppressing slavers, or in promoting survey and exploration, in time to show their fighting qualities in the Russian War, the Indian Mutiny and the Second China War.[30]

By mid-century religion had become an unmistakable element in naval life. The chaplaincy was revitalised along the lines that Middleton had desired, with a regular pastoral and sacramental ministry. Sunday service was compulsory throughout the navy, and various ships introduced voluntary daily prayers. The custom became so popular with the lower deck that the Admiralty eventually incorporated it into daily routine. When training ships were introduced in the 1850s to induct the new long-service ratings into naval ways, religious instruction formed a significant part of the general education programme, with chaplain-schoolmasters much in evidence. Victorian England was always going to find a place for religion, but it did not have to be the low-church piety of evangelicalism. In the end, however, the form that the Church took in the navy was largely modelled on ideas first canvassed by the Blue Lights.

This is hardly surprising, since they had devised the mechanisms that really worked. Their record of successful innovation is astonishing. In pursuit of its programme naval evangelicalism had pioneered a series of measures which collectively amounted to a radical transformation of religion at sea and the concept of the church afloat. These were:

1. Bible distribution for private ownership
2. Instructions for the chaplains, 1806
3. First use of punishment returns
4. Introduction of all-rank shipboard groups for prayer and fellowship
5. Ships' libraries
6. Voluntary religious gatherings in leisure hours

To this list would be added in the post-war era major projects of social welfare through Sailors' Homes and shore accommodation. New vehicles for evangelism and pastoral support came through Scripture Readers and the Naval Prayer Union. The Church afloat was progressively strengthened by a series of measures, including the first RN Confirmation Service and more frequent celebrations of

[30] Rear-Admiral Sir Edward Parry (1790–1855): Arctic voyages 1819–20 (as second to John Ross), 1821–3 (furthest west), 1824–5, 1827 (furthest north); hydrographer 1823–9; commissioner of Australian Agricultural Society 1832–7; controller of steam machinery 1837–46; superintendent Haslar hospital 1846; d. as lieutenant governor Greenwich 1854.

Holy Communion. Later, chaplains were allowed to choose the cabin best placed for pastoral work, and in all HM Ships a place was set aside for private prayer. Evangelical influence was the force that called into being the Sailors' Homes, the Scripture Readers and the Prayer Union, and it was arguably the prime mover in every one of the other developments. Surprisingly perhaps, it was an Evangelical admiral who first embarked a Catholic priest to minister as an unofficial chaplain to a fleet at sea. Evangelical influence gave a huge boost to the temperance movement, and founded the RN Temperance Society to run alongside the RN Christian Union – both the result of Agnes Weston's work with her incomparable Sailors' Rests. In many other matters, such as restored Sunday worship and then daily prayers, or the encouragement of Holy Communion, or the Portsmouth RN Club, they collaborated with others, but a list of measures where Blue Lights took the lead indicates how far-sighted and ultimately beneficial the movement became.[31]

Their further hope that Christian sailors would become worldwide ambassadors for the Gospel was strikingly expressed by Penrose in 1813 in one of his letters to *The Naval Chronicle*: 'Nelson and his followers would have harassed our enemies beyond their resources by carrying a British army from place to place with ease and rapidity … And by proper attention we might spread the power of the gospel to all nations and languages by the same means.'[32] The great Protestant missionary expansion of the nineteenth century was spearheaded by Britain, greatly facilitated by the freedom of ocean travel which her maritime supremacy conferred. Not only did the navy support British missionaries – politics as well as religion helped determine that policy, of course – but naval officers pioneered the first Protestant mission to Japan by raising the funds, appointing the missionary and administering their own society. The more conventional church organisations were not yet ready for such a visionary incursion into a new culture.[33]

The Blue Lights, and more generally the evangelicalism from which they sprang, promoted humanity, compassion and benevolence. Besides the well-known anti-slavery movement there were the prison reforms of John Howard and Elizabeth

---

[31] A brief chronology should include: first Confirmation, 1843; Naval Prayer Union, 1851; Royal Portsmouth Sailors' Home (later the Portsmouth Royal Naval Club), 1852; Scripture Readers began 1854 and formed into recognised society 1860; chaplain's preferential choice of cabin, 1868; provision of screened place of prayer, 1870; RN Temperance Society, 1873; RN Christian Union, 1870s or early 80s (date unclear in Weston autobiography); first Sailors' Rest opened at Devonport, 1876; RC priest embarked in Mediterranean Fleet, 1888.

[32] *NC*, XXIX (1813), p. 476.

[33] Loo Choo Naval Mission (to Okinawa), 1843–61.

Fry, the changed treatment of the mentally sick, the later Mines and Factories Acts associated with Lord Shaftesbury – and in fact the 'ten thousand compassions and charities' that one twentieth-century historian credited to them.[34] Humanity of a kind, rather like liberty, could be nurtured by Jefferson's 'inalienable rights' – even though his definition was restricted enough to allow room for slavery – or it could be derived from the French concept of the Rights of Man and of Citizen. By contrast, the evangelical agenda of social reform was derived from a biblical concept of mankind, men and women made in the image of God, sharing common membership of the human family, all beloved of the God who had showed his love in the redemption of the world through his Son. Godfearing people had to combine faith and compassion, as defined, for instance, by the prophet Micah: 'what does the Lord require of you but to act justly, to love mercy and to walk humbly with your God?'[35] The Old Testament ordered the people of God to love their neighbours as they loved themselves, and to show practical support for aliens, widows and orphans, every vulnerable member of society, while Jesus enlarged the sphere of loving obligation to include even enemies. The New Testament stressed the intrinsic worth of every soul, each one uniquely loved of God and destined for immortality. Compassion and Christianity cannot be prised apart.

Not every professing Christian society or individual has lived up to these searching principles, particularly when zeal has blurred the distinction between the proper spheres of public law and private morality. Not every evangelical earned a reputation for benevolence: Samuel Marsden, the 'flogging parson' of New South Wales, or Sir George Arthur, the governor of Van Diemen's Land, were often seen as over-severe. Aware perhaps of the rising tide of piety afloat, *The Naval Chronicle* in 1812 expressed its distaste for 'the sour discipline of the puritans or the dogmatic severity of fanatics'.[36] In fact the Blue Lights purveyed a different spirit and (as this study has shown) were prominent in efforts to improve conditions of service and to develop a fair and even merciful code of discipline.

Humane attitudes were implicit in Barham's *Regulations*, explicit in AFY's proposals, and personified by Duncan and Saumarez. They were given wide currency by examples of officers in command of ships and fleets, and by the way numbers of young officers were inducted into gentler methods through their experiences under Saumarez, Gambier, Pellew, Penrose, Hillyar, Maude, Coote and a galaxy of others. Pellew's determination to bring the Bantry Bay conspirators to justice looks vindictive until set in its 1797 context of threatening mutiny and invasion,

---

[34] Ford K. Brown, *Fathers of the Victorians* (Cambridge, 1961), p. 317.

[35] Micah 6:8; Leviticus 19:18; Exodus 23:9; Deuteronomy 24:19, 22; Matthew 5:44.

[36] *NC*, XXVIII (1812), p. 424n.

and Austen may have been severe to the point of excess. Yet Pellew introduced the system of quarterly returns that eventually proved to be one of the most progressive disciplinary developments of the Great Wars. It was this reform that made Austen accountable to the Admiralty, and even if he is exonerated by the delinquent state of his ship's company, he remains an awkward exception to the record of Blue Lights in command. He did not reverse the tidal flow of evangelicalism in the direction of humanity.

Compassionate reform became more prominent after the wars, when evangelicalism drove forward the Sailors' Cause, and pioneered the schemes of welfare which were eventually to be found in every major port – cheap and alcohol-free accommodation, games and reading rooms, floating chapels and seamen's missions. Where the state was slow to recognise its obligations to sailors' dependants, the churches channelled funding into orphanages, ragged schools and support for widows. Many of these schemes were run by officers on half-pay, as they carried forward their evangelistic mission from wartime gatherings afloat to shore-based charities.

Evangelicals supported these practical schemes of welfare without abandoning their conservative attitudes towards social and political structures. In general they were happy with the authority of captains and officers, including powers of awarding corporal punishment, so long as it was just and tempered with mercy: discipline could only be relaxed once lower-deck conduct improved. Although this summary is not unfair to their overall position, it does not do justice to the enlightened methods of some outstanding Blue Lights – officers like Edward Parry, Bartholomew Sulivan and William Peel – who brought the insights of a Duncan or a Penrose to a new generation. Whether on the progressive wing or amongst the more reactionary, their attitudes were tempered by a sense of accountability to Almighty God.[37]

Emphatically the Blue Lights were not just a wartime flare of religion that lasted till peace and then went out. Men of this conviction were still serving in later decades, some as long-lived survivors (like Austen or Henry Hope) but many more as new recruits (like Trotter and Fishbourne, Otter and King-Hall).[38] The

[37] Parry, Arctic explorer, see n. 30 above; Admiral Sir Bartholomew Sulivan (1810–90), known for his surveys of the approaches to Bomarsund and Helsingfors under fire in the Russian War; Captain Sir William Peel (1824–58), one of the first naval VCs, commander of the *Shannon*'s naval brigade in the Indian Mutiny.

[38] Sir Francis Austen (1774–1865), admiral of the fleet; Sir Henry Hope (1787–1860) retired admiral. Henry Dundas Trotter (1802–59) and Edmund Fishbourne (1811–87) survived the disastrous Niger expedition of 1841 and reached admiral's rank (retired). Admiral H. C. Otter was a distinguished surveyor in the Baltic

moral and spiritual values which they had cherished survived, grew in strength, and then became well-nigh commonplace in the later Victorian navy – Sunday worship, daily prayers, voluntary religious gatherings, an active chaplains' branch. Would these things have happened without them? Probably so, eventually and to some degree, for religion ran strong in Victorian society. But the Blue Lights had always pressed for religious observance to be part of corporate life at sea, and the way this came about in the nineteenth century exactly fulfilled the original Kempenfelt–Middleton manifesto. Whereas High Church piety and middle-of-the-road churchmanship stressed sacraments and liturgy, naval religion retained some of the features more obviously derived from evangelicalism – Bible distribution, Scripture Readers, study groups, prayer meetings – and perhaps we should add impromptu sermons and rousing hymns. The chaplains' branch developed much as the Blue Lights had hoped, with a pastoral, preaching, priestly ministry, a spiritual role shorn of extraneous duties, a man of God accessible to all aboard, as Middleton and Penrose had advocated.

More subtly the Blue Lights influenced the thinking of the officer corps, partly by the power of *Regulations and Instructions*, but indirectly too through the example of professionally competent commanders like Duncan, Saumarez and Penrose. They had proved under the demands of war that it was possible to govern a ship without profanity, and that drunkenness and immorality were not inseparable from the characters of sailors. The power of their example was magnified by the eminence of their rank. For several years Blue Lights were commanders-in-chief of the Channel, Mediterranean, Baltic and East Indies fleets; the captains they appointed and the officers who in turn followed them would impart a tone to the navy for years to come.

Young officers were taught their trade at sea. For them the ship was the practical academy in which they learned seamanship, navigation, all the rudiments of their profession, and any smatterings of general education which they might acquire on the way. They formed the junior members of a captain's entourage. From him and from the other officers they learned what they could about management and command. There was no Dartmouth in the Napoleonic War, but only a vast number of individual gunrooms and captains. Officer training followed no syllabus other than the topics required for passing as lieutenant. The personal influence of a commanding officer would determine much about the future career of his *protégés*. It would be a worthwhile task to trace the origins and

---

campaign and of the western coast of Scotland; Sir William King-Hall (1816–86) served as flag captain in the Baltic campaign and the Second China War before becoming C-in-C The Nore 1877–9.

track the careers of officers who owed their positions to Gambier, Saumarez and Pellew, and those who were closely influenced by them during time in their flagships. Within two or three decades the navy itself became uncommonly like the Blue Lights in its outward conduct – although there is evidence that things were not like this when sailors went ashore!

A little anecdote from a forgotten book of Victorian reminiscences gives an instance of how this education might work. Admiral John Moresby in his book *Two Admirals* recalls the early career of his father, Admiral of the Fleet Sir Fairfax Moresby. As a young midshipman in Captain Peter Parker's frigate *Amazon* he became so desperately unhappy that he found the courage to desert. Fortunately for him he was found by Captain Vansittart of *La Fortunée* (Blue Light and SPCK subscriber), who took the despondent youngster to his own ship and elicited his story. He gave the lad a Bible and bade him make it his guide through life. He interceded with Parker on his behalf and ensured his trouble-free return to the *Amazon*. Moresby never forgot that lesson in simple Christian kindness, and sought to base his own standards upon it. Years later, as captain of the *Menai*, he had to deal with a sailor whose carelessness had caused a potentially disastrous fire: when the ship had been saved, the punishment grating was rigged and the hands assembled. But Moresby declared the culprit pardoned: 'It is not 24 hours since God forgave us all', he declared. 'It is fitting I should now forgive you. Pipe down.' When in his turn the son had his own command, the gunboat *Snake* (1862–3), he was happy to allow a voluntary Bible study group for a quarter of the ship's crew, in remarkable similarity to the psalm-singing circle of the Napoleonic War.[39]

Many officers who came under Gambier's influence spread their evangelical convictions widely in the navy and in the new evangelistic and philanthropic maritime societies ashore. Evangelicals were the first to tackle the social problems of the maritime milieu and the difficulties for sailors' dependants. They had an honourable record in pressing for reforms in the navy itself – pay, leave, discipline, rewards.

The Blue Lights had been searching for humane methods of control from the days of Kempenfelt. By introducing many more rewards for reliable service – enhanced pay, good conduct badges, some exemption from flogging – the navy gradually adopted the philosophy which Penrose had argued, and with it came a gentler but carefully regulated disciplinary code. Quarterly returns led on to punishment warrants, a defined code of penalties, and at last the suspension of peacetime flogging.

39 Admiral John Moresby, *Two Admirals* (1909; rev. edn 1913), pp. 15, 25.

After 1853, Continuous Service contracts dispensed with the old method of enlistment for a single commission and made it possible for the lower deck to enter for a career.[40] Thereafter the navy had to train its own personnel, and that included teaching moral and religious values from chaplain-schoolmasters in the training ships which were now the nursery for the fleet. The Blue Lights had consistently looked for 'better men' in the service, and with the coming of the long-serving professional bluejacket their hope was realised. Kempenfelt and Penrose might have recognised the mid-Victorian rating as the man they had wished to see – unattainable in 1780 or 1800 but a living reality in 1860. The aspirations of the original Blue Lights were amply fulfilled when their Christian values became hard-wired into the Victorian naval profession.

[40] After prolonged consideration the navy began to recruit and train its own seamen, instead of relying upon the national pool of seafarers that traditionally provided men for merchant shipping, fishing fleets and the Royal Navy. No longer were naval ratings discharged into civilian life on the conclusion of a commission when her crew paid off: instead they belonged to the navy and were expected to serve for the full term of their contract, i.e. they had enlisted for 'continuous service'. The system was launched in 1853 but took several years to become the standard form of recruitment. See Bromley, *Manning Pamphlets*.

Bibliography

Archive Sources

BRITISH LIBRARY

Add. MS 23207	Original Despatches of Naval Victories, 1793–1815
Add. MS 33124	Pelham Papers (Miscellaneous)
Add. MS 36604	Log Book of HMS *Agamemnon*, 1793–4
Add. MS 36605	Log Book of HMS *Agamemnon*, 1794–5
Add. MS 38258	Liverpool Papers, vol. lxix
Add. MS 41079	Melville Papers (Series II), vol. i (Barham)
Add. MS 41083	Melville Papers (Series II), vol. v
Add. MS 41365	Martin Papers, vol. xx
Add. MS 41366	Martin Papers, vol. xxi
Add. MS 41367	Martin Papers, vol. xxii
Add. MS 41369	Martin Papers, vol. xxiv

EAST SUSSEX RECORD OFFICE, LEWES

Locker Lampson Papers, including correspondence of Edward Hawke Locker

NATIONAL ARCHIVES: PUBLIC RECORD OFFICE

Admiralty records all prefixed ADM

ADMIRALTY IN-LETTERS

1/411	Despatches to the Admiralty concerning the Trafalgar campaign
1/2501, 2503, 2504	Letters from captains to Secretary of Admiralty (Nepean), 1801
1/3928	Greenwich Hospital Correspondence
1/4476	Letters to Secretary of the Admiralty (Samuel Cole to Barrow)
1/4971	Letters to Secretary of the Admiralty (John Owen to Barrow)

ADMIRALTY MINUTES

3/174	Correspondence of the Chaplain General, John Owen, including Minutes of the Admiralty Board concerning the status of chaplains, 1812

COURTS MARTIAL

1/5299	Proceedings of Court Martial aboard *Arundel*, 10 January 1760
1/5339	Minutes of Courts Martial, 6 April – 30 June 1797
1/5459	Minutes of Courts Martial, including the Rev. P. Pounder, 24–8 December 1818
12/27B	Digest of Courts Martial: Admiralty 'Black Book', vol. 1 – Officers not to be employed again
12/27C	Digest of Courts Martial: Admiralty 'Black Book', vol. 2 – Officers not to be employed again

MUSTER BOOKS AND PAY LEDGERS

35/504	Pay ledger	*Defence*	1793–1794
36/12569	Muster book	*Defence*	1794–1794
36/5094	Muster book	*Expedition*	1800–1
37/119	Muster book	*Conqueror*	1806

LOG BOOKS – ADMIRALS' JOURNALS

| 50/43 | Saumarez | *Diomede* | 1803 |
| 50/44 | Pellew | *Culloden* | 1805–6 |

LOG BOOKS – CAPTAIN'S LOGS

51/3770	*Arundel*	1747–1756
51/1001	*Torbay*	1755–1763
51/307	*Elizabeth*	1757–1758
51/3771	*Arundel*	1757–1760
51/3998	*Valiant*	1763–1764
51/56	*Ardent*	1775–1776
51/94	*Bedford*	1776–1783
51/1036	*Victory*	1778–1783
51/88	*Barfleur*	1780–1783
51/4193	*Formidable*	1782–1783
51/4193	*Fortune*	1782
51/1104	*Agamemnon*	1793
51/1159	*Crescent*	1793–1794
51/1162	*Adventure*	1793–1794
51/4435	*Defence*	1793–1794
51/1162	*Bellerophon*	1794
51/1198	*Q. Charlotte*	1794–1795
51/4490	*Q. Charlotte*	1794–1795
51/1214	*Venerable*	1796–1798
51/1369	*Courageux*	1801
51/1585	*Conqueror*	1806–1807
51/1734	*Conqueror*	1807–1808
51/1979	*Conqueror*	1808–1809
51/1826	*St Albans*	1808
51/1734	*Caledonia*	1808–1809
51/2344	*Elephant*	1812–1813

LOG BOOKS – MASTERS' LOGS

52/1086	*Valiant*	1760–1761
52/1568	*Ardent*	1775–1776
52/3505	*Defence*	1793–1794
51/2219	*Conqueror*	1808–1809
51/2220	*Conqueror*	1809–1820

OTHER ADMIRALTY RECORDS

| 107/30 | Admiralty Passing Certificates (No. 31: R. Marks to Lieut.) |
| Ind 9229 | List of Chaplains eligible for bounty, 1836 |

NATIONAL MARITIME MUSEUM, GREENWICH

PERSONAL COLLECTIONS

Barham Papers	MID/2/28	Letters to C. I. Latrobe
Duncan Papers	DUN/19	Public and Private Correspondence, 2 vols
	DUN/31	Memorandum book of Captain Adam Duncan
Keats Papers	KEA/6	includes letters from Saumarez
	KEA/7	includes letters from Gambier
	KEA/8	includes letters from Pellew
Yorke Papers	YOR/6	includes letters from Gambier
	YOR/14	includes letters from Pellew, Penrose and Spencer Percival
	YOR/16 (a) and (b)	includes letters from Saumarez
	YOR/19	includes letters from Wilberforce

JOURNALS

Phillips 89/14 (Nel/1)	Nelson's Journal, 27 June 1793 – 24 March 1794
JOD 23	The Rev. R. Vyvyan, *Nonsuch*, 1780
JOD 47	George Gould, *Mercury*, 1800–2
JOD 34	A passenger, HM Store-ship *Dromedary*, 1811–12
LOG NC. 41	Midshipman's log, Arthur Burgh, *Conqueror*, 1808–11

OTHER DOCUMENTS

RUSI MSS A29B, NM 35	Memorandum book of Naval Signals
LBK/21	Letter book of Rear Admiral Sir Charles Penrose, 1813–14
BGR/2	'Memoirs of James Trevenen', by C. V. Penrose
SCO/1–4	Papers of the Rev. A. J. Scott
BOS/14 and 15	Marine Society papers of Captain H. T. A. Bosanquet
NM 137 A and B	Kealy MSS concerning Naval Chaplains
CAD/A/11	'Memoirs of the Royal Navy,' by Charles Derrick, 1789 [MS from library of Lord Barham]

MEDWAY ARCHIVES, STROOD, KENT

Parish records of St Margaret's Church, Rochester relating to Andrew Burn

PRIAULX LIBRARY, ST PETER PORT, GUERNSEY

Saumarez family papers

RHODES HOUSE, UNIVERSITY OF OXFORD

Manuscript volume written by James Ramsay, chiefly concerned with his Abolition interests: MSS. Brit. Emp. s.2 f.83 1787

ROYAL MARINES MUSEUM, EASTNEY

ARCH 11/45	Chatham Division Letter Book 1782–4
ARCH 2/20	reference to Andrew Burn

SHRUBLAND HALL, IPSWICH, SUFFOLK

Private letters and papers of James, first Lord de Saumarez

THE SOCIETY FOR PROMOTING CHRISTIAN KNOWLEDGE
SPCK, Holy Trinity Church, Marylebone Road, London NW1
Minutes Books, vols. 27–35 (1776–1812)

SUFFOLK PUBLIC RECORD OFFICE, IPSWICH
Letter books and official correspondence of Lord de Saumarez, Baltic, 1808–12. HA 93.

MSS IN PRIVATE OWNERSHIP
Capt. P. L. Saumarez, DSC, RN (Rtd): two letters from Richard Saumarez

Periodicals

The Naval Chronicle, 40 vols., 1799–1818.
Joshua Larwood, 'Navy Chaplain Schoolmasters', VII (1802), pp. 372–87.
Prayer used in British fleet after the Battle of the Nile, IV (1801), p. 367.
Record of Court Martial of Admiral Lord Gambier, XXII (1809), pp. 107–30, 215–42.
Letters of 'AFY' [C. V. Penrose], XIX (1808), pp. 196, 286, 289, 382, 460; XX (1808), pp. 23, 115, 202–5, 296ff.; XXI (1809), pp. 28, 109–12, 199–202, 473, 464ff.; XXIX (1813), pp. 390, 399–402, 475ff.; XXX (1813), pp. 51f., 130, 136ff., 404f., 480–4; XXI (1814), p. 36.

PERIODICALS EDITED BY BO'SUN SMITH
The New Sailor's Magazine, 1827, 1828, 1831, 1852, 1856, 1858.
The Soldiers and New Sailor's Magazine and Naval Chronicle, 1828.
The Sailor's Asylum, n.d. but bound with the above in BL copy.

Report of Proceedings of the Naval and Military Bible Society, biennially 1805–10, annually 1811–70.

Report of Proceedings of the Society for Promoting Christian Knowledge, 1811–15.

The Gentleman's Magazine, 1830, 1846, 1863, 1865. Obituary of Bo'sun Smith, 1863, I, pp. 260, 390f. Review of two publications concerning Methodists, 1830, II, pp. 242f.

Statutes and Regulations

Statutes of the Realm, V (1819).
Calendar of State Papers, Domestic Series, of the Reign of Charles II (M. A. E. Green, ed.), 1862, vols. xcix, c (1663–4), cxviii (1664–5), cliii (1665–6).
The Laws of War and Ordinances of the Sea, 1652; B. L., Thomason Tracts 684 (9).
Regulations and Instructions Relating to His Majesty's Service at Sea, 1731; 2nd edn, 1734; 2nd edn, 1734 with MS additions; 3rd edn, 1740; 4th edn, 1743; 6th edn, 1746; 6th edn, 1746 with MS additions; 7th edn, 1747; 9th edn, 1757; 10th edn, 1766; 11th edn, 1772; 12th edn, 1787; 13th edn, 1790; 13th edn, 1790 with MS additions ['Mr. Derreck's Copy'].
Regulations and Instructions Relating to His Majesty's Service at Sea, 1806; 2nd edn, 1808.
Additional Regulations and Instructions Relating to His Majesty's Service at Sea, 1813.

Printed Publications

Aliquis: see Marks, Richard.
Allen, Joseph, *Battles of the British Navy*, 2 vols., 1852.
Allen, W. O. B., and Edmund McClure, *Two Hundred Years: The History of the Society for Promoting Christian Knowledge, 1698–1898*, 1898.
Anderson, R. C., and C. Lloyd (eds.), *A Memoir of James Trevenen, 1760–1790*, NRS, 1959.
Andrews, Stuart, *Methodism and Society*, Harlow, 1970.
Anon., 'Drake's Voyage Round the World', in J. Hampden (ed.), *The Tudor Venturers*, 1970, pp. 143–67, the Folio Society edn of R. Hakluyt, *Principal Navigations, Voyages, Traffics and Discoveries of the English Nation*, 1589.
—— *A declaration of the officers and company of sea-men aboard His Majesties ships the Constant Reformation, the Convertine, the Swallow, the Antelope, the Satisfaction, the Hynd, the Roe-buck, the Crescent, the Pellican, the Blackmore Lady lately rescued for His Majesties service, with an invitation to the rest of the fleet and their brethren on land to joyne with them in their just undertakings*, printed in Holland and reprinted in London 1648; BL Thomason Tracts, vi (4 Apr – 12 Aug 1648), 669, f. 12.
—— *An Inquiry into the Causes of our Naval Miscarriages*, 2nd edn, 1707; originally *The Old and True Way of Manning the Fleet*, 1707 (BM Catalogue of Printed Books, LXIV, 2504).
—— *An Answer to the Rev. James Ramsay's Essay, by Some Gentlemen of St. Christopher*, Basseterre, 1784.
—— [probably James Tobin], *A short rejoinder to Mr. Ramsay's reply*, 1787.
—— *The Bye-Laws and Regulations of the Marine Society*, 1772; 4th edn, 1792.
—— *A Prayer for the Safety of our Fleets, by His Majesty's Special Command, 9th March 1796*, 1796, printed on card.
—— *A Form of Prayer and Thanksgiving to Almighty God, to be used on Tuesday 19th December 1797*, 1797.
—— *An Authentic Narrative of Proceedings of His Majesty's Squadron under the Command of Sir James Saumarez, by an Officer of the Squadron*, 1801.
—— *An Account of the Naval and Military Bible Society from its Institution in 1780 to Lady-Day 1804*, 1804.
—— *Minutes of the Proceedings of a Court Martial for the trial of Sir Robert Calder, Bart., Vice-Admiral of the Blue*, 1806.
—— *An Address to the Officers of His Majesty's Navy, by an Old Naval Surgeon*, Dublin, 1824.
—— *An Appeal on Behalf of the Naval and Military Bible Society*, 1834.
—— 'Memoir of the Late Lord De Saumarez', *Guernsey and Jersey Magazine*, November 1836, pp. 298–324.
—— [J.B.I.], *Faithful unto Death: A Memoir of William Graeme Rhind*, RN, 1863.
—— *A Catalogue of Graduates … in the University of Dublin*, Dublin, 1869.
Anson, Peter F., *The Church and the Sailor*, 1948.
—— *The Sea Apostolate in the Port of London*, Glasgow, 1991 [text 1971].
Baker, Norman, 'Changing Attitudes towards Government in Eighteenth-Century Britain', in Ann Whiteman, J. S. Bromley and P. G. M. Dickson (eds.), *Statesmen, Scholars and Merchants: Essays in Eighteenth Century History presented to Dame Lucy Sutherland*, Oxford, 1973.
Balleine, G. R., *A History of the Evangelical Party in the Church of England*, 1908; new edn 1951.
Baring-Gould, S., *Cornish Characters and Strange Events*, 1908; 2nd series 1925.

Barker, A. E., *The SPCK and the Armed Forces*, SPCK leaflet, n.d.
Barrow, Sir John, The *Mutiny and Piratical Seizure of HMS Bounty*, 1831; new edn 1976.
Bateman, J. P., *Remarks on a Pamphlet written by J. Ramsay*, 1784.
Baugh, D. A. (ed.), *Naval Administration, 1715–1750*, NRS, 1977.
Baynham, Henry, *From the Lower Deck: The Old Navy, 1780–1840*, 1969.
—— *Before the Mast: Naval Ratings of the Nineteenth Century*, 1971.
Bechervaise, John, *Thirty-Six Years of a Seafaring Life, by an Old Quarter Master*, Portsea, 1839.
—— *A Farewell to my old Shipmates and Messmates, by the Old Quarter Master*, Portsea, 1847.
Berkmann, Evelyn, *The Hidden Navy*, 1973.
Best, G. F. A., 'The Evangelicals and the Established Church in the early Nineteenth Century', *Journal of Theological Studies* (NS), x (1959), pp. 63–78.
—— *Temporal Pillars: Queen Anne's Bounty, the Ecclesiastical Commissioners and the Church of England*, Cambridge, 1964.
Bible Society, *Account of the Naval and Military Bible Society from its Inception in 1780 to Lady-Day 1804*, 1804, and *Account of the 38th Anniversary of the Naval and Military Bible Society*, 1818.
Boys, Commander Edward, RN, *Narrative of a Captivity and Adventure in France and Flanders between the Years 1803 and 1809*, 1827; 2nd edn 1831.
Bradley, Ian, *The Call to Seriousness: The Evangelical Impact on the Victorians*, 1976.
Brenton, Edward Pelham, *The Naval History of Great Britain from 1783 to 1836*, 2 vols., 1837.
Brenton, Rear-Admiral Sir Jahleel, *An Appeal to the British Nation on Behalf of her Sailors*, 1838.
—— *The Hope of the Navy*, 1839.
Bromley, J. S. (ed.), *The Manning of the Royal Navy: Selected Public Pamphlets, 1693–1873*, NRS, 1974.
Brown, Ford K., *Fathers of the Victorians*, Cambridge, 1961.
Bruce, Michael R. (ed.), 'The Escape of Midshipman Thomas Blakiston, RN', *MM*, LIX (1973), pp. 209–17, 335–42.
Burn, Andrew, *The Christian Officer's Panoply: containing Arguments in favour of Divine Revelation, by a Marine Officer* [pubd. Anon.], 1789; reissued as *The Christian Officer's Complete Armour*, by Col. A. Burn of the Royal Marines, 2nd edn 1806.
—— *Who Fares Best, the Christian or the Man of the World? Or The Advantages of a Life of real Piety to a Life of fashionable Dissipation, By a Marine Officer*, 1789; 2nd edn 1806; 3rd edn 1810.
—— *Memoirs of the Life of the late Major General Andrew Burn of the Royal Marines, collected from his Journals with copious Extracts from his Principal Works on Religious Subjects*, 2 vols., 1815.
Byrn, John D., Jr, *Crime and Punishment in the Royal Navy: Discipline on the Leeward Islands Station, 1784–1812*, Aldershot, 1989.
Cabantous, Alain, *Le Ciel dans la mer, christianisme et civilisation maritime, XVIe–XIXe siècle*, Paris, 1990.
—— and Françoise Hildesheimer (eds.), *Foi chretienne et milieux maritimes, XVe–XXe siècles: Actes du colloque, Paris, Collège de France, 23–25 septembre 1987*, Paris 1989.
Camperdown, R. A. H. P. [Earl of Duncan], *Admiral Duncan*, 1898.
'Captain in the Royal Navy, A' [R. Grant according to cover of BL copy], *Observations and Instructions for the use of the commissioned, the junior and other Officers of the Royal Navy*, 1804; new edn 1807.

Carr Laughton, L. G. (ed.), *The Life of a Sea Officer, by Jeffery, Baron de Raigersfeld*, privately pubd., *c.* 1830; 1929.
Carretta, Vincent, *Equiano, the African: Biography of a Self-Made Man*, Athens, Georgia, 2005.
Cecil, Richard *Memoirs of the Rev. John Newton*, 1808; reissued with new material as *The Life of John Newton*, ed. Marylynn Rouse, Fearn, Ross-shire, 2000.
Charnock, John, *Biographia Navalis*, 6 vols., 1794–1798.
Chatterton, Lady Henrietta Georgina (ed.), *Memorials Personal and Historical of Admiral Lord Gambier*, 2 vols., 1861.
Childers, Spencer (ed.), *A Mariner of England: An Account of the Career of William Richardson from Cabin Boy in the Merchant Service to Warrant Officer in the Royal Navy (1780–1819) as told by Himself*, 1908.
Clarke, The Rev. James Stanier, *Naval Sermons Preached on Board His Majesty's Ship the Impetueux, in the Western Squadron, During its Services off Brest*, 1798.
—— and John McArthur, *The Life of Admiral Lord Nelson KB, from His Lordship's Manuscripts*, 2 vols., 1809.
Claxton, Lieutenant C., RN, *The Naval Monitor*, 1821; 2nd edn, 1833.
Clayton, Tim, and Phil Craig, *Trafalgar: The Men, the Battle, the Storm*, 2004.
Clowes, W. Laird, *The Royal Navy, a History from the Earliest Times to the Present*, 7 vols., 1897–1903.
Coad, F. Roy, *A History of the Brethren Movement*, Exeter, 1968.
Cobbett, William, *Parliamentary Debates*, 1st Series, XXI (7 Jan 1812 – 16 Mar 1812), 1812.
—— *The Parliamentary History of England*, XXXIII (3 Mar 1797 – 13 Nov 1798), 1813.
Cochrane: see Dundonald.
Coleman, Terry, *Nelson: The Man and the Legend*, 2001.
Collingwood, Newnham, *Correspondence of Admiral Lord Collingwood*, 1829; 4th edn, 1829.
Collins, Lieutenant F., RN, *Voyages to Portugal, Spain, Sicily, Malta, Asia Minor, Egypt, in HMS Dolphin, from 1796 to 1801*, 1807.
Conolly, M. F., *Biographical Dictionary of Eminent Men of Fife*, Edinburgh, 1866.
Corbett, J. S. (ed.), *Signals and Instructions, 1776–1794*, NRS, 1908.
Cordingly, David, *Billy Ruffian: The Bellerophon and the Downfall of Napoleon*, 2003.
Cornwall, The Rev. Alan, *Recollections of an Address at the Funeral of the Rev. Edward Ward, 28 March 1835*, 1835.
Costin, W. C., and J. Steven Watson, *The Law and Working of the Constitution: Documents, 1660–1914*, 2 vols., 1952.
Crofts, B. D., A. K. Stanley, and P. Jefferies, *Upon this Rock*, Gibraltar 1969.
Cummins, John, *Francis Drake*, 1995; pbk edn 1997.
Delafons, John, *A Treatise on Naval Courts Martial*, 1805.
Dennis, T., A *Systematic Plan for Bettering the Condition of British Seamen*, 1819.
Dictionary of National Biography, ed. Leslie Stephen and Sidney Lee, 1885–1900; new edn in 21 vols. and *Supplement to the DNB*, 1908–9.
Douglas, J. D. (ed.), *The New International Dictionary of the Christian Church*, Exeter, 1974.
Dugan, James, *The Great Mutiny*, 1866.
Duncan, Neil, *Duncan of Camperdown*, Diss, 1995.
Duncan, R. A. H. P., Earl of Camperdown, *Admiral Duncan*, 1898.
Dundonald, Admiral the Earl of, *Observations on Naval Affairs*, 1847.
—— *The Autobiography of a Seaman*, 2 vols., 1860; republished in one vol. with intro. by R. Woodman, 2000.
Earle, Peter, *Sailors: English Merchant Seamen 1650–1775*, 1998.

Equiano, Olaudah, *The Interesting Narrative of the Life of Olaudah Equiano, or Gustavus Vassa, the African, Written by Himself*, 1789, pbk edn 2001.
Forester, C. S. (ed.), *The Adventures of John Wetherell*, 1954.
Foster, Joseph (ed.), *Alumni Oxonienses, 1715–1886*, 4 vols., Oxford, 1887, 1888;.
Furneaux, Robin, *William Wilberforce*, 1974.
Gardiner, Robert (ed.), *The Naval War of 1812*, 1998.
Gardner, James Anthony, *Above and Under Hatches*, ed. Christopher Lloyd, 1955.
Gilbert, A. D., *Religion and Society in Industrial England: Church, Chapel and Social Change, 1740–1914*, 1976.
Gillespie, L., *Advice to the Commanders and Officers of His Majesty's Fleet serving in the West Indies, on the Preservation of the Health of Seamen*, 1798.
Graham, G. S., *Great Britain in the Indian Ocean, 1810–50*, Oxford 1967.
Grant, R.: see 'A Captain in the Royal Navy.'.
Griffin, John, *Memoirs of Captain James Wilson*, 1815.
—— *The British Officer* [the life of Lieutenant Tucker Mends, RN], 1818.
Gurney, W. B., *Minutes of a Court Martial Taken in Shorthand by Mr. W. B. Gurney*, Portsmouth, 1809 [the Gambier Court Martial].
Gwyn, Julian (ed.), *The Royal Navy and North America: The Warren Papers, 1736–1752*, NRS, 1973.
Haldane, A., *Lives of Robert and James Alexander Haldane*, 1852.
Hampden, J. (ed.), *The Tudor Venturers*, 1970.
Hanway, Jonas, *Letter from a Member of the Marine Society*, 1757.
Harris, Mark, 'Naval Chaplains in the late Seventeenth and early Eighteenth Century', *MM*, LXXXI (1995), pp. 207–10.
Hawker, Edward, *Statement of Certain Immoral Practices Prevailing in His Majesty's Navy*, 1821; 2nd edn 1822 [pubd. Anon.].
Hawker, The Rev. Robert, *The Sailor Pilgrim* 1806, 1810.
Hay, M. D. (ed.), *Landsman Hay: The Memoirs of Robert Hay, 1789–1847*, 1953.
Heasman, Kathleen, *Evangelicals in Action*, 1962.
Hennell, Michael, *John Venn and the Clapham Sect*, 1858.
Hibbert, Christopher, *Nelson: A Personal History*, 1994.
Hinchliffe, G., 'Some letters of Sir John Norris', *MM*, LVI (1970), pp. 77–84.
Hiney, Tom, *On the Missionary Trail*, 2000, pbk edn 2001.
Historical Manuscripts Commission, *Report on Papers of James Saumarez, 1st Baron de Saumarez – Baltic Naval Papers 1808–27*, 2 vols., 1975.
Hoare, Prince, *Memoirs of Granville Sharp*, 2 vols., 1820.
Hodges, H. W., and E. A. Hughes, *Select Naval Documents*, Cambridge, 1922; 2nd edn, 1936.
Hodgskin, Thomas, *An Essay on Naval Discipline, shewing part of its evil effects on the minds of the officers, on the minds of the men, and on the community; with an amended system by which pressing may be immediately abolished*, 1813.
Hoste, Lady (ed.), *Memoirs and Letters of Captain Sir William Hoste, Bt., RN, KCB, KMT*, 2 vols., 1833.
Howell, John (ed.), *The Life and Adventures of John Nicol, Mariner*, Edinburgh, 1822; ed. Tim Flannery, Canongate, 2000.
Howse, Ernest Marshall, *Saints in Politics: The 'Clapham Sect' and the Growth of Freedom*, Toronto 1952; Open University pbk edn 1971.
Hubback, J. H., and C. Edith, *Jane Austen's Sailor Brothers*, 1906.
Hunt, W. R., 'Nautical Autobiography in the Age of Sail', *MM*, LVII (1971), pp. 135–42.

Hunter, Richard A., and Ida Macalpine, 'The Reverend William Pargeter, BA, MD (1760–1810), Psychiatrist', *St. Bartholomew's Hospital Journal* LX (1956), pp. 52–60.
Hutchins, John H., *Jonas Hanway, 1712–1786*, 1940.
Index Ecclesiaticus, 1800–1840, 1890.
James, William, *The Naval History of Great Britain from 1793 to the Accession of King George IV*, 5 vols., 1822–4; new edn, 6 vols., 1847.
James, Admiral Sir William, *Old Oak, the Life of John Jervis, Earl of St. Vincent*, 1950.
Johnson, R. F., *The Royal George*, 1971.
Kealy, A. G., *Chaplains of the Royal Navy, 1626–1903*, Portsmouth 1905.
Keevil, J. J., *Medicine and the Navy, 1200–1900*, 4 vols., Edinburgh and London, 1957–63: I: *1200–1649*, 1957; II: *1649–1714*, 1958. See also under Lloyd and Coulter.
Kemp, P. K., *The British Sailor: A Social History of the Lower Deck*, 1970.
Kempenfelt, Admiral Richard [as 'Philotheorus'], *Original Hymns and Poems*, Exeter 1777; reprinted 1861.
Kirk, Rudolf, *Mr. Pepys upon the State of Christ-Hospital*, Philadelphia, 1935.
Knight, R. J. B., 'Sandwich, Middleton and Dockyard Appointments', *MM*, LVII (1971), pp. 175–92.
Knight, Roger, *The Pursuit of Victory: The Life and Achievement of Horatio Nelson*, 2005.
Knowles, Vice-Admiral Sir Charles, *Observations*, 1830.
Kverndal, Roald (ed.), 'Memoirs of the Founder of Seamen's Missions in 1801', *MM*, LXII (1976), pp. 47–51.
—— 'The 200th Anniversary of Organized Seamen's Missions, 1779–1979', *MM*, LXV (1979), pp. 255–63.
—— *Seamen's Missions: Their Origin and Early Growth*, Pasadena, 1986.
Larsen, Timothy (ed.), *Biographical Dictionary of Evangelicals*, Leicester, 2003.
Laughton, J. K. (ed.), *State Papers Relating to the Defeat of the Spanish Armada, 1588*, NRS, 2 vols., 1895–1900, reissued 1981.
—— (ed.), *Letters and Papers of Charles, Lord Barham, 1758–1813*, NRS, 3 vols., 1907–11.
Le Fevre, Peter, and Richard Harding (eds.), *Precursors of Nelson: British Admirals of the Eighteenth Century*, 2000.
—— *British Admirals of the Napoleonic Wars: The Contemporaries of Nelson*, 2005.
Lewis, Donald M. (ed.), *Blackwell Dictionary of Evangelical Biography, 1730–1860*, 2 vols., Oxford, 1995.
Lewis, Michael A., *England's Sea Officers: The Story of the Naval Profession*, 1939.
—— (ed.), *A Narrative of my Professional Adventures, by Vice-Admiral Sir William Henry Dillon (1790–1839)*, NRS, 2 vols., 1953–6.
—— *A Social History of the Navy, 1793–1815*, 1960.
—— *Napoleon and his British Captives*, 1962.
—— *The Navy in Transition, 1814–64*, 1965.
Liddell Hart, B. H. (ed.), *The Letters of Private Wheeler, 1809–28*, 1951.
Lindwall, Ake, 'The Kempenfelt Family', *MM*, LVII (1971), pp. 379–83.
Lloyd, Christopher, *Lord Cochrane*, 1947.
—— *The Navy and the Slave Trade*, 1949.
—— (ed.), *The Naval Miscellany*, IV, NRS, 1952.
—— *The Nation and the Navy*, 1954.
—— (ed.), *The Health of Seamen*, NRS, 1965.
—— *St. Vincent and Camperdown*, 1963.
—— *The British Seaman, 1200–1860: A Social Survey*, 1968.

―― and J. L. S. Coulter, *Medicine and the Navy, 1200–1900*: III: *1714–1815*, 1961; IV: *1815–1900*, 1963. See also under Keevil.

Lloyd Phillips, I., 'The Evangelical Administrator: Sir Charles Middleton at the Navy Board, 1778–1790', DPhil thesis, Oxford University, 1978.

―― 'Lord Barham at the Admiralty, 1805–1806', *MM*, LXIV 64 (1978), pp. 217–33.

Locker, Edward Hawke, *Popular Lectures on the Bible and Liturgy*, 1821.

Lowe, J. A. (ed.), *Records of the Portsmouth Division of Marines, 1764–1800*, Portsmouth, 1990.

Lowther Clarke, W. K., *A History of the SPCK*, 1959.

McGowan, Alan, 'The First HMS *Implacable*', *MM*, XCI (2005), 294–308.

Mackay, Ruddock F., *Admiral Hawke*, Oxford 1965.

Mahan, A. T., *Types of Naval Officers*, 1902.

Manwaring, G. E. (ed.), *The Diary of Henry Teonge, Chaplain on board HM Ships Assistance, Bristol and Royal Oak, 1675–79*, 1927.

―― and Bonamy Dobrée, *The Floating Republic: An Account of the Mutinies at Spithead and the Nore in 1797*, 1935; new imp. 1966.

Marcus, G. J., *Heart of Oak: A Survey of British Sea Power in the Georgian Era*, 1975.

Markham, Sir Clements (ed.), *Selections from the Correspondence of Admiral John Markham, 1801–1804, 1806–1807*, NRS, 1904.

Marks, Richard ['Aliquis'], *Nautical Essays, or a spiritual View of the Ocean and maritime Affairs, with reflections on the Battle of Trafalgar and other events*, 1813; reissued as *The Ocean Spiritually Reviewed*, 1824; 7th edn 1848.

―― *The Retrospect, or Review of Providentia Mercies, with Anecdotes of various Characters, and an Address to Naval Officers*, 1816; 20th edn 1842.

Marsden, The Rev. J. B., *Two Sermons on the Life, Death and Ministry of the Late Reverend Richard Marks*, 1847.

Marshall, John, *Royal Naval Biography*, 7 vols., 1823–30.

Martin, Bernard, *John Newton*, 1950.

―― and Mark Spurrell, *The Journal of a Slave Trader: John Newton, 1750–54*, 1962.

Meyerstein, E. H. W. (ed.), *Adventures by Sea of Edward Coxere* [written between 1685 and 1694], Oxford, 1945.

Miller, Robert, *From Shore to Shore: A History of the Church and the Merchant Seafarer*, privately printed, 1989.

Moresby, Admiral John, *Two Admirals*, 1909; revised edn 1913.

Neale, W. Johnson: *History of the Mutiny at Spithead and the Nore* [pubd. Anon.], 1842.

Newton, The Rev. John, *An Authentic Narrative of Some Remarkable and Interesting Particulars in the Life of the Reverend John Newton*, 1764; reprinted as *Out of the Depths*, Chicago, 1964.

―― *Thoughts upon the African slave trade*, 1788, reprinted in Martin and Spurrell, pp. 97–113.

Nicolas, Paul Harris, *Historical Record of the Royal Marine Forces*, 2 vols., 1845.

Noll, Mark A., *The Rise of Evangelicalism*, Leicester, 2004.

O'Byrne, W., *A Naval Biographical Dictionary*, 1849.

Ogg, David, *England in the Reigns of James II and William III*, Oxford 1955, pbk edn 1969.

Oman, Carola, *Nelson*, 1947; Reprint Soc. edn 1950.

Oppenheim, Michael, *A History of the Administration of the Royal Navy from 1509 to 1660*, 1896.

Osler, E., *The Life of Admiral Viscount Exmouth*, 1861.

Oxford Dictionary of National Biography, ed. H. C. G. Matthew and Brian Harrison, 60 vols., Oxford 2004.
Pack, Captain S. W. C., *Admiral Lord Anson*, 1960.
Padfield, Peter, *Broke and the Shannon*, 1968.
—— *Maritime Supremacy and the Opening of the Western Mind*, 1999.
Parkinson, C. Northcote, *Edward Pellew, Viscount Exmouth*, 1934.
—— *Britannia Rules: The Classic Age of Naval History, 1793–1815*, 1977.
Parry, The Rev. Edward, *A Brief Memoir of Rear-Admiral Sir Edward Parry*, King's Lynn, 1857.
Penrose, C. V. [Admiral Sir Charles], *A Short Address to the Unlearned on the Advantage of Possessing the Holy Scriptures, and the Best Use to be Made of that Possession*, Bodmin, 1820.
—— *A Friendly Address to the Seamen of the British Navy, by A real Friend to British Seamen*, Bodmin, 1820 [pubd. Anon.].
—— *Observations on Corporal Punishment, Impressment and other Matters*, Bodmin, 1824.
—— *Observations on the Impressment of Seamen, on the Means of Manning the Navy generally, and the Means whereby Desertion and Discontent may be Best Obviated*, Bodmin, 1824.
—— *The Danger of the Church Considered, By an Old Member of the Establishment*, 1829 [pubd. Anon.].
Penrose, The Rev. John, *The Lives of Admiral Penrose and Captain Trevenen*, 1850.
Philippart, J., *The Royal Military Calendar*, 3 vols., 1815.
Pollock, John, *George Whitefield and the Great Awakening*, 1972.
—— *Wilberforce*, 1977, p.b. edn 1978.
—— *Amazing Grace: John Newton's Story*, 1981, pbk edn 1985.
Pollock, Tom, *The Young Nelson in the Americas*, 1980.
Powell, J. R. (ed.), *The Letters of Robert Blake*, NRS, 1937.
—— *Robert Blake, General-at-Sea*, 1972.
Raikes, The Rev. Henry (ed.), *Memoirs of the Life and Services of Vice-Admiral Sir Jahleel Brenton* (abridged by his son), 1855.
Ralfe, James, *The Naval Biography of Great Britain, consisting of historical memoirs of those officers of the British Navy who distinguished themselves during the reign of George III*, 4 vols., 1828.
Ramsay, The Rev. James, 'A Letter from Mr James Ramsay, Surgeon, on Copper Vessels, to George Macaulay, MD, read on 2 Oct. 1758', in *Medical Inquiries and Observations*, n.d. [copy in RNM library].
—— *Sea Sermons, or a Series of Discourses for the Use of the Royal Navy*, 1781.
—— *An Essay on the Treatment and Conversion of African Slaves in the British Sugar Colonies*, 1784.
—— *An Inquiry into the Effects of putting a Stop to the African Slave Trade*, 1784.
—— *An Address on the proposed Bill for the Abolition of the Slave Trade*, 1788.
—— *An Examination of Mr Harris's scriptural Researches on the Licitness of the Slave Trade*, 1788.
—— *Objections to the Abolition of the Slave Trade, with Answers*, 1788.
—— 'Sermon on Redemption', in The Rev. James Walker, *Sermons*, 1829.
Rappoport, Angelo S., *Superstitions of Sailors*, 1928.
Rawson, G. (ed.), *Nelson's Letters*, Everyman edn, 1960.
Rediker, Marcus, *Between the Devil and the Deep Blue Sea: Merchant Seamen, Pirates and the Anglo-American World, 1700–1750*, Cambridge, 1987.

Rhind, W. G., *The Magnet, the Life of the Mariner's Compass*, 1853.
Roberts, William, *Memoirs of the Life and Correspondence of Mrs Hannah More*, 4 vols., 1834.
Rodger, N. A. M., *The Admiralty*, Lavenham, 1979.
—— (ed.), *The Naval Miscellany*, V, NRS, 1984.
—— *The Wooden World: An Anatomy of the Georgian Navy*, 1986.
—— *The Insatiable Earl: A Life of John Montagu, Fourth Earl of Sandwich, 1718–1792*, 1993.
—— 'The Naval Chaplain in the Eighteenth Century', *British Journal for Eighteenth Century Studies*, XVIII (1995), pp. 33–45.
—— *A Naval History of Britain*, I: *The Safeguard of the Sea, 660–1649*, 1997.
—— *A Naval History of Britain*, II: *The Command of the Ocean, 1649–1815*, 2004.
Rolleston, W. (ed.), 'Some letters of Mrs Richard Saumarez', *Transactions of La Societe Guernesiase*, XI (1933), pp. 319–47.
Ross, Sir John, *Memoirs and Correspondence of Admiral Lord de Saumarez*, 2 vols., 1838.
Royle, Edward, *Radical Politics, 1790–1900: Religion and Unbelief*, 1971.
Ryan, A. N., 'The Melancholy Fate of the Baltic Ships in 1811', *MM*, L (1964), pp. 123–4.
—— (ed.), *The Saumarez Papers: Selections from the Baltic Correspondence of Vice-Admiral Sir James Saumarez, 1808–1812*, NRS, 1968.
Schama, Simon, *Rough Crossings: Britain, the Slaves and the American Revolution*, New York 2006.
Shyllon, Folarin, *James Ramsay, the Unknown Abolitionist*, Edinburgh 1977.
—— *Black People in Britain, 1555–1833*, 1977.
Smith, Alan, *The Established Church and Popular Religion, 1750–1850*, 1971.
Smith, the Rev. George Charles [Bo'sun Smith], *The Boatswain's Mate, The Quarter Master, The Sailors on Shore, Jack Tars at Plymouth, TheDreadnought, The Royal George, Torbay – or the Fleet at Anchor*, all by 'A Naval Officer,' n.d. but from 1811 onwards.
—— *Minehead and Watchet Officers and the Bethel Flag*, Bristol, 1823.
—— *Windsor, or an Humble Appeal to His Gracious Majesty George IV, inviting Inquiry respecting an Order of HRH the Duke of Clarence as Lord High Admiral, prohibiting the Circulation of Religious Tracts in the British Navy Without the Permission of the Rev. Mr. Cole, Chaplain of Greenwich Hospital*, 1828.
—— *Portsmouth, or the First Part of an Humble Address to the Lord Bishop of London concerning the Fatal Licence given to the General Admission of Unmarried Females into British Ships of War*, 1828.
Smith, Theophilus Ahijah, *The Great Moral Reformation of Sailors: Prospectus*, 1874.
Smith, Waldo E. L., *The Navy and its Chaplains in the Days of Sail*, Toronto 1961.
—— *The Navy Chaplain and his Parish*, Ottawa 1967.
Smyth, Charles, *Simeon and Church Order, a Study of the Origins of the Evangelical Revival in Cambridge in the Eighteenth Century*, Cambridge, 1940.
Smyth, John, *In this Sign Conquer*, 1968.
Snape, Peter, *The Redcoat and Religion*, 2005.
Southam, David, *Jane Austen and the Navy*, 2000, pbk edn 2005.
Southey, Robert, *The Life of Nelson*, 1831.
Spavens, William, *Memoirs of a Seafaring Life*, 1796: ed. N. A. M. Rodger, Folio Soc. edn 2000.
Steel, David, *Steel's Original and Correct List of the Royal Navy, 1782, 1795–1816*, [1783]–1816.
Sugden, John, *Nelson: A Dream of Glory*, 2004.
Sullivan, F. B., 'The Naval Schoolmaster during the Eighteenth Century and the early Nineteenth Century', *MM*, LXII (1976), pp. 311–26.

―― 'The Royal Naval Academy at Portsmouth, 1729–1806', *MM*, LXIII (1977), pp. 311–26.
Sykes, Norman, *Church and State in England in the Eighteenth Century*, Cambridge 1934.
Syrett, David, and R. L. DiNardo (eds.), *The Commissioned Sea Officers of the Royal Navy, 1660–1815*, NRS, 1994.
Talbott, John E., *The Pen and Ink Sailor: Charles Middleton and the King's Navy, 1778–1813*, 1998.
Tanner, J. R. (ed.), *A Descriptive catalogue of the Naval Manuscripts in the Pepysian Library at Magdalen College, Cambridge*, NRS, 4 vols., 1903–24.
―― *Samuel Pepys's Naval Minutes*, 1926.
Taylor, Gordon, *The Sea Chaplains: A History of the Chaplains of the Royal Navy*, Oxford, 1978.
Taylor, James Stephen, *Jonas Hanway, Founder of the Marine Society*, 1985.
Thursfield, H. G. (ed.), *Five Naval Journals, 1789–1817*, NRS, 1951.
Tobin, James [as 'A Friend to the West India Colonies'], *Cursory remarks upon the Rev. Mr. Ramsay's Essay*, 1785.
―― *A Farewell Address to the Rev. Mr. James Ramsay*, 1788.
Trotter, Dr Thomas, *Medicina Nautica*, I: *An Essay on the Diseases of Seamen*, 1797.
―― *A Practicable Plan for Manning the Royal Navy without Impressment*, 1819.
Tunstall, Brian (ed.), *The Byng Papers*, 3 vols., III, NRS, 1932.
―― *Naval Warfare in the Age of Sail: The Evolution of Fighting Tactics, 1650–1815*, ed. Nicholas Tracy, 1990.
Urquhart, Thomas, *The Substance of a Letter to Lord Viscount Melville*, 1815; *A Letter to W. Wilberforce, Esq. MP, on the Subject of Impressment*, 1816; both reprinted in *The Pamphleteer*, XXIV (1824), pp. 384–402, 464–76.
Vale, Brian, *The Audacious Admiral Cochrane*, 2004.
Venn, J. A. (ed.), *Alumni Cantabrigienses*, Part 2: *1752–1900*, 6 vols., Cambridge, 1940.
Vesey Hamilton, R. (ed.), *Journals and Letters of Admiral of the Fleet Sir Thomas Byam Martin, 1773–1854*, NRS, 3 vols., 1898–1903.
Walsh, J. D., 'Origins of the Evangelical Revival,' in G. D. Bennett and J. D. Walsh (eds.), *Essays in Modern English Church History in Memory of Norman Sykes*, 1966.
Ward, The Rev. Edward, *Sermon Preached in the Parish Church of Iver, Bucks., on Sunday 28th April 1833 on the Occasion of the Death of the Rt. Hon. Lord Gambier, Admiral of the Fleet*, 1833.
Wareham, Tom, *The Star Captains: Frigate Command in the Napoleonic Wars*, 2001.
Warner, Oliver, *A Portrait of Lord Nelson*, 1958, Reprint Soc. edn 1959.
―― *The Glorious First of June*, 1961.
―― *William Wilberforce*, 1962.
―― *Nelson's Battles*, 1965.
―― *The Life and Letters of Vice-Admiral Lord Collingwood*, 1968.
Watkins, J., and F. Shoberl, *A Biographical Dictionary of the Living Authors of Great Britain and Ireland*, 1816.
Watt, Surgeon Vice-Admiral Sir James, 'James Ramsay, 1733–1789: Naval Surgeon, Naval Chaplain and Morning Star of the Anti-Slavery Movement', *MM*, LXXXI (1995), pp. 156–70.
―― 'Surgery at Trafalgar', *MM*, XCI (2005), pp. 266–83.
Wauchope, Admiral Robert, *A Short Narrative of God's Merciful Dealings* (printed for private circulation), 1862.
Wesley, The Rev. John, *Journals, 1738–1791*, Everyman edn, 4 vols., n.d.
Weston, Agnes, *My Life among the Blue-Jackets*, 1909; 13th imp., 1913.

Whitefield, The Rev. George, *Journals, 1738–1741* [seven journals reissued with additional autobiographical material], 1960.
Wilberforce, R. I. and S., *The Life of William Wilberforce*, 5 vols., 1838.
Williams, Glyndwr (ed.), *Documents Relating to Anson's Voyage Round the World, 1740–1744*, NRS, 1967.
Wilson, William, *A Missionary Voyage to the Southern Pacific Ocean in the Years 1796, 1797, 1798, in the Ship Duff, Commanded by Captain James Wilson*, 1799.
Wolfe, The Rev. R. B., chaplain, *English Prisoners in France, containing Observations on their Manners and Habits, principally with reference to the Religious State during nine years' Residence in the Depots of Fontainebleau, Verdun, Givet and Valenciennes*, 1830.
Wood, A. Skevington, *The Inextinguishable Blaze: Spiritual Renewal and Advance in the Eighteenth Century*, 1960.
—— *The Burning Heart: John Wesley, Evangelist*, Exeter, 1967.
Woodman, Richard, *The Victory of Seapower: Winning the Napoleonic War, 1806–1814*, 1998.
Woodward, The Rev. Josiah, DD, *The Seaman's Monitor, or Advice to Sea-faring Men, with Reference to their Behaviour before, in and after their Voyage* 1700; 20th edn 1812.
Wright, Lieutenant J., RN, *Narrative of the Loss of HMS The Proserpine*, 1799.
Wright, R. F., 'The High Seas and the Church in the Middle Ages', *MM*, LIII (1967), pp. 3–31, 115–35.

Compact Disks

The State Funeral of Horatio, Lord Viscount Nelson, KB, ed. Colin White, Herald AV Publications, 1999.
The Complete Navy List of the Napoleonic Wars, 1793–1815, ed. Patrick Marioné, SEFF, Brussels, 2003.
The Mariner's Mirror on CD-ROM, 1911–2000, ed. John P. Bethell, 2002.

Index

British and foreign merchant and warship names are listed under 'ships'.
Known Blue Lights and Psalm-singers appear in bold type.

'A., Robert' (*Conqueror* sailor) 256–8
Aberdeen 38, 57
abolition of slavery, movement for 41, 114, 284
  Middletons' role in 41, 67, 68
  naval contribution to 63–8, 112, 223
  Newton's influence 284
  Wilberforce and 67
Addington, Henry, Viscount Sidmouth (1757–1844; prime minister 1801–4) 179, 196
administrations, Government, listed 198 n. 25
Admiralty, Board of 124
  composition and duties 196
  relationship with Navy Board 43
  First Lords, listed 198 n. 25
  regulations *See* Regulations and Instructions
  Black Book of officers not to be employed again 86
  circulars 172 and n. 58
  punishments monitored by 187–8, 292
Adour River 166
African Institution 223
'A.F.Y.' (pseudonym) *See* Penrose, Captain Charles
Against Enthusiasm (SPCK pamphlet) 221
Aix, Île d' 209–10, 215, 216, 217
Aix Roads, Action of (1809) 174, 190–4, 202–21 *passim*
  sketch map 216
Akers, Rebecca (Mrs James Ramsay) 65
Alexander I (1777–1825; tsar of Russia 1801–25) 175, 200, 201
Algeciras, Battle of (1801) 181, 183
  See also Gibraltar, Gut of
Algiers
  expedition to (1620) 14
  bombardment of (1816) 77, 166, 182, 268
Allemand, Zacharie (1762–1828; French admiral) 205, 209

American Independence, War of (1775–83) 2, 5, 21, 34, 42, 47, 48 n. 23, 53, 54, 70, 71, 79, 80, 82, 96, 98, 115, 131, 133, 158, 183, 185, 269
Amiens, Peace of (1802) 98, 129, 131, 140, 165, 226, 243
Anderson, Richard (*Conqueror* seaman) 259
Anglicanism (Church of England) 28, 50, 82, 140, 172, 232, 235, 243, 275, 284
  theory of establishment 32
  as bulwark of state 12, 15, 21, 22, 82, 99, 144, 153
  aboard ship 12, 13, 15, 22, 63, 84, 144
  neglect of seafarers' spiritual needs 16, 21, 32, 86
  and evangelical movement 26, 27, 29, 99, 184, 235
  See also evangelicalism
Anglo-Dutch Wars 14, 70
Anne, Queen (1665–1714; r 1702–14) 15, 20 n. 21
Anson, George, Admiral Lord (1697–1762) 23, 43, 47, 124
Antinomianism 28
Appeal to the British Nation (pamphlet by Admiral Brenton) 10 n. 5, 185
Arbuthnot, Vice-Admiral Marriot (1711–94) 115
Armada, Spanish (1588) 13, 17 n. 17
Arminianism ('free will') 28
Army, British 162, 165–6, 175
  religious interest amongst Redcoats 32, 80, 240–2
Arthur, Sir George (1784–1854; governor of Van Diemen's Land) 289
Articles of War 14, 18, 24, 91, 92, 99, 102
  read to ships' company 69, 71, 72, 84
atonement 27
  expression of faith in, by: Burn 109–10; Duncan 273; Hillyar 186; Marks 252–3; Newton 283–4; Pellew 181–2; Penrose 272; Saumarez 129; Ward 107
Austen, Captain [later Rear-Admiral] Charles (1779–1852) 189 n. 21

Austen, Captain [later Admiral of Fleet Sir] **Francis** (1774–1865) 187–90, 268
 background and service career 187–9
 religious beliefs and evangelical association 189, 240
 humanity and severity 187–9, 290
 links with Gambier 187, 189
 support for Cochrane 220 n. 56
Austerlitz, Battle of (1805) 200

Ball, Captain [later Rear-Admiral Sir] Alexander (d. 1809) 125
Baltic 130, 175–9, 185, 187, 196
 importance to Britain 175, 177, 200–1
Baltic Fleet 211, 291
Baltrum (island) 248
Bantry Bay, Ireland 93 n. 41, 132, 133 n. 44, 181, 289
Baptist Missionary Society 233
Baptists *See* Dissenters
Barcelona 264
Bardsey Island 11
Barham, Lord *See* Middleton, Captain Charles
Barham Court, Kent 40
 inherited by Middleton 41, 57, 67, 68
Barrington, Admiral Samuel (1729–1800) 58, 100, 161
Barrow, Sir John (1764–1848; second secretary at Admiralty) 286
Basque Roads, action (1809) *See* Aix Roads
Batavia 180
Beatty, William (surgeon) 146
Bechervaise, John (sailor and writer) 256
Bedford, Captain [later Vice-Admiral] William (1764–1827) 83, 175, 208, 218, 269
Beechey, Sir William (1753–1839; painter) 197
Belle Isle, capture of (1761) 133
Benbow, Admiral John (1653–1702) 96
Benevolent Institution 223
Berkeley, Admiral [later Sir] George (1753–1818) 259, 263
Berlin Decree 175
Beresford, Captain [later Admiral Sir] John 217
Bernadotte, Jean, Marshal of France (1763–1844; Crown Prince of Sweden 1810–18, King Charles XIV 1818–44) 177
Bethel Union, Bethel flag 223, 236, 275
Birt, The Rev. Isaiah (1758–1837; Baptist minister) 232, 277 n. 10

Blake, Robert (1599–1657; Commonwealth admiral) 15
blasphemy and profanity 8, 9, 19 n. 20, 118, 230, 250, 251
 prohibited by custom and regulations 22
 punishments for 22, 118 and n. 24, 259
Bligh, Captain [later Vice-Admiral] William (1754–1817) 217, 218
blockades *See* Brest; Cadiz; Texel; Toulon
Blue Lights 29
 name 30, 225
 enablers and activists 229
 minority 268, 273, 286
 aims and beliefs
  promotion of public worship 34, 63, 105, 269
  evangelism, proselytism 31, 95, 222
  morality 105, 117, 269
  reform 222, 262
  theological convictions 272–3
 'manifesto' of movement 36, 62–3, 138, 153, 269, 291
 methods 55, 95, 104, 105, 118, 138–9, 141, 153, 222, 287–8
 growth of humanity 62, 63, 105, 138–9, 288–90, 292
 social background and membership 30–1, 33, 105, 242, 268–9
 four phases 273–5
 See also conversion; evangelicalism; prayer groups
Book of Common Prayer 12, 13, 14, 99, 172
Boswell, James (1740–95; writer) 41
Botany Bay (convict settlement) 62
Bouverie, Elizabeth (d. 1798; Evangelical landowner) 38, 40, 41, 67
Bowen, Captain Thomas (d. 1809) 73
Boyart Shoal 210, 215, 216, 218
Boys, Captain Edward (1785–1866) 244
Brazil 220
Breda, Carl Frederik von (1759–1818; painter) 59
Brenton, Captain Edward Pelham (1774–1839; historian and philanthropist) 183, 184, 214, 218, 221
Brenton, Captain [later Vice-Admiral] **Sir Jahleel** (1770–1844) 183–5, 268
 conversion 184, 279
 naval service 183–4, 279 n. 15
 prisoner of war 183–4, 243, 244, 245 n. 35
 writings 10 n. 5, 185
Brest, blockade of 101, 128, 175, 205, 255
Bridport, Admiral Sir Alexander, Viscount (1726–1814) 133

Bristol 11, 64, 68
Bristol Tract Society 267
British and Foreign Bible Society (1805) 112, 234, 268
Broke, Captain [later Rear-Admiral Sir] Philip (1776–1841) 103, 172
Broughton, Captain William (1762–1821; at Gambier court martial) 216–18
Brueys, François-Paul de (1753–98; French vice-admiral) 125–6, 127
brutality 7, 92, 155–7, 163
See also humanity; punishment
Buckingham, George Villiers, Duke of (1592–1628) 14
Buenos Aires 210
Bunker Hill, Battle of (1775) 113
Bunyan, John (1628–88; puritan writer, author of *Pilgrim's Progress*) 253
Burder, The Rev. George (1752–1832; author of sermons) 102, 252, 265
Burdett, Sir Francis (1770–1844; Radical MP) 213
Burmese War, Second (1852) 189 n. 21
Burn, Major-General Andrew (1742–1814; Royal Marines) 24, 108–14, 137, 230, 268, 282
  career 81, 108–11
  conversion and religious experience 72, 109–10, 281
  writings 80, 95, 111–14, 112 n. 13
Byrn, John, Jnr (historian) 155–7

Cadiz 14, 128
  blockade of 187, 248
Calder, Admiral Sir Robert (1745–1818) 193
Callao 271
Calvinism ('election') 28, 52, 110
Cambrai 244
Cambridge 27, 67, 249, 280 n. 16
Campbell, The Rev. John (1766–1840; Dissenting minister) 225–6, 235
Campbell, Lieutenant Patrick (d. 1798) 116 n. 19
Camperdown, Battle of (1797) 136, 139, 232
Cape Finisterre, Battle of (1747) 124
Cape of Good Hope 111, 184
Cape Horn 185
Cape St Vincent, Battle of (1797) 106, 111, 125, 127, 181, 183
Cape St Vincent, Moonlight Battle of (1780) 133
Cape Town 180, 184
Capisterre, St Kitts 65

captains
  moral and religious duties
    customary responsibilities 9, 18–19, 21
    duties as perceived by Middleton 56, 62–3, 153–5
    neglect of religion in 18th century 23–4, 69–72
    renewed interest in 1790s and beyond 72–4
  accountability and exercise of authority 155–8
  educating aspiring young officers 59–60, 289, 291–2
Caracciolo, Francesco (d. 1799; Neapolitan admiral) 143
Cathcart, William, Lord (1755–1843; general at Copenhagen, 1807) 200
Catholicism, Roman
  as a threat to Protestant England 12, 13, 24
  in England 32, 63, 82, 170
  in France 11 n. 7, 141
  in Royal Navy 3, 8–9, 11, 14, 15, 16–17, 86, 172, 288
  in navies of Catholic nations 5–6, 8, 12, 16, 55
Cavanagh, John (sailor and prayer-group leader) 240
Chabert, Marquis de (French naval officer, capturer of Gambier) 115
Channel Fleet 5, 54, 73, 86, 87, 134, 174, 198, 199, 202, 204, 208, 210, 218
Channel Islands 81, 115, 125, 129, 174, 175
chaplains, naval
  effectiveness 24–5, 76–7, 79, 161
  ministry opportunities
    spiritual 161
    sacraments 25, 76, 287–8
    in action 76, 106, 161
    visiting sick 107
    comforting the dying 76, 106
    educational 161, 293
    other roles 76, 107, 161 n. 38
  recruitment and scarcity of 20, 21, 24, 25–6, 74–5, 79–81
  rewards for 22, 25, 74–5, 106, 160–3
  instructions for, 1806 61, 154–5, 159–61
  criticisms of: Jervis 85–6 ; Marks 79; Smith 233
  Chaplain General and central organisation 162–3, 291
Charente, River 212
Charles I (1600–49; r 1625–49) 14
Charles II (1630–85; r 1660–85) 15, 18

Charleston, capture of (1780) 115
Chatham (naval dockyard) 108, 110
Chatham, 2nd Earl of (1756–1835; First Lord of Admiralty) 43
Chatham Chest 17
Chatterton, Lady Georgina (biographer of Gambier) 114, 194, 214, 217, 221
Cherbourg 183
Chile 220
China War, Second 287, 291 n. 38
Christian Officer's Panoply, The (pamphlet by Burn) 111
Christian Union, Royal Naval (Weston) 288
Chronicle, The Naval 76, 101, 149–50, 166–7, 223, 248, 289
  foundation and publication details 166
  importance of, for professional thinking 166–7
  letters of A.F.Y. 131, 167–73, 288, 289
Church of England *See* Anglicanism
Church Missionary Society 50, 130, 223
CHURCHES AND CHAPELS
  Cambridge, Holy Trinity 27
  Capisterre, St John's 65
  Charles parish, Plymouth 182
  Clapham parish 41
  Great Missenden parish, Bucks 249
  Iver parish, Bucks 106, 224
  Kingsland chapel, London 225
  Mariners', Wellclose Square 223, 275
  Merton parish 144
  Octagon chapel, Penzance (Baptist) 232
  Old Stoke parish 253
  Olney parish 284
  Orange Street chapel, Portsea 114
  St John's, Devonport 234
  St John's, Jamaica 75
  St Mary's Woolnoth 284
  St Peter's, Ipswich 278
  Teston and Nettlestead 58, 67
Churchill, Sir Winston (1874–1965) 201
Clapham, Clapham Sect 27, 41, 62, 114, 163, 182, 194, 235
Clarence, Duke of, Prince William Henry (1765–1837; *r* as William IV 1830–37) 153, 286
Clark, John (sailor and prayer-group leader) 238
Clarke, The Rev. James Stanier (chaplain from 1795 and writer, founder of *The Naval Chronicle*) 101, 103, 149–50, 151, 153, 166, 173

Clarkson, Thomas (1760–1846; Abolitionist) 41, 67, 68
Clarkson, Lieutenant John (1764–1828) 68
Cobbett, William (1762–1835; Radical MP) 204, 213
Cochrane, Admiral Sir Alexander (1758–1832) 98
Cochrane, [Thomas] Captain Lord [later Admiral the 10th earl of Dundonald] (1775–1860)
  career to 1809 184
  character 165, 204–5, 213–14, 220
  leads fireship attack at Aix Roads 205, 211–13
  criticises Gambier over tracts 203–4
  Aix Roads operations 206, 209–10, 215, 217
  vote of thanks 212–13
  alleges foul play at court martial 219, 219–20 n. 56
  disgrace, dismissal and later career 214, 220
  implicated in alleged Stock Exchange fraud 205, 220
  Autobiography of a Seaman (1860) 192, 203, 205, 221
Codrington, Captain [later Admiral Sir] Edward (1770–1851) 142
Colby, Captain Charles (post 1741, d. 1772) 69
Cole, The Rev. Samuel (chaplain from 1790) 76, 77 n. 17, 86 n. 34, 153, 286
Collingwood, Vice-Admiral Cuthbert Baron (1748–1810) 22, 33, 141, 148–51, 163, 166, 248, 264, 265
  piety 33
  applies to NMBS 98
  orders thanksgiving after Trafalgar 148–9
Collins, Lieutenant Francis (d. 1824; evangelist and literature distributor) 235, 250
Commonwealth 18, 19, 87
Communion, Holy *See* sacraments
Comptroller of the Navy, head of the Navy Board 5
  See also Middleton, Sir Charles
Comyn, The Rev. Stephen (chaplain from 1798) 145
confirmation 76, 287
Congregationalists *See* Dissenters
Congreve rockets 190, 206
Connecticut River 265

Continental System (Napoleon's economic war against Britain) 175, 200–1
Continuous Service contracts 89–90, 169, 293
conversion (key evangelical experience) 28, 100, 102, 275
  exemplified by: Brenton 184, 279; Burn 109–10; Leech 280; Marks 250–3; Newton 282–5; Rhind 279–80; Smith 276–7; Stokes 278; Wauchope 280
  analysis of the process 251, 276–85
convicts 62, 77, 289
Coote, Captain Richard (1782–1814) 264–6, 280
Copenhagen, Battle of
  Nelson's battle (1801) 98, 232, 276
  Gambier's action (1807) 175, 192, 193, 200–2, 206, 210
Corbett, Thomas (d. 1751; secretary of the Admiralty 1741–51) 22
Cornwallis, Admiral the Hon. Sir William (1744–1819) 192, 199
courts martial 83, 85, 133, 134, 188, 208
  principles of operation 155–7
  of Gambier 193, 194, 205, 213–21
  of Pounder 280
Cox, Lieutenant John (1765–1839; distributor of literature) 234–5
Coxere, Edward (1633–94; Quaker sailor) 19
Craven, Captain Charles (d. 1821; SPCK applicant) 83 n. 28
Creevey, Thomas (1768–1838; MP and diarist) 45
Cromwell, Oliver (1599–1658) 14, 145
Crosfield, Robert (d. c. 1705; writer on naval matters) 19
Cumby, Lieutenant [later Captain] William Pryce (1771–1837) 86
Cuxhaven 248

Danloux, Henry Pierre (1753–1809; painter) 135
Dawe, Captain (SPCK applicant) 83 n. 28
Deism 9, 24, 26, 28, 109, 110, 154, 253, 267, 282
delegates (sailors' elected representatives during mutinies) 87, 91, 93, 136
Denmark 175, 196, 199, 200–2
desertion 89, 156
Devonport naval dockyard *See* Plymouth
Dillon, Vice-Admiral Sir William (1779–1857) 116–23 *passim*, 190, 192

discipline
  curbing disorder at sea 5, 7, 18, 22, 24, 155–7
  naval system of law 155–8
  contribution of religion to 5, 52, 55, 61–2
  gradual humanisation of naval practice 157–9
  See also divisions; humanity; punishment
Dissenters (Baptists, Congregationalists, Presbyterians, religious Nonconformity) 26, 32, 82, 98, 102, 103, 114, 137, 140, 223, 225, 228, 232–6, 244, 267, 275, 277
  See also Anglicanism, Catholicism, Methodists, Moravians, Quakers
divisions, divisional system (basic RN way of organising a ship's company)
  origins 55 n. 37
  advocated by Kempenfelt 42, 55
  used by Middleton 42
doctrines *See* Antinomianism; Arminianism; Atonement; Calvinism; Catholicism; Deism; Evangelicalism; Pacifism; sinless perfection
Doddridge, The Rev. Philip (1702–51; Dissenting minister and author) 32, 256, 257 n.54
Doeg, Thomas (sailor and spiritual influence on Bo'sun Smith) 93–4
Dogger Bank, Battle of (1781) 124
Domett, Admiral [later Sir] William (1754–1828; on Admiralty Board 1808–13) 162 n. 39
Douarnenez Bay 128
Drake, Sir Francis (c. 1543–96) 12–13, 14
Duckworth, Captain [later Admiral Sir] John (1748–1817) 83, 187
Duncan, Adam, Admiral Lord (1731–1804) 133–9, 228, 268, 272, 289, 290, 291
  portrait 135
  career 81, 133
  character and religious faith 70, 73, 133, 136, 137, 149–51
  advocate of reform 95, 134, 138
  humanity of 137, 139
  blockade and mutiny 1797 134–6, 139
  See also Camperdown, Battle of
Duncan, The Rev. Alexander (chaplain from 1778) 135, 137
Dundas, Henry *See* Melville, Lord
Dundee 109, 133
Dungeness, Battle of (1652) 14
Dunsterville, The Rev. John (chaplain) 103

Earle, Augustus (1793–1838; painter) 270–1
Earle, Peter (historian) 8–9
East India Company 9, 38, 42, 113
East Indies 53, 54, 111, 179–80, 181, 291
East Indies Fleet 181, 182, 185
education
 at sea 6, 59–60, 117, 134, 160, 161, 162, 171, 186, 255–6, 289, 291
 amongst prisoners of war in France 244
 in training ships 90, 287, 293
Edwards, The Rev. Jonathan (1703–58; American theologian) 27
Edwards, Robert (sailor) 259–60
Egyptian campaign (1801) 185, 248, 250
Elbe, River 246, 248
Elliot, Commander Robert James (d. 1849; philanthropist) 223, 275
Enlightenment, 18th-century European 24, 64, 111, 154
enlistment *See* manning and enlistment
Episcopal Floating Church Society 223
Equiano, Olaudah (1745–97; African Abolitionist and former sailor) 68 and n. 53
Essay on Treatment ... of African Slaves (by Ramsay) 66
Estaing, Charles Henri, Comte d' (1729–94; French admiral) 115
ethos
 of officer corps 58, 61, 134, 153, 163, 165, 166–8, 291–2
 of navy generally 47, 61, 140, 173, 291–3
'Eugenius' *See* Maude, Ashley
evangelicalism
 origins of movement 27, 29
 relationship to Methodist revival 28
 distinctive characteristics
  authority of Scripture 29
  belief in justification by faith 147
  belief in conversion 27, 28
  concern for evangelism and mission 29, 107, 138, 269, 288
  compassion 29, 288–90
  social conservatism 29
 entry into 18th-century navy 35–6, 80
 See also Blue Lights (for officers); Psalm-singers (for the lower deck)
evangelism
 definition 29
 witness and personal evangelism 107, 226
 See also NMBS; preaching; tracts
Eylau, Battle of (1807) 200

Fairfax (master of Channel Fleet at Aix Roads) 215
Farne Islands 11
Fellowes, Captain [later Rear-Admiral Sir] Thomas (1778–1853) 258, 261, 263
Ferdinand IV (1751–1825; king of Naples and Sicily 1759–1825) 143
Fielding, Sir John (d. 1780; magistrate and philanthropist) 35
fire-ships 124, 205–7, 211, 215, 217, 220
First Fleet (conveying convicts to Australia, 1787) 62
First Lords of the Admiralty, listed 198 n. 25
Fishbourne, Admiral Edmund (1811–87) 290
Fitzmaurice, Lieutenant George 261
Fletcher, The Rev. Francis (chaplain on Drake's voyage) 13–14
Fletcher, The Rev. John (1729–85; Evangelical vicar of Madeley) 28, 52, 53
floating chapels 223, 275, 290
Floating Republic 87, 92
France, and the French navy 5, 12, 54, 141, 160 n. 36
French Revolutionary War (1793–1802) 72, 82, 98–9, 104, 140–1
Fresselicque, The Rev. John (chaplain from 1793) 72, 101
Frew, The Rev. John (chaplain from 1771) 71
Friedland, Battle of (1807) 200
Frobisher, Sir Martin (*c.* 1535–94) 12, 13 n. 9
Frowd, The Rev. John (chaplain from 1811) 77 and n. 17
Fry, Elizabeth (1780–1845; prison reformer) 288
Fuller, The Rev. Andrew (1754–1815; Baptist minister) 233, 235

Gambier, Captain George Cornish (1795–1879; philanthropist) 223, 275
Gambier, Baron James (1756–1833; Admiral of the Fleet)
 portrait 197
 background, upbringing and marriage 44, 114–15, 189
 career 48, 80, 81, 115, 137, 187, 196–9, 268
 caricatured 191
 character and religious beliefs 45, 70, 72–3, 98, 114, 116, 119, 122–3, 272
 criticisms of 115–16, 141, 174, 190–5, 203, 206–8
 captain of *Defence* 116–24

(Gambier, James, *continued*)
  at Glorious First of June 119–22
  tributes to courage 116 n. 19, 121, 122, 123
  member of Admiralty Board 196, 198–9
  governor and C-in-C Newfoundland
    (1801–4) 198
  controversies surrounding
    promotion 48, 192–3, 195–6
  tract distribution 95, 194, 203–4
  Copenhagen action (1807) 175, 200–2
  Aix Roads action (1809) 202–21 *passim*
  court martial 214–21
  supports chaplain Hawtayne 117, 118, 225
  pay reform 162
  subsequent service 193
  support for the sailors' cause 194, 196, 221–4
  definitive Blue Light 141, 174, 187, 189, 286, 289, 292
Gambier, Margaret *See* Middleton, Lady
Ganteaume, Honoré (1755–1818; French vice-admiral) 264
Gardiner, Commander Allen Francis
  (1794–1851; pioneer missionary) 185
Gardiner, Colonel James (1688–1745;
  evangelical military hero) 32, 33 n. 36
Gardner, Commander James Anthony
  (1770–1846; writer) 26, 79
Garlies, Viscount George, Captain
  [later Admiral the Earl of Galloway]
  (1768–1834; member of Admiralty
  Board 1805–6) 198
Garrick, David (1717–79; actor) 41
Geary, Admiral Sir Francis (*c.* 1710–96) 54, 71
Genoa 252, 259
Gentleman's Magazine, The 174
George III (1738–1820; r 1760–1820)
  20 n. 21, 30, 86
George IV *See* Prince Regent
Ghent, Treaty of (1814) 193
Gibraltar 30, 50, 56, 71, 127, 128, 133, 165, 183, 238, 249, 255, 259, 265
  Gut of, action (1801) 128, 130, 181, 183
Gironde, River 166
Givet (site of detention of British
  prisoners of war) 184, 243, 244
Glorious First of June, Battle of (1794) 72, 117–23, 185
  illustrated 121
Gordon, The Rev. Patrick (chaplain from 1694) 20
Gordon Riots (1780) 96

Gorman, Patrick (sailor on *Conqueror*) 261 and n. 62
Gothenburg 175
Graham, Captain Lord George (1715–47) 77
  portrait 78
Granville (French port) 174
Great Awakening 27
Greathead, Samuel (d. 1823; former army
  officer and evangelist) 233–4, 235
Greece 220
Greenwich, Greenwich Hospital 17,
  77 n. 17, 163, 184, 286, 287 n. 30
Grenville, William Wyndham (1759–1834) 41
grievances, sailors' 87–8, 91, 92, 134, 135, 138, 280
Guadeloupe 212
Guernsey *See* Channel Islands
Guichen, Luc Urbain, Comte de (1712–90;
  French vice-admiral) 56, 124
Gwenap (Cornish open-air site of
  Methodist gatherings) 52

Halliday, The Rev. Evan (chaplain from
  1793; Holliday in Kealy) 77, 107
Halliday, Captain [either Michael,
  1765–1829, or John (Vice-Admiral),
  1772–1837] 234
Halloran, The Rev. Laurence (chaplain
  from 1798) 77
Hallowell, Captain [later Admiral Sir]
  Benjamin (1761–1834; SPCK applicant) 83 n. 28
Hamilton, Lady Emma (1765–1815) 127, 143, 144, 145
Hanway, Jonas (1712–86; philanthropist and
  founder of the Marine Society) 35 and
  n. 1, 41 and n. 7, 80
Hardy, Admiral Sir Charles (*c.* 1716–80) 54, 133
Hardy, Captain [later Admiral Sir] Thomas
  Masterman (1769–1839) 143, 286
Harvey, Admiral Sir Eliab Harvey
  (1758–1830) 190, 192, 193, 199, 205
  career and character 203, 209 n. 41
  criticism of Gambier 203, 208–9
  court martial 208
  SPCK membership 221
Haslar Naval Hospital 123, 287 n. 30
Hatherall, The Rev. William (chaplain
  from 1779; Hatherill in Taylor) 94
Havana, capture of (1762) 133

Hawke, Admiral Lord (1705–81) 23, 76, 109, 124
Hawker, Captain [later Admiral] **Edward** (*c.* 1782–1860; pamphlet writer) 268, 286
Statement concerning certain Immoral Practices 286
Hawker, The Rev. Robert (1753–1827; vicar of Charles and tract writer) 113, 182 and n. 12, 249
Hawkins, Sir John (1532–95) 13
Hawtayne, The Rev. William (chaplain from 1793) 86 n. 34, 107, 118, 225–6
Hay, Robert (1789–1847; seaman and writer) 103
health 7, 57, 134, 158–9
  See also surgeons
Heasman, Kathleen (historian) 227
Henry VIII (1491–1547; r 1509–47) 12
Herbert, Admiral Arthur, Earl of Torrington (1648–1716) 15
Herbert, George (1593–1633; poet) 52
Hext, The Rev. John (chaplain from 1690) 20
Hicks, Captain, prob. Thomas [later Rear-Admiral] (1731–1801; SPCK applicant) 83 n. 28
Hillyar, Captain [later Admiral] **Sir James** (1769–1843)
  background and career 185 and n. 16, 269 and n. 1
  character and religious faith 186
  encourages prayer group aboard *Phoebe* 186, 240
  promotes shipboard education 186
  wary of seaport culture 186
Hitchins, The Rev. Thomas (1776–1830) 234
Hoare, William Henry (1776–1819; evangelical banker) 235
Hodgskin, Thomas (1787–1869; naval officer and Radical critic) 165
Hogarth, William (1697–1764; artist) 77, 78, 161
Hood, Admiral Lord (1724–1816) 81
Hope, Captain [later Admiral Sir] George (1767–1818)
  At Trafalgar 248; supports Marks 249; rebukes Austen 187
Hope, Captain [later Admiral Sir] Henry (1787–1863; frigate captain) 290
Hope of the Navy, The (pamphlet by Brenton) 185
Hoste, Captain Sir William (1780–1828; frigate captain) 33, 142

hostels and homes, sailors' 223, 275, 287, 288
Howard, John (1726–90; prison reformer) 41, 79, 288
Howard, Thomas, Lord, of Effingham (1536–1624; 1st Earl of Nottingham) 13, 17
Howe, Admiral Earl (1726–99) 43, 45, 48, 56, 72, 91, 122, 124, 133, 151, 152, 198
Hubback, John (1774–1810; evangelical master) 234, 238, 239 n. 26
humanity
  found generally in navy 155–9
  Nelson's attitude 142, 143
  in 1806 *Regulations* 61–2, 158–9, 289
  example of Duncan 133–9
  advocated by Penrose 95, 131, 169–70
  other instances amongst Blue Lights 1–2, 106–7, 139, 179, 186, 288–90, 292
Hume, David (1711–76; Scottish philosopher) 64
Huntingon, Selina, Countess of (1707–91; sponsor of evangelical worship) 28
Hutt, Captain John (1746–94; SPCK applicant) 83 n. 28
Hyder Ali, Indian prince 114
hypocrisy, allegations against evangelicals 192, 200, 208–9, 237, 238

impressment *See* manning and enlistment
Indian Mutiny (1857) 287, 290 n. 37
Inquiry into Naval Miscarriages (pamphlet) 19 and n. 20
Inscription Maritime 89
inshore squadrons 128, 179
Ireland, Irish 3, 32, 82, 86, 132, 133, 196
  United Irishmen 31, 86, 93
Iver, Bucks. 106, 224

Jacobinism 29, 82, 93, 141, 165, 289
Jacobite cause 22
Jamaica 76, 107, 109, 138
James II (1633–1701; r 1685–8) 15
James, William (naval historian) 192, 214, 221
Japan 189, 288
Java 180, 185
Jefferson, Thomas (1743–1826; US president 1801–9) 64, 289
Jellicoe, Earl (1859–1935; Admiral of the Fleet) 218
Jena, Battle of (1806) 200
Jersey *See* Channel Islands

Index 317

Jervis, Sir John, Earl St Vincent (1735–1823; Admiral of the Fleet) 43, 99, 101, 111, 125, 127, 128, 140–1, 161, 174, 194, 196, 213, 219, 227
   maintenance of discipline 84, 133
   religious attitudes 73, 84–6
   contrasted with Blue Lights 33
   directs chaplain's sermons 85
   critical of chaplains 85–6
   dislike of Middleton and Gambier 45, 84
   parodied by Cumby 86
Johnson, Samuel (1709–84; lexicographer) 41, 47, 155
Jones, Captain Jenkin (d. 1843) 98 n. 49
Joyce, Valentine (leader of Spithead mutineers) 91, 93
justification by faith *See* evangelicalism
Jutland, Battle of (1916) 218

Keats, Captain [later Admiral Sir] Richard (1757–1834) 128, 142, 210
Keith, Admiral Viscount (1746–1823) 127, 213
Keppel, Admiral the Hon. Augustus, Viscount (1725–86) 133
Kempenfelt, Captain [later Rear-Admiral] **Richard** (1718–82) 6, 10, 12, 41, 69, 71, 80, 81, 83, 105, 124, 133, 138, 172
   portrait 51
   career and character 39, 54, 56
   correspondence with Middleton 5, 50, 54
   progressive thinker 50, 52, 54–6
   advocates compulsory religious observance 50, 52
   evidence of personal beliefs 39
   religious verse 52–3
   support for NMBS 56
Kerr, Captain Alexander Robert (d. 1831) 217
Kettle, Tilly (1735–86; painter) 51
King-Hall, Admiral Sir William (1816–86; Victorian evangelical) 290 and n. 38
Knight, Captain [later Admiral Sir] John (1745–1831; SPCK applicant) 83 n. 28
Kverndal, Roald (historian and missiologist) 4, 227, 237 n. 21, 245 n. 35

Laforey, Admiral Sir John (*c.* 1729–96) 49 and n. 27
Lambert, Andrew (historian) 192, 196
Lancaster system of education 171
Languedoc 184
Larwood, The Rev. Joshua (chaplain from 1783) 76

laity, responsibility for religion afloat 18, 74
Latrobe (or La Trobe), Benjamin (1728–86; Moravian minister) 41, 67
Latrobe (or La Trobe), Ignatius (1758–1836; Moravian minister) 41, 50, 67
Laughton, Sir John Knox (naval historian) 40, 42, 45, 61, 192, 196, 214
Leech, Samuel (sailor and writer) 280
Leeward Islands 36, 57, 65, 156
Leissègues, Corentin de (1758–1832; French rear-admiral) 187
Lewis, Michael (naval historian) 116, 192, 243
Linois, Charles, Comte de (1761–1848; French rear-admiral) 128
Linzee, Captain [later Vice-Admiral] Samuel (1773–1820; SPCK applicant) 83 n. 28
Lisbon 177, 259, 263 n. 64
literacy
   rates of, amongst sailors 107, 241, 256
   reading classes 186, 189 n. 21, 244, 249, 273
   libraries at sea 255–6
   evangelical provision of reading material 265, 267
   See also NMBS; SPCK; tracts
Liverpool 64, 68, 284
Liverpool, Lord (1770–1828; prime minister 1812–27) 178
Lloyd, Christopher (naval historian) 214
Lock Hospital (charitable foundation) 223
Locker, Edward Hawke (secretary to Pellew, lecturer on Bible) 181, 182 n. 12
log books 23, 69–74, 187–9, 259–63
London, Bishop of, licensing clergy to serve afloat 16, 74
London Missionary Society 114
Longwy (site for detention of prisoners in France) 244
Loo Choo Naval Mission (to Okinawa, Japan) 189, 288 and n. 33
Louis XIV 160
Louis, Rear-Admiral Sir Thomas (1759–1807) 187
Lovegrove, John (sailor) 277 n. 10
Lundie 137
Luther, Martin (1483–1546; German reformer) 28

'Macarius' *See* Coote, Captain Richard
McArthur, John (Nelson's biographer) 143, 166
Mahan, Captain Alfred Thayer (naval historian) 127

Mahon, Port, Minorca 184, 247, 259, 264
Malcolm, Captain [later Admiral Sir] Pulteney (1768–1838) 216
Malham, The Rev. John (aspiring naval chaplain) 100–1
Malta 247, 248
Mangin, The Rev. Edward (chaplain from 1812 and writer) 79, 103, 107, 171
manning and enlistment
  conditions of service 89, 230
  hire and discharge (enlisted for one commission) 21, 89, 169, 293 n. 40
  wartime expansion and need for manpower 54, 88, 188
  volunteers 88
  impressment 54, 88, 89, 90, 91, 134
  desertion 89, 156
  issue of popularity of navy 89–90, 169–70
  leave to go ashore 42, 54, 87–8, 131, 134, 156, 165, 168
  French *Inscription Maritime* 89
  Continuous Service contracts 89–90, 169, 293
  See also Royal Naval Reserve
Marine Society 35 and n. 1, 223
Marines, Royal ('Marines' until 1802) 72, 80, 108, 109, 111, 112, 113, 131, 133, 137, 144, 178, 182, 238, 265
Marks, The Rev. Richard (1778–1847) 24, 79, 173, 245–67, 268, 277, 281, 285
  background and naval career 248–9
  shipwrecked 246, 248
  at Trafalgar 248–9
  promoted lieutenant 249
  conversion 250–3
  takes prayers at sea 73, 254
  organises *Conqueror*'s 'wingers' (prayer group) 255–9
  knowledge of prayer groups 228, 234, 236, 253–9
  relations with 'Methodists' 229, 257
  ordination and parish work 246 n. 36, 249, 255
  writings 245–6, 247, 250, 255, 266–7
  importance of 206–7, 250, 260, 263
Marsden, The Rev. Samuel (1765–1838) 289
Martin, Captain [later Admiral of the Fleet Sir] Thomas Byam (1773–1854) 180, 210–11 and n. 46
Martinique 212, 221
Mary I (1516–58; *r* 1553–58) 12
Mathew, Louisa (Gambier's wife) 115
Maude, Captain Francis (1798–1886; NMBS secretary) 98

Maude, Captain the Hon. Sir James Ashley (1786–1841) 264, 280
Mauritius 185
Maxwell, Captain (SPCK applicant) 83 n. 28
medicine at sea *See* health
Mediterranean 125–6, 187, 196, 234, 248, 250
Mediterranean Fleet 84, 106, 111, 164, 166, 180, 182, 269, 280, 288, 291
Melville, Viscount (Henry Dundas) (1742–1811; secretary of state for war 1794–1801, First Lord of Admiralty 1804–5) 41, 43, 44, 45, 48, 196, 198
messes (sailors' basic lower deck community) 32, 35, 230–1
  'pious' messes 35, 231
Methodism, Methodists (term often used for any strong piety) 26, 37, 79, 80, 140, 208, 229–32, 231, 232, 238, 240, 243, 257, 280
  radical tendencies 30
  appeal to soldiers 32
  possible involvement in 1797 mutinies 93
  model for prayer groups 230
Middleton, Captain [later Admiral Sir] **Charles, Lord Barham** (1726–1813) 10, 69, 81, 105, 124, 138, 150–1, 289, 291
  portrait 37
  character
    integrity 42
    religious beliefs 40, 43, 47, 49–50, 95
    aptitude for business 42, 45
    hasty temper 43, 45
    growing amiability 44, 50
  career 35, 36, 40, 42, 61, 140
  conversion 37–9
  marriage 38–40, 44; tribute to his wife 38
  religious observance afloat as a captain 23, 35–6, 69–70
  correspondence with Kempenfelt 5, 50, 54
  memorandum 'Duties of Captains' 36, 56, 61, 62, 153, 155
  Comptroller of the Navy 5, 42, 46, 48
  centralising authoritarianism 43, 45, 46
  resigns office 48–9, 61
  production of new *Regulations* 61, 153–5
  First Lord of Admiralty 61, 140, 153, 198
  Ramsay's influence and collaboration 58
  supports Abolition movement 44, 58, 67
  'Manifesto' and importance for evangelical movement in RN 36, 62–3
  death 268

Middleton, Lady [Margaret Gambier]
  family background, courtship and marriage 38–41, 114
  instrumental in Charles Middleton's conversion 37–9
  inducts Middleton into evangelical society 40–1
  cultivated home life 41 and n. 7
  birth of daughter (Diana) 44
  beneficial influence on her husband's character 44
  encouragement of Abolition movement 44, 67
  upbringing of James Gambier 114
midshipmen, training of 59, 116, 117, 134, 161, 265, 291–2
Milan Decree 175
Miller, Captain Ralph (1762–99) 126
Millingchamp, The Rev. Benjamin (chaplain from 1778) 77 and n. 20
Minorca 252
Missions to Seamen (Anglican) 275
morality 5, 42, 55, 195
  See also seaport culture; women
Moravians, Moravian Brethren (mission movement) 41, 50, 66, 67
More, Hannah (1745–1833; evangelical writer) 29, 41, 44, 49, 68, 202
Moresby, Admiral of the Fleet Sir Fairfax (1787–1877) 292
Moresby, Admiral John (b. 1830; officer and writer) 292
Morgan, The Rev. William (chaplain from 1778, served under Jervis) 85, 101–2
Morriss, Roger (historian) 45, 47
Mosse, Captain James Robert (1746–1801; SPCK applicant) 83 n. 28
Mulgrave, Henry Phipps, 1st Baron (1755–1831; First Lord of Admiralty 1807–10) 198, 199, 205, 206–7, 208, 213
Muncaster, Lord (d. 1813; friend of Wilberforce) 148
Murray, Sir Oswyn (historian) 45
mutinies *See* Nore, The; North Sea Fleet; Spithead

Naples 127, 143, 184, 200, 279
Napoleon (1769–1821; French emperor 1804–15) 175–8, 200–1, 202
Napoleonic Wars (1803–15) 177, 200–1
Nash, Commander James (d. 1827) 240–2
'Nastyface, Jack' (sailor and writer) 206

Naval and Military Bible Society (NMBS) 106, 268, 274
  foundation 96
  supplies fleet 33, 56, 98, 181, 255
  contribution to Thames Revival 236–7
  supported by: Saumarez 179; Pellew 181; Hillyar 186
Naval Charitable Society 223
Naval Prayer Union 189, 286, 287, 288
Navarino, Battle of (1827) 264, 280
Navy Board
  responsibilities and relationship with Admiralty Board 43
  headed by Comptroller of the Navy 5
  Middleton as head of Navy Board *See* Middleton, Sir Charles
Navy List 141, 198, 248, 249
Neale, Captain [later Admiral Sir] Harry Burrard (1765–1840) 73, 210, 217
Nelson, The Rev. Edmund (father of Lord Nelson) 143 and n. 5
Nelson, Lady Frances 143
Nelson, Vice-Admiral Viscount Horatio (1758–1805)
  religious convictions 144–7
  distinct from Blue Lights 144, 147, 194
  support for SPCK 83, 144
  moral flaws 143–4
  prayers of
    after Nile 145–6
    before Trafalgar 146
    at death 144, 146, 147
  piety and patriotism 82, 145
  religious effects of his death 147–51, 152
  general influence of on navy 142–3
  popularisation of religion 140–1, 143, 227
Nelson, The Rev. William (1757–1835; brother of Lord Nelson [later 1st Earl], chaplain from 1784) 77
New England 27
New Sailor's Magazine 231, 233
New South Wales 62, 289
Newfoundland 198
Newton, The Rev. John (1725–1807) 24, 41, 50, 52, 68, 151, 277, 281–5
Newton, Mrs Mary 283
Ney, Marshal (1769–1815) 178
Nile, Battle of the (1798) 126–7, 181
Nonconformists *See* Dissenters
Nore, The 42, 290 n. 38
  Mutiny 87, 91–4, 130, 136–7, 139, 196, 232
Norris, Admiral Sir John (1660–1749) 23
Northesk, Admiral the 7th Earl of (1756–1831) 141, 269

North Sea Fleet 133–6, 139, 232
  Mutiny 87, 134–6

Ocean Spiritually Reviewed, The (book by Marks) 151, 246–7
officers, naval
  social background 33, 35, 81
  conservatism 33–4, 82–3
  Duties and Qualifications of a Sea Officer 58–9
  ethical values 21–2, 90–1, 156–7
  half pay 81, 290
  learning lessons from mutinies 227–8
  'improved tone' noted by Marks 228, 263–4
  ethos developed by Penrose 163–73 *passim*
  training by example 59–60, 289, 291–2
  See also captains
Olonne, Sables d' 212
Oran 201
Orde, Admiral Sir John (1751–1824) 193
order book, captain's 42, 80
Otter, Captain [later Admiral] **H. C.** (Victorian evangelical) 290
Owen, Archdeacon John (d. 1825; chaplain general) 162, 221

Pacifism 111, 266
Padfield, Peter (historian) 13
Padstow, Cornwall 165
Pakenham, Captain John (1790–1876; NMBS supporter) 122 n. 28, 231, 234
Pakenham, Captain the Hon. [later Admiral Sir] Thomas (1757–1836) 122
Palles Shoal 210, 212
Parker, Admiral Sir Hyde (1739–1807) 75
Parker, Captain Sir Peter (1786–1814; frigate captain) 292
Parker, Richard (leader of mutineers at The Nore) 93, 94
Parkinson, Northcote (historian) 181, 182
Parliament
  thanks Gambier 212–13
  Cochrane expelled from 220
Parry, Lieutenant [later Rear-Admiral Sir] **Edward** (1790–1855; polar explorer) 189, 265–6, 286–7, 290
Patton, Captain [later Admiral] Philip (1739–1815; member of Admiralty Board 1804–6) 91, 158 n. 32, 198
Peel, Captain Sir William (1824–58; notable Victorian officer) 290

Pellew, Admiral Sir Edward, Viscount Exmouth (1757–1833) 73, 84, 130–3, 174, 179–83, 289–90
  career 131–2, 166, 179–80, 268
  character 131, 132, 139, 180, 182–3
  Bantry Bay episode 1799 132–3, 133 n. 44, 289
  rescue of *Dutton* 132, 182
  question of over-severity 132–3, 139, 289–90
  nepotism 132, 180
  religious convictions 181, 182
  support for NMBS 98, 181
  support for Locker's ministry 181, 182 n. 12
  quarterly punishment returns 181, 290
  rivalry with Saumarez 180–1
Pellew, Captain Fleetwood (1789–1861) 180 and n. 7
Pellew, Captain [later Admiral] **Sir Israel** (1758–1832)
  career 249
  disciplinary record 261
  support for Marks 73, 239
  religious convictions 249, 254
Pellew, Captain Pownall (1786–1833) 180 and n. 7
Peninsular War 162, 165–6, 175, 177
Penrose, Captain [later Admiral Sir] **Charles Vinnicombe** (1759–1830) 130–1, 137, 138, 268, 272, 291
  portrait 164
  career 131, 165–6
  letters of A.F.Y. 131, 167–73, 288, 289
  other writings 167, 170
  philosophy of management with humanity 95, 131, 167–73, 292
  shore leave an entitlement 131, 165, 168–9
  supports religious policies 171–3
Penzance 232, 235
Pepys, Samuel (1633–1703; naval administrator) 18, 19, 47, 74
Perceval, Spencer (1762–1812; prime minister 1809–12) 163
Peyman, General Ernst (governor of Copenhagen, 1807) 201
Phillips, Thomas (master-lighterman and Thames evangelist) 266
'Philo Nauticus' (pseudonymous author) 150
'Philotheorus' *See* Kempenfelt, Captain Richard
Pilgrim's Progress (book by Bunyan) 253
Pinder, Captain (SPCK applicant) 83 n. 28

Index

Pitcairn Island 98
Pitt, William, the Younger (1759–1806; prime minister 1783–1801, 1804–6) 41, 45, 46, 47, 48, 62, 114, 138, 140, 192, 195, 196, 198
Platen, Baron (Swedish statesman) 177 n. 3
Plymouth 132, 178, 181, 182, 229, 279
Pocock, Nicolas (1740–1821; painter) 120–1
Pole, Captain [later Admiral of the Fleet Sir] Charles (1757–1830; SPCK applicant) 83 n. 28
Pollock, John (writer) 38–9
Popham, Captain [later Rear-Admiral] Sir Home (1762–1820) 198, 210
Porter, Captain David, USN 185
Porteus, Beilby (1731–1808; Bishop of London) 41, 67, 202
Portland, Lord (1738–1809; prime minister 1783, 1807–9) 196, 198, 199, 200, 201
Porto Farina, battle of (1655) 15
Portsmouth 123, 229, 288
Portugal 177, 240
Pounder, The Rev. Patrick (schoolmaster) 280
prayer
  examples of prayers: Duncan 70, 137; Gambier 70; Hillyar 186; Nelson 144–7; Saumarez 129, 130
  liturgical worship at sea 9, 12, 15, 22, 55, 71, 84–7, 99, 113, 117, 130, 144, 172–3, 188, 189, 203, 241, 249, 262–3, 265, 287
  place of prayer appointed (1870) 288
  See also Book of Common Prayer; Supply of Prayer
prayer groups
  purpose and character 225, 230, 236, 255–7
  origins and first examples 225–6
  growth in numbers 226–7, 238, 239
  eighty by 1815 2, 228 n. 4, 238
  direct evangelism of lower deck by 226
  officer links 228–9, 238, 239
  evidence for 228, 231, 233
  encouragement by certain captains 228, 238
  suspicions of 237
  abuse of privilege by 238
  instances of suppression of 238, 258
  crossing ranks 30, 239
  disappearance at end of war 269
preaching
  by 16th–17th-century 'preachers' 14, 17, 18
  sermons required by Regulations 22, 61, 153–5
  first printed collection 100

(preaching, *continued*)
  problems of assessing quality 99
  examples of sermons: Ramsay 60, 100; Clarke, Stanier 101, 103, 149–50; Fresselicque 101; Malham 100–1; Dunsterville 103; Scott 103; Burder (printed collection) 102
Presbyterians *See* Dissenters
Prince Regent (1762–1830; *r* as George IV 1820–30) 153, 166
Pringle, Captain [later Vice-Admiral] Thomas (d. 1803) 123
prisoners of war 159, 242–5, 267, 274–5
Proclamation against Vice
  William III 20
  Anne 96
  George III 21 n. 21
Proclamation Society (Wilberforce) 31
profanity *See* blasphemy
proselytism *See* evangelism
Prussia 177, 178, 200
'Psalm-singers' 30, 226, 232, 237, Chapter 7 *passim*
  abuse of 230, 237–8
  See also prayer groups
punishment
  flogging 7, 42, 89, 92, 118 n. 24, 134, 186, 256, 259, 280
  Penrose's views 170
  Israel Pellew's record 261
  Austen's record 187–9
  Conqueror's log 259–63
  executions 85, 92, 94, 106, 133, 170
  punishments for blasphemy 22, 118 and n. 24, 259
  severity of Navy's record, yet struggle for fairness 155
  monitored by Board of Admiralty 187–8, 292
  moderating influence of quarterly returns 158, 181 and n. 10
  other humanizing tendencies 134, 165, 170

Quakers 19, 64, 66
'Quartermaster, The Old' *See* Bechervaise, John
Quiberon Bay, Battle of (1759) 76
Quota Acts 1795 90, 91, 169

Radicals, Radicalism 29, 30, 31, 83, 107, 165, 204, 213, 221
Rae, Malcolm (historian) 139
Ramsey, Captain (maybe David Ramsay, d. 1818; SPCK applicant) 83 n. 28

Ramsay, The Rev. James (1733–89) 57–68
  passim, 80, 81
  portrait 59
  character 57, 60, 62, 66, 68
  medical career 57, 64, 65
  visit to slaver 64
  suffers injury and leaves navy 64–5
  ordination 58, 65
  ministry in West Indies 60
  naval chaplaincy 1778 58
  opposition to plantation slavery 60, 65–6
  pamphlet controversy 67 and n. 50
  Middleton's confidential secretary 57
  influence upon Middleton 41, 58, 62
  writings
    Duties and Qualifications of a Sea Officer 58–9
    Sea Sermons 60, 100, 102
    Essay on Interest 66
    Essay on ... African Slaves 66
Reading, Berks. 277 and n. 10
Rediker, Marcus (historian) 7–8, 10, 30
Reformation, English 9, 10, 12–17
Regulations and Instructions
  1731 volume 22, 55, 60, 61, 76, 100, 118, 140, 273
  1806 revision 58, 61, 140, 153–5, 195, 198–9, 289, 291
  1868 edition 172
religion, progress of
  by 1783 80
  after 1803 227
  by 1815 274–5
Religious Tract Society 102 and n. 57, 112, 235, 250, 255, 274
Retrospect, The (book by Marks) 246, 247, 248, 257, 259
Reynolds, Captain John (d. 1788) 69
Reynolds, Sir Joshua (1723–92; artist) 41
Rhé, Île de 14
Rhind, Lieutenant William (1794–1863) 279–80, 281, 284
Richardson, Captain [later Vice-Admiral Sir] Charles (d. 1851) 204
Richardson, William (warrant officer and writer) 204
Rio de Janiero 271
Roberts, Hugh (sailmaker) 234
Robinson, Captain Hercules (1789–1864) 280
Rochelle, La 14
Rochefort 215
Rodger, N. A. M. (historian) 13, 45, 155–7, 276

Rodney, Admiral, 1st Baron (1719–92) 70, 124, 133
Rooke, Admiral Sir George (1650–1709) 20, 23, 96
Rosas Bay action (1809) 264
Ross, Captain [later Rear-Admiral] Sir John (1777–1856; Arctic explorer) 129, 179, 238, 287 n. 30
Royal Marines *See* Marines
Royal Naval Academy, Portsmouth 166
Royal Naval Christian Union (Weston) 288
Royal Naval Reserve 90
Royal Naval Temperance Society (Weston) 288
Royal Navy in the Victorian era
  religion a significant feature 172, 195, 275, 287–8, 291, 293
  punishment and discipline 158, 290
  manning 169, 293
  branches 161
Royal Sailors' Rests 288
Russia 175, 177, 178, 200, 201
Russian War (1854–6) 90, 287, 290 n. 37
Rutland, 6th Earl of 14
Ryan, A. N. (historian) 127

Sabbath observance *See* Sunday
sacraments 12, 14, 16, 18, 20, 25, 62, 76, 110, 144, 160, 244, 287, 288
Sailor Pilgrim, The (tract by Hawker) 113
sailors, general characteristics 8, 9, 10 and n. 5, 16
  attitude to comrades and communal life 9, 230–1
  responses to danger 6, 251, 278
  moral values 230
  sense of religion and superstition 7–10
Sailors' Cause (evangelical post-war reform movement) 17, 194, 195, 196, 222–4, 273–5, 290
  links with wartime religion 275
Sailors' Rests 288
St Bartholomew's Hospital, Bristol 11
St Christopher's Island (St Kitts, West Indies) 58, 60, 65, 68
Saint-Malo 174
St Vincent, Earl *See* Jervis, Sir John
Saints, Battle of The (1782) 70, 124, 181
San Domingo, Battle of (1806) 187
Sandwich, James Montague, 4th Earl of (1718–92; First Lord of Admiralty) 42, 43, 44
Sankerson, Captain (commands *Arundel* in Seven Years War) 69

Index

Santa Cruz da Teneriffe, Battle of (1657) 15
Saratoga, Battle of (1777) 131
Sardinia 125, 259
Saumarez, Admiral Sir James, Baron de Saumarez (1757–1836) 80, 84, 124–30, 226, 268, 279, 289, 291, 292
  portrait 176
  early naval career 81, 124–5
  character and religion 72, 95, 127–8, 129–30, 175, 178–9, 210–11
  commands ships of the line in battles of
    The Saints (1782) 80, 124
    Cape St Vincent (1797) 125, 127–8
    The Nile (1798) 126–7
  commands inshore squadron 128, 179
  actions at Algeciras and in Gut of Gibraltar (1801) 128–9, 130, 272
  C-in-C Baltic 175–9
  loss of the Baltic ships (1811) 178, 278
  rivalry with Pellew 178, 180–1
  support for Bible Societies and mission 98, 179
Saumarez, Captain Philip (1710–47; uncle of Lord de Saumarez) 124
Saumarez, Midshipman Richard [later Admiral Rtd] (d. 1864; nephew of Lord de Saumarez) 279 n. 15
Saumarez, Captain Thomas (d. 1766; uncle of Lord de Saumarez) 124
Sawyer, Captain [prob. later Admiral Sir] Herbert (d. 1833; SPCK applicant) 83 n. 28
schoolmaster, naval 76, 161, 293
Scilly Islands 268
Scoresby, The Rev. William (1789–1857; Arctic scientist and sailors' minister) 275
Scott, The Rev. Alexander (chaplain from 1793) 75, 76, 102, 103, 144, 146–7, 161
Scripture Readers 287, 288, 291
Scripture texts quoted
  Job (27 v. 5) 94
  Psalms (51 vv. 1, 2) 94, (103 v. 2) 246
  Proverbs (3 vv. 13, 16) 143 n. 5
  Ecclesiastes (11 v. 1) 246
  Micah (6 v. 8) 289
  Matthew (24 v. 40) 246
  Mark (12 vv. 38–40) 209
  John (1 v. 29) 279, (11 v. 25) 149
  Acts (16 v. 31) 253
  2 Timothy (1 v. 12) 249
  Hebrews (3 vv. 13–15) 143 n. 5, (12 v. 6) 122
  Apochrypha (1 Maccabees) 149
scurvy *See* health

Sea Fencibles (maritime militia) 165
Seaman's Christian Friend, The (pamphlet by Hanway) 80
Seaman's Friend Society, British and Foreign (Smith) 223, 236
Seaman's Monitor, The (pamphlet by Woodward) 20, 80, 82, 95–7, 99, 138, 182, 267
  illustrated 97
Seamen's Missions (book by Kverndal) 4
'seaport culture' 6, 17, 123, 222–3, 229–30, 274, 292
  need for reform in 4th phase of Evangelicalism 274–5, 287, 290
Searle, Captain [later Rear-Admiral] Thomas (1777–1849), depicted 271
Serle, Ambrose (1742–1812; naval administrator) 41, 47, 48 n. 23
sermons *See* preaching
Seven Years War (1756–63) 32, 50, 69, 70, 98, 109
Seymour, Captain [later Admiral of the Fleet Sir] George (1787–1870; frigate captain) 217–18
Seymour, Vice-Admiral Lord Hugh (1759–1801) 131
Seymour, Captain [later Rear-Admiral Sir] Michael (1768–1834; frigate captain) 272
Shaftesbury, Lord (1671–1713; deistic writer) 282
Shaftesbury, 7th Earl of (1801–85; evangelical social reformer) 289
Sharp, Granville (1735–1813; Abolitionist) 41, 66, 68
Sharp, W. (*fl.* 1830; painter) 164
Sheerness 71, 108, 112, 189 n. 21
SHIPS
(All Royal Navy, except where stated.)
  Adamant (4th rate) 136
  Adventure (5th rate) 72
  Agamemnon (64; 3rd rate) 83 n. 28, 93, 98, 144, 232, 277 and n. 10
  Alcide (3rd rate) 83 n. 28
  Amazon (frigate) 132, 292
  Amethyst (5th rate) 272 n. 2
  Amphion (5th rate) 83 n. 28, 103, 249
  Anson (4th rate) 39, 52
  Ardent (3rd rate) 42, 50, 56, 61, 65, 71, 80, 105, 272
  Arundel (6th rate) 36, 57, 64, 69, 70
  Barfleur (2nd rate) 71, 106, 183, 225, 237, 263 n. 64
  Bedford (3rd rate) 71

(ships, *continued*)
  Bellerophon (3rd rate) 72, 101, 230
  Berwick (74; French) 248
  Blenheim (2nd rate) 133
  Borer (brig) 265
  Bounty (armed transport) 98 and n. 49
  Britannia (1st rate) 83 n. 28, 77
  Caesar (80; 3rd rate) 107, 128, 183, 204, 217, 218
  Calcutta (56; French, ex-British) 219
  Caledonia (1st rate) 73, 118, 187, 208 210, 215, 217, 269 n. 1
  Canopus (2nd rate) 187
  Carnatic (3rd rate) 106
  Centurion (4th rate of 1691) 21 n. 21
  Chesapeake (US frigate) 103
  Christian VII (3rd rate) 234
  Cleopatra (5th rate) 131
  Cléopâtre (French frigate) 131
  Clipper (French prize) 259
  Colossus (3rd rate) 83 n. 28
  Conqueror (3rd rate) 73, 173, 232, 233, 239, 247, 249, 253, 255, 257, 259–63
  Constant (French privateer) 259
  Constant Reformation (42–gun ship of 1619) 14
  Courageux (3rd rate) 73
  Crescent (36; 5th rate) 72, 125
  Culloden (3rd rate) 182 n. 12
  Defence (3rd rate) 72, 107, 115, 116–23, 137, 178, 248
    illustrated 121
  Dolphin
    (6th rate) 144
    (5th rate) 250
    (revenue cutter) 232
  Dreadnought (2nd rate) 230, 249, 278
  Droits de l'Homme (French 3rd rate) 132 and n. 42
  Druid (5th rate) 125
  Duff (missionary ship) 114
  Dutton (troopship) 132, 139, 182
  Edgar (3rd rate) 81
  Elephant (3rd rate) 187–9
  Elizabeth (3rd rate) 232, 238
  Emerald (28; 5th rate) 37
  Essex (US frigate) 85
  Euryalus (5th rate) 148
  Eurydice (20; 6th rate) 125
  Expedition (4th rate) 248, 250, 252
  Favorite (6th rate) 280
  Formidable (2nd rate) 70, 83, 106, 107, 188
  Fortune (sloop) 71
  La Fortunée (5th rate) 234, 292

(ships, *continued*)
  Le Franklin (80; French) 126
  Ganges (3rd rate) 232, 238, 259
  General Mifflin (20; US warship) 115
  Genoa (3rd rate) 279
  Glasgow (5th rate) 264
  Gloucester (3rd rate) 25 n. 31
  Golden Hind 14
  Goliath (3rd rate) 111, 126
  Greyhound
    (5th rate) 249
    (merchant ship) 283
  Hannibal (3rd rate) 128, 183
  Harwich (4th rate) 283
  Hero (3rd rate) 178
  La Hogue (3rd rate) 265
  Hussar (6th rate) 244
  Hyperion (frigate) 270–1
  Imperieuse (5th rate) 184, 211, 212, 215, 217, 218, 219
  Impetueux (3rd rate) 101, 240
  Indefatigable (38; heavy frigate, cut-down 74) 132
  Invincible (3rd rate) 122
  Jean Bart (74; French) 212
  Leopard (4th rate) 263 n. 64
  La Ligurienne (French brig) 187
  Lord Mulgrave (prob. Indiaman) 83 n. 28
  Macedonian (5th rate) 279, 280
  Mars (64; French) 124
  Menai (6th rate) 292
  Milford (6th rate) 72
  Minerva (38; frigate) 118 n. 24
  La Minerve (5th rate) 183
  Monarch (3rd rate) 77 n. 17, 286 n. 29
  Namur (2nd rate) 189 n. 21
  Nassau (3rd rate) 248, 251–2
  Neptune (2nd rate) 198
  Nottingham (60) 124
  Nymphe (5th rate) 83 n. 28, 131, 182
  L'Ocean (120; French 1st rate) 212
  L'Orient (120; French 1st rate) 126
  Orion (74; 3rd rate) 83, 126, 226
  Pallas (5th rate) 217
  Peacock (sloop) 264 n. 66, 265
  Peterel (sloop) 187
  Le Peuple Souverain (French 3rd rate) 126
  Phoebe (5th rate) 185, 238, 240
  Plantagenet (3rd rate) 198
  Powerful (3rd rate) 83 n. 28
  Prince George (2nd rate) 106
  Prince of Wales
    (3rd rate) 100
    (2nd rate) 106, 175, 238

(ships, *continued*)
  Princess Amelia (3rd rate) 21
  Proserpine (6th rate) 246, 247, 248
  Queen
    (2nd rate) 83 n. 28, 123
    (sloop) 83 n. 28
  Queen Charlotte (1st rate) 72, 106
  Raleigh (frigate) 115
  Redoubtable (74; French) 203
  Repulse (3rd rate) 232–3, 233 n. 14, 234 n. 15, 238
  Resolution (3rd rate) 83 n. 28, 112
  Réunion (French frigate) 125
  Revenge (3rd rate) 217, 218, 240, 269 n. 1
  Royal George (1st rate) 56, 98, 109, 232
  Royal Oak (3rd rate) 232
  Royal Sovereign (1st rate) 83, 249
  Russell (3rd rate) 81
  St Albans (64; 3rd rate) 187–9, 240
  St George (2nd rate) 178, 232, 233 n. 12
  Salisbury (4th rate) 20
  San Ildefonso (Spanish 3rd rate) 249
  San Josef (2nd rate) 174
  San Juan 165
  Sandwich (2nd rate) 83 n. 28, 93, 94
  Sans Pareil (3rd rate) 106, 107
  Sceptre (3rd rate) 83 n. 28
  Scipio (3rd rate) 232
  Shannon
    (5th rate) 103, 172
    (steam frigate) 290 n. 37
  Snake (steam gunboat) 292
  Spartan (5th rate) 184, 279 n. 15
  Speaker (12; brig) 36
  Speedy (brig) 183 and n. 13
  Superbe (3rd rate) 77
  Swift (slaver) 64
  Téméraire (98; 2nd rate) 203
  Theseus (3rd rate) 126, 217
  Thétis (40; French warship) 272 n. 2
  Thunder (bomb-ketch) 115
  Le Tigre (3rd rate) 188
  Tonnant (80; 3rd rate) 232, 234
  Torbay (3rd rate) 69
  Trimmer (small warship) 83 n. 28
  Triton (5th rate) 198
  United States (US frigate) 279, 280
  Valiant (3rd rate) 69, 73, 123, 133, 217
  Vanguard (3rd rate) 125, 144, 145
  Venerable (3rd rate) 135, 136
  Victory (100; 1st rate) 5, 56, 71, 83 n. 28, 143, 144, 146, 175, 203, 238
  Ville de Paris (2nd rate) 113, 259, 264, 265
  Virginie (44; French) 132
  Wasp (US brig) 265
  Yarmouth (3rd rate) 114
  Zealous (3rd rate) 126, 232
Shovell, Admiral Sir Cloudisley (1659–1707) 20, 96
Shrubland Hall 129
Sicily 53, 127, 143
Sierra Leone 62, 284
signalling at sea 30, 54, 56, 60, 130, 136, 193, 198, 210, 275
Simeon, The Rev. Charles (1759–1836; Evangelical leader) 27, 28, 95, 280 n. 16
sinless perfection, doctrine of 52, 53, 257
slavery, slave trade 57, 64, 66, 68, 283, 284
See also abolition
Smith, The Rev. George Charles, 'Bo'sun Smith' (1782–1863; sailor, minister, reformer, writer)
  naval career 98–9, 232
  conversion 94, 276–7 and n. 10
  Baptist ministry 232
  'Naval Correspondence Mission' 232, 235, 269
  knowledge of prayer groups afloat 228, 231, 232
  contribution to Thames Revival 275
  post-war social reform – the Sailor's Cause 223, 268
  tracts 112–13, 267
  writes for *New Sailor's Magazine* 231, 233
Snape, Michael (historian) 32
Society for Promoting Christian Knowledge [SPCK] (1698) 20, 21, 22, 33, 71, 82, 83
Society for the Propagation of the Gospel [SPG] (1701) 20 and n. 21, 179
Solent 116
Somerset House 46
Somerville, Sir James (1882–1949; Admiral of the Fleet) 201
South Carolina 264 n. 66, 265
Southey, Robert (1774–1843; early biographer of Nelson) 143
Spain 5, 12, 14, 54, 75, 87, 128, 165, 175
Spanish Succession, War of (1702–13) 20
SPCK *See* Societiy for Promoting Christian Knowledge
SPG *See* Society for the Propagation of the Gospel
Spencer, 2nd Earl (1758–1839; First Lord of the Admiralty) 45, 49, 196
Spithead 56, 117, 123, 237
  Mutiny 72, 87–8, 91–2, 94, 130, 134, 136, 168, 196, 286 n. 29

Statement concerning certain Immoral Practices (pamphlet by Hawker) 286
Steel's Navy List See Navy List
Stock Exchange, alleged fraud concerning Cochrane 205, 220
Stokes (master of *Caledonia*) 210
Stokes, Samuel (sailor and writer) 278
Stopford, Admiral Sir Robert (1768–1847) 204, 209, 210, 212, 215, 217, 218, 269
Suckling, Captain Maurice (1728–78) 42
Sugden, John (historian) 82
Sulivan, Admiral Sir Bartholomew (1810–90; noted Victorian officer) 290
Sunday, Sabbath observance 18, 19, 22, 23, 33, 34, 35, 36, 55, 63, 69–73, 85, 99, 116, 117, 119, 122, 130, 154, 241, 244–5, 248, 269, 274
Supply of Prayer for Ships [without] Ministers (1646) 14
surgeons, naval 13, 263
  trusted by lower deck 60
  Ramsay's contribution to ethos 60
  instructions regarding cleanliness and compassion 1806 61, 158–9
Surinam 232
Sweden 175–8
Symons, The Rev. J. (preacher of a Trafalgar-memorial sermon) 150–1
Syrett, David (historian) 46

Tahiti 114, 238
Talbott, John E. (historian) 43, 45, 47, 48
Taylor, The Rev. Gordon (author of *The Sea Chaplains*) 166 n. 42, 174, 192
Taylor, John (sailor) 244
Teonge, The Rev. Henry (17th-century chaplain) 19
Terrot, The Rev. William (chaplain from 1806) 231, 233, 234
Teston, Kent 38, 67
Texel, blockade of the 73, 134–6, 251;
Thames Revival 223, 236–7, 245, 250, 266, 275
Thompson, Vice-Admiral Sir Charles (c. 1740–99) 85, 193
Thomson, Sir John Deas (secretary to Middleton) 38, 39 n. 5, 45
Tierra del Fuego 185
Tilsit, Treaty of (1807) 175, 200–1
Times, The 220
Tomlinson, Lieutenant Robert (evangelical and writer) 112
Toplady, Augustus Montague (1740–78; hymn writer) 281

Torrington, George Byng, Admiral Viscount (1663–1733) 22
Toulon 185, 233
  blockade of 125, 180
tracts
  SPCK tracts widely used in War of Spanish Succession 20, 96
  favoured method of evangelism 80, 95, 138, 250, 255, 274
  attractiveness of presentation 112, 267
  appeal to the mind 96, 194
  distributed by Gambier 95, 194, 202–3
  circulated amongst newly pressed men by Cox 234–5
  encouraged by Lieutenant Francis Collins 235, 250
  popularity amongst sailors 266
  huge circulation 20, 95, 250, 267
  post-war restrictions on, by Cole and Clarence 286
  opposed by Cochrane 203–4
  available in HMS *St Albans* 189
  authors and their writings: Woodward 20, 95–7; Burn 111–12; Hawker 113, 267; Marks 112–13, 250, 267; Smith 112–13, 267; Penrose 167
  See also Religious Tract Society; Seaman's Monitor
Trafalgar, Battle of (1805)
  campaign 50, 187
  Nelson's death at 144, 146–7
  sermons based on 149–51
  poster's religious appeal 151–2
  Richard Marks at 248–9
  Collingwood's signal for divine service after 33, 148–9
  Wilberforce overcome by news of 148–9
  reference to made by Marks and Newton 151
training ships 90, 287, 293
Trevenen, Captain James (1760–90) 131, 165 n. 41
Trotter, Captain Henry Dundas (1802–59; Victorian Blue Light) 290
Trotter, Thomas (1760–1832; naval physician) 229
Troubridge, Rear-Admiral Sir Thomas (c. 1758–1807) 84, 179–80
Turner, The Rev. John (chaplain from 1806) 263
Two Admirals (book by Moresby) 292
Two Dialogues (tract by Burn) 112

Index

United Irishmen 31, 86, 93
United Service Journal 186
United States of America 90, 156 n. 27, 193, 265, 279, 280
See also American Independence, War of; War of 1812
Ushant, Battle of (1781) 56, 124
Utrecht, Treaty of (1713) 21

Valenciennes (site of detention for prisoners of war) 244
Valparaiso 185
Van Diemen's Land 289
Vansittart, Captain [later Vice-Admiral] Henry (1777–1843) 234, 292
Vason Bay, Guernsey 125
Venice 282
Venn, The Rev. John (1759–1813; vicar of Clapham) 41
Verdun (site of detention for prisoners of war) 244, 245 n. 35
View of Christianity (book by Wilberforce) 264
Villeneuve, Pierre-Charles (1763–1806; French admiral) 126, 187, 249
Vinga Sound ('Wingo' to British sailors) 175
voluntarism, voluntary religious practices
  Penrose supports principle against overmuch compulsion 172–3
  voluntary as well as compulsory under Gambier 194–5
  meetings led by Marks 254–5
  informal meetings in wartime 244, 274, 287

Walcheren expedition (1809) 240
Waldegrave, Admiral Sir William, Baron Radstock (1753–1825) 106
Wallis, Captain James (d. 1808) 248
Ward, The Rev. Edward (chaplain of 1796) 83 and n. 30, 106–8, 138
War of 1812 (1812–14) 185, 193, 265, 279, 280
Warwick, Sir Robert Rich, 2nd Earl of 14
Watson, George (sailor and writer) 281
Watts, Isaac (1674–1748; hymn writer and Nonconformist divine) 124, 129, 232
Wauchope, Captain [later Admiral] **Robert** (d. 1862) 30, 280–1, 286
  conversion 280
  encounters opposition to beliefs 286

Wellington, Duke of (1769–1852) 142, 165–6, 175, 200, 240
Wesley, The Rev. Charles (1707–88; hymn writer) 27, 232, 285
Wesley, The Rev. John (1703–91) 27, 28, 35, 52, 229
West Indies 35, 42, 46, 49, 50, 54, 57, 58, 64, 65, 66, 67, 68, 107, 109, 112, 124, 187, 205, 212, 219, 220
Western Squadron 73, 101, 102, 132
Weston, Dame Agnes (1840–1918; philanthropist and reformer) 288
Wetherell, John (sailor and writer) 244
Wheeler, Private William (letter writer) 240–2
Whitby, Captain John (1775–1806) 118 n. 24
Whitefield, The Rev. George (1714–70) 27–8, 30, 38–9, 52
Who Fares Best? (tract by Burn) 111–12
Wilberforce, William (1759–1833) 31, 41, 50, 67, 68, 114, 123, 148–9, 202, 264
Willaumez, Jean-Baptiste (1763–1841; French rear-admiral) 205, 212
William III (1650–1702; r 1689–1702) 15, 20, 31
William IV See William Henry, Prince
William Henry, Prince (1765–1837; r as William IV 1830–37) 153, 286
Williams, Charles (1797–1830; caricaturist) 191
Williams, Edwin (19th century; painter) 176
Wilson, Captain James (1760–1814; mission ship master) 113
Winter, Vice-Admiral Jan Willem de (1761–1812; Dutch) 139
Wolfe, The Rev. Robert (chaplain to prisoners of war at Givet) 184, 234, 243–4, 279
women, admission to HM ships 42, 116, 118, 230, 286
Woodman, Richard (historian) 192, 214
Woodward, The Rev. Josiah (1657–1712; author of *The Seaman's Monitor*) 20, 95–7, 167
Woolwich 108, 111

Yorke, Charles Philip (1764–1834; First Lord of Admiralty 1809–12) 162 n. 39